INCIVILITIES: REGULATING OFFENSIVE BEHAVIOUR

Prohibitions against offensive conduct have existed for many years, but their extent and use were on the decline. Recently, however, several jurisdictions, including England and Wales, have moved to broaden the reach and severity of measures against incivilities. New measures include expanded targeting of unpopular forms of public conduct, such as begging, and legislation authorising magistrates to issue prohibitory orders against anti-social behaviour. Because these quality-of-life prohibitions can be so restrictive of personal liberties, it is essential to develop adequate guiding and limiting principles concerning state intervention in this area. This book addresses the legal regulation of offensive behaviour. Topics include: the nature of offensiveness; the grounds and permissible scope of criminal prohibitions against offensive behaviour; the legitimacy of civil orders against incivilities; and identifying the social trends that have generated current political interest in preventing incivilities through the intervention of law. These questions are addressed by eleven distinguished philosophers, criminal law theorists, criminologists, and sociologists. In an area that has attracted much public comment but little theoretical analysis to date, these essays develop a fuller conceptual framework for debating questions about the legal regulation of offensive behaviour.

Studies in Penal Theory and Penal
Ethics: Volume 3

Studies in Penal Theory and Penal Ethics

A Series Published for
the Centre for Penal Theory and Penal Ethics
Institute of Criminology, University of Cambridge

GENERAL EDITORS:
ANDREW VON HIRSCH, ANTHONY E BOTTOMS

Ethical and Social Perspectives on Situational Crime Prevention
edited by Andrew von Hirsch, David Garland and Alison Wakefield

**Restorative Justice and Criminal Justice: Competing or
Reconcilable Paradigms?**
edited by Andrew von Hirsch, Julian Roberts, Anthony E Bottoms,
Kent Roach and Mara Schiff

Incivilities:
Regulating Offensive Behaviour

Edited by
ANDREW VON HIRSCH
and
AP SIMESTER

·HART·
PUBLISHING

OXFORD AND PORTLAND, OREGON
2006

Published in North America (US and Canada)
by Hart Publishing
c/o International Specialized Book Services
920 NE 58th Avenue, Suite 300
Portland, OR 97213-3786
USA
Tel: +1 503 287 3093 or toll-free: (1) 800 944 6190
Fax: +1 503 280 8832
E-mail: orders@isbs.com
Website: www.isbs.com

Hart Publishing, 16c Worcester Place, Oxford, OX1 2JW
E-mail: mail@hartpub.co.uk
Telephone: +44 (0)1865 517530 Fax: +44 (0)1865 510710

Website: http://www.hartpub.co.uk

British Library Cataloguing in Publication Data
Data Available

ISBN-13: 978-1-84113-499-4 (hardback)
ISBN-10: 1-84113-499-6 (hardback)

Typeset by Compuscript, Shannon, Ireland
Printed and bound in Great Britain by
Biddles Ltd, King's Lynn, Norfolk

Preface

Prohibitions against 'offensive' conduct, such as indecent exposure, have existed for many years. Until recently, it had been assumed that their extent would decrease, in keeping with liberal trends toward decriminalisation. Now, however, several jurisdictions, including England and Wales, are extending the reach and severity of regulation as part of a government-led campaign to improve the quality of public environments. Included are expanded measures against intrusive and non-intrusive begging, and legislation authorising magistrates to issue prohibitory orders against 'anti-social' conduct. Because the scope of such quality-of-life prohibitions is potentially so broad, it is essential to develop principles that define and limit their scope.

This volume explores such principles. Topics covered include the conception of offensiveness itself; what mediating principles, such as principles of tolerance, should restrict the criminalisation of offensive conduct; the legal regulation of offence in England and Wales and in Germany; and the social factors that have generated the current political interest in 'cracking down' on incivilities.

The chapters of this volume began as presentations at two colloquia held in Cambridge. The first was held in October 2002; a second meeting, reviewing and discussing papers, took place a year later. We are grateful to everyone who attended these seminars—the resulting chapters have benefited greatly from participants' comments, and from the stimulus of those discussions.

Funding for the project was provided by the Centre for Penal Theory and Penal Ethics, of the Institute of Criminology, Cambridge University.

We would like to thank Helen Griffiths for organising the two colloquia, and Ann Phillips for her work in editing the chapters and preparing the work for publication.

AvH
APS
Cambridge

Easter Term, 2005

Contents

Preface   v

List of Contributors   ix

1 Penal Offence in Question: Some Reference Points
   for Interdisciplinary Conversation   1
   Paul Roberts

2 How Offensive Can You Get?   57
   RA Duff and SE Marshall

3 Disgust: Metaphysical and Empirical Speculations   91
   Douglas Husak

4 Penalising Offensive Behaviour: Constitutive and
   Mediating Principles   115
   Andrew von Hirsch and AP Simester

5 Legal Regulation of Offence   133
   Tatjana Hörnle

6 Crimes of Offence   149
   John Tasioulas

7 Regulating Offensive Conduct through Two-Step
   Prohibitions   173
   AP Simester and Andrew von Hirsch

8 'No Spitting': Regulation of Offensive Behaviour
   in England and Wales   195
   Elizabeth Burney

9 Social Capital, Trust and Offensive Behaviour   219
   Bryan S Turner

10 Incivilities, Offence and Social Order in Residential Communities   239
   Anthony E Bottoms

   Index   281

List of Contributors

Sir Anthony Bottoms is Wolfson Professor of Criminology, University of Cambridge, and Fellow of Fitzwilliam College. He is Associate Director of the Centre for Penal Theory and Penal Ethics.

Elizabeth Burney is Senior Fellow at the Institute of Criminology, University of Cambridge.

Antony Duff is Professor of Philosophy, University of Stirling.

Andrew von Hirsch is Honorary Professor of Penal Theory and Penal Law, University of Cambridge, and Honorary Fellow of Wolfson College. He is Director of the Centre for Penal Theory and Penal Ethics.

Tatjana Hörnle is Professor of Law, University of Bochum, Germany.

Douglas Husak is Professor of Philosophy, Rutgers University, USA.

Sandra Marshall is Professor of Philosophy, University of Stirling.

Paul Roberts is Professor of Criminal Jurisprudence, University of Nottingham.

Andrew Simester is Professor of Legal Philosophy, University of Nottingham, and Senior Fellow of the Centre for Penal Theory and Penal Ethics.

John Tasioulas is CUF Lecturer in Philosophy, University of Oxford, and Fellow of Corpus Christi College.

Bryan Turner is Professor of Sociology, National University of Singapore.

1

Penal Offence in Question: Some Reference Points for Interdisciplinary Conversation

PAUL ROBERTS[1]

I. WHY ARE WE TALKING ABOUT OFFENSIVE CONDUCT, WITH WHOM, AND WHAT FOR?

O FFENSIVE CONDUCT IS an especially promising topic for interdisciplinary scholarly investigation, for at least two, mutually reinforcing reasons. First, offensiveness as the specific target of criminal prohibition is largely unexplored terrain, by comparison with the more familiar, relatively well-mapped, territory of criminalised harms. Pioneers, in scholarship as elsewhere, may reasonably hope that venturing into the unknown will bring suitably handsome rewards, in the form of new theoretical knowledge (with or without immediate policy applications).

Secondly, embarking upon a new field of inquiry may be expected to open up novel standpoints and fresh perspectives from which prevailing wisdom may be challenged and established learning reconsidered. Thinking more seriously and systematically about offensive conduct could ultimately reveal as much about criminalisation in general as it does about offensive crimes in particular. Careful examination of this hitherto neglected dimension of penal regulation might prompt us to revise some of what we thought we already knew about the scope and content of the criminal law.

If a third reason for paying closer attention to the criminalisation of offensive conduct were needed, it is readily available in the preoccupations of contemporary English penal policy, a major strand of which is currently

[1] I am grateful for the many comments and suggestions received from participants at the October 2003 colloquium, and in particular to my discussant on that occasion, John Tasioulas, for forcing me to clarify a number of important points of method and substance. My remarks on criminological research benefited from discussions with Nottingham colleagues Peter Bartlett and Dirk van Zyl Smit, neither of whom should be assumed to endorse the opinions I express. The final draft was much improved by the sterling efforts of both editors.

directed towards 'taking a stand against' (Home Office, 2003a) and 'tack-ling' (Armitage, 2002) anti-social behaviour. This flagship policy initiative recently culminated in the enactment of the Anti-Social Behaviour Act (ASBA) 2003, a major legislative intervention which builds on previous meas-ures, notably those contained in Part I of the Crime and Disorder Act 1998 and Part I of the Criminal Justice and Police Act 2001. It is characteristic of the present government's anti-social behaviour legislation to be both inno-vative in design and sweeping in effect, and the ASBA 2003 exemplifies both trends, for good or ill. Several commentators have been deeply unim-pressed. Andrew Ashworth (2004: 287) has described such measures as 'incoherent, potentially oppressive, and contrary to both the spirit and the letter of the European Convention on Human Rights'. Roger Smith (2005: 19), the Director of the law reform campaigning group JUSTICE, recently lambasted Anti-Social Behaviour Orders as 'a jurisprudential Frankenstein, cobbled together in the satanic mills of the Home Office out of disparate parts of the justice system'. Nicola Padfield (2004: 727) concludes that the 2003 Act epitomises 'Nanny State' legislation, which in this instance is also 'unnecessary, unduly complex and unclear. It may even prove counter-productive'. Supporters of the current policy offensive against anti-social behaviour might regard these assessments as too pessimistic or uncharita-ble, but nobody can deny that the government has introduced controversial legal powers with significant implications for individual rights and com-munity interests. These new measures demand close scrutiny and careful evaluation.

Offensiveness and anti-social behaviour are distinct, but overlapping, concepts. As the following discussion should make clear, not everything that is anti-social is also 'offensive' in any theoretically illuminating or prac-tically useful sense, but much that is offensive is also anti-social. The over-lap explains why the distinct concepts of 'offensive conduct' and 'anti-social behaviour'[2] are often run together in policy discourse and sometimes appear to become entangled in academic literature. This suggests that the two concepts may profitably be analysed in tandem, not least so that they can be prised apart again and properly differentiated as occasion demands.

Although issues of policymaking are intermittently addressed in the fol-lowing discussion, this chapter is principally concerned with theoretical, disciplinary, and methodological questions, and is addressed primarily to scholars working in the broad field of criminalisation (see Lacey, 1995). At

---

[2] Nothing turns for present purposes on the shift from 'conduct' to 'behaviour'. I am mere-ly adopting the now-standard terminology of 'anti-social behaviour' (as opposed to 'anti-social conduct', which is hardly ever used) in a way which also usefully serves to accentuate the real contrast I want to make between conduct/behaviour that is 'offensive', and conduct/behaviour that is 'anti-social'.

risk of stating explicitly what could safely be taken as read, let me add that I reject any notion of a strict separation between 'theory' and 'practice', and with it the lazy assumption that narrowly-focused scholarly endeavours must necessarily be aridly scholastic. Thinking *is* practice (or, if you prefer, praxis) in my book. The following discussion is consequently intended to be theoretically illuminating *and* pertinent to policymaking, even whilst theory and methodology rather than policy choices are its principal focus. By the same token, this exploratory analysis does not claim to say all that there is to say about criminalising offence, as if anything omitted must necessarily be marginalised as unimportant, or that the material included could not have been presented in other illuminating ways, with different emphases and from different perspectives. This would not merely be an uncharitable reading: it would directly contradict the fundamental commitment to methodological pluralism from which this chapter proceeds.

II. FACING UP TO THE CHALLENGES OF INTERDISCIPLINARY CONVERSATION

Interdisciplinary scholarship always presents difficulties of communication between the disciplines. How can scholars addressing a multi-disciplinary audience be confident that what is heard by colleagues from other disciplines equates with what was said? How can a scholarly audience be sure that the messages its members reconstruct from within their own disciplinary frames of reference are faithful to the speaker's communicative intentions? A single message may fragment into multiple, competing meanings when communicated, or rather *not* communicated, across disciplinary boundaries. Messages get corrupted in translation, or distorted by 'noise'. This is not just a matter of each academic tribe employing its own esoteric code of technical terms and concepts. Much more than just a distinctive professional vocabulary, disciplinary affiliation signifies a shared background of training, methodology, and standards of conduct and critical evaluation. Being a lawyer or a philosopher or a sociologist, etc, profoundly influences how one thinks and views the world.

Formative disciplinary influences on the character of scholarly inquiry and communication are often subtle and therefore frequently unnoticed, which only serves to increase their potency. Legal scholars (to reach, predictably, for the example most natural to me) are able to take for granted a shared background of discipline-specific assumptions, priorities, and insider-information when communicating with other lawyers. Having all undergone the same more-or-less standard initiation to law (itself partly determined by the demands of a professional qualification), every English lawyer is broadly familiar with a basic canon of concepts and doctrines—contract, tort, property, trust, judicial review, legal personality, right, remedy, reasonable expectations, the Rule of Law, natural justice, etc—which structure a distinctively legal universe of thought, meaning, and conventional understanding. The relationships between a discipline's foundational concepts form a dynamic and productive network of complex doctrinal compounds and well-rehearsed debates, an intellectual structure more substantial and compelling than the sum of its individual component parts. When the concept of 'intention' is mentioned, for example, a synaptic reflex takes me back to undergraduate encounters with intention in the crime of murder, the criterion of intentionality in the formation of trusts, and various contractual doctrines including the 'intention to create legal relations'. Years later, the old material on trusts and contracts, though barely revisited since Finals, remains vivid, and doubtless at some level influential. If other lawyers do not instinctively make the same or similar associations, they will at least know exactly what I am talking about. Non-lawyers, of course, are excluded from this intimate legal colloquy, just as lawyers would be excluded from the coded conversations of professional sociologists or philosophers.

Once initiated into a particular disciplinary mind-set there is, in a sense, no going back. The best one can hope for is to keep moving forward, intellectually, morally, and in any other way that matters. Having abandoned the fantasy of an Archimedean Point beyond culture from which one may report an objective 'view from nowhere',[3] the question for scholars is not *whether* to interpret the world through the prism of professional acculturation, but *which* disciplinary perspective or combination of perspectives to adopt, to the extent that this can ever be a matter of deliberate choice. At the very least one ought to try to recognise the disciplinary perspectives that have shaped one's own approach to research and scholarship. Whether the protocols of a particular discipline produce enlightenment or prejudice (or what marxists call 'ideology') is a topic of perennial scholarly concern. Time and again questions of methodology are the flashpoint—or pretext— for localised border disputes between established disciplines. Methodological disagreement also frequently fuels internecine rivalry between opposing factions within the same discipline, each claiming to be the true guardian of orthodoxy or nurturing irredentist ambitions for independent recognition.

The relationship between offensive conduct and penal regulation offers a fascinating case-study in the perils and possibilities of interdisciplinary scholarship. This is clearly a topic in which a diverse range of disciplines and sub-disciplines is likely to declare an interest. Criminalising offence predictably poses bread-and-butter questions for philosophers, lawyers, sociologists, psychologists, political scientists and historians, especially those

---

[3] I take it that we can all agree on this much, though that assumption may depend on individual readers' disciplinary affiliations.

working in more narrowly focused sub-disciplines including criminal law theory, penology, criminal procedure, human rights law, policing studies, social policy, regulation theory, crime prevention, and socio-legal studies. This list is intended to be indicative, rather than exhaustive, and contains at least one glaring omission. Criminologists, too, have an obvious stake in the penal dimensions of offensive and anti-social behaviour. However the composition and boundaries of Criminology are defined (a conundrum taken up again in § IV, below), it is a reasonable working assumption that a discipline devoted to the study of crime and offending might contribute indispensable knowledge and know-how to our interdisciplinary conversation. It is therefore apparent that the topic of this volume presents pervasive and fundamental challenges of successful interdisciplinary communication.

The demand is not merely for bi-lateral translation, arising at the interface between two disciplinary traditions with a mutual interest in offensive conduct, but an exponentially more complex multi-lateral affair involving a host of contributing disciplines and sub-disciplines. And because offensive conduct is a neglected backwater of scholarly investigation, there is no extant *lingua franca* or common currency of concepts and terminology to which contributors to a nascent interdisciplinary conversation can agree in advance to subscribe. Small wonder, then, that our first forays into the criminalisation of offence at the initial Cambridge workshop held in October 2002 generated a certain degree of misunderstanding and argument at cross purposes between participants. Precisely because the territory is largely uncharted, however, there should be few disciplinary conceits or previously staked-out positions to challenge or defend. Scholars remain at liberty to explore the new terrain in a co-operative spirit of shared inquiry, inevitably filtering their perceptions through potentially distorting disciplinary lenses, but keeping an open mind regarding substantive issues of penal offence.

Yet, in addition to goodwill on all sides, meaningful co-operation implies the need for a shared frame of reference and conceptual language through which pertinent ideas, arguments, data, and experiences can be expressed intelligibly and communicated across disciplinary boundaries. It is to this preliminary task of developing a shared conceptual vocabulary and establishing some useful reference points for further interdisciplinary discussion that this introductory chapter is devoted. An immediate test for this type of theorising will be whether it assists readers to interpret and evaluate the more substantive data, arguments, and debates presented in subsequent chapters of this volume.

The following discussion is organised around three stylised disciplinary approaches to the criminalisation of offensive conduct, which I will call 'Philosophy', 'Criminology', and 'Jurisprudence'. My aim is to develop a functional taxonomy of ideal-types, in which each label picks out a recognisable disciplinary core of research and writing. Disciplinary affiliation within this taxonomy is intended to be sufficiently inclusive to embrace the bulk of contemporary research activity and scholarship self-consciously contributing towards the relevant disciplinary tradition, but at the same time sufficiently discriminating to accentuate significant contrasts of method and focus which ultimately account for each discipline's distinctive character. So long as these definitions meet a threshold level of descriptive accuracy, the three 'disciplines' are not just something conjured out of thin air, with no recognisable referent in the real-world of scholarship; albeit that, in reality, disciplinary borders constantly shift and overlap and are endlessly disputed. For present purposes at least, borderline disputes and hard-cases—does scholar X or research report Y 'count as' Criminology or Jurisprudence?— are both pointless and irrelevant.[4] An idealised disciplinary typology succeeds to the extent that it encapsulates and clarifies the core focus, method, data, and conclusions that should be regarded as each discipline's distinctive and possibly unique contribution to an informed appreciation of penal offence.[5]

Of course, this structuring typology is artificially neat for the purposes of exposition. Dynamic scholarly traditions in reality overlap and intersect, allowing data, perspectives, methodologies, and arguments developed within one particular discipline to be exported and shared with others. Far from conceiving of academic disciplines as sharply differentiated or entirely self-absorbed, the following discussion is intended to facilitate a productive process of interdisciplinary exchange, adaptation, and cross-fertilisation of ideas, concepts, methods, and data. Philosophy, Criminology, and Jurisprudence have been singled out for their potential to contribute significantly to a shared understanding of penal offence. No other well-established

---

[4] Judging by the hostile reactions they are prone to encounter, functional definitions of a field of scholarship sometimes appear to be mistaken for normative criteria of membership, as though they were devised and wielded to reclassify certain methodologies ('that's jurisprudence, not philosophy') or disqualify particular scholars from their chosen disciplinary affiliation ('you're not a proper criminologist'). But since the boundaries of any scholarly discipline are always fluid, contested, and ultimately arbitrary, why would anybody want to embark upon the ridiculous and pointless, not to mention arrogant, exercise of telling scholars what they are 'really' doing, or who they 'really' are? People can categorise their work in any way they like, but those who want to be understood beyond their circle of confederates should take care to define their terms.

[5] Readers who doubt that my disciplinary typology fails to satisfy even a threshold level of descriptive accuracy are free to interpret the following sections as developing a non-discipline specific conceptual analysis of penal offence. The three disciplinary perspectives could be renamed entirely neutrally as 'A', 'B', and 'C' without changing the substance of the literature, data, concepts, issues, questions, arguments, and analyses presented in each section, regardless of the academic discipline—if any—to which these intellectual resources might be ascribed. In my view, there is enough descriptive truth in the typology to qualify the labels 'Philosophy', 'Criminology', and 'Jurisprudence' as illuminating and useful signposts, but it is not necessary to accept this proposition in order to follow the main thrust of the exposition.

disciplinary traditions or fields of inquiry have an obviously stronger claim on our attentions, even if potential alternatives—history? political science? economics? theology?—might have proved equally illuminating. Philosophical analysis is a convenient point of departure, not least because philosophy generates indispensable conceptual clarifications and refinements that can later be usefully employed in criminological and jurisprudential exposition. Still, the order in which the three disciplinary perspectives are presented does not carry any implicit message about their relative importance in the larger scheme. What follows is not a sports commentary in which coming first means awarding a gold medal to Philosophy, silver to Criminology, with Jurisprudence bringing up the rear for the bronze.

Proceeding in this fashion will allow us to explore potential contributions to an interdisciplinary conversation addressing the penal regulation of offensive conduct and anti-social behaviour, and to pose a series of follow-up questions for further investigation and discussion. If the enterprise undertaken in this chapter itself needs to lay claim to any disciplinary pedigree, it is probably best regarded as an exercise in applied conceptual taxonomy and the philosophy of method.

III. QUESTIONS FOR PHILOSOPHY

With the conspicuous exception of Part II of Joel Feinberg's wide-ranging, instructive, and frequently entertaining treatise on *The Moral Limits of the Criminal Law* (1985), legal philosophers have paid scant attention to the criminalisation of offensive conduct. These days, following Feinberg, it is common to find references in criminal law scholarship to the so-called 'Offence Principle', but this concept generally receives little if any elucidation.[6]

Such neglect is partly attributable to the historical preoccupations of Anglo-American criminal jurisprudence. What is known, following Williams (1961), as the General Part of the criminal law has tended to predominate in modern scholarship and teaching, and the General Part is typically treated as being synonymous with general principles of criminal liability (see, further, Shute and Simester, 2002; Gardner, 1998). The bulk of English criminal law scholarship in fact focuses even more narrowly on a handful of *mens rea* terms—especially intention and recklessness—flanked by a smattering of miscellaneous writings on general defences, principles of auxiliary liability ('aiding and abetting', etc), and inchoate offences like attempts, conspiracy, and incitement. Causation is one of the few *actus reus* terms to have benefited from sustained theoretical analysis (see, especially, the classic

---

[6] Simester and von Hirsch, 2002 is a recent exception, notable in part precisely for the novelty of the questions it raises.

study by Hart and Honoré, 1985). Offensive conduct has barely figured in all of this because principles of criminalisation, generally, have been neglected. Legal philosophers and criminal law theorists, collectively, have not systematically applied themselves to the question: what kinds of conduct ought to be proscribed by the criminal law?

It is worth pausing a moment to underline the significance of this omission. Perhaps it will come as a surprise to scholars working in other, related fields, and who have always assumed that principles of criminalisation were somebody else's business, to learn that, in fact, no field of scholarship has ever really come forward to claim this topic, despite its manifest importance. Contemplating criminal law teaching in US law schools, Doug Husak (2002: 19) has recently lamented the 'appalling prospect that professors might teach and students might learn about both the general and special parts of criminal law without paying any attention to the crucial issue of what conduct should or should not be criminalized'. Yet Husak's appalling prospect is apparently the reality in the majority of US law schools. And if, in England and Wales, law teachers and their students are arguably better served by criminal law texts (see e.g. Ashworth, 2003: chs 2–3; Simester and Sullivan, 2004: chs 1–2; Lacey and Wells, 1998; cf Alldridge, 1990), it is difficult to quibble with Husak's broad comparative evaluation that '[d]espite its central importance, criminalization remains the single most widely neglected issue among contemporary criminal theorists' (Husak, 2002: 20).

To the extent that the moral limits of the criminal law are ever seriously questioned in academic writing, the standard liberal reply, drawing inspiration from Mill (1962 [1859]) and popularised by Feinberg (1984), is that the criminal law legitimately sanctions *harmful* conduct.[7] It is sometimes added, almost as an afterthought and without much in the way of an articulated rationale, that certain types of offensive conduct may also justifiably be criminalised.[8] Philosophical justification for criminalising harms is not difficult to discern. Human beings have vital 'welfare interests' (Feinberg, 1984: 37–8) in life, bodily integrity and function, freedom of movement, shelter, sustenance, freedom from debilitating pain, the opportunity to form valuable relationships with other people, and so forth.[9] These vital interests are a prerequisite to leading any kind of valuable or fulfilling life, a common set of basic requirements for pursuing whatever other, more complex, goals or aspirations each of us might have for ourselves as individuals or as valued members of a collectivity (family, neighbourhood, community, profession,

---

[7] In fact, if one were trying to elaborate a systematic account of criminalisation from first principles, harmful conduct might not be the best place to start, since '[f]ocusing on the harms tends to occlude the wrongfulness of the act itself' (Gardner and Shute, 2000: 196).

[8] If this is an indictment, I might have to plead guilty to it myself: see Law Commission, 1995: Appendix C. But I was in good company in treating offensive conduct as a proper object of criminal prohibition: in addition to Feinberg, 1985, see Packer, 1969: ch 16.

[9] Cf the enumeration of 'basic human goods' by Finnis (1980: chs III–IV), and Hart's influential discussion of the 'minimum content of natural law' (1961: 189–95).

club, society, church, state, nation, humanity...). If the criminal law should protect any personal interests at all, it should surely protect these vital welfare interests.

Timeless criminal prohibitions against murder, assault, rape, burglary, and theft are logical extensions of individual rights to life, bodily integrity, and security of person and property. In the Anglophone tradition these rights have crystallised into common law principles and doctrines, latterly cemented (to a greater or lesser extent in different jurisdictions) by modern criminal legislation and the emergent law of human rights. For the purposes of legal proceedings, and to those of a legalistic bent, the identification of pertinent legal rights and duties might be as far as the analysis needs to go. For those with a more inquiring disposition, the vast vista of moral and political philosophy (including moral epistemology) awaits, with its meandering pathways, serial switchbacks, and beguiling promises of enlightenment. Suffice it here to say that treating murder as a proper object of criminal prohibition is about as certain and well-founded as anything in life ever is. I might be mistaken about the criminalisation of murder, but then I might also be mistaken in believing that the world is round, or in thinking that you or I exist. For present purposes, we must bracket-off these and other similarly tempting philosophical diversions, in order to stay focused on the questions in hand.

The next step in clarifying the philosophical foundations of criminalisation is to interpret 'harm' as a composite concept with two components: injury— or, more neutrally, 'a set-back to interests' (Feinberg, 1984: ch 1)—and wrongfulness.[10] It is not murder to kill a person in reasonable self-defence, or

---

[10] Decomposing 'harm' into set-backs and wrongfulness is vulnerable to the criticism that harm is being conceived reductively, in terms of an exclusively 'consequentialist' function of physical or material set-backs to welfare interests. As Duff (2001) maintains, an important dimension of criminal victimisation—at least with regard to crimes with identifiable victims—is the intrinsic harmfulness inflicted by a deliberate, hostile assault on one's person or possessions which seems to convey the message that one's interests count for less than they should. On this view, *the meaning* of crime, as purposive human conduct, is part of what makes crime so especially hurtful and harming, more harmful than otherwise similar set-backs to one's interests caused accidentally. What might be called the 'intrinsic moral harm' of crime is a powerful idea, suggesting that one function of punishment should be to restore the moral balance by negating the offender's false message of denigration with a reassertion of the moral truth about values, including, in particular, the inherent equal worth of all human lives (see Murphy and Hampton, 1988, reviving an Hegelian theme in the philosophy of punishment). However, as Gardner and Shute (2000: 216) and Simester and von Hirsch (2002: 284) contend against Duff (and Feinberg), expanding the concept of harm to include moral harm collapses the analytical distinction between harming and wronging, with the consequence that the Harm Principle is no longer able to play its traditional exclusionary role in liberal accounts of criminalisation. Wrongs are now deemed harmful, just by virtue of the fact that they involve wrongdoing, which opens the door to unbridled legal moralism. Both conceptualisations are *conceptually* plausible. The choice between them turns on the comparative uses and usefulness of concepts of harm, and these are normative, rather than strictly conceptual, considerations. That is to say, the best concept of 'harm' depends on what you want your concept of harm to achieve.

by accident during a risky surgical operation or whilst participating in dangerous contact sports, or to kill oneself. Although dying usually[11] constitutes a (grievous) set-back to one's interests, death is not necessarily a *wrongful* set-back. It is morally permissible, within limits, to kill an aggressor in self-defence, and to mortally injure a person who has given full and informed consent to be exposed to certain risks of death, in the operating theatre or on the sports field. If the ghosts of people who died in such circumstances could come back and confront their killer, they might reasonably say that their surgeon or opposing prop-forward had seriously set back their interests, but they could not legitimately complain that they had been wronged at his hands. These familiar examples illustrate, first, that penal law proscribes only what legislators regard as *wrongful* set-backs to interests, as opposed to set-backs *simpliciter*; and, secondly, that the scheme of criminal prohibitions reflects gradations of moral wrongdoing—murder came to be recognised, almost universally in modern legal codes, as more heinous than suicide.[12]

Two further questions are prompted by this analysis: Is a wrong a necessary condition of criminalisation? Is a wrong a sufficient condition of criminalisation? The second question is by far the easier; the answer is, No. There are many types of wrong that properly fall outside the ambit of the criminal law, either because they are not in principle the sort of thing that should be criminalised, or because, even though they might in principle be criminalised, it would be too difficult, too costly, counterproductive, or improper, all things considered, to apply the criminal law to that end. An example of the first type of wrong is speaking ill of one's friends when their backs are turned, which is morally delinquent—a betrayal—but not something that should generally result in criminal sanctions. An example of the second type is making an excessive profit from arm's length commercial transactions with vulnerable but competent individuals, which exemplifies the moral wrong of extortion, but is effectively impossible to police in a rapidly globalising capitalist market economy. Adultery and recreational

---

[11] Not always: it is possible to imagine scenarios in which a person's prospects are so bleak that he would be better off dead, and this, in the final analysis, regardless of whether he shares this evaluation of his situation. However, a person's subjective evaluation is one ingredient in the objective assessment of their circumstances, so that a person who wants to die may be better off dead whilst another in an almost identical position may be better off alive if he wants to live. (For the avoidance of doubt, I should add that the fact that somebody would be better off dead provides no warrant whatever for somebody else to kill him.)

[12] Suicide is not a crime in English law, though it used to be regarded as 'self-murder' (Williams, 1961: 392–3), and its criminalisation has been a prominent feature of European legal culture (Neeley, 1995). However, it is a long time since *felo de se* was regarded as a crime of equivalent gravity to murder. Williams (1961: 393, n 7) reports that the stringency of the punishment for self-murder at common law was already being mitigated by the early eighteenth century, citing Hawkins, *Pleas of the Crown* (1716). In *R v Burgess* (1862) L & C 258; 169 ER 1387 the Court for Crown Cases Reserved held that attempted suicide did not amount to attempted murder within the meaning of the relevant statute.

drug use could arguably fall within either class of wrongs that ought not to be criminalised, depending on the proper moral evaluation of such conduct and the salient features of particular sets of circumstances and factual scenarios.

Whether a wrong is a necessary condition of criminalisation is more difficult to determine. One set of complications arises from the fact that penal law, like law generally, is a dynamic constituent of certain moral wrongs. Thus, there is no general moral prohibition against driving on the right-hand side of the road (if there were, most countries in the world would be damned on that account), but once the law of England and Wales has declared that everybody must drive on the left, it would then be culpably immoral behaviour to risk life and limb through deliberate or reckless disobedience. Likewise, offences against the administration of justice only get off the ground, morally speaking as well as in a practical sense, after the relevant institutions and procedures of civil society have been established by law. But once a legitimate[13] political authority has legislated for police, courts, trials, and prisons, it is thereafter immoral to obstruct a police officer in the course of his duty (without good cause), to bear false witness (perjury), to intimidate a juror, or to escape from prison.

With the diffidence appropriate to the difficulty of this question, I am inclined to think that wrongfulness *is* a prerequisite to legitimate criminalisation. Penal censure is easier to justify, other things being equal, when it applies to morally wrongful conduct (allowing that the law itself could be partly constitutive of the wrong). However, this principled constraint admittedly creates practical difficulties for criminal legislation and its enforcement.

It follows from the fact that legal rules are always over-inclusive (Schauer, 1991: ch 2) that even prohibitions with cogent rationales tend to draw morally neutral, or even praiseworthy, conduct into the net of criminality. Most non-wrongful conduct within the *prima facie* scope of a legitimate criminal prohibition can still be shielded from penal censure, in the first instance by appropriately tailored criteria of liability and the application of criminal law defences, backed-up (in common law jurisdictions)[14] by prosecutorial discretion and the ultimate safety-net of *ad hoc* judicial equity (including jury nullification in trials on indictment: see Roberts and

---

[13] There is much to unpack in this qualification, but suffice it here to observe that an illegitimate political authority, such as a brutal military dictatorship or a regime built on systematic oppression, might be disqualified from issuing morally binding laws. This is not an all-or-nothing question. Certain laws, may bind certain citizens, some of the time.

[14] The legality principle—*Legalitatsprinzip*—of compulsory prosecution is the norm in continental jurisdictions (Nelken, 2002; Fionda, 1995), though there are important exceptions (eg, there is significant prosecutorial discretion in the Netherlands: Fionda, 1995; ch 4) and much debate regarding whether in reality practice matches theory (see, for a pronounced contrast, Di Federico, 1998).

Zuckerman, 2004: § 2.3) for exceptional cases where no recognised defence is available on the facts. Yet the conceptual possibility remains that a legitimate criminal prohibition could be applied to censure and punish morally neutral or even praiseworthy conduct. This would occur whenever, and for whatever reason, none of the established normative or institutional mechanisms for keeping the criminal law focused exclusively on wrongful conduct is capable of operating legitimately and successfully. How often, if ever, this conceptual possibility materialises in practice could only be answered by systematic empirical investigation of criminal adjudication in particular jurisdictions.[15] Perhaps one is forced into the seemingly paradoxical conclusion that not every lawful application of a morally legitimate law is itself morally legitimate. But we must leave these puzzles for another day. Ultimately the thought is: if criminal conviction and punishment involve public censure for wrongdoing (von Hirsch, 1993), how could it ever be legitimate to condemn a person as a criminal offender unless he or she has perpetrated a wrong, over and above the mere fact of having broken a formally valid law? Mandela broke the law of the land but subsequently became President of his country and a secular saint in global opinion, whilst those who *obeyed* Nazi law were the criminals, morally speaking. Something more than the thin, formal 'ought' of positive law is required for these purposes, a substantive moral judgment to underpin the law's claim to legitimate (moral) authority when penal law is invoked to condemn criminality. The moral wrongfulness of criminalised conduct plays an essential legitimising role in criminal adjudication and sentencing, helping to differentiate justified state punishment from the brute force of naked coercion or political domination.

A conceivable counter-example is suggested by the situation where, under emergency conditions, it is thought necessary to proscribe membership of a hitherto lawful political or cultural association suspected of infiltration by terrorists.[16] Proscription of the association might lead to those wholly innocent of any terrorist connection being condemned as criminals purely on account of continuing membership. But even this is not a clear-cut case of crime without immorality. If the association has truly become a terrorist threat, it might be regarded as immoral to remain a member of it after the threat has been adequately publicised, not least by reclassifying the association as a criminal organisation. If, conversely, there are no reasonable

---

[15] One clue (though certainly not a self-sufficient litmus test, since penal censure is sometimes *per se* sufficient punishment for criminal wrongs) would be the frequency with which courts impose either no material sanction or purely nominal punishments on convicted offenders, assuming that such disposals are available in particular legal systems. In 2002 19,000 offenders (a little over one per cent of all sentenced offenders) in England and Wales received an absolute discharge, with a further 98,700 (about 7 per cent) sentenced to a conditional discharge (Home Office, 2003b: 78, Table 4A).

[16] Cf s 11 of the Terrorism Act 2000.

grounds for believing that the association poses a genuine threat, in the absence of a material risk of harm the argument for criminalisation falls away.

What if, in circumstances of extreme terrorist alert, the government were to proscribe membership of an effectively non-elective group, like being a Muslim or an Iraqi national? This is the limiting case. Although it is permissible to do things in an emergency that would ordinarily be intolerable, condemning someone as a criminal purely on account of their religion or nationality is categorically beyond the pale for any state with even minimally liberal pretensions. Internment is one thing (and to this day we are still arguing about the rights and wrongs of what was done to German nationals living in Britain in the 1940s); criminal censure of the entirely blameless, in the knowledge that they are entirely blameless,[17] is quite another.

Let us now relate the conceptual fruits of general theorising specifically to questions of offensive and anti-social behaviour. This topic should be of prime interest to penal philosophers, both for the ways it does and does not comport with harm-based accounts of legitimate criminalisation, and for the light it refracts back onto the broader analytical frameworks of criminal law theory.

1. Crime and Offence

Those few philosophers who have addressed offensive conduct directly have tended to concentrate on factors that apparently distinguish harm from offence, whether or not this methodological bias is explicitly acknowledged or even noticed. The selectivity of this approach merits emphasis, since its significance and limitations are easily overlooked—partly, I suspect, because we conventionally refer to all crimes, generically, as 'criminal *offences*'. This turn of phrase is perfectly innocuous in general usage, but could be a trap for the unwary in the present context, because references to 'criminal offences' in the generic sense are much too blunt to facilitate illuminating conceptual analysis of offensive conduct.

When criminal law theorists ask, 'Is *x* offensive?' they generally mean: 'Is *x* offensive, *given that* x *is not harmful*?' This rather refined interpretation of the question is driven by theorists' engagement with the moral limits of the criminal law. Since it is already well-established in the philosophical literature

---

[17] The blameless are censured whenever innocent people are convicted. This must be a routine occurrence in any human system of justice, and probably happens more often than we would like to think. Crucially, however, we do not convict the blameless *on purpose*. If the mistake is discovered, a wrongful conviction will be quashed, monetary compensation may be paid, and these days English judges even sometimes say that they are sorry that a mistake has been made.

that harms to vital interests are legitimate objects of criminalisation, offensive harms seem relatively uninteresting from a philosophical perspective. 'Should racist murder be a criminal offence?' is the type of question that Americans call a no-brainer. The more interesting test-cases for criminalisation, from a philosophical point of view, are instances of non-harmful offensiveness, of which public copulation (cf Roberts, 2001a: 52–55; Brants, 2001: 137–8) and Holocaust denial (Swart, 2001) are good examples (as good as it gets: most offensive conduct can also be regarded, with a little imagination, as posing risks of diffuse or remote harms, such as inciting copycat violence through bad example or corrupting others' moral virtue). Though it turns out, on further analysis, that the grounds for criminalising offensiveness are philosophically more instructive than is at first sight apparent, it is perfectly understandable, viewed in the light of traditional disciplinary preoccupations, why *harmless* offensive conduct should particularly pique the interest of criminal law theorists; to the extent that penal offence has attracted any philosophical attention at all.

Under the standard (Feinbergian) conception of harm outlined above, varieties of offensiveness could be considered harmless on one or both of two grounds. Either it would not be wrongful to give offence of a particular type, or such offence would not set back anybody's interests. As before, the second component of the harm couplet is easier to dissect than the first, inasmuch as certain forms of offence clearly do not set back anybody's interests, on any analytically useful conception of a 'set-back'. This is because, as Feinberg (1984: 188–90) explained, the liberal presumption against state coercion places a *de minimis* limitation on the notion of a set-back. The criminal law should not concern itself, even *prima facie*, with very trivial annoyance or disappointments. Thus, there is no criminal offence of being rude to one's parents or work colleagues, no crime of being late for appointments or meetings; and if my barber gives me a slightly less satisfactory hair cut than last time, he might miss out on a generous tip, but he need not fear blazing police sirens and prosecution for making me too self-conscious to enjoy my next evening out. Let us take a moment to recapitulate why such restraint in criminalisation is a leading article of faith in a liberal society.

Criminal law is expensive to enforce and heavy-handed in its methods—a blunderbuss, rather than a rapier, of moral discrimination. Even the most authoritarian government has weighty instrumental reasons for not resorting to a penal sledgehammer to crack a trifling peanut of moral delinquency. But in democratic polities proclaiming the virtues of political liberty and personal autonomy (see Raz, 1986: especially Part V), the capacity of criminal prohibitions and their enforcement severely to curtail citizens' freedom provides an even more compelling reason for keeping the ambit of the criminal law confined to what is strictly necessary to satisfy the dictates of good order, security, and justice. This idea is encapsulated in the political and juridical doctrine of penal minimalism (Ashworth, 2003: 32–37; 2000a:

83–84). In open, tolerant, liberal societies, people need to rub along togeth-er and take a certain amount of, even wrongful, annoyance and disappoint-ment on the chin. Penal minimalism can be seen at work, for example, in *Collins v Wilcock*,[18] where Lord Justice Robert Goff implied a *de minimis* condition into the legal concept of a battery. His Lordship was understand-ably anxious to avoid the plainly ludicrous result that every accidental but foreseen bodily contact in a busy street, shopping mall, or football stadium might constitute the crime of common assault. Extrapolating more broad-ly, that same doctrine of penal minimalism—underpinned by the positive argument for protecting and promoting personal autonomy (Raz, 1986)—explains liberal thinkers' attachment to the Harm Principle (Raz, 1987) and their principled opposition to criminalising harmless wrongdoing (Feinberg, 1988). These are the normative assumptions behind criminal law theorists' standard conceptual preference for excluding *de minimis* inconvenience from the concept of a set-back to interests.

But couldn't a particularly nasty or prolonged bout of offensive behaviour still constitute a substantial, non-*de minimis* set-back to somebody's inter-ests? What about cases of 'neighbours from hell' who diminish the quality of life in local communities with their selfish, bombastic, menacing behav-iour, or stalkers who turn pestering letters and gifts and abusive phone calls into campaigns of terror? Do the victims of such offensive behaviours not suffer persecution, loss of amenity, and declining health, ultimately leading in some cases to nervous breakdown or even suicide? Sadly, they do. However, set-backs to interests in psychological or emotional well-being of this nature easily qualify as harms,[19] whether or not they also manifest phys-ical symptoms or consequences. But the philosophers' question was whether there are any instances of *non-harmful* offence that might be considered legitimate candidates for criminalisation. Cases in which the victim unar-guably suffers harm are beside the point from this perspective.

Turning to the more intractable half of the harm couplet, the wrongfulness of offence poses deeper philosophical puzzles. Some offensive behaviour, like a racist, sexist, or otherwise discriminatory insult, is clearly wrongful. For those who believe in human dignity and equality—which in any event is the official, legally-enshrined creed of all western democracies—it is

---

[18] [1984] 1 WLR 1172, 1177, DC: 'most of the physical contacts of ordinary life are not actionable because they are impliedly consented to by all who move in society and so expose themselves to the risk of bodily contact. So nobody can complain of the jostling which is inevitable from his presence in, for example, a supermarket, an underground station or a busy street, nor can a person who attends a party complain if his hand is seized in friendship, or even if his back is (within reason) slapped.... Although such cases are regarded as examples of implied consent, it is more common nowadays to treat them as falling within a general excep-tion embracing all physical contact which is generally acceptable in the ordinary conduct of daily life.'

[19] As English law well recognises: see, eg, *R v Chan-fook* [1994] 1 WLR 689, CA.

morally wrong to criticise or verbally abuse a person on the basis of an unchosen and permanent characteristic[20] like skin colour, religious or cultural background, gender, or sexual orientation. Such characteristics are not appropriate objects of blame or criticism. If they were, that would imply that people with certain identities are inherently less worthy of concern and respect than others; that white people, or Christians, or men, or heterosexuals are less human than others. Giving wrongful offence of this kind strikes at the very root of human dignity and equal citizenship in a liberal democratic society.

It is equally clear, however, that giving offence—even serious offence, which might drive those offended close to apoplexy—is not necessarily wrongful. It was recently reported that a white South African rugby player was dropped from the national touring squad following allegations that he refused to share a hotel room with a black team-mate (Colquhoun, 2003; Malone, 2003).[21] The idea of sharing hotel facilities with a black man was apparently deeply offensive to this rugby player's racist sensibilities, though presumably his personal apartheid did not extend to refusing to pass the ball to black team-mates (which would have been an even better reason for dropping him from the team). One can imagine that the rugby player was sincerely and deeply affronted by the prospect of inter-racial communal living, since racism is far from a transitory or trifling matter. But he was not wronged by being offended: on the contrary, he was an unwitting beneficiary of a valuable lesson. In being forced to confront the unacceptability of his racist beliefs, presumably a by-product of up-bringing and social milieu which the rugby player did not choose for himself in any straightforward sense, he may come to appreciate the deeply offensive nature of racism and learn the moral irrelevance of skin-colour. The incident, in other words, provided the rugby player with an opportunity for greater moral insight, which is an educational advantage—albeit an unsolicited benefit—rather than an injurious psychic assault.

---

[20] Strictly speaking I should say *to all intents and purposes* unchosen and permanent, since there are—usually costly and sometimes extreme—ways of altering all these characteristics in some measure. But this is a minor qualification. For it would just as surely strike at the root of liberal values if human dignity and full citizenship were for some people conditional on their undertaking extreme and costly measures to alter a fundamental aspect of their personal identity, unless that characteristic was itself morally repugnant and illiberal—eg a propensity for cold-blooded murder, or child abuse.

[21] It should be said that the player in question consistently denied any racial animus, and that a subsequent inquiry by the South African Rugby Football Union's disciplinary committee failed to find conclusive proof of racism (Colquhoun, 2004). However, it should also be said that the incident prompted the immediate resignation of the Springboks' communications director, who left protesting that he 'could no longer be part of a squad in which prejudice is tolerated, wished away and excused'. Nor is this the first time that allegations of racism have been levelled: see eg, Carroll, 2003, detailing various unsavoury incidents; and Jackson, 2004, reporting that 1995 World Cup-winner Chester Williams was called 'fucking kaffir' by a Springboks team-mate, and challenged: 'Why do you want to play our game? You know you can't play it.'

This anecdote exposes a pivotal distinction between the subjective state of feeling, or just being, offended, and the objective criterion of moral wrongfulness. For wrongful offence to be given, it seems, the subjective experience must coincide with its objective moral appraisal. Offence is closely related to (and perhaps in some measure constituted by) a loosely articulated collection of other emotional reactions, including distress, anger, indignation, frustration, disgust,[22] fear, suspicion, disorientation, angst, alienation, possibly even hatred or guilt (self-hatred). Relative to some normative standard of what would offend the hypothetical person of reasonable sensibility and psychological fortitude, conduct may be offensive without actually offending anybody. However, offence is only actually given if somebody experiences the emotions constituting the subjective psychological state of being offended. In this subjective sense one either takes offence, or not, as a simple question of fact. It would neither be natural in everyday language nor analytically illuminating to interpose an objective criterion of evaluation between a person's authentic (not faked) experience of feeling affronted and the status of being offended, as though some neutral arbitrator could usefully differentiate between those who have 'really', truly, been offended, and those who only mistakenly think they have taken offence.[23] An essentially subjective conception of being offended allows conceptual room for one to say 'X took offence unreasonably', whereas if taking offence

---

[22] The focus of Doug Husak's contribution to this volume.

[23] Cf Simester and von Hirsch's potentially ambiguous remark that, although a person exposed to a disgusting foul stench might loosely describe the assault on her senses as 'offensive', yet she still 'may not describe herself as "offended"' by it (2002: 273, n 11). Of course, there has to be some reason—'something more', as Simester and von Hirsch rightly insist— before a stimulus one dislikes can intelligibly be regarded as offensive (and not just unpleasant), but this is a general property of any state of affairs for which responsibility could be attributed. It is not a special feature of taking offence. Being offended implies that, somewhere along the chain of causation, somebody is regarded as being responsible for the stimulus found offensive, if not for creating it in the first place, then at least for failing to abate it or clean it up afterwards. Thus, if horses run wild in the field next-door to my house, I might be physically disgusted by the stench of their excrement, but I would not be *offended* by it because horses are not agents capable of giving offence. However, if I believe that the stench is the fault of my neighbour for failing to muck-out his stables regularly enough, then I might well find the stench offensive; and it would also then be natural to say that I am offended by it. This conclusion holds, moreover, even if my neighbour is violating nobody's rights and perpetrating no wrong— say, because I am hyper-sensitive to the smell of horse manure and have completely unreasonable expectations of country living. As usual, however, the instrumental value of particular conceptualisations, rather than the conventions of ordinary language, must be decisive in conceptual analysis. The better approach, which achieves conceptual clarity without violating the canons of everyday speech, is to allow that being offended is purely a matter of psychological reactions, whilst insisting that only *wrongful* offence is a plausible candidate for criminalisation. This is consistent with the argument developed by Simester and von Hirsch (2002), provided that their 'something more' contemplates general features of attributing responsibility to agents, rather than building any objective criterion of evaluation into the concept of being offended.

were, by conceptual definition, subject to an objective criterion of reasonableness such commonplace descriptions of events would be nonsensical, or at least oxymoronic. In responding unreasonably to a stimulus subjectively experienced as offensive, X would on that account have failed to take offence in the stipulated sense, though she might erroneously believe herself to have been offended. This would be a strange way of characterising the world with no obvious analytical merit. People usually know whether they have taken offence or not, and there is, generally speaking,[24] nothing to be gained by attempting to second-guess their self-knowledge in this matter. But whether a person behaved reasonably or unreasonably in taking offence is another matter entirely. Such normative evaluations are best kept analytically distinct from the prior question of whether or not offence was taken, just as the subjective and objective dimensions of being offended are normally held separate in the conventions of ordinary language conversation.

It follows from these conceptual clarifications that identifying the subjective condition of being offended is only the first step in developing a philosophically robust account of penal offence. To substantiate the argument for criminalisation, being offended *per se* will never be enough. Only wrongful offence is a plausible candidate for legitimate criminalisation, and appeals to wrongfulness necessarily imply moral discrimination between the categories and sources of offence. Offence might be taken at just about anything. It always remains to be asked, therefore, whether one's reaction in taking offence was *justified*, which is to say that one had *good reason* to be offended. And one has good reason to be offended by conduct that is *wrongfully* offensive.

This analysis explains why hate speech and other racial insults are amongst the forms of (non-harmful) offensive behaviour most often criminalised in liberal democracies. Racism is an easy case, because it goes to the heart of liberal political morality as previously observed. Few will dissent from the linked propositions that racism is wrongfully offensive, and that the (subjective) offence taken by the racist, far from being wrongfully injurious, is itself an appropriate target for (objective) moral criticism. This is not yet to say that racial insults should be criminalised, all things considered, only that at this preliminary stage of the inquiry racial insults remain a plausible candidate for criminalisation. Less clear-cut instances of wrongful offence are correspondingly more difficult to place on either side of the fine moral line which differentiates those types of offensive conduct that a liberal society might conceivably criminalise, from relatively trivial wrongful affronts that should not be brought within the ambit of the criminal law.

---

[24] I am not entirely ruling out exotic psychological possibilities such as states of denial, sublimated offence, or offence which only registers at a subconscious level hidden from conscious self-realisation (without the aid of a therapist?), but I think we can safely ignore these borderline cases for the purposes of a general discussion.

Before arriving at any firm conclusions either way, one should seriously entertain the possibility that to be offended from time to time, even wrongfully offended, might be socially beneficial and healthy for personal growth and well-being.

Occasional offence challenges comfortable preconceptions, sharpens moral intuitions, and keeps the mind alive to new ways of thinking and acting. Nobody enjoys a monopoly of moral wisdom, just as nobody is entirely free from the distortions of accumulated prejudice. Without exposure to new experiences, some of which might initially seem disconcerting or distasteful by virtue of their very unfamiliarity, neither individual sensibilities nor societal mores would develop and mature. From a twenty-first century perspective, it is just as well that the limits of 1950s decency were tested by Elvis' gyrating pelvis, and that the Victorians' horror of female hemlines above the ankle was confronted and overcome. This strikes me as a highly salient distinction between offence and harm. It is not only that non-harmful offence is, in general, less serious than a (harmful) set-back to one's interests. The suggestion is that experiencing offence could be positively beneficial, both to the moral development of the individual and to the cultural health of a flourishing society. Even experiencing *wrongful* offence could help to re-establish legitimate moral boundaries and entrench socially functional taboos by preserving cherished values from enervating complacency, not least by providing exemplary occasions for their public reassertion in criminal trials. There are no obvious parallels to harmful conduct. It is not considered healthy to be beaten up from time to time in order to be reminded why physical assault is wrongful, or to experience periodic burglaries as a prophylactic against losing sight of the value of property. More frequent incentives to count one's material blessings would doubtless benefit most of us, but nobody who has read victims' accounts of the devastating experience of being burgled will regard criminal victimisation as an appropriate means to this end.

Perhaps it is also significant that criminal proscriptions targeting harmful conduct are typically underpinned by a widespread and relatively stable social consensus acknowledging the seriousness of the harm(s) in question and the propriety of their criminalisation. The boundaries and content of (wrongfully) offensive conduct are, by contrast, typically controversial and sometimes hotly disputed. Designations of wrongful offence are more obviously a function of time and place than the standard catalogue of criminalised harms. It is plausible to infer that the moral status of many potential sources of offence is more difficult to judge than the obvious immorality of much harmful conduct. If legislators derive any moral reassurance from the fact that the nature of criminal harm has been relatively stable through the centuries (albeit frequently extended by analogy to meet modern exigencies), the fact that perceptions of what is offensive appear to shift with the fashions of the times should, by parity of reasoning, give serious pause for thought before the decision is taken to extend criminal sanctions to new or previously unpenalised forms of offensive conduct. It must surely count against criminalising particular (*ex hypothesi*, unharmful) conduct that the legislature is unsure how to appraise it, the more so where society at large remains confused and deeply divided in its moral evaluations of the conduct in question.

The equivocal morality of much conduct giving (subjective) offence, reinforced by the potential value of the experience of being offended once in a while, together strongly suggest that, in principle, a legislature should deliberate very carefully and be sure to have regard to the full range of potential costs and benefits before opting to criminalise arguably wrongful offence. This is an argument, expressed in positive terms, for a general presumption against criminalising conduct that does no harm to others. In other words, philosophical investigation of the grounds for criminalising offence leads, by an indirect route, to a novel reaffirmation of the Harm Principle. The remainder of this section will further explore the concept of offensiveness, its relationship with harm, and the pivotal role of moral wrongs in the criminalisation of offence. Additional, more legalistic, constraints on criminalisation are canvassed as questions of Jurisprudence, in § V below.

2. Offence, Communication, and Intention

Offence cannot be taken before it has been communicated. Ignoring exotic psychoanalytic possibilities,[25] one cannot be offended by something of which one is ignorant. Offensive things may be said or done behind one's back but one cannot actually be offended by them unless and until the conduct in question is brought to one's attention. This is patently not true of physical injury or material loss. A blow from behind may be every bit as injurious as a full frontal assault, whilst the carefully concealed depredations of the sneak-thief or housebreaker can be just as effective in appropriating one's property as daylight robbery. *In extremis*, victims of homicide who never knew what hit them are no less deceased than those who, moments or hours beforehand, looked doom in the eye.

From this genuine difference in the respective *modus operandi* of harm and offence, it is tempting to infer that there is something *distinctively* communicative about offensive behaviour. But that premature conclusion stands in need of major qualification. For one thing, much harmful conduct could equally be regarded as communicative. Nor is this a unique characteristic of peculiarly communicative harms such as blackmail, threats to kill, or racially-motivated assault. Any crime with an identifiable victim

---

[25] See n 24, above.

usually communicates clearly enough that the perpetrator cares nothing for the victim's well-being and is prepared to use illegitimate means to advance his own interests at the victim's expense (see, further, Murphy and Hampton, 1988). Paradigmatic criminal offences like rape (Gardner and Shute, 2000) or wounding may convey such messages with especially piquant clarity, so much so that one might want to insist, with Duff (2001), that the communicative aspect of wrongdoing is a crucial dimension of the 'harm' that such offences inflict.[26] Conversely, offensiveness (harmful or otherwise) is not conceptually tied to *intended* communications. The idea of giving offence *un*intentionally is perfectly familiar, as where something is said without knowing that a person who might be offended by it happens to be within earshot. Whether an individual could properly be blamed for causing unintended offence, and the further question whether blameworthy unintended offence could ever be a proper object of criminal prohibition, cannot be settled by acontextual generalisations. One would need to examine specific types of unintentionally offensive behaviour, and the attendant circumstances and consequences of that behaviour, in detail. The essential point to notice is that the same broad questions of blameworthiness and the limits of criminalisation also arise in relation to harmful conduct. These questions are far from unique to the criminalisation of offence. So the putative distinction between harm and offence as communicative conduct amounts to no more than this, as a broad theoretical proposition: offensive conduct is by definition communicative (even when the actor has no intention to communicate anything), whereas harmful conduct is not communicative by conceptual necessity, but virtually always does in fact convey information about the actor's values, priorities, and motivation, at least whenever it is harmful conduct that might qualify as a proper object of penal regulation in a liberal society.

It is possible to construct a further argument according to which criminalisation of non-wrongful offence might conceivably be consistent with liberal principles, notwithstanding the strictures of penal minimalism. Suppose that Albert knows that Victoria is idiosyncratically offended by something perfectly innocuous, like the sight of novelty socks. One day Albert sets out with the express purpose of offending Victoria by sporting, along with short trousers for maximum impact, patterned socks depicting characters from an obscure 1970s cartoon show. Albert knows that Victoria regards cartoon-show novelty socks as the epitome of bad taste. Sure enough, Victoria is mightily offended by Albert's hosiery, and spends the rest of the day trying to avoid him. Now, it is not morally wrong (though it may be a kind of fashion crime) to wear Hong Kong Phooey socks, so we cannot say that Victoria has suffered wrongful offence. Yet Albert's conduct

---

[26] But see n 10, above.

might still be vulnerable to moral criticism, depending on further information establishing his precise motivation. Were Albert exploiting Victoria's peculiar vulnerability to novelty socks purely out of spite, for example, his conduct might fairly be regarded as petty, insensitive, and cruel. If we are precluded, both by a desire for conceptual clarity and by ordinary linguistic convention, from describing Victoria as having suffered wrongful offence, we might nonetheless still insist that Victoria has been offended wrongfully. The wrongfulness in this case inheres in the morally delinquent quality of Albert's reason for acting, rather than in the nature of the conduct giving offence.

But there is no need, for present purposes, to try to determine whether the Albert-and-Victoria hypothetical picks out a morally interesting case, or just a diverting scholastic abstraction. In terms of the political morality of criminalisation, the limited theoretical purchase of such scenarios stems from their sheer triviality. Whatever Albert's motivation, he is perfectly entitled to dress in whatever way he likes, and there is no question of framing a criminal prohibition dictating sartorial choice in order to accommodate anybody's idiosyncratic propensities to be offended by another's appearance. This is not, first and foremost, a question of practical feasibility, much less of conceptual possibility: as a matter of fact, in earlier historical periods clothing styles and colours have been minutely regulated and penalised by so-called 'sumptuary laws' (see Hunt, 1996). The point is that penal regulation of clothing is, within limits,[27] a moral non-starter in a liberal society where self-expression and freedom of choice must be respected by the legislature unless a pressing need for constraints is clearly established.

Offence always takes a particular object. One is offended *by* something or someone, not offended at large. However, as we have seen, subjective personal sensibilities could in principle be offended *by almost anything*, so that the scope of the criminal law would in no time become intolerably expansive were it to cater for every situation in which offence might conceivably be taken. To remain true to the autonomy-preserving, democratic principle of penal minimalism, prohibitions on offensive conduct must be tightly circumscribed. This is the conceptual labour assigned to an objective criterion of wrongfulness, which reiterates why only *wrongful* offence should be a plausible candidate for legitimate criminalisation in a liberal democracy.

---

[27] A leather jacket adorned with protruding razor blades is straightforwardly ruled out by the risk of harm to others, ie criminalisation satisfies the Harm Principle. More controversially, there are also limits of decency. I cannot choose to go entirely naked (except in properly designated naturist areas), though the letter of the law would probably only be enforced in certain contexts (perhaps not on the beach, but almost certainly in my lectures), which is further evidence of the relativity and flexibility of acceptable standards bearing on the reasonableness of taking offence. Be that as it may, Albert's tragically unfashionable footwear does not even come close to raising a threshold question of criminalisation.

3. Varieties of Offence Principle

As well as clarifying the legitimacy of existing or proposed criminal prohibitions targeting (arguably) offensive conduct, conceptual analysis of the nature of offence can also profitably inform general theorising on the moral limits of the criminal law. We have seen that non-harmful offence has served penal philosophy as a kind of test-case, potentially pushing the boundaries of the criminal law beyond the limits imposed by the Harm Principle. If there are categories—or even, I suppose, just one category—of non-harmful offence that might properly be criminalised in a liberal democracy, there would be room in the basic conceptual toolkit of criminal law theory for a distinct Offence Principle, following Feinberg (1985) and others (also see Simester and von Hirsch, 2002: 292–5). One or more variants of the Offence Principle might then stake their claim for inclusion in the authorised canon of general principles of criminalisation, which both facilitates theoretical analysis and provides practical guidance to policymakers in the art of principled legislation.

Plausible candidates for criminal sanctions can readily be envisaged. The Offence Principle might be satisfied, for example, by the sort of insult that is especially wrongful because grossly disrespectful and morally obnoxious, even though a mere insult does not directly set back anybody's interests ('sticks and stones may break my bones, but words can never harm me ...').[28] Perhaps certain racial epithets or sexist put-downs are insults of this kind. Whether this or any other set of examples ultimately succeeds in justifying the retention of a separate Offence Principle can only be determined by extended, properly contextualised moral argument and empirical analysis, which are beyond the scope of this chapter's general discussion. But suppose it turns out that convincing examples cannot be identified. Would that put an end to the fledgling intellectual career of the Offence Principle? Not necessarily. Even if non-harmful offensive conduct never merits criminalisation in a liberal society, the Offence Principle could still be analytically useful.

Suppose, for example, that particular forms of harmful offence exhibit special characteristics that are worth emphasising by distinguishing *within* the category of harmful conduct between offensive harms, and others of the regular, 'non-offensive' kind. One might then propound a reformulated Harmful Offence Principle (HOP). In adopting this approach, one would no longer be stretching the moral limits of the criminal law in the way in which legal philosophers have previously utilised the Offence Principle, as

---

[28] The proposition is *not* that mere words can never set back interests: consider an allegation—true or false—of corruption levelled against a public official, various forms of incitement, etc. But, for the purposes of this argument, one needs to identify offensive conduct (which could be mere words, like an insult) that is not harmful—does not set back anybody's interests—but which could nonetheless be a plausible *prima facie* candidate for penal sanctions.

traditionally conceived. But HOP might nonetheless still perform a useful function in the design and evaluation of schemes of criminalisation.

At this point it is pertinent to recall our previous observation that, contrary to what might be imagined, the essentially communicative character of offensive conduct does not robustly differentiate wrongful offence from non-offensive harms and wrongs. However, there may be other characteristic features of offensive harms of particular types, or which typically occur in distinctive circumstances, which general principles of criminalisation could usefully highlight and reinforce.

One intriguing possibility is that a reformulated Offence Principle might incorporate a zoning dimension, by which specified offensive conduct is restricted to designated premises or districts, in preference to its outright abolition. In its proper place,[29] zoning presents itself as an intuitively appealing, tolerant, and accommodating response to potentially offensive conduct in pluralistic societies. To the extent that offensive conduct may be regarded as harmful only because it might be imposed on the sensitive, the youthful, the impressionable, the strongly dissenting, or the unwary, removing the conduct to places where only well-informed consenting adults risk exposure could even render the conduct in question harmless. It is notable, however, that zoning has few, if any, plausible applications to traditional criminal harms. For as Simester and von Hirsch (2002: 295) observe, 'It is no answer to the argument for criminalising assaults on 15th Street that anyone can walk safely down 14th or 16th Streets; that 15th Street is avoidable. By contrast, indecent exposure ... may be permitted at designated beaches....' To emphasise this distinction, the Offence Principle might be said to apply to that category of penal offence, including offensive harms, which is amenable to zoning.

Another subdivision of potentially harmful offensive conduct that might require special treatment concerns communications with an overtly political dimension. It is at least arguable that colourably political communications should attract special immunity from criminal prohibition in the name of promoting democratic participation in the political process. Thus, one might still prefer, on balance, to allow the Ku Klux Klan to have their fancy-dress parades and to let Holocaust-deniers travestise history, even whilst abhorring the racist politics of such groups and even though there is a real risk of public disorder arising out of clashes with those whom Nazis and white supremacists most seriously offend. The argument would be that political participation is worth protecting even when consequential harm is

---

[29] Zoning is neither a ubiquitous nor a cost-free response to (arguably) offensive conduct. As a matter of political morality, imposing official restrictions on behaviour, stopping well short of criminalisation, may still be challenged as illegitimate, for example because zoning restrictions impose unfair costs on those who wish to participate in the behaviour in question and perhaps discourage some would-be participants altogether. Zoning may also have undesirable sociological and cultural side-effects, such as ghettoisation, social exclusion, or discriminatory treatment of those who engage in regulated pursuits.

clearly foreseeable. This is not a trivial proposition. If a material risk of public disorder were enough in itself to criminalise expressions of political viewpoints, that would also put an end to peaceable civil rights marches, demonstrations against war in Iraq, and meetings of the World Trade Organization. On the assumption that a variant of the Offence Principle such as HOP could be a legitimate principle of criminalisation, it should perhaps be qualified by POP—the Political Offence Principle—to preserve politically motivated wrongful offence from the ambit of criminal sanctions. Whereas HOP would be an essentially inclusionary principle specifying the legitimate extent and conditions of criminalisation, POP would function as an exclusionary principle placing designated conduct beyond the reach of penal sanctions.

In the USA, First Amendment jurisprudence appears to operate somewhat in the manner of an exclusionary POP, limiting the scope of criminal prohibitions to categories of constitutionally unprotected expression (see e.g. Dworkin, 1996: Part II). This idea might usefully be developed in general theorising on the moral limits of the criminal law, and possibly translated into doctrines of positive law with practical purchase in legal proceedings. In England and Wales we do not have the First Amendment to the US Constitution, but we do now have, via the Human Rights Act 1998, Article 10 of the European Convention on Human Rights and its associated jurisprudence guaranteeing the right to freedom of expression. And beyond the realms of anything that could sensibly be regarded as political participation, perhaps there are additional principles of criminalisation, concerning such matters as freedom of religion (protected by ECHR Article 9) or artistic expression, that a suitably-tailored Offence Principle could be adapted to serve.

These sketchy suggestions plainly require a great deal more thought and elaboration before any firm conclusions can be drawn. In the absence of any knock-down arguments for retaining a discrete Offence Principle, a simple functional test is proposed: theoretical concepts are worth retaining if, and just insofar as, they serve a useful analytic purpose. If, conversely, theoretical concepts merely generate gratuitous complexity and empty neologisms, they should be discarded without a moment's hesitation or sentimentality. Whether the Offence Principle ultimately passes this functional test for the utility of concepts is a question for another occasion. For present purposes we may conclude, as a general proposition, that philosophical analysis of the moral limits of the criminal law is far from self-evidently exhausted by an undifferentiated Harm Principle.

IV. QUESTIONS FOR CRIMINOLOGY

Although it is perilous to attempt to define a discipline as nebulous and contested as 'Criminology', it is essential to establish some broad definitional parameters for this discussion. Bearing in mind that such definitions are always *stipulations* minted to serve particular purposes (cf Roberts and MacMillan, 2003), I will characterise Criminology as a descriptive discipline primarily concerned with explaining the meaning, nature, causes, and consequences of crime. This definition deliberately excludes from the ambit of Criminology many descriptive issues concerned with criminal process and penal policy, as well as the bulk of normative questions relating to crime and punishment, which could be regarded as criminological in the broader sense. The discipline of Criminology is an exceedingly moveable feast, which makes it vibrant, innovative, and exciting (as well as perennially contested and sometimes fraught). However, the decisive objection to adopting an expansive definition, for present purposes, is that Criminology would then potentially swallow up everything remotely connected with crime and punishment, including the matters allocated to questions of Philosophy in the last section, and those to be addressed as questions of Jurisprudence in the next. In order to emphasise distinctive features of disciplinary method and tradition it is necessary to ascribe to Criminology a more limited frame of reference, and correspondingly deflated aspirations. In my view, it is both descriptively justifiable and conceptually illuminating to regard normative issues of crime and punishment as belonging to a distinct, emerging discipline of Criminal Justice (Roberts, 1998; cf Zedner, 2004; Sanders and Young, 2000). But there is no need to insist on that more controversial claim here. Criminology must undoubtedly be included as a valued and active participant in any interdisciplinary conversation on the topic of penal offence, even when Criminology is defined relatively narrowly as an essentially descriptive enterprise.

Developing this theme, there are at least two types of description, both with important policy implications, that Criminology might contribute to an understanding of the criminalisation of offensive conduct. A first set of criminological questions concerns the nature and extent of particular offensive behaviours. This type of description should always precede policymaking for the simple reason that, before attempting to throw laws or policemen at problematic behaviour, one should always first at least try to ascertain the true nature and extent of the problem and gauge its tractability to reform. A second set of research questions, addressing and investigating the causes of crime, ties in with Criminology's more ambitious projects of social, political, cultural, historical, and psychological analysis and explanation. Whilst criminological description features prominently in several subsequent chapters of this volume,[30] the discussion in this section must be limited to providing a few illustrations, drawn primarily from recent policy initiatives, of the type of scholarship that I claim is paradigmatically criminological.

---

[30] See, in particular, the chapters by Tony Bottoms and Elizabeth Burney.

Before engaging with this corpus of work in detail, however, we must grapple with one further preliminary question of definition.

Rather than 'offensive conduct' *per se*, it is the notion of 'anti-social behaviour' that has recently assumed a high profile in the UK government's legislative agenda, culminating in the Anti-Social Behaviour Act 2003. References to 'anti-social behaviour' have become a staple of policy discourse, with regular press briefings promoting new policing initiatives (e.g. Labour Party, 2003a and b) and concerted community action directed towards 'taking a stand against anti-social behaviour' (Labour Party, 2004). In January 2003 a dedicated Anti-Social Behaviour Unit was created within the Home Office, supported by a linked website,[31] to lead policy and disseminate best practice. Steps have been taken to encourage the police and local authorities to make greater use of their new powers, not least through financial incentives. It is no exaggeration to say that tackling anti-social behaviour constitutes a major plank in the government's multifaceted legislative programme to 'extend security and opportunity for all in a changing world'.[32] Four additional Bills on Clean Neighbourhoods and Environment, Management of Offenders, Road Safety, and Youth Justice were announced in the Queen's Speech at the State Opening of Parliament on 23 November 2004,[33] prominently including further anti-social behaviour measures to be taken forward in the ensuing parliamentary session.

Now, offensiveness and anti-social behaviour are clearly not synonymous concepts. Much that is regarded as anti-social is also unarguably harmful, whether or not it is offensive as well. Indeed, *all* crime, including the most harmful criminality, is arguably 'anti-social behaviour' in a straightforward, literal sense. References to offensive conduct nonetheless appear to crop up with some frequency in this connection, if only because the label 'anti-social behaviour' is applied so promiscuously to a very broad spectrum of activities, some of which can be seriously harmful whilst others barely justify a penal response. In the White Paper preceding the 2003 Act the Home Office provided the following elaboration:

Anti-social behaviour means different things to different people. It reflects a range of activities. These include:
- Harassment and intimidating behaviour
- Behaviour that creates alarm or fear
- Noisy neighbours
- Drunken and abusive behaviour

---

[31] http://www.homeoffice.gov.uk/crime/antisocialbehaviour/index.html (last visited 4 April 2005).

[32] A press briefing continues: 'Opportunity and progress can only be built in a safe and secure society where government and the criminal justice system are on the side of the law-abiding citizen. To ignore security concerns is to let communities and the country down.... In a changing and uncertain world, both opportunity and security are vital for the future of Britain's hard working families.'

[33] http://www.number10.gov.uk/output/page6654.asp (last visited 4 April 2005).

- Vandalism, graffiti and other deliberate damage to property
- Dumping rubbish or litter

Though there are many different forms of anti-social behaviour, a definition given in the Crime and Disorder Act 1998 is that 'a person has acted in a manner that caused or was likely to cause harassment, alarm or distress to one or more persons not of the same household as himself'. Anti-social behaviour is a problem manifested in hundreds of ways and locations....

Without attempting any further conceptual refinement, the ASBA 2003 subsequently launched straight into detailed measures to regulate particular types of conduct singled out by Parliament as anti-social (see Padfield, 2004). The definition given in the 1998 Act, and quoted in the White Paper, consequently remains the primary point of reference for those in search of authoritative guidance. On this freewheeling definition, however, any behaviour likely to cause alarm or distress to anyone who is not one's cohabitee is anti-social. Taken literally, this would include wholly innocuous and even positively praiseworthy conduct, such as intervening to break up a street-fight, 'have-a-go-hero'-style, which some onlookers might regard as alarming or distressing. It would certainly include attacking a burglar in one's own home, despite the fact that the right to repel intruders, if need be with fatal force, has been promoted as something akin to an Englishman's constitutional prerogative in certain sections of the media.[34] Without more, it would also extend to the performance of certain professional, official, or employees' duties,[35] though provision would presumably be made to exempt *bona fide* cases, if not from *prima facie* application of the label 'anti-social behaviour', then at least from any further penal consequences. This nebulous concept of 'anti-social behaviour' is at any rate broad enough to cover most, if not all, offensive conduct that might plausibly be targeted for criminalisation. Conduct liable to give offence will nearly always, and without seriously taxing the legal imagination, also seem capable of causing distress to a hypothetical onlooker.

As consumers of this policy agenda, citizens (voters) might reasonably infer that they have every reason to be alarmed about the incidence and severity of anti-social behaviour in their midst. According to an October 2003 press release, 'A snap-shot survey showed that in one day last month,

[34] The lawful extent of reasonable self-defence briefly threatened to become an election issue in early 2005, before Labour decided that it would not pursue the legislative option in this instance. New guidance was instead issued jointly by the Crown Prosecution Service and the Association of Chief Police Officers on the meaning and application of the existing law: see *Householders And the Use of Force Against Intruders* (2005), on-line at http://www.cps.gov.uk/publications/ prosecution/index.html (last visited 4 April 2005). The next morning, several national dailies, including the *Express*, *Daily Mirror*, and *London Evening Standard* ran the front-page headline 'You *Can* Kill a Burglar'.

[35] For example, in my experience informing a student that they have failed their degree is always a distressing, if not alarming, prospect.

local agencies dealt with more than 60,000 reports of vandalism and anti-social behaviour—more than one report every two seconds' (Labour Party, 2003c). The Home Secretary admonished: 'It's time to stop thinking of anti-social behaviour as something that we can just ignore. Anti-social behaviour blights people's lives, destroys families and ruins communities. It holds back the regeneration of our disadvantaged areas and creates the environment in which crime can take hold' (Home Office, 2003a: Ministerial Foreword). Policies to tackle anti-social behaviour are thus predicated on empirical claims about the nature and extent of the problem of anti-social behaviour and its consequences. This is the point at which Criminology becomes indispensable, both to policymaking and to scholarship.

1. The Nature and Extent of (Offensive) Anti-Social Behaviour

Modern, rational, enlightened public policymaking is supposedly 'evidence-based'. Nobody today thinks that 'The Way of The Baffled Medic—prescribe first, diagnose later (if at all)' (Twining, 1994)—is an appropriate approach to penal policymaking. But then, in light of successive waves of policy initiatives to tackle anti-social behaviour, one is entitled to ask: where are the criminological data establishing the need for these measures? For despite the flurry of recent legislative activity, and its accompanying bluster of alarm and resolve, methodologically robust empirical information describing the character of anti-social behaviour rarely puts in an appearance, in government publications or—for that matter—in criminological journals. Sophisticated analysis of what is specifically *offensive* in current patterns of criminal or anti-social behaviour is virtually non-existent.

Common sense and informed speculation suggest some points of departure for further conceptual analysis and empirical research. Technology-dependent modes of giving offence, like abusive e-mails or nuisance telephone-texting, can only be genuinely novel phenomena of our times; other types of offensive conduct, such as racial abuse, have probably been occurring in their modern guises for decades, but have only recently registered in the public consciousness. Still others, like public nudity, disgusting displays, neighbourhood noise, obstruction of the highway, aggressive begging, pornography, profanity, and blasphemy are almost certainly as old as civilisation itself. Yet activities such as these have attracted little sustained attention from criminologists and other social scientists. In what is probably the leading British textbook on Criminology, running to over 1,200 pages, Anti-Social Behaviour Orders attract just two brief mentions, whilst there is no index reference whatsoever to 'anti-social behaviour', 'offence', 'offensiveness', or 'offensive conduct' (Maguire *et al*, 2002). Offensive conduct and even 'anti-social behaviour' have presumably been regarded as too trivial to inspire the criminological imagination. This state of affairs is perfectly understandable, since offensiveness *is* relatively trivial in the greater scheme of criminality and did not figure prominently in modern penal policymaking until the twilight of the twentieth century. But now that anti-social behaviour has become a prime target of penal regulation, following New Labour's landslide election victory in 1997, it is a legitimate and pressing question whether criminal justice policymaking is running too far ahead of its supporting evidential foundation in criminological research.

This is not to deny that certain criminologists at various times have taken a keen interest in anti-social behaviours, counter-cultures, marginal forms of illegal conduct, 'deviant' lifestyles, and the like. The sociological canon boasts numerous classics of ethnography shedding light on the *demi-monde* of arguably offensive or anti-social behaviours (e.g. Shaw, 1966 [1930]; White, 1993 [1943]; Humphreys, 1970), stretching back at least to the pioneering work of the Chicago cultural anthropologists of the 1920s and 30s. Forty years later, on this side of the Atlantic, the whole centre of gravity of British Criminology appeared to shift from 'crime' to 'deviance'—a modest academic accommodation of '1968 and All That' (Downes and Rock, 1998; Sumner, 1994). Yet each successive generation of researchers must replicate and adapt the work of their teachers to modern conditions if criminological knowledge is to remain valid and applicable to contemporary problems of crime and justice. Today, it is an open question whether British criminology has the motivation, institutional structure, and capacity to satisfy contemporary theorists' and policymakers' on-going demands for current, up-to-the-minute empirical data. Ethnographic work, in particular, is time-consuming, demanding, and unpredictable, sometimes even dangerous (cf Wardhaugh, 2000; Winlow *et al*, 2001; Sharpe, 2000). There are easier ways to forge a successful academic career as a criminologist, for example by specialising in government-sponsored evaluation research.

Even if pertinent criminological data of the right sort and in sufficient quantities were being produced, considerable logistical problems of access and availability are posed by the rather disparate nature of this work, spread as it is across intersecting fields of sociology, social policy, cultural anthropology, social geography, urban studies, experimental psychology, etc. Needless to add, even if data were readily available and policymakers knew where to look for them, there is no guarantee that the findings of criminological research would actually be taken on-board by government, especially if research evidence seems to embarrass prevailing political agendas (including politicians' desire to appear 'tough on crime' in order to get re-elected).[36] A combination of scarcity, disaggregation, and political

---

[36] Despite modern government's ostensible allegiance to evidence-based policy-making, many UK-based academic criminologists have apparently become pessimistic, if not cynical, about policymakers' real attitudes towards criminological research. See eg, Hillyard *et al*, 2004; Tonry, 2004; Morgan, 2000; Garland and Sparks, 2000; Jefferson and Shapland, 1994; Radzinowicz, 1991; but cf Hood's more bullish appraisal (2002).

inconvenience therefore conceivably accounts for the notable absence of empirical data cited in support of recent legislative and other policy initiatives to tackle anti-social behaviour. Whatever the true explanation for this 'data gap', penal policymaking cannot claim to be fully 'evidence-based' until it incorporates systematic empirical investigation of the offensive and anti-social behaviours that are said to require remedial penalisation, utilising the full range of triangulating research methods available to social scientists.[37] The Labour government's expanding corpus of anti-social behaviour legislation does not even approach this ideal standard for evidence-based policymaking.

In addition to not knowing very much about the prevalence and character of different forms of anti-social and offensive conduct, there is little concrete information about what actually offends people in Britain today, with what frequency, and how seriously. To be sure, there is plenty of anecdotal chatter in the public domain, but this is typically refracted through the media's distorting lens and is nearly always equivocal and inconclusive. 'Does this offend you?' demanded an inch-high banner headline of *The Independent* newspaper of 14 January 2005. The front-page reproduced an almost life-size cropped photograph of the swastika armband sported by Prince Harry as part of a fantasy Nazi outfit, resembling something in-between the uniforms of the Afrika Korps and the Hitler Youth, which the prince was snapped wearing to a private fancy-dress party. World War II veterans expressing divergent viewpoints were quoted at length.[38] Lord Janner, the former war crimes investigator, regarded the episode as 'utterly offensive', but the Editor of *Jewish News* was 'disappointed more than outraged'. The consensus of expert and celebrity opinion elaborated on the inside pages was that the Prince's conduct had been foolish rather than offensive, calling for education ('I wish I could take him to Auschwitz and show him what went on...') rather than punishment.

---

[37] There is no implication that all questions can be settled by empirical investigation. Normative questions patently demand normative—eg, moral, political, or juridical—analysis. Moreover, as Doug Husak's contribution to this volume helpfully reminds us, even questions that initially *appear* empirical might turn out on further analysis to be settled by moral or conceptual argument. I would only add that, even here, empirical investigation can be useful in establishing its own limitations, and sometimes plays a crucial role in informing moral or conceptual analysis. Part of the essential justification for undertaking empirical investigation is that its results are not fully predictable in advance.

[38] Former Navy gunner Harry Marrington, 80, was mightily offended: 'I don't know what's wrong with the boy. At 20, he should have grown out of that. We were already fighting a war at 17 and 18.... We fought a war to try to stop this business.... I cannot imagine what people who have lost their families in the Holocaust must feel.' However, Jim Ratcliffe, 82 and a veteran of D-Day, was not offended by the incident: 'I just thought, "You silly lad". It is a storm in a teacup.... It was in bad taste, but all this was 60 years ago. I think we should all move on.... I've got a swastika upstairs as a souvenir. I recently spoke to some Scouts and took it with me for them to see; they had never seen one before. It is a piece of history.'

Recent performances of *Behzti* (*Dishonour*), a play by the female Sikh playwright Gurpreet Kaur Bhatti which depicts murder and rape in a Sikh temple, and the BBC's controversial decision to screen the expletive-laden *Jerry Springer—The Opera*, provoked similarly polarised public reactions. Some (potential) viewers expressed deep offence and demanded that blasphemy and indecency laws should be enforced to the letter;[39] others took up the cudgels for liberal values of free speech and artistic integrity. There is no doubting the intensity of the passions inflamed, or their tangible penal consequences: both the playwright Bhatti and the BBC executives who commissioned *Jerry Springer* were subsequently subjected to death threats and harassment, and *Behzti* had to be cancelled after crowds of protestors stormed the theatre and smashed its windows (Dodd, 2005; Deans, 2005). But what these anecdotal episodes tell us about the sources of offence in a pluralistic, multi-cultural, religiously diverse, twenty-first century Britain is more difficult to discern. Perhaps the securest inference is that public opinion is deeply divided on such contentious issues.

Some limited attempt has been made to investigate public attitudes towards anti-social behaviour more systematically. Answers to the existing diet of questions in the British Crime Survey, almost inevitably given the inherent limitations of survey research, provide only sketchy and inconclusive indications of the nuances of public opinion (Nicholas and Walker, 2004; Budd and Sims, 2001). What, for example, is one supposed to make of the statistic that, 'A third of people perceived vandalism (35%), litter (33%), teenagers hanging about (33%) and drug use or dealing (32%) to be a very or fairly big problem in their area' (Thorpe and Wood, 2004: 55)? That litter is a 'worse problem' than drug-dealing? That 'hanging about' should be criminalised, but only for 'teenagers'? Are these behaviours understood to be harmful, or offensive, or both, or neither?

The temptation to be excessively dismissive of statistical surveys of popular attitudes should be resisted. Such data are meaningful and can be instrumentally useful, both in scholarship and policymaking, provided that their limitations are fully acknowledged and appreciated. It is, for example, a suggestive (if entirely predictable) finding that, whilst people in affluent areas are most exercised by rubbish, vandalism, and rough-sleepers, council estate dwellers perceive teenagers hanging about and drug use/dealing as

---

[39] Prior to transmission the BBC received 45,000 e-mails, phone calls, and letters objecting to the screening of *Jerry Springer*, in what appears to have been an unprecedented campaign orchestrated by a lobby group called Christian Voice. Another 1,400 calls were received after transmission, 40% of which were in favour of the screening and 60% against. Christian Voice was forced to remove the home contact details of BBC executives which it had published on its website, after abusive and threatening calls were made to the executives and their families, but its Director, Stephen Green, has vowed to press on with a private prosecution for blasphemy (Deans, 2005).

the biggest problem in their neighbourhoods (Thorpe and Wood, 2004: 59 61). Raw statistics of this nature should be exploited as a platform for further research endeavouring to 'get behind' the superficial appearances of highly-structured and relatively mechanical responses to tick-box questionnaires. Without exploring respondents' understandings of the issues and questions, their motivations, points of comparison, sources of information, and personal prejudices and preoccupations, survey results remain equivocal as criminological knowledge and precarious as a basis for policymaking. Meanwhile, in the absence of illuminating follow-up interviews or other supplementary qualitative studies, 'public opinion' regarding anti-social and offensive conduct falls hostage to the projections of the leader writers and the idiosyncratic contents of MPs' postbags endlessly recycling respectable fears (Pearson, 1983).

The evident methodological limitations of existing anecdotal and survey data are exacerbated by unresolved issues of conceptual definition. To the limited extent that policy-orientated qualitative research has been undertaken, it has tended to lump together incidents 'described variously as anti-social behaviour, incivility, minor disorder, or "quality of life" issues' (Bland and Read, 2000). This is said to reflect a 'pragmatic "common sense" view based primarily on the operational realities':

> So, for the police at a local level, 'anti-social behaviour' is a description of whatever 'minor' problems intrude on the daily life of communities and lead to calls for police service.... [I]n many cases, 'anti-social' served as a generic term for problems with young people. (*Ibid*: 5, 12.)

Another empirical study commendably employed a range of complementary research methods, but proceeded from the vacuous premise that '[a]nti-social behaviour includes behaviour that puts people in fear of crime' (S Campbell, 2002: 1). It was discovered that Anti-Social Behaviour Orders—the 'ASBO', which is discussed in the next section—frequently target a range of traditional crimes including assault, racial harassment, criminal damage, public disorder, arson, 'shoplifting' (theft), drunk and disorderly behaviour, and street prostitution (*ibid*: 13–17). This research report unwittingly exposes the frustratingly elusive quality of 'anti-social behaviour' as an operational concept. How can we ever hope to describe or measure particular behaviour accurately if we cannot even define what it is? That which puts people in fear of crime is hardly an illuminating definition of anti-social behaviour. People are put in fear of crime by internet fraud and international terrorism, but not necessarily by noise, high hedges, or other forms of sub-criminal annoyance which the government's anti-social behaviour legislation has targeted. In their efforts to inform policymaking in relation to anti-social behaviour, it would appear that criminologists might have something valuable to learn from the exacting standards of conceptual rigour and definitional precision which characterise philosophical analysis of offensive conduct.

2. Crime Causation and Criminological Theory

Criminology has been preoccupied with questions of crime causation since the birth of the modern discipline, arguably traceable to the criminal anthropology of Cesare Lombroso towards the end of the nineteenth century (Garland, 2002). Causal analysis plays a central role in criminological theory, just as it ought to be indispensable to rational penal policymaking (one needs to know *how* and *why* something occurred before formulating a rational response to it). Causal analysis also implicitly underpins most ascriptions of criminal liability in individual cases (if the accused did not bring about the proscribed outcome, he should not be punished for it). There is therefore plenty of scope for instrumentally useful, as well as theoretically illuminating, criminological explanation of the behavioural and circumstantial precursors to offensive conduct.

Unfortunately, causal analysis of crime is too often tendentious or reductive. One (admittedly rather uncharitable) way of characterising the history of Criminology would be as a series of failed attempts to extrapolate from a plausible analysis of what causes *some* crimes to an inevitably reductive general theory of *all* crime. It ought to be clear by this stage in the evolution of the discipline, not least from the wreckage of discarded theories in Criminology's extensive back-catalogue (for surveys, see e.g. Vold *et al*, 2002; Morrison, 1995), that there can be no comprehensive causal explanations for behaviour as utterly diverse and differentiated as criminal offending. The only sensible response to the loaded question, 'What causes crime?' is a request for further clarification: 'What do you mean by "crime"?' Conduct which might arguably be regarded as offensive, for example, covers a vast array of activities, with no obviously uniform characteristics other than their shared propensity for causing offence. It follows that causal explanations must be particularistic, tailored to specific forms of offensive or anti-social conduct. With this caveat in mind, we may turn to consider how criminological analysis might challenge or confirm the causal claims that have been advanced in partial justification of the government's crackdown on anti-social behaviour.

According to David Blunkett, the Home Secretary responsible for placing the ASBA 2003 on the statute-book:

> The anti-social behaviour of a few, damages the lives of many. We should never underestimate its impact. We have seen the way communities spiral downwards once windows get broken and are not fixed, graffiti spreads and stays there, cars are left abandoned, streets get grimier and dirtier, youths hang around street corners intimidating the elderly. The result: crime increases, fear goes up and people feel trapped.... Anti-social behaviour blights people's lives, destroys families and

ruins communities. It holds back the regeneration of our disadvantaged areas and creates the environment in which crime can take hold. (Home Office, 2003a: Ministerial Foreword.)

This sequence of causal claims rings true at a superficial level: the behaviour of a few upsets many; decline in the built environment produces a vicious cycle of more crime and further decline; and finally, completing the cycle, crime and disorder hamper belated attempts at urban regeneration, entrenching social exclusion. Plausible causal hypotheses are one thing, however; evidence-based policymaking is quite another. Only systematic, methodologically rigorous criminological research, which was notably absent from the government's White Paper preceding the ASBA 2003, could confirm whether these speculations are a sound basis for policymaking, or just another set of unfounded assumptions contradicted by empirical reality.

The causes of crime need not be mysterious or arcane. Individuals commit crimes, including offensive crimes, for the familiar range of prosaic reasons: greed, laziness, spite, prejudice, boredom, opportunity, to feed a drug habit, or just to make a living. Prostitutes walk the streets to put food on the table; kids vandalise housing estates because they don't know any better and don't have anything better to do. These facts are evident to people who never consult criminology books, including journalists, taxi-drivers, and most politicians. Yet such common sense causal hypotheses require systematic empirical investigation to pinpoint the causal dynamics at work in particular contexts. Common sense theories are often well-founded, but they are also sometimes ill-informed, misconceived, biased, or prejudiced (Allen, 2001; MacCrimmon, 2001). The discipline of more systematic and methodologically rigorous inquiries is needed to provide an essential supplement and corrective to pop-criminology. By investigating the ways in which individuals' choices and psychology are moulded by socio-economic environment and public policy interventions, criminological researchers extend the time-honoured scholarly tradition of teasing out and articulating the more complex, interwoven, and extended chains of crime causation.

Why do the kids have nothing better to do than wreck the estate where they live and make their neighbours' lives a misery? Why is their home environment so damaging, and their educational and cultural horizons so constrained? Unless one believes that middle-class children are genetically programmed to be better behaved, it is impossible to ignore socio-economic factors in explanations of juvenile crime. What does it say about a person's opportunities for gainful employment that she chooses to become a sex worker? Can we be confident that there is any genuine choice in the matter? Single mums, even those with a crack addition to feed, still might be said to 'choose' their occupation (though whether this 'choice' retains enough volition to be an adequate basis for criminal censure is another question). But the same cannot be said for Eastern European women tricked or kidnapped into prostitution and trafficked to the UK as sex slaves, unable to escape the tutelage of violent criminal gangs and, as illegal immigrants, almost equally fearful of deportation should the opportunity to seek official protection ever arise (Kelly and Regan, 2000). And why are people-trafficking gangsters able to operate at all, if not because some regions of the world are wealthy and attractive destinations for all kinds of illicit job-seekers, whilst others are impoverished, economically weak, institutionally corrupt, war-torn (Jamieson, 1998), in short, easy-pickings for organised criminals? As the Prime Minister has himself said on more than one occasion (e.g. Blair, 2001), drug-fuelled burglaries and other everyday crimes on British streets must be understood within a global economy of incentives and opportunities.

Post-War criminological theory has gone through a series of transformations, which some might describe as intellectual progress, and others as a weakness for passing fads and fashions. Marxist social explanation is no longer in vogue today (cf Taylor *et al*, 1973 and 1975), but has bequeathed to criminological theorising a strong tradition of linking the definition and causes of crime to patterns of production and consumption, economic policy, and the business cycle (e.g. Ruggiero, 2000; Box, 1987). Feminist criminology (Gelsthorpe, 2002; Gelsthorpe and Morris, 1990) subsequently located (certain) crime in sexism, male violence, and oppressive and discriminatory social relations and cultural practices, a perspective subsequently extended to racist crime (Phillips and Bowling, 2002; Cook and Hudson, 1993). Contemporary criminological theory is characterised by diversity. Whilst the postmodern tendency disengages from anything quite so prosaic as investigating the causes of crime, instrumental 'administrative' criminologies such as 'situational crime prevention' and 'routine activity theory' have addressed themselves primarily to policymakers in the self-effacing conviction that, '[c]rime is crass, and crime science must be, too' (Felson, 2002: 37; for general discussion and critique, see von Hirsch *et al*, 2000; Garland, 2001: 127–31, 182–92). Meanwhile, Criminology's valuable tradition of critical social explanation is preserved, for example, in Jock Young's recent work on social exclusion (Young, 1999; Young and Matthews, 2003; Young, 1998).

Government policy on anti-social behaviour occasionally betrays its debt to criminological theory. In the passage quoted earlier from David Blunkett's Ministerial Foreword (Home Office, 2003a), the general notion that incivilities, if left unchecked, are the precursors of more serious offending, along with particular idiomatic references to 'the way communities spiral downwards once windows get broken and are not fixed', are borrowed directly from Wilson and Kelling (1982)'s celebrated 'Broken Windows' article. The fact that Wilson and Kelling's thesis was more in the nature of an interesting hypothesis than an empirically proven causal axiom underlines the need for policymakers to be discriminating in their choice of criminological theory. There is doubtless some truth in Broken Windows, but its credentials as a comprehensive causal theory of nuisance offending are suspect. One might also question the extent to which criminological theories of crime causation are amenable to transatlantic extension, without paying closer attention to the comparative cultural nuances of time and place (for further discussion of comparative methodology, see Nelken, 2002 & 2000; Newburn and Sparks, 2004; Roberts, 2002).

At other points in the discussion, the same White Paper appears to supplement the nostrums of administrative Criminology with a more fully contextual analysis of the causes of anti-social behaviour:

> Family problems, poor educational attainment, unemployment, and alcohol and drug misuse can all contribute to anti-social behaviour. But none of these problems can be used as an excuse for ruining other people's lives. Fundamentally, anti-social behaviour is caused by a lack of respect for other people.

> No one in this country should beg—it is degrading for them, embarrassing for those they approach and often a detriment to the very areas where environmental and social improvements are crucial to the broader regeneration of the community itself. We need to tackle the nuisance and intimidation caused to those going about their lawful business, by people who persistently beg.... The reality is that the majority of people who beg are doing so to sustain a drug habit, and are often caught up in much more serious crime. When members of the public give them money on the street it does not help them deal with their problems. (Home Office, 2003a: 7; paras 3.40–3.41.)

Notice, however, that the White Paper soon abandons its apparent commitment to contextual empirical analysis by reverting to a sequence of wholly untested moralising assertions. It is true that 'rotten social background' cannot be an all-purpose excuse for offensive or anti-social behaviour (broadly for the reasons rehearsed by Morse, 2000), and it certainly would be nice to think that nobody in twenty-first century Britain need resort to begging to survive—just as it would be nice to think that in this day and age nobody should be starving to death in Africa. It remains unclear, however, why lack of respect for others should be singled out as *the fundamental cause*. Might lack of respect not be a *symptom* of defective moral education in the home, in school, and in the wider community? Nor is the bald assertion that begging in Britain today is an entirely optional career choice entirely convincing—even if we conveniently overlook, as most people do, the plight of teenage runaways and illegal immigrants who must fend for themselves outside the formal safety-net of social welfare provision.[40] These

---

[40] When I lived in Oxford in the late 1980s, career beggars were at work on Broad Street, middle-aged men with council houses who would freely admit that embarrassed tourists and the occasional kind-hearted don were a soft touch. Like the Man with the Twisted Lip (Conan Doyle, 1981 [1930]), begging was, for them, a profitable and even enjoyable occupation. But the young people who today huddle under damp blankets next to cashpoint machines in Nottingham city centre, with their pathetic dogs on string-leads, do not appear to me to be living the lives that they would ideally choose for themselves.

passages inadvertently demonstrate how truncated analysis of the causes of crime, coupled with moralising common sense assumptions, pave the way to short-sighted, and possibly unjustifiable, penal policies.

From its first days in office the current Labour administration set out its stall to socialise criminal justice policy—in Tony Blair's endlessly recycled slogan, to be 'tough on crime, and tough on the causes of crime'. New penal initiatives have frequently been allied, at least rhetorically, to measures in related fields of social policymaking including the family, education, employment, housing, health, and community regeneration. This is unequivocally a welcome change of direction from the later Thatcher and Major governments of the 1990s which deprecated efforts to understand the causes of crime, preferring instead to call for harsher sentences and build more prisons.[41] However, evidence-based analyses of crime causation are seemingly in competition with a more populist penal agenda, in which the government promises 'to shift the culture away from protecting the rights of the perpetrator towards protecting the rights of decent people' (Home Office, 2003a: para 1.3). When penal populism gains the upper hand, concrete policy prescriptions predictably gravitate towards greater toughness on crime and away from tough-minded policies to tackle the causes of crime. Measures intended to combat nuisance begging illustrate this general trend in microcosm. The White Paper's rhetorical commitment to 'addressing the underlying causes and tackling its persistent nature' (*ibid*: para 3.43) laid the foundation, not for intensive social assistance or more inclusive housing policies, but for reclassifying begging as a recordable offence (*ibid*: paras 3.43–3.44).[42] Beggars will henceforth be fingerprinted without their consent[43] and acquire a formal criminal record, with the possibility of drug treatment or other suitable rehabilitative community sentence only on conviction for a fourth offence.[44]

On a common sense view, crime is the product of individual choice and, perhaps, social circumstances, and penal policy is merely reactive in its efforts to get to grips with 'the crime problem'. But this is a naïve perspective, which fails to appreciate the extent to which government policy and administration may themselves be 'criminogenic' in creating or causing

---

[41] Eager to be seen as getting tough with young thugs, John Major declared that it was 'time to condemn more, and understand less', which must be—in a very strong field—just about the most bone-headed comment that a politician has ever uttered regarding penal policy. Condemnation, of whatever magnitude and no matter how justified, is never an alibi for ignorance.

[42] Effected by the National Police Records (Recordable Offences) (Amendment) Regulations (SI 2003/2823), amending the schedule of specified offences listed in the National Police Records (Recordable Offences) Regulations (SI 2000/1139).

[43] Police and Criminal Evidence Act 1984, s 61(3).

[44] Section 151 of the Criminal Justice Act 2003 permits a court to impose a community sentence 'in the interests of justice' on offenders who have been fined on three previous occasions, in respect of a current offence, or offences, which would otherwise only be serious enough to attract another fine.

crime. Criminologists have demonstrated that changes in penal policy—whether effected through primary legislation, or more informally—and their translation into practical law-enforcement must be included as part of the broader picture of crime causation. As labelling theory and symbolic-interactionist criminologies of the 1960s and 1970s taught (Morrison, 1995: ch 14; Matza, 1969; Becker, 1963), the social and institutional processes of criminalisation through which particular conduct is designated 'criminal', and dealt with accordingly, is a composite of precipitating actions and official reactions. In this expanded frame of reference, it is perfectly intelligible to speak of education, housing, employment, or social welfare policies as 'causes' of crime, in addition to recognising the criminogenic potential of much criminal justice and penal policymaking in the narrow sense (prisons as 'universities of crime', etc). The reflexive nature of both offending behaviour and criminal justice policy and practice, whereby changes in one often produce adaptive changes in the other, greatly complicates analyses of crime causation.

Episodes of social interaction do not stand still in order to allow themselves to be caught, as it were, in freeze-frame and measured accurately by patient social scientists armed with compass and magnifying glass. Criminologists have nonetheless made significant strides in theorising this fundamental methodological challenge, and in devising research strategies to cope with it (generally, see King and Wincup, 2000; Jupp *et al*, 2000). Far removed from the simplistic image of researchers gathering up facts like so many pebbles on a beach (a fantasy which the *cognoscenti* deride as 'positivism'), producing descriptions of crime and offending that are faithful to the complexities of human interaction in particular social and institutional settings calls for expertise, determination, and ingenuity in the application of interpretative, (de)constructionist, or 'hermeneutic' methods (Taylor, 1985; Webber, 2004). Cultural criminology is the latest self-conscious innovation in criminological theorising to announce itself ready, able, and willing to strive to overcome the methodological obstacles to authentic description (Hayward and Young, 2004; Kane, 2004; also see Nelken, 2004).[45]

The normative philosophical, legal, and penological tasks of designing criminal prohibitions, apportioning blame, and prescribing appropriate

---

[45] At the October 2003 colloquium I was chided by one friendly critic for presenting Criminology as a mundane, low-level, empirical science conceived to be conducted by administratively-minded researcher-drones. Philosophy and Jurisprudence had supposedly been assigned all the best tunes in my taxonomy of disciplines. Once the methodological complexity of description is appreciated, however, I cannot see how this accusation can be made to stick. If it is true, as some have provocatively claimed, that 'the majority of mainstream criminological scholarship today can only be described as ... boring' (Ferrell, 2004: 295), this is not because Criminology is, in my terms, an essentially descriptive enterprise. Description can certainly be boring, just as it can be done badly, but it need not be either. Indeed, description is more likely to be interesting when it is done well.

sanctions and remedies must proceed on the firm basis of evidence and knowledge about crime causation, rather than on the speculative hopes of inflated political rhetoric, common sense preconceptions and prejudices, or uninformed guesswork. Criminologists' descriptive labours are consequently an indispensable precursor to rational criminal legislation and policy-making. Neither policymakers nor scholars can afford to leave Criminology out of their interdisciplinary conversations on the topic of penal offence.

V. QUESTIONS FOR JURISPRUDENCE

Several years ago, BBC2's *Newsnight* programme brought together a retired senior judge and a representative of a pressure group to debate how the law should respond to women who kill their abusive spouses. The judge sought to temporise, but the lobbyist would not be deflected from advocating a new, dedicated criminal law defence to absolve battered women who kill. At the height of the debate, when the judge was just about as worked up as retired judges should ever get on live television, he demanded to know: 'How would such a defence be drafted?' This seemingly pettifogging objection doubtless appeared eccentric to the majority of the viewing public, and in its bloodless and legalistic preoccupations, provided ample confirmation that the judiciary is hopelessly 'out of touch' with the concerns of ordinary people. Yet the judge was making an important jurisprudential point, the significance of which is too often overlooked. Questions of legislative drafting may be relatively arcane, but they are pivotal to the enterprise of successfully translating moral precepts and conceptual distinctions into workable rules of law.

A defence for battered women who kill, for example, could not be drafted to apply to 'any woman who kills her spouse' (too broad, by common consent), 'any woman whom the judge thinks has a meritorious defence' (too reliant on untrammelled judicial discretion), or 'any woman whom representatives of women's groups think has a meritorious defence' (nobody seriously contends that the application of the criminal law should be determined by lay people representing sectional interests). Any such defence would have to be restricted to particular situations or types of relationship, which themselves would have to be carefully specified in advance. Who should qualify as a 'battered spouse'? How should one characterise a 'battering relationship'? By the number of battering incidents, by the duration of the relationship, or a mixture of both? Does the concept of battering cover psychological or emotional abuse as well as physical harm? The fundamental dilemma, as the judge was trying to explain to *Newsnight's* audience, is that any such defence would inevitably be criticised for being ungenerously narrow if it were drafted restrictively, but might become available to almost all domestic—and even possibly some non-domestic—murderers were it drafted more expansively. None of this establishes conclusively that a dedicated defence for battered spouses who kill is legally untenable, but it does illustrate why the impact of pragmatic drafting considerations on the scope and content of the criminal law should never be under-estimated. Legislators must walk a fine line between excessive rigour and incontinence in the penal law.

These general observations apply with particular force to the criminalisation of offensive conduct. The initial problem, which we have already encountered from a philosophical perspective, is to frame an appropriately circumscribed general prohibition, or battery of specific prohibitions targeting particular types of offensive conduct, given that literally almost anything could be experienced as offensive by somebody or other. For the reasons previously stated in § III, liberal legislators can legitimately limit their attentions to *wrongful* offence, but this is only the first step in meeting the drafting challenge.

Simply criminalising 'offensive conduct' (not to mention 'anti-social behaviour') and leaving the details to be worked out by individual police officers, prosecutors, and fact-finders in the application of the prohibition manifestly will not pass muster. To satisfy Rule of Law requirements of prospectivity, legal certainty, democratic accountability, and fair warning (Ashworth, 2003: 69–78; Raz, 1977), now reinforced in England and Wales by Article 7 of the European Convention on Human Rights,[46] it will be necessary to specify the nature of criminal offensiveness in some detail. How is this to be done, without getting into the open-ended and faintly ridiculous business of designating proscribed words, phrases, and gestures in criminal legislation? Micro-policing the content of expression is a job for which the criminal law is spectacularly ill-suited. Added to which, in the UK context, there is no parliamentary time for continually updating a secular Index of proscribed gestures or communications (a task of immense proportions, given the speed and ingenuity with which new insults and obscenities are incessantly being coined), and the whole enterprise would be at odds with the modernist aspiration, currently to the fore in English penal policy, to produce a simplified criminal law amenable to restatement in a handy-to-use Code (CJS, 2002: paras 0.25, 4.5.1; Auld, 2001: ch 1, paras 35–36; Roberts, 2001b: Part IV).

A possible riposte to these pragmatic objections would be to draft an open-ended prohibition criminalising anything that would be considered seriously offensive by the reasonable person, as determined after-the-fact by the court. There is a precedent for this drafting strategy in the English law

---

[46] Article 7(1) provides that, 'No one shall be held guilty of any criminal offence on account of any act or omission which did not constitute a criminal offence under national or international law at the time it was committed.'

offence of causing 'harassment, alarm or distress' contrary to section 5 of the Public Order Act 1986. However, it is debatable whether this formulation is fully compliant with Articles 7 and 10 of the ECHR (Ashworth, 2003: 25–26, 77–78), and section 5 itself might have to be reconsidered under the Human Rights Act in the near future.

Another tempting legislative strategy for keeping the criminal law confined within reasonable bounds would be to limit the scope of any prohibition to *intentionally* offensive behaviour. This tactic reprises and generalises the Albert-and-Victoria hypothetical discussed in § III, where the argument was limited to *non-wrongful* offence. A requirement of intentionality would exclude from the realm of penal censure cases of adventitious over-hearing, mistaken indecent exposure, casually insensitive remarks and the like, a limitation which makes sense if the primary objective is to proscribe deliberately offensive conduct and one is content to let accidentally-inflicted wrongful offence pass without penal remedy on *de minimis* grounds. It would not, however, solve the problem of protecting legitimate political or cultural expression, for which dedicated defences would presumably need to be carved out of any general prohibition (with or without the analytical assistance of some variation on the Offence Principle, such as HOP or POP).

Every such limitation or exception would incrementally increase the enforcement costs of criminal prohibitions aimed at penalising offensive conduct. The long-running saga of the meaning of 'intention' in the crime of murder (Ashworth, 2003: 173–80; Simester and Sullivan, 2003: 126–36, 334–8) should be a strong hint for prosecutors of the practical difficulties to be overcome in proving a deliberate intention to cause offence in any particular case. Meanwhile, the notorious obscenity trials of the 1960s and early 1970s (the *Lady Chatterley's Lover* and *Oz* trials in Britain; contested censorship of the works of Allen Ginsberg, William Burroughs, Jack Kerouac, and Henry Miller in the USA: see Kearns, 1998; de Grazia, 1991; McGaffey, 1974–5) still stand as a warning of what lies in wait for those foolhardy enough to seek to determine the limits of legitimate artistic expression through criminal litigation. At some point it must become doubtful whether a prohibition that was so limited in scope and so difficult to enforce in practice could really justify all the time and effort that would be needed to get it onto the statute-book in the first place.

Advocates of criminalisation also need to consider the practical realities of policing and criminal investigations. If a particular prohibition could only be enforced by morally odious means or at great cost to related objectives or values, then even a penal statute that could be justified in principle should not be enacted. Practical objections loom especially large where the principled argument for criminalisation is finely balanced. This will often be the case, as we have seen, when attempting to appraise the merits of non-harmful or only marginally harmful offensive conduct. If the enforcement of prohibitions against such conduct would require major sacrifice of other important values at play in criminal investigations and prosecutions, that consideration might tip the scales decisively against criminalisation. Sanford Kadish (1987: 24) once directed this kind of argument against homosexual importuning offences:

> To obtain evidence, police are obliged to resort to behaviour that tends to degrade and demean both themselves personally and law enforcement as an institution. However one may deplore homosexual conduct, no one can lightly accept a criminal law that requires for its enforcement that officers of the law sit concealed in ceilings, their eyes fixed to 'peepholes', searching for criminal sexuality in the lavatories below; or that they loiter suggestively around public toilets or in corridors hopefully awaiting a sexual advance.

An extreme illustration of the wholly disproportionate side-effects that may be triggered by such policing methods is provided by the cautionary tale of the Beverly Hills undercover officer who arrested popstar George Michael for indiscretions in a public convenience (Wallace and North, 1998). This highly publicised celebrity arrest led to a $10 million law-suit in which the police officer in question sought compensation for 'emotional and mental distress' and reduced career prospects (Campbell, 2002 & 1999).[47] Vice cops are always prone to bribery and corruption, owing to the company they are obliged to keep and the potentially compromising situations in which they regularly find themselves. Even those who think that gay sex in public toilets is gravely immoral and offensive, and believe that tax revenue is well spent on catching offenders, still need to ask themselves whether the law enforcement means are capable of satisfying the ends of penal justice, bearing in mind that criminalisation will almost inevitably lead to police officers' routine degradation and exposure to corrupting influences.

To this point I have been assuming that criminal prohibitions are designed to be enforced. It is conceivable, however, that the criminalisation of offensive conduct might be intended as an essentially symbolic gesture to signal society's abhorrence of egregiously wrongful forms of offence. Ignore for now the question whether this would be an appropriate use of scarce legislative resources.[48] The main objection to purely symbolic penal legislation is

---

[47] George Michael was convicted of 'disorderly behaviour', for which he was fined $810 and ordered to perform 80 hours' community service. He subsequently satirised the incident in the video for his next single release, 'Outside', which featured glitter-ball silver urinals in disco-lit public toilets, extravagant sexual innuendo, and mincing dancers wearing cut-down police uniforms. The arresting officer interpreted this spectacle as public ridicule, and also took exception to George Michael's chat show allegations of active entrapment: 'He played a game called "you show me yours, I'll show you mine" ... I responded to a handsome American cop. They don't send Colombo in to do this....'

[48] Though this is a serious objection in the English context, given that parliamentary time apparently cannot be found to enact long-overdue criminal law reforms, like modernising our antiquated Offences Against the Person Act 1861 (see Roberts, 2001b: Part IV).

that symbolic gestures are not cost-free, nor necessarily cost-effective. Supposedly symbolic gestures may even be directly counter-productive, as where a new criminal prohibition draws attention to undesirable conduct that previously went largely unnoticed, only to appear to condone the conduct through under-enforcement. What messages do unenforced or unenforceable symbolic laws convey, if not an invitation to perpetrators to mock the justice system, thus bringing the law into (greater) disrepute amongst victims of crime and their supporters? American criminal laws proscribing race-hatred, for example, are said to have produced a litany of counter-productive effects, 'exacerbating social divisions rather than contributing to social solidarity' and letting 'politicians off the hook too easily' (Jacobs and Potter, 1998: 91):

> One potential unintended result is that people will take symbolism too seriously and assume that denouncing the problem through hate crime laws effectively addresses the problem.... Throwing laws at a problem costs no money and requires no real political energy.

Besides, penal legislation is rarely, if ever, promoted by policymakers as a purely symbolic gesture. Politicians typically promise voters effective policies to combat crime, and penal administrators and criminal justice professionals are expected to make a real difference to crime control in practice.

Anticipated enforcement difficulties have encouraged legislators to look for ways of evading due process constraints on criminal investigations and prosecutions. Recent initiatives to tackle anti-social behaviour in England and Wales, which have been condemned for their 'subversion of human rights' (Ashworth, 2004), exemplify this tendency. Fixed penalty notices issued by the police, which hitherto were confined to minor road traffic offences, have been extended to cover a much broader range of quality-of-life crimes and categories of offender;[49] though, for the time being at least, police officers have not been given the widely-touted power to march hoodlums directly to a cash-point machine to collect on-the-spot fines (Leading Article, 2003; Hooper and White, 2000).[50] Such informal sanctioning schemes divert cases out of the criminal justice process at the earliest opportunity, utilising a kind of systematic pre-emptive charge-bargaining effectively beyond the purview of judicial supervision. In similar vein, Part 2 of the ASBA 2003 recruits social housing policy into the programme of measures to tackle anti-social behaviour (complementing related provisions of

---

[49] Anti-Social Behaviour Act 2003, ss 23, 43 and 87; Criminal Justice and Police Act 2001, ss 1–11.

[50] It is tempting to surmise that politicians must have noticed that loitering by cash-machines had not proved an especially rewarding strategy for the homeless. But in reality on-the-spot fines were doomed as soon as senior police officers publicly pronounced the idea 'not a goer ... a dead duck' (Ford, 2000).

the Homelessness Act 2002), and consideration is being given to withholding housing benefit from 'problem tenants' (Home Office, 2003a: para 4.48: generally, see Padfield, 2004; Brown, 2004) Indeed, local authorities are under a statutory duty to promote crime prevention and to consider how best to reduce disorder in relation to *all* their powers of local government.[51] Needless to add, such broadly integrated social policy initiatives are typically unfettered by the presumption of innocence, the privilege against self-incrimination, rights to legal advice and representation, and most of the other procedural hallmarks of orthodox criminal prosecutions in modern liberal democracies.

The Anti-Social Behaviour Order, or 'ASBO', introduced by section 1 of the Crime and Disorder Act 1998 is the acme of this new enforcement philosophy. Ostensibly a civil law order akin to an injunction, the ASBO empowers a magistrates' court at the behest of the police or local authority to impose tailor-made restrictions on the future conduct of a person who has been proved[52] to have engaged in any one of a broad range of 'anti-social' behaviours, some, but by no means all, of which are also independent criminal offences. The scope of an ASBO can extend far beyond merely directing desistance from the particular anti-social behaviour in question. An ASBO may impose restrictions on a person's movements, for example by excluding individuals from specified public locations like parks, shopping malls, or sports stadia. Other conditions could include a curfew, or even, in principle, a prohibition on place of residence preventing a person from continuing to live in their own home. The order remains on foot for a minimum of two years, but has no maximum duration and could therefore impose permanent civil disabilities, 'a kind of internal exile' (Ashworth *et al*, 1998: 9). Most controversially of all, breach of an ASBO is a criminal offence carrying a maximum penalty of five years' imprisonment. This puts the crime of ASBO-breach on a par with traditional criminal offences of medium seriousness like assault occasioning actual bodily harm, malicious wounding, and theft.[53]

It would be simplistic and unfair to dismiss the new package of diversionary mechanisms as nothing more than a cynically-motivated attempt by illiberal politicians to evade the traditional protections for suspects, the

---

[51] Crime and Disorder Act 1998, s 17.

[52] Proof was originally assumed to require the civil 'balance of probabilities' standard, but in *McCann v Manchester Crown Court* [2003] 1 AC 787; [2002] UKHL 39, the House of Lords held that the criminal standard of proof must be satisfied in ASBO applications. In other respects, however, these remain civil proceedings, so that, for example, the hearsay rule applicable in criminal trials does not apply.

[53] Theft in fact carries a maximum sentence of seven years' imprisonment, but the 'typical' or statistically average theft attracts far less severe punishment. Fewer than one in three (27.9%) offenders convicted of theft or handling stolen goods in 2002 were sentenced to immediate custody, with an average sentence length of 7–22 months, depending upon plea, precise charge and the circumstances of the offence (Home Office, 2003b: Tables 4D and 4.2).

accused, and convicted offenders enshrined in criminal procedure law. For there are genuine problems of detection, delay, proof, and general under-enforcement in the administration of the criminal law—'the justice gap' (CJS Framework Document, 2002)—which do call for imaginative solutions. If minor infractions can be dealt with satisfactorily through fixed penalty notices, cautions, reprimands, and final warnings, there is no sense in dragging the matter out unnecessarily at greater cost. Such intermediate, quasi-criminal sanctions are an established feature of many continental European legal systems (see Hörnle, 2001: 271–4; and, more generally, Fionda (1995), comparing diversionary mechanisms in England and Wales, Scotland, the Netherlands and Germany), and their extension was urged by Lord Justice Auld's *Review of the Criminal Courts in England and Wales* (2001: ch 9). Nor is it desirable that prolific offenders should have to wait many months before being brought to trial, at risk of further offending whilst on bail and without receiving positive penal interventions to promote their rehabilitation and desistance from crime.

But identifying a genuine shortfall in the administration of justice is not the same thing as devising legislative remedies or implementing practical solutions. In pronounced contrast to other areas of social policymaking, in which it is acceptable to make direct trade-offs between citizens' competing interests in pursuit of aggregate social welfare, criminal law involves publicly blaming and punishing individual moral wrongdoers, which can only be done legitimately in accordance with certain substantive moral precepts and procedural guarantees. The guilty, and only them, must be punished only in accordance with their just deserts, and no lawful punishment may be exacted until culpable breach of a prospective, well-defined, and properly advertised criminal prohibition has been publicly demonstrated in a fair trial, to a demanding level of proof, and after strenuous efforts have been made to avoid wrongful conviction of the innocent (Roberts and Zuckerman, 2004: chs 1 and 8). Excessive haste and inattention to detail, on the other hand, are precisely the characteristics that give 'summary justice' its pejorative connotations.

Legal protection of fundamental freedoms in England and Wales has been underpinned by the passage of the Human Rights Act 1998, conferring a newly-elevated status in English law on the European Convention on Human Rights. Article 5 of the Convention protects against unlawful deprivations of liberty, whilst Article 6 guarantees the right to a fair trial, including the presumption of innocence[54] and the privilege against self-incrimination in criminal proceedings.[55] Significantly, the Strasbourg-based European Court of Human Rights adopts an 'autonomous interpretation'

---

[54] Article 6(2).
[55] *Saunders v UK* (1996) 23 EHRR 313; *Funke v France* (1993) 16 EHRR 297.

of the concept of a criminal charge in Article 6,[56] so that States Parties to the Convention cannot circumvent fair trial rights by the simple expedient of re-branding criminal prosecutions as civil enforcement proceedings. This stricture has particular salience for hybrid penal measures like the ASBO. The Strasbourg Court could decide that, if it looks like a penal order, and is enforced by penal institutions, and involves onerous sanctions of a penal character, then the ASBO is a criminal penalty, regardless of what the UK government might choose to call it, and there must consequently be compliance with the full range of Article 6 protections before an ASBO can lawfully be imposed. The House of Lords has recently determined otherwise,[57] confirming the formal status of the ASBO as a non-penal civil order in English law. However, the Strasbourg judges are not obliged to endorse their Lordships' question-begging reasoning (see Macdonald, 2003) and will doubtless be called upon to reconsider the issue in due course.[58]

There is a fundamental tension, or contradiction, at the heart of the government's policy on tackling anti-social behaviour, which echoes the conceptual confusions and misunderstandings that sometimes plague inter-disciplinary academic discussions of 'offensive conduct'. On some occasions, and for certain purposes, it is emphasised that anti-social behaviour 'blights people's lives, destroys families and ruins communities' such that '[t]here must be a consistent message that sanctions against anti-social behaviour are *extremely serious* and that breach of them will lead to unwelcome consequences for the perpetrators' (Home Office, 2003a: para 1.13, emphasis supplied). This message is accompanied by pessimistic diagnoses (for the most part lacking empirical substantiation, as we observed in § IV) of 'the spiral of anti-social behaviour', according to which '[e]nvironmental decline, anti-social behaviour and crime go hand in hand and create a sense of helplessness that nothing can be done' (*ibid*: para 1.8). Yet policymakers' insistence on the seriousness of anti-social behaviour is difficult to square with the marginal penal significance of most (non-harmful) offensive conduct. If anti-social behaviour truly produces such dire consequences, why is it not already catered for by criminal prohibitions penalising personal injury, damage to property, harassment, public disorder, endangerment, and interference with the administration of justice? With upwards of 8,000 separate criminal offences on the statute-book, at a conservative estimate (Ashworth, 2000b: 226), English law is certainly no slouch in the criminalisation

---

[56] *Benham v UK* (1996) 22 EHRR 293.

[57] *McCann v Manchester Crown Court; Clingham v Kensington Royal LBC* [2003] 1 AC 787.

[58] It is fair to say that the existing Strasbourg authorities are inconclusive on the precise point in issue: compare *Steel v UK* (1998) 28 EHRR 603, with *Raimondo v Italy* (1994) 18 EHRR 237 and *Guzzardi v Italy* (1980) 3 EHRR 333. For further conceptual discussion, see Simester and von Hirsch in this volume.

stakes.[59] If unexpected chinks from time to time appear in the criminal law's existing armoury, targeted statutory amendment or, if amendment would be insufficient or unsuitable, tailor-made additions to the current scheme of offences would be the obvious remedies. A persuasive case for adopting radically novel enforcement strategies remains to be made.[60] Moreover, if anti-social behaviour produces seriously harmful consequences meriting stern public disapprobation and severe punishments, how could it ever be legitimate to deal with such behaviour except within the framework of regularly-constituted criminal proceedings, affording due process of penal law and full compliance with fundamental human rights? Minor offences would presumably be more promising candidates than grave crimes for experimental diversion from formal criminal process.

By which circuitous route we return, almost full-circle, to the philosophers' central preoccupation with identifying grounds for criminalising non-harmful offensiveness in the strict, narrow sense previously distilled in § III of this chapter. Perhaps all the dire predictions of remote harms (cf. von Hirsch, 1996) flowing from offensive conduct are just so much smoke and mirrors to divert attention from the illiberality of criminalising non-harmful offence. In that case, however, warnings of 'extremely serious' sanctions threaten to envelop anti-social behaviour more deeply within the toils of penal regulation and to talk its punishment much further up the sentencing tariff than could ever be consistent with liberal principles of autonomy, human rights, and penal justice.

There is one further possibility, and one last question. It is possible that the seriousness of anti-social behaviour has failed to register in traditional responses to crime because the criminal law primarily targets discrete, one-off events involving individual perpetrators. With its pronounced emphasis on individuation it may be difficult for criminal law to accommodate the full impact of on-going conduct or concerted group activity—by a 'gang' or 'problem family', for example—which cumulates over time. But even if there is some truth in this accusation, it still remains to be shown how novel measures to combat anti-social behaviour can deliver justice according to law, rather than merely seeking to impose social order any which way. This

---

[59] The extent of criminalisation in England and Wales is not widely appreciated. When I invite first-year undergraduate lecture groups to guess how many different criminal offences exist in English law, bidding starts at around ten and rarely ventures above 1,000. (The editors wish me to add, for the avoidance of doubt, that Criminal Law is taught in the second year at the University of Nottingham.)

[60] A further influential consideration may have been that it was often too difficult to secure evidence of anti-social behaviour that would satisfy a criminal court, partly as a result of alleged witness intimidation (S Campbell, 2002: ch 6; cf *McCann v Manchester Crown Court; Clingham v Kensington Royal LBC* [2003] 1 AC 787, at [16]–[17], [44], [85]). This is a serious concern, but the solution comes perilously close to saying that, since evidence of offending cannot be assembled, we will simply dispense with the need for proof and proceed directly to 'punishment': cf Ashworth, 2004: 278–9.

has been, in various guises, a recurring central question for the jurisprudential analysis undertaken in this section: how can legitimate penal censure be
imposed without complying with the normal procedural guarantees and
fundamental process rights sanctified by our political traditions as the
authentic characteristics of criminal prosecution, trial, and conviction?
Stripped of its procedural pedigree, criminal process is seemingly reduced to
a degenerate mongrel.

VI. QUESTIONS BEFORE ANSWERS

By exploring the distinctive types of questions that different disciplines tend
to frame about the relationship between crime, offence, and anti-social
behaviour, this chapter has endeavoured to convey a sense of the broader
institutional context, objectives, methodology, and significance of alternative perspectives and complementary approaches. An interest in questions is
usually motivated by a desire for answers. However, in venturing into still
largely uncharted and at times disorientating territory, it is far too early to
be confident, let alone dogmatic, about one's ultimate destination. A sensible preparatory step would be to identify and organise the available intellectual resources into a useful inventory. This calls for a mapping exercise,
a kind of disciplinary cartography, to supply some fixed points of reference
to facilitate productive interdisciplinary conversation.

In taking up the challenge of placing penal offence in question, this chapter expounded the merits of three, broadly conceived, disciplinary traditions. Philosophy, I sought to demonstrate, brings conceptual rigour and the
guidance of moral and political principle to discussions of criminalisation.
Philosophical rationalisation locates penal offence within a broader framework of values, and establishes links with fundamental questions of political authority and human flourishing. Broadly speaking, western, liberal,
analytical philosophy (to be a little more explicit about this chapter's
inevitably partial definition of Philosophy) promotes conceptual clarity and
the priority of moral principle over political opportunism. Whilst it sometimes does—and arguably often should—draw upon empirical information,
however, philosophical inquiry is predominantly normative. For informa-
tive and reliable empirical data, one must look elsewhere.

Criminology, conceived as an essentially descriptive enterprise, supplies the methodological tools and research data to generate detailed and
sophisticated accounts of the prevalence, causes, and effects of offensive
criminality and anti-social behaviour. Building on its critical tradition of
dissecting the socially-constructed meanings of 'crime', Criminology could
also shed important light on the nature and extent of offensiveness in modern society. To produce authentic descriptions of complex social interactions and cultural meanings demands self-reflexive interpretative acumen

and methodological expertise, ingenuity, and perseverance. Criminology boasts a unique repository of vital methodological resources. Unfortunately, the potential of criminological research to illuminate offensive conduct and anti-social behaviour remains largely unrealised at the present time.

Finally, Jurisprudence cultivates essential expertise in the techniques of legislation and principles of enforcement, linking up with related contributions from penal theory and criminal policy studies. Jurisprudence focuses on the practical legal expression of the moral limits of the criminal law, including principles of criminalisation and criteria of liability and moral culpability. The tasks for Jurisprudence have lately become significantly more complex and demanding, as a consequence of the human rights revolution and the creeping constitutionalisation of penal law. But here again, there is considerable untapped potential for applying jurisprudential method to unravelling the mysteries of penal offence.

A multi-disciplinary inquiry, harnessing the strengths of each of these disciplinary traditions (amongst others) must surely, in the long run, provide superior answers to questions of criminalising offensive conduct than any single scholarly methodology with limited intellectual horizons and a tendency, by dint of disciplinary specialisation, towards parochial preoccupations. By taking the time to understand each other's questions on topics of mutual concern, an inclusive interdisciplinary community of scholars might work towards formulating answers capable of satisfying our shared theoretical curiosity. Such a project, no less urgently, might generate cogent, principled, and empirically substantiated recommendations for reform that could be ignored only with a bad conscience and at policymakers' peril.

REFERENCES

ALLDRIDGE, P (1990) 'What's Wrong with the Traditional Criminal Law Course?' *Legal Studies* 10: 38.

ALLEN, RJ (2001) 'Common Sense, Rationality, and the Legal Process' *Cardozo Law Review* 22: 1417.

ARMITAGE, R (2002) *Tackling Anti-Social Behaviour: What Really Works*. London: NACRO.

ASHWORTH, A (2000a) *Sentencing and Criminal Justice* (3rd edn). London: Butterworths.

—— (2000b) 'Is the Criminal Law a Lost Cause?' *Law Quarterly Review* 116: 225.

—— (2003) *Principles of Criminal Law* (4th edn). Oxford: Oxford University Press.

—— (2004) 'Social Control and "Anti-Social Behaviour": The Subversion of Human Rights' *Law Quarterly Review* 120: 263.

ASHWORTH, A, GARDNER, J, MORGAN, R, SMITH, ATH, VON HIRSCH, A and WASIK, M, 'Neighbouring on the Oppressive: The Government's "Anti-Social Behaviour Order" Proposals' *Criminal Justice* 16(1): 7.

AULD, LJ (2001) *Review of the Criminal Courts in England and Wales.* London: TSO.

BECKER, HS (1963) *Outsiders.* New York: Free Press.

BLAIR, T (2001) Speech to the Labour Party Conference, Brighton.

BLAND, N and READ, T (2000) *Policing Anti-Social Behaviour,* Police Research Series Paper 123. London: Home Office.

BOX, S (1987) *Recession, Crime and Punishment.* London: Macmillan.

BRANTS, C (2001) 'The State and the Nation's Bedrooms: The Fundamental Right of Sexual Autonomy', in P ALLDRIDGE and C BRANTS (eds), *Personal Autonomy, the Private Sphere and Criminal Law: A Comparative Study.* Oxford: Hart Publishing.

BROWN, AP (2004) 'Anti-Social Behaviour, Crime Control and Social Control' *Howard Journal of Criminal Justice* 43: 203.

BUDD, T and SIMS, L (2001) *Antisocial Behaviour and Disorder: Findings from the 2000 British Crime Survey,* RDS Findings No 145. London: Home Office.

CAMPBELL, D (1999) 'George Michael Faces $10m Claim by Officer who Arrested Him' *The Guardian,* 15 September.

—— (2002) 'Policeman sues George Michael' *The Guardian,* 5 December.

CAMPBELL, S (2002) *A Review of Anti-Social Behaviour Orders,* Home Office Research Study 236. London: Home Office RDS.

CARROLL, R (2003) 'The Black Pack: Rugby in South Africa is One of the Last Bastions of the White Man, and Still Rife with Racism. But Things are Changing' *The Guardian,* G2, 29 September.

CJS (2002) *Justice for All,* Cm 5563. London: TSO.

CJS Framework Document (2002) *Narrowing the Justice Gap,* on-line via: http://www.cjsonline.gov.uk/njg/index.html.

COLQUHOUN, A (2003) 'Luyt Shocked by Racism Row' *The Guardian,* 9 September.

—— (2004) 'Rugby Union: South Africa Clear Cronje' *The Guardian,* 10 March.

CONAN DOYLE, SA (1981 [1930]) 'The Man with the Twisted Lip', in *The Penguin Complete Sherlock Holmes* (Harmondsworth, Penguin).

COOK, D and HUDSON, B (eds) (1993) *Racism and Criminology.* London: Sage.

DE GRAZIA, E (1991) 'Freeing Literary and Artistic Expression during the Sixties: The Role of Justice William J Brennan, Jr' *Cardozo Law Review* 13: 103.

DEANS, J (2005) 'BBC Acts Over Threats to Executives' *The Guardian,* 10 January.

DI FEDERICO, G (1998) 'Prosecutorial Independence and the Democratic Requirement of Accountability in Italy' *British Journal of Criminology* 38: 371.

DODD, V (2005) 'Author Facing Death Threats Breaks Silence to Defend Play' *The Guardian,* 13 January.

DOWNES, D and ROCK, P (1998) *Understanding Deviance: A Guide to the Sociology of Crime and Rule Breaking* (3rd edn). Oxford: Oxford University Press.

DUFF, RA (2001) 'Harms and Wrongs' *Buffalo Criminal Law Review* 5: 13.

DWORKIN, R (1996) *Freedom's Law: The Moral Reading of the American Constitution.* Oxford: Oxford University Press.

FEINBERG, J (1984) *The Moral Limits of the Criminal Law, Volume One: Harm to Others.* Oxford: Oxford University Press.

—— (1985) *The Moral Limits of the Criminal Law, Volume Two: Offense to Others.* Oxford: Oxford University Press.

—— (1988) *The Moral Limits of the Criminal Law, Volume Four: Harmless Wrongdoing.* Oxford: Oxford University Press.

FELSON, M (2002) *Crime and Everyday Life* (3rd edn). Thousand Oaks, CA: Sage.

FERRELL, J (2004) 'Boredom, Crime and Criminology' *Theoretical Criminology* 8: 287.

FINNIS, J (1980) *Natural Law and Natural Rights*. Oxford: Oxford University Press.

FIONDA, J (1995) *Public Prosecutors and Discretion: A Comparative Study*. Oxford: Oxford University Press.

FORD, R (2000) 'Police Chiefs tell Blair Spot Fines are "Not a Goer"' *The Times*, 4 July.

GARDNER, J (1998) 'On the General Part of the Criminal Law', in A DUFF (ed), *Philosophy and the Criminal Law: Principle and Critique*. Cambridge: Cambridge University Press.

GARDNER, J and SHUTE, S (2000) 'The Wrongness of Rape', in J HORDER (ed), *Oxford Essays in Jurisprudence*, Fourth Series. Oxford: Oxford University Press.

GARLAND, D (2001) *The Culture of Control: Crime and Social Order in Contemporary Society*. Oxford: Oxford University Press.

—— (2002) 'Of Crimes and Criminals: The Development of Criminology in Britain', in M Maguire, R MORGAN and R REINER (eds), *The Oxford Handbook of Criminology* (3rd edn). Oxford: Oxford University Press.

GARLAND, D and SPARKS, R (2000) 'Criminology, Social Theory, and the Challenge of Our Times', in D GARLAND and R SPARKS (eds), *Criminology and Social Theory*. Oxford: Oxford University Press.

GELSTHORPE, L (2002) 'Feminism and Criminology', in M MAGUIRE, R MORGAN and R REINER (eds), *The Oxford Handbook of Criminology* (3rd edn). Oxford: Oxford University Press.

GELSTHORPE, L and MORRIS, A (eds) (1990) *Feminist Perspectives in Criminology*. Milton Keynes: Open University Press.

HART, HLA (1961) *The Concept of Law*. Oxford: Oxford University Press.

HART, HLA and HONORÉ T (1985) *Causation in the Law* (2nd edn). Oxford: Oxford University Press.

HAYWARD, KJ and YOUNG, J (2004) 'Cultural Criminology: Some Notes on the Script' *Theoretical Criminology* 8: 259.

HILLYARD, P, Sim, J, TOMBS, S and WHYTE, D (2004) 'Leaving a "Stain Upon the Silence": Contemporary Criminology and the Politics of Dissent' *British Journal of Criminology* 44: 369.

Home Office (2003a) *Respect and Responsibility—Taking a Stand Against Anti-Social Behaviour*, Cm 5778. London: TSO.

—— (2003b) *Criminal Statistics England and Wales 2002*, Cm 6054. London: TSO.

HOOD, R (2002) 'Criminology and Penal Policy: the Vital Role of Empirical Research', in A BOTTOMS and M TONRY (eds), *Ideology, Crime and Criminal Justice: A Symposium in Honour of Sir Leon Radzinowicz*. Cullompton, Devon: Willan.

HOOPER, J and WHITE, M (2000) 'Blair wants On-the-Spot Fines for Louts' *The Guardian*, 1 July.

HÖRNLE, T (2001) 'Offensive Behavior and German Penal Law' *Buffalo Criminal Law Review* 5: 255.

HUMPHREYS, L (1970) *Tearoom Trade: A Study of Homosexual Encounters in Public Places*. London: Duckworth.

HUNT, A (1996) 'Regulating Taste', in L BENTLY and L FLYNN (eds), *Law and the Senses: Sensational Jurisprudence*. London: Pluto.

HUSAK, DN (2002) 'Limitations on Criminalization and the General Part of Criminal Law', in S SHUTE and AP SIMESTER (eds), *Criminal Law Theory: Doctrines of the General Part*. Oxford: Oxford University Press.

JACKSON, P (2004) 'Will Rainbow Nation turn to Chester, the Star they called Kaffir?' *Daily Mail*, 4 February.

JACOBS, JB and POTTER, K (1998) *Hate Crimes: Criminal Law and Identity Politics*. New York: Oxford University Press.

JAMIESON, R (1998) 'Towards a Criminology of War in Europe', in V RUGGIERO, N SOUTH and I TAYLOR (eds), *The New European Criminology: Crime and Social Order in Europe*. London: Routledge.

JEFFERSON, T and SHAPLAND, J (1994) 'Criminal Justice and the Production of Order and Control: Criminological Research in the UK in the 1980s' *British Journal of Criminology* 34: 265.

JUPP, V, DAVIS, P and FRANCIS, P (eds) (2000) *Doing Criminological Research*. London: Sage.

KADISH, S (1987) *Blame and Punishment: Essays in the Criminal Law*. Basingstoke: Macmillan.

KANE, SC (2004) 'The Unconventional Methods of Cultural Criminology' *Theoretical Criminology* 8: 303.

KEARNS, P (1998) 'Obscenity Law and the Creative Writer: The Case of DH Lawrence' *Columbia-VLA Journal of Law and the Arts* 22: 525.

KELLY, L and REGAN, L (2000) *Stopping Traffic: Exploring the Extent of, and Responses To, Trafficking in Women for Sexual Exploitation in the UK*, Police Research Series Paper 125. London: Home Office, on-line via http:// www.home-office.gov.uk/prgpubs.htm.

KING, RD and WINCUP, E (eds) (2000) *Doing Research on Crime and Justice*. Oxford: Oxford University Press.

Labour Party (2003a) 'Anti-Social Behaviour Powers to Offer Parents Support and Sanction', Press Release, 26 February 2004, via http://www.labour.org.uk.

—— (2003b) 'Fines for Anti-Social Behaviour', Press Release, 14 May 2004.

—— (2003c) 'Government Targets Nightmare Neighbours', Press Release, 14 October.

—— (2004) 'Citizens Rewarded for Taking a Stand Against Anti-Social Behaviour', Press Release, 22 December 2004.

LACEY, N (1995) 'Contingency and Criminalisation', in I LOVELAND (ed), *Frontiers of Criminality*. London: Sweet & Maxwell.

LACEY, N and WELLS, C (1998) *Reconstructing Criminal Law: Text and Materials* (2nd edn) London: Butterworths.

Law Commission (1995) *Consent in the Criminal Law*, Consultation Paper No 139. London: HMSO.

Leading Article (2003) 'Another of Mr Blunkett's Gimmicks Hits the Streets' *The Independent*, 15 May.

MACCRIMMON, M (2001) 'What is "Common" About Common Sense?: Cautionary Tales for Travelers Crossing Disciplinary Boundaries' *Cardozo Law Review* 22: 1433.

MACDONALD, S (2003) 'The Nature of the Anti-Social Behaviour Order—*R (McCann & Others) v Crown Court at Manchester*' *Modern Law Review* 66: 630.

MAGUIRE, M, MORGAN, R and REINER, R (eds) (2002) *The Oxford Handbook of Criminology* (3rd edn). Oxford: Oxford University Press.

MALONE, A (2003) 'Racism Tarnishes "Rainbow Rugby"' *The Observer*, 7 September.

MATZA, D (1969) *Becoming Deviant*. Englewood Cliffs, NJ: Prentice Hall.

McGAFFEY, R (1974–5) 'A Realistic Look at Expert Witnesses in Obscenity Cases' *Northwestern University Law Review* 69: 218.

MILL, JS (1962 [1859]) *On Liberty*. London: Fontana.

MORGAN, R (2000) 'The Politics of Criminological Research', in RD KING and E WINCUP (eds), *Doing Research on Crime and Justice*. Oxford: Oxford University Press.

MORRISON, W (1995) *Theoretical Criminology: From Modernity to Post-Modernism*. London: Cavendish.

MORSE, SJ (2000) 'Deprivation and Desert', in WC HEFFERNAN and J KLEINIG (eds), *From Social Justice to Criminal Justice*. New York: Oxford University Press.

MURPHY, JG and HAMPTON, J (1988) *Forgiveness and Mercy*. Cambridge: Cambridge University Press.

NEELEY, GS (1995) 'The Right to Self-Directed Death: Reconsidering an Ancient Proscription' *Catholic Lawyer* 36: 111.

NELKEN, D (2002) 'Comparing Criminal Justice', in M MAGUIRE, R MORGAN and R REINER (eds), *The Oxford Handbook of Criminology* (3rd edn). Oxford: Oxford University Press.

—— (2004) 'Using the Concept of Legal Culture' *Australian Journal of Legal Philosophy* 29: 1.

—— (ed) (2000) *Contrasting Criminal Justice: Getting from Here to There*. Aldershot: Ashgate.

NEWBURN, T and SPARKS, R (eds) (2004) *Criminal Justice and Political Cultures: National and International Dimensions of Crime Control*. Cullompton, Devon: Willan.

NICHOLAS, S and WALKER, A (eds) (2004) *Crime in England and Wales 2002/2003, Supplementary Volume 2: Crime, Disorder and the Criminal Justice System—Public Attitudes and Perceptions*, RDS Report 02/04. London: Home Office.

PACKER, H (1969) *The Limits of the Criminal Sanction*. Palo Alto, CA: Stanford University Press.

PADFIELD, N (2004) 'The Anti-Social Behaviour Act 2003: The Ultimate Nanny-State Act?' *Criminal Law Review* 712.

PEARSON, G (1983) *Hooligan: A History of Respectable Fears*. London: Macmillan.

PHILLIPS, C and BOWLING, B (2002) 'Racism, Ethnicity, Crime, and Criminal Justice', in M MAGUIRE, R MORGAN and R REINER (eds), *The Oxford Handbook of Criminology* (3rd edn). Oxford: Oxford University Press.

RADZINOWICZ, L (1991) 'Penal Regressions' *Cambridge Law Journal* 50: 422.

RAZ, J (1977) 'The Rule of Law and its Virtue' *Law Quarterly Review* 93: 195.

—— (1986) *The Morality of Freedom*. Oxford: Oxford University Press.

—— (1987) 'Autonomy, Toleration, and the Harm Principle', in R GAVISON (ed), *Issues in Contemporary Legal Philosophy: The Influence of HLA Hart*. Oxford: Oxford University Press.

ROBERTS, P (1998) 'On the Preconditions and Possibilities of Criminal Law Theory' *South African Journal of Criminal Justice* 11: 285.

—— (2001a) 'Privacy, Autonomy and Criminal Justice Rights: Philosophical Preliminaries', in P ALLDRIDGE and C BRANTS (eds), *Personal Autonomy, the Private Sphere and Criminal Law: A Comparative Study*. Oxford: Hart.

—— (2001b) 'Philosophy, Feinberg, Codification, and Consent: A Progress Report on English Experiences of Criminal Law Reform' *Buffalo Criminal Law Review* 5: 173.

—— (2002) 'On Method: The Ascent of Comparative Criminal Justice' *Oxford Journal of Legal Studies* 22: 539.

ROBERTS, P and MACMILLAN, N (2003) 'For Criminology in International Criminal Justice' *Journal of International Criminal Justice* 1: 315.

ROBERTS, P and ZUCKERMAN, A (2004) *Criminal Evidence*. Oxford: Oxford University Press.

RUGGIERO, V (2000) *Crime and Markets: Essays in Anti-Criminology*. Oxford: Oxford University Press.

SANDERS, A and YOUNG, R (2000) *Criminal Justice* (2nd edn) London: Butterworths.

SCHAUER, F (1991) *Playing by the Rules: A Philosophical Examination of Rule-Based Decision-Making in Law and Life*. Oxford: Oxford University Press.

SHARPE, K (2000) 'Sad, Bad, and (Sometimes) Dangerous to Know: Street Corner Research with Prostitutes, Punters, and the Police', in RD KING and E WINCUP (eds), *Doing Research on Crime and Justice*. Oxford: Oxford University Press.

SHAW, CR (1966 [1930]) *The Jack-Roller: A Delinquent Boy's Own Story*. Chicago: University of Chicago Press.

SHUTE, S and SIMESTER, AP (eds) (2002) *Criminal Law Theory: Doctrines of the General Part*. Oxford: Oxford University Press.

SIMESTER, AP and SULLIVAN, GR (2003; revised 2004) *Criminal Law: Theory and Doctrine*. Oxford: Hart.

SIMESTER, AP and VON HIRSCH, A (2002) 'Rethinking the Offense Principle' *Legal Theory* 8: 269.

SMITH, R (2005) 'Shocking Behaviour' *Law Society Gazette*, 17 March.

SUMNER, C (1994) *The Sociology of Deviance: An Obituary*. Milton Keynes: Open University Press.

SWART, B (2001) 'Denying Shoah', in P ALLDRIDGE and C BRANTS (eds), *Personal Autonomy, the Private Sphere and Criminal Law: A Comparative Study*. Oxford: Hart.

TAYLOR, C (1985) 'Interpretation and the Sciences of Man', reprinted in *Philosophy and the Human Sciences: Philosophical Papers 2*. Cambridge: Cambridge University Press.

TAYLOR, I, WALTON, P and YOUNG, J (1973) *The New Criminology: For a Social Theory of Deviance*. London: Routledge.

TAYLOR, I, WALTON P and YOUNG J (eds) (1975) *Critical Criminology*. London: Routledge.

THORPE, K and WOOD, M (2004) 'Antisocial Behaviour', in S NICHOLAS and A WALKER (eds) (2004), Crime in England and Wales 2002/2003, Supplementary Volume 2: Crime, Disorder and the Criminal Justice System—Public Attitudes and Perceptions, RDS Report 02/04. London: Home Office.

TONRY, M (2004) *Punishment and Politics: Evidence and Emulation in the Making of English Crime Control Policy*. Cullompton, Devon: Willan.

TWINING, W (1994) 'The Way of the Baffled Medic: Prescribe First; Diagnose Later—If At All', in *Rethinking Evidence: Exploratory Essays*. Evanston, IL: Northwestern University Press.

VOLD, GB, BERNARD, TJ and SNIPES, JB (2002) *Theoretical Criminology* (5th edn). New York: Oxford University Press.

VON HIRSCH, A (1993) *Censure and Sanctions*. Oxford: Oxford University Press.

——(1996) 'Extending the Harm Principle: "Remote" Harms and Fair Imputation', in AP SIMESTER and ATH SMITH (eds), *Harm and Culpability*. Oxford: Oxford University Press.

VON HIRSCH, A, GARLAND, D and WAKEFIELD, A (eds) (2000) *Ethical and Social Perspectives on Situational Crime Prevention*. Oxford: Hart.

WALLACE, R and NORTH, N (1998) 'Three Sleazy Minutes that Brought an Idol's World Crashing Down: George Michael's Sex Shame—George Michael Weeps after Gay Sex Charge' *The Mirror*, 9 April.

WARDHAUGH, J (2000) '"Down and Outers": Fieldwork Amongst Homeless People', in RD KING and E WINCUP (eds), *Doing Research on Crime and Justice*. Oxford: Oxford University Press.

WEBBER, J (2004) 'Culture, Legal Culture, and Legal Reasoning: A Comment on Nelken' *Australian Journal of Legal Philosophy* 29: 27.

WHITE, WF (1993 [1943]) *Street Corner Society: The Social Structure of an Italian Slum* (4th edn). Chicago: University of Chicago Press.

WILLIAMS, G (1961) *Criminal Law: The General Part* (2nd edn). London: Stevens.

WILSON, JQ and KELLING, GL (1982) 'Broken Windows' *Atlantic Monthly* (March), 29.

WINLOW, S, HOBBS, D, LISTER, S and HADFIELD, P (2001) 'Get Ready to Duck: Bouncers and the Realities of Ethnographic Research on Violent Groups' *British Journal of Criminology* 41: 536.

YOUNG, J (1998) 'From Inclusive to Exclusive Societies', in V RUGGIERO, N SOUTH and I TAYLOR (eds), *The New European Criminology: Crime and Social Order in Europe*. London: Routledge.

—— (1999) *The Exclusive Society: Social Exclusion, Crime and Difference in Late Modernity*. London: Sage.

YOUNG, J and MATTHEWS, R (2003) 'New Labour, Crime Control and Social Exclusion', in R MATTHEWS and J YOUNG (eds), *The New Politics of Crime and Punishment*. Cullompton, Devon: Willan.

ZEDNER, L (2004) *Criminal Justice*. Oxford: Oxford University Press.

2

How Offensive Can You Get?

RA DUFF AND SE MARSHALL*

FEINBERG'S OFFENCE PRINCIPLE was intended as a necessary supplement to the Harm Principle: it legitimates, in principle, the criminalisation of conduct that does not cause or threaten harm to others, but that does or might cause serious offence to others (Feinberg, 1984: 45–51; 1985: xiii). Such a principle will be attractive to those who worry about the extent of 'offensive' behaviour and its impact on the lives of its victims, but will arouse the anxiety of liberals who rightly worry about extending the heavy-handed reach of the criminal law; about increasing the potentially oppressive discretion allowed to law enforcement officers (since 'offensive behaviour' offences will predictably be enforced even more selectively than are other parts of the criminal law); and about sanctioning an illiberal lack of acceptance or toleration of others' ways of life.

In this chapter we offer cautious support for the idea that the criminal law can properly be used to deal with some kinds of offensive conduct, even if they are not strictly harmful. To that end, in § I we discuss some of the different species and structures of offensiveness that must be distinguished if we are to be clear about the possible grounds for criminalising offence. In § II, we discuss some possible responses to behaviour that is genuinely offensive, and argue that criminalisation ought to be a 'last resort'.[1] In § III, we discuss two hybrid responses that have recently come to the fore in Britain, Anti-Social Behaviour Orders (ASBOs) and Acceptable Behaviour Contracts (ABCs), as well as the older hybrid device of injunctions: whilst ASBOs are open to some by now familiar, and devastating, objections, injunctions that prohibit offensive conduct on pain of criminal sanctions if

* Thanks are due to participants in the Cambridge workshop for which this chapter was first written, and in workshops at Manchester Metropolitan University and at the University of Stirling where drafts were discussed. Antony Duff's thanks are due to the Leverhulme Trust for the award of a Major Research Fellowship, during which this chapter was written.

[1] This will also help to clarify one sense of that familiar but notoriously obscure slogan: see Husak, 2004; Jareborg, 2005.

they are breached can play a proper role; but a suitably enriched version of ABCs—one that takes seriously the idea of a contract as a two-way affair— could offer a more useful way of responding to some worrying kinds of offensive behaviour.

I. STRUCTURES OF OFFENCE

Those who worry that an Offence Principle would open the door to an oppressive expansion of the criminal law might be tempted to fall back on the Harm Principle, and to argue that we should criminalise offensive conduct only if it is also harmful.[2] Now the kinds of offensive conduct that we ourselves would in the end favour criminalising might also be classifiable as 'harmful' under a plausible conception of harm, but this is not a route that we wish to follow. Were we to follow it, we would have to ask, as anyone seeking to apply the Harm Principle must ask, first what kinds of lasting impact (since a merely fleeting impact is not harm) on what kinds of interest should be taken to constitute harms, and then what kinds of harm should concern the criminal law (since not all kinds of harm create even a *prima facie* ground for criminalisation). It will, however, be simpler to ask directly what kinds of impact, on what kinds of interest, offensive conduct should have if it is to be apt for criminalisation, without worrying about whether or not such impact counts as harm.[3]

A second obvious way of limiting the scope of an Offence Principle is to insist that only offensive conduct that is also wrongful—or, yet more restrictively, that wrongs those whom it offends—is even in principle apt for criminalisation (see Feinberg, 1985: 1–2; Simester and von Hirsch, 2002: 273–9). The simple reason for this restriction is that the criminal law condemns conduct that it defines as criminal, and the courts censure those whom they convict for engaging in such conduct; were the conduct not wrongful, that condemnation and censure would not be just.[4] However, this requirement for wrongfulness as a necessary condition of criminalisation leads us to the first of several important distinctions between different types or structures of offensiveness in relation to wrongfulness.

---

[2] See eg, Simester and von Hirsch, 2002; but they would retain a distinct Offence Principle, to mark the distinctive structure of offensive harms.

[3] Compare Hörnle, 2001, especially at 268–70, arguing that we should focus on rights and interests rather than on 'harm'.

[4] The wrongfulness that justifies condemnation and censure could of course, as in the case of *mala prohibita*, be consequent upon, rather than a reason for, the legal regulation of the conduct in question, but it must be prior to its criminalisation: see Duff, 2002.

1. Mediated and Immediate Offence[5]

Sometimes what is offensive is *immediately* offensive, in that the offence is not logically mediated by a judgment that it violates some standard. We can take noise as a good example of this: noise that offends not because of its meaning (as racist hate speech offends), but simply by virtue of its character as noise—its particular sound (as when a finger scratches a slate), or its volume or intrusiveness. Conduct that is in this way offensive can of course be harmful: a loud enough single noise can cause physical damage; a persistent and unavoidable noise can make sleep impossible and seriously impair one's ability to lead a decent life. But the relevant point for our purposes is that noise, especially persistent, loud noise, can have a serious impact on significant interests, whether or not we should count that impact as 'harm'.

Now immediately offensive conduct is wrongful, if it is wrongful at all, only because it is offensive: what makes it wrong to engage or persist in noisy conduct (if that is wrong) is that the conduct offends others. By contrast, *mediately* offensive conduct is offensive because it is wrong by some relevant standard that it violates: the wrongfulness is constitutive of the offensiveness, rather than being consequent upon it as in the case of immediate offence. The case of the naked rambler provides a paradigm example of mediated offence. Stephen Gough spent seven months walking naked (apart from boots, socks, and hat) from Lands End to John O'Groats.[6] He was not a sexual exhibitionist; his purpose was rather to publicise the merits of naturism, and to show up the absurdity (as he saw it) of the conventions that he was violating. His trip took that long because he was arrested seventeen times, and served two short terms in prison, for conduct liable to cause a breach of the peace and for breaching his bail conditions. Many people were no doubt in fact offended by (or took offence at) his behaviour: not because nudity is immediately offensive, but because they saw it as violating an important standard. Indeed, it is only in virtue of others' strong reactions to such a perceived violation that such conduct might cause a breach of the peace.

The standard whose violation causes mediated offence may be a moral standard: this was, no doubt, true of the naked rambler (people were offended because they believed such a public display of what properly belonged in private to be immoral). Mediated offence can also arise, however, from the violation of non-moral standards: we can be offended by aesthetic failings, as when a neighbour paints her front door a glaringly inappropriate colour; or by breaches of etiquette or style; or by the breach of any

---

[5] Compare Feinberg, 1985: 10–12, 14–16, on offences to 'sensibilities' or to the senses.

[6] See news.bbc.co.uk/1/hi/scotland/3420685.stm; the case was also reported in, e.g., *The Guardian*, 4 October 2003 and 23 January 2004, and *The Independent,* 23 January 2004.

standard that we take seriously (philosophers might be offended by some crass philosophical error). More precisely, what is offensive is not the mere violation of the standard, but the disregard or even contempt for the standard and for the values it represents that the violation displays—the neighbour's utter disregard for the aesthetics of housing, or the erring philosopher's contempt for the demands of the discipline.

Conduct is mediately offensive if it offends only in virtue of its (contemptuous) breach of an important standard, whether that standard be moral or non-moral. However, if our interest is in possible grounds for criminalisation, it must be in morally wrongful offence: we should, therefore, distinguish three types of offensive conduct:

(A) conduct that is mediately offensive because of the contempt that it displays for moral values or standards;
(B) conduct that is mediately offensive because of the contempt it displays for non-moral standards;
(C) conduct that is immediately offensive.

The important distinction, for the question of criminalisation, is that between (A) on the one hand and (B) and (C) on the other: that distinguishes the two different ways in which offence and moral wrongfulness can be connected. Conduct of type (A) is offensive because it is morally wrongful: the wrongfulness constitutes the offence. Conduct of type (B) or type (C), by contrast, whether the offence is immediate or mediated, is morally wrong (if it is) because it is offensive and because it is morally wrong to offend in that way: the offence grounds the wrong. Conduct of type (A), we might say, is offensively wrongful, whereas conduct of type (B) or (C), if it is morally wrong at all, is wrongfully offensive.

Intrinsic to mediated offence (whether of type (A) or type (B)) is a normative judgment, that what I find offensive violates some standard or value that I take seriously, and that I can cite my reason for finding X offensive. No such judgment is essential to immediate offence; I need have no reason to be offended by X.[7] Although this distinction is analytically clear, it is in practice quite often blurred. In particular, the character of immediate offence can be modified by one's normative perspective on the behaviour that caused it. If I am disturbed by an—as I at first hear it—offensively raucous noise outside

---

[7] Norms and values, ideas of what is proper or improper, will often figure in the genetic explanation of immediate offence: although I have no reason to be offended by a sound or smell that immediately offends me, the reason why my sensory responses are so ordered that I am thus offended might have to do with the contingent association between that sound or smell and something of normative significance in my culture or in my own life; see Husak, this volume: nn 29–36. However, this does not show the offence to be mediated rather than immediate: it shows, we might say, that there is a reason why I am (immediately) offended, not that I have reason to be offended; but I am mediately offended only when I have, or suppose that I have, reason to be offended—that reason consisting in the violation of a standard.

my house, not only my further response to it, but also how I hear it (indeed, what I hear), might well differ as between the case in which I find that it is being made by 'a gang of louts', and that in which I find that it is being made by my children celebrating a birthday, especially if the noise persists: in the former case, I might become increasingly disturbed by what I hear as loutish-ly inconsiderate and even threatening noise; in the latter, I might come to take pleasure in this manifestation of my children's pleasure. Insofar as offence is in this way partly mediated, the points we will make about mediated offence apply to it; but, for the sake of simplicity and analytic clarity, we will focus initially on clear-cut cases of either mediated or immediate offence.

2. Intended and Unintended Offence

Cutting across the distinction between mediated and immediate offence is that between intended and unintended offence. I can offend others without intending to do so, and without even realising that I am doing so; or I can set out to offend them by behaving in a way that I believe will offend them, either mediately or immediately.[8] Intended offence can of course be valu-able, in part because it offends: it can shock, and challenge our deep-root-ed prejudices, in morally or aesthetically serious ways. When it lacks such value, however, intended offence, even if initially immediate, acquires a dimension of mediated offensiveness: what offends is now not just the immediately offensive sight or sound or smell, but (mediately) the rudeness (or worse) involved in the intention to offend.

Insult is a paradigm example of intended mediated offensiveness.[9] Insults, by words or deeds, range across a wide spectrum, from friendly mutual insults between friends in a pub, through the mildly insulting epithet I might throw at someone who cuts me up in traffic, or the more hostile, angry insults that disputatious neighbours might exchange, to campaigns of vio-lently racist, xenophobic, or homophobic abuse directed against those whom the insulters portray, in their insults, as aliens or outcasts. Serious insults, those that go beyond mutually friendly banter, are offensive by virtue of their meaning, because they flout moral standards of respect and politeness;[10] they are also typically attacks on the people who are insulted,

---

[8] Others might be (mediately) offended only because they mistakenly believe that I intend to offend; but such offence, if it is truly mediated by that belief, should vanish when the mis-take is discovered.

[9] See Feinberg, 1985: *passim*, but especially 218–38; also Simester and von Hirsch, 2002; von Hirsch and Simester, this volume: § III. 1.

[10] Even insults exchanged in what is mutually understood to be mere friendly banter can be offensive, to others, if not to the participants. Even if they are not intended to offend, they may be offensive by virtue of the attitudes they display towards other groups—think, for instance, of a group of (often ostentatiously) heterosexual men whose banter includes accusing each other, in demeaning and derogatory tones, of homosexuality.

and perhaps on the group to which they belong—they are intended to hurt or humiliate. They are offensive even if those who are insulted do not realise that they are being insulted, or are not offended: for we may say that both the insulted person and others *should* be offended by them.[11]

Insults and other kinds of intended offence are—if they cannot be justified—distinctively wrongful as attacks on the senses or sensibilities of others. This is not to imply, however, that unintended offence cannot be wrongful in its own ways: it can be wrong to act in ways that I know will offend others, even if I do not intend that offence, and to act in ways that I should realise might offend others.

3. Reasonable, Unreasonable, and Necessary Offence

Immediate offence is in itself neither reasonable nor unreasonable; it just occurs. This is not to say that we are helpless in relation to it: we sometimes can, and sometimes should, train ourselves not to be (so) offended by what in fact offends us. So far as that is possible, our continuing offendedness might be judged reasonable, or unreasonable, in a less direct way, on the basis of a judgment about whether we could and should have trained ourselves out of it. In itself, however, such offence is not a matter of reason.

Mediated offence, however, *is* a matter of reason. If I am mediately offended I have—or must suppose that I have—reason to be offended, grounded in the offender's violation of a norm or value that should be taken seriously; my offence is subject to critical evaluation, and is liable to be judged as reasonable or unreasonable. I am still offended, even if my offence is rightly judged to be unreasonable, but we cannot now say that what I am offended by is offensive: for to call something offensive is to say not merely that it offends, but that it is something by which it is reasonable to be offended. What is immediately offensive, by contrast, is what is in fact likely to offend most ('normal') people. Immediate offensiveness is thus analogous to visibility, whereas mediated offensiveness is analogous to desirability.[12]

We should note two different grounds on which someone's actual offence can be judged to be unreasonable, with the implication that what offended her is not offensive. The obvious first ground is that her judgment is misguided: the standards that she takes to have been violated are not

---

[11] See § I.3 below. Insults might not be intended to offend, since they can be unintentional. An insulter might be ignorant of the local conventions given which his words or conduct bear an insulting meaning, or he might be culpably insensitive to the insulting character of the joke he is telling: but he still insults, however unwittingly or inadvertently. Only when the insult is intended does it constitute an attack.

[12] *Pace* JS Mill, who notoriously treated the logic of visibility as being the same as that of desirability: see Mill, 1998 [1861]: ch 4.

standards that it is reasonable to hold, or to treat as binding on the conduct of others; or the conduct that she finds offensive did not flout those standards; or, even if it did violate a legitimate standard, that standard (or its violation) is not as significant as her offence portrays it as being. The other ground is that, even if the conduct that she finds offensive flouts some legitimate standard, it is none of her business to judge it, or to be offended by it. If I criticise my neighbour's choice of interior décor, which I can see through her window, as aesthetically offensive, she might respond, not by defending her taste, but by arguing that how she chooses to decorate her house is none of my business—a response that might generate argument about what is, and what is not, a matter of proper 'public' interest in this context.

If something is mediately offensive, it is reasonable to be offended by it. But we must also distinguish merely 'reasonable' from 'necessary' offence. In many cases, whilst it is quite reasonable to be offended by X, it is equally reasonable not to be offended by it. My more aesthetically concerned friends may be offended by an aesthetically displeasing choice of external decoration for a house, and I would not say that it is not their business or that they are misjudging the décor (by which I mean that their offence is not, on either of those grounds, unreasonable). But I am not offended by it myself—either because I do not care much about such aesthetic matters, or because I am more inclined to think that people should please themselves when it comes to choosing their home décor; and I would object if my friends told me that I *should* be offended, or criticised me for not being offended. Sometimes, however, we think not just that it is reasonable to be offended by X, but that one *should* be offended by it: if someone was not offended by a crudely racist joke (especially perhaps if the joke was told within earshot of a member of the insulted group) we would be more inclined to criticise his lack of sensitivity and respect than to admire such open-minded acceptance of others' sense of humour.[13] To call something 'necessarily' offensive, as we use the term here, is thus to imply that it flouts standards that people ought to care about, in a way that people ought to find offensive (even if they are not in fact offended by it).[14]

[13] If a victim of the joke is not offended by it, our judgment should be more careful. We might wonder whether his lack of offence displays a lack of self-respect—an acceptance of the devaluation or contempt expressed by the insult: compare Murphy, 1988. But it might instead reflect a moral self-confidence that does not allow such insults to impinge.

[14] We should emphasise, especially in relation to the category of the necessarily offensive, that offensiveness can be a morally very serious matter. Sometimes 'offensive' is used, implicitly, to mean something like 'merely offensive', but that is not how we are using the term: some kinds of offensive conduct, including racist insults, are not 'merely' offensive, but outrageously or intolerably offensive. (Thanks to Andrea Baumeister for forcing us to make this clearer; see also Feinberg, 1985: ch 9, on 'profound' offence.)

Such judgments of the reasonableness or the necessity of offence are, of course, liable to be controversial.[15] The naked rambler would no doubt argue that the offence that others certainly felt or took at his conduct was unreasonable, on the grounds that such public nudity should be accepted, even welcomed, as a celebration of our bodies; or on the grounds that what clothes one wears in public, indeed whether one wears clothes at all, should be recognised as private matters that do not concern other people. Others would see the offence he aroused as being at least reasonable, as a matter either of manners or of morals:[16] the conventions that forbid such nudity are entrenched, and not clearly unreasonable; it was not unreasonable for those who saw him to take at least mild offence. Others would see his conduct as necessarily offensive—as something by which any decent person should and would be offended.

It is not our purpose here to argue for one of these views of the naked rambler (our sympathy lies with the second); our aim so far has been only to distinguish some of the different ways in which offence can be caused, structured, and evaluated. We turn now to the question of how it might be appropriate to respond to offensive conduct, and in particular the question of whether or under what conditions it might be appropriate to mobilise the criminal law.

II. RESPONDING TO OFFENCE

Behaviour can, as we have seen, offend without being offensive. Our concern here, however, must be with behaviour that is genuinely offensive, that is, that reasonably or necessarily offends. If someone is (unreasonably) offended by behaviour that is not offensive, there is no question to be asked about how she should respond to it *qua* offensive behaviour: she has no legitimate claim that those engaged in it should desist, and she should try to persuade or train herself not to be thus unreasonably offended by it. When behaviour is genuinely offensive, however, that gives those engaged in it reason to desist, and gives others (at least those who are offended by it) *a* reason to do something about it—which is not to say that it always gives them strong, let alone conclusive, reason: if

---

[15] But they are not inherently more controversial than other matters of value. In talking of 'reasonable' or 'necessary' offence, we are not taking a stand on the metaphysical issues that Husak (this volume) discusses: all we are committed to, as anyone who engages in normative debate must be committed, is the possibility of rational discussion about issues of value—including issues about what it is reasonable or unreasonable, necessary or unnecessary, to find offensive.

[16] We need not explore here the question of whether his conduct was aesthetically offensive or, if it was thus offensive, morally wrongful because aesthetically offensive.

something is offensive, we have reason to prefer its absence to its presence; and that (reasonable) preference gives us reason to act so as to secure its absence.[17]

The reasons that the agent has to desist from offensive behaviour, and that others have to seek to prevent it, are of course stronger when the offensive behaviour is morally wrong—whether wrong because offensive, or offensive because wrong. Since we take it to be a basic principle constraining criminalisation that only morally wrongful conduct should be criminalised,[18] we will therefore focus on behaviour that is either wrongfully offensive or offensively wrongful. To identify those two categories properly would require a detailed discussion of the kinds of offence that are wrongful, and of the ways in which wrongs can be offensive—a discussion that we cannot embark on here. We should, however, say a bit about each category of wrong.

As far as offensive wrongs are concerned, we should not count *all* moral wrongs as offensive, *qua* wrongs. What offends, we suggested, is not the mere fact of contravening some standard, but the contemptuous disregard for the standard or for the values it expresses that wrongdoing can display; but not all moral wrongdoing displays such contempt.[19] Furthermore, often what is salient, morally and as a ground for criminalisation, is not the offensiveness of the wrong: a rape or assault might be offensive, but our moral and legal focus will be on the wrong whose contemptuous commission makes it offensive, not on its offensiveness. We will be tempted to mobilise the Offence Principle only when we do not already have good reason, independently of its offensiveness, to criminalise the conduct that offends: typically, when the conduct does not cause or threaten one of the familiar kinds of harm that concern the criminal law. That is why insult is a good example of offensive wrong: even a sustained campaign of serious racial insults against an individual or group might not cause or threaten any of the familiar kinds of material harm that usually ground criminalisation;[20] but its

---

[17] This way of putting the matter assumes that whilst we can sometimes justify either the offensive behaviour itself, or a refusal to intervene to try to prevent it, the form of such justification will always be, 'Admittedly, the behaviour is offensive, but...'. It might be argued that in some cases of justified offensiveness (if, eg, one justifiedly *intends* to offend) its offensiveness provides *no* reason against the offensive action: nothing crucial to our overall argument would be lost if we admitted this.

[18] See text preceding n 4 above.

[19] Some accounts of the nature of immorality might suggest that all wrongdoing is offensive as such (see Hampton 1989, 1990, on immorality as 'defiance'); such monistic accounts are not, however, plausible (for a useful critique of Hampton, see Murphy, 1998).

[20] Or the kind of 'psychiatric injury' that can, in English law, ground a charge of inflicting 'bodily harm' (Offences Against the Person Act 1861, ss 20, 47; see *Burstow* [1998] AC 147; Simester and Sullivan, 2003: 387–91). Such conduct can, of course, cause material (if it incites racial violence) and psychological harm: our argument is that we have reason to criminalise it independently of the fact or likelihood of any such consequential harm.

moral offensiveness as a symbolic attack on the victim's status as a fellow citizen provides some reason to criminalise it.[21]

As for wrongful offence, that is, immediately or non-morally mediately offensive behaviour that is morally wrong only because it is offensive, there is plenty of room for controversies over what kinds and degrees of offensiveness are wrong. The general nature of the wrong is not problematic, although its details need careful analysis.[22] Offensive conduct is wrong when it constitutes a morally unacceptable and not reasonably avoidable intrusion into others' lives—when it forces uncomfortable and disturbing experiences on them, to a degree or in a context that they should not be expected to accept; its wrongfulness is aggravated when, through its persistence, it impairs their ability to lead or to enjoy their ordinary lives—as when persistent noise makes the lives of those subjected to it increasingly difficult. Such conduct is culpable if it displays a lack of due respect and consideration for the interests of those affected by it. If it is intended to offend, it has the moral character, and wrongfulness, of an attack; absent such an intention, it is culpable if the agent acts knowingly, recklessly or negligently as to its offensiveness.

Even if we can agree, however, that certain kinds of conduct are wrongfully offensive, or offensively wrongful, this is a long way from agreeing that they should be criminalised. In the rest of this section, we will look at a range of possible responses to wrongful offensive conduct, to try to work out more clearly when, and why, criminalisation might be legitimate as, we will argue, a 'last resort'.

1. Toleration

Offensive conduct should sometimes simply be tolerated: those offended by it ought not to attempt to dissuade or prevent it (beyond, perhaps, a simple and polite request), but instead put up with it with as good a grace as they can muster. Since toleration is often preached as a core liberal value, however, we should be clear about what it involves.[23]

Sometimes we ought to refrain from attempting to dissuade or prevent conduct that offends us because we should realise that it is not offensive, that our offence is unreasonable. This is a matter not of toleration, but of

---

[21] See § II.5 below. Given the lack of a clear legal definition of 'harassment', it is not clear whether a charge of 'racially aggravated' harassment (Protection from Harassment Act 1997, ss 1–2; Crime and Disorder Act 1998, s 32: see Simester and Sullivan, 2003: 397–401) could be made out.

[22] Some of which is provided by Feinberg, 1985, and by Simester and von Hirsch, 2002.

[23] See Mendus, 1988, for a useful collection of readings.

open-mindedness—a willingness to recognise that activities or modes of life that at first repel us might be worthwhile, although we would not engage in them ourselves: we tolerate only that to which we have (or think we have) good reason to object, but we have no good reason to object to conduct that is not offensive. We should note, however, that the 'reasons to object' that toleration presupposes need not be moral reasons: I might tolerate—refrain from objecting to or from commenting adversely on—my neighbour's ill-chosen colour for his front door, when my objections to it are aesthetic rather than moral.

Sometimes we should refrain from attempting to dissuade or prevent conduct that is indeed offensive, because there is nothing (or nothing that would not probably make matters worse) we can do about it. This is not a matter of toleration either: we tolerate only what we could try to do something about;[24] and toleration, if it is anything more than a merely behavioural matter, is motivated not just by a concern to avoid immediate harm, but by a more positive concern to promote such values as diversity, freedom, and mutually respectful co-operation—or at least a respect for such values.

We will not tackle here the question (more accurately, the wide and diverse set of questions) of what kinds of offensive conduct we should tolerate. We want, instead, to look at the kinds of response that might be appropriate to offensive conduct that we should not be expected to tolerate. Two important points to note are, first, that to say that we need or should not tolerate a particular type of behaviour is not yet to say that we may or should use coercion to prevent it:[25] even when non-toleration involves an attempt to prevent, that need amount to no more than attempts at rational moral persuasion or at peaceful negotiation.[26] Second, when we ask what 'we' should or should not tolerate, we must distinguish the informal actions (individual or collective) of citizens from the formal (typically coercive) actions of the state: it is one thing to argue that those who are affected by offensive behaviour may or even should take informal steps to dissuade or prevent it; it is quite another to argue that the state should wield its formal power, in particular the power of the criminal law, to that end. In

[24] Although we focus on when we could legitimately try to prevent offensive conduct, the 'something' that I could try to do about what I tolerate need not involve trying to prevent it: I can display tolerance by not commenting adversely on or retaliating against offensive conduct that I could not even try to prevent.

[25] A point missed by those who think that we tolerate only that which we have the power to prevent: see eg, Raphael, 1988.

[26] Some take 'toleration' to include attempts at rational persuasion, and to preclude only coercive or non-rational methods of prevention; for our purposes, however, the important distinction here is between 'toleration' as precluding any attempt to dissuade or prevent, and all the kinds of attempt to dissuade or prevent that we go on to discuss.

what follows we look first at some kinds of informal response that citizens might make.[27]

2. Negotiation

The simplest non-tolerant response to offensive conduct is to ask the agent to desist from it, and if necessary try to persuade her to do so, by pointing out its offensiveness. Such requests might, however, mark the start of a longer process of discussion and negotiation: they might provoke the response that there was no good reason for the complainant to be offended (that the conduct was not offensive); or an explanation of how important this admittedly offensive behaviour is to the life of those engaged in it; or counter-complaints about the complainant's own behaviour. If the complainant is to treat the offending agent with the respect due to her as a fellow citizen, he must then either withdraw his complaint or be prepared to engage in a serious discussion of her response.

That discussion might resemble the kind of mediation process often favoured by advocates of 'restorative justice': a process that looks to repair harm done, and to reconcile those who find themselves in 'conflict' with each other, rather than to punish wrongs.[28] Whatever doubts one might have about the adequacy of such processes as responses to crime, they can surely have a role in this context, when what is most important for the parties involved might be to work out a tolerable *modus vivendi* for the future. Mediation seems especially appropriate if some or all of the following conditions are met—conditions which militate against a criminal law response that seeks to allocate blame for past wrongdoing. First, whatever wrongs were done were not so serious that any adequate response to the problem must make them salient: for if they were serious, they might inhibit the kind of negotiated compromise that mediation seeks. Second, there is room for discussion about how unreasonably offensive the conduct was, and perhaps about whether the complainant has also engaged in offensive conduct.[29]

---

[27] In discussing possible responses to offensive behaviour we leave aside other methods of trying to prevent it, in particular those that involve identifying and tackling its underlying causes, or removing its more immediate stimuli and opportunities (as with measures of 'situational crime prevention'). The first of these possibilities is particularly important when those causes involve unjust disadvantage or exclusion suffered by those who now behave offensively; we comment briefly on it in § III.3. The second possibility raises its own set of ethical issues, which we cannot discuss here (see von Hirsch *et al*, 2000, for a useful collection of critical papers).

[28] On 'conflict', see Christie, 1977; see also Hulsman, 1986, on talking of 'troubles' rather than 'crimes'. For the central arguments for and against 'restorative justice' in relation to crime, see Johnstone, 2002; von Hirsch *et al*, 2003.

[29] That is to say, there is room for the kind of discussion that Christie envisages for crimes in general, about 'How wrong was the thief, how right was the victim?' (1977: 8).

Third, since the disputants are neighbours (in a broad sense) who must find a way to live, if not together, then at least in reasonably peaceful proximity, it is less important to rehearse past complaints than to negotiate a way forward: a negotiation that might require both sides to make compromises in how they behave themselves, and in what behaviour they will or will not put up with from each other.[30] If some or all of these conditions are satisfied, as they surely are in many cases of offensive behaviour, we should see less room or need for the coercive and condemnatory intervention of the criminal law. The mediation could be facilitated by the state, for instance through the availability of trained and publicly funded mediators; but it needs to be informal, consensual, and non-coercive if it is to promote a genuine agreement between the disputants.

We should note a further point about cases in which the offended party is or claims to speak for a collective—a local community, a group of tenants, the owners and users of a shopping mall. It might turn out that the offending behaviour flows, at least in part, from features of the social environment that the offended parties can do something about, or for which they might be at least partly responsible—that, for a simple example, youths' offensive behaviour on the streets is partly explained by the lack of any other social space in which they can gather, or of social facilities that they can use. Such explanations might suggest, first, that the behaviour is not as unreasonably offensive as might at first appear, since the extent to which my behaviour is unreasonable depends in part on the alternatives available to me; second, that responsibility for the offensive behaviour might lie partly with the offended, if they should have made more and better social provision for the offenders; and third, that whether or not such retrospective responsibility should be assigned, a suitable way forward might involve the provision of such facilities.[31] We return to this point in § III.3.

Negotiated settlements will, however, not always be possible or appropriate. They depend on the willingness of all the parties to take a serious part in the process, to show respect for each other, and to refrain from attempts at bullying or manipulation; but such willingness will not always exist. They depend on reaching an uncoerced agreement about the way forward—an agreement that will require some or all of those involved to restrain their offensive behaviour, and to put up with some continuing offensive behaviour from others; we cannot be confident that such agreement will always (or even often?) be possible. They depend on agreement that the offending behaviour is not so categorically wrong that it *must* be condemned; but such agreement will not always be likely, or appropriate,

---

[30] On this type of 'civil' (as opposed to 'criminal') mediation, see Duff, 2003: 49–53.
[31] For an all too typical fulmination that ignores this obvious point, see Magnet, 2004.

especially when the conduct is offensively wrongful or purposely offensive—imagine asking the victims of a campaign of racist abuse to enter into negotiation with the abuser, with a view to finding some satisfactory resolution to their 'conflict'.[32] Their success depends on whatever agreement is made being kept by all those bound by it, or at least not being violated so flagrantly and regularly that it collapses; but such agreements will sometimes, even often, collapse. When such negotiated agreements are impossible, or fail, we must look to other kinds of response.

3. Civil Law Remedies

One kind of alternative response would involve taking a civil law route. Individuals or groups who suffered from others' offensive conduct could seek an injunction requiring the offenders to desist from such conduct, or sue for damages on the basis of the offensive conduct. If they had engaged in a negotiation that led to a legally binding agreement, their case would rest on the terms of that agreement—on the offenders' agreement to refrain from the specified types of offensive conduct. Absent such a binding agreement, they would have to find grounds for their case in the law's existing range of recognised civil wrongs.

Several aspects of the civil law route need not concern us here. Legally binding agreements, and the civil remedies that may be sought for their breach, raise no special issues here. We comment on injunctions in more detail later (§ III.2). Claims for compensation or damages become legitimate only when some loss, of a kind that could in principle be compensated by a monetary payment,[33] can be proved: they are therefore more appropriate in response to conduct that is consequentially harmful, than to conduct that is intrinsically offensive.[34] Two questions are directly relevant to the present discussion. First, when (if ever) could it become appropriate to use the law at all to try to prevent offensive conduct, rather than relying solely on informal persuasion and negotiation? Second, if and when it is appropriate to use the law, what kinds of consideration should guide the choice between a civil law route and a criminal law route?

We can offer no determinate answer to the first question. The crucial first issue is whether the behaviour about which the complainant complains

---

[32] This is not to say that some kind of mediation might not be appropriate in relation to such wrongdoing. We can see a useful role for victim-offender mediation, or 'conferencing', in the aftermath of crime, but its character and aims will be quite different from those of the kind of non-criminal mediation envisaged here, in part because it will presuppose a non-negotiable condemnation of the offender's conduct; see Duff, 2003: 50–56.

[33] We cannot enter here into the debate about when compensation is, or is not, possible or even intelligible: see Goodin, 1991.

[34] An adequate discussion of this issue would need to attend carefully to the tort of nuisance, but that is not something we can embark on here.

is indeed wrongful—wrongfully offensive or offensively wrongful. If the judgment that it is wrongful is to ground a legal complaint, it must also be grounded in a process that can give it legitimate authority as law —a process of authoritative legislation, or of legal interpretation by a court.[35] It might be tempting to say that if the conduct is properly, and publicly, judged to be wrongful in one of these two ways, and if negotiation is not feasible or is unsuccessful, there is good reason to provide for a legal remedy: there might be stronger reasons, especially reasons of material or moral cost, against providing for such a remedy, but it would in principle be appropriate. This would, however, be too swift: a threshold of seriousness (and perhaps also of persistence) should be crossed before we think of mobilising the ultimately coercive power of the law; there will be kinds of offensive conduct that others should be expected, if not to tolerate, at least to put up with if attempts at informal persuasion and negotiation fail.

Just where that threshold should be set must be a matter for public debate, but some offensive conduct will surely cross it: some conduct is so offensively wrongful or wrongfully offensive that others should not be expected to put up with it without legal recourse. This leads into the second question: how should we decide between a civil and a criminal (or quasi-criminal; see § II.4 below) mode of legal response?

For present purposes there are two key differences between a criminal and a civil procedure. First, a civil procedure is under the control of the victim-plaintiff: it is up to her to bring and pursue the case, or to drop it if she so wishes. A criminal procedure, by contrast, is under the control of the state, which decides whether to prosecute, and either pursues or drops the case: this relieves the victim-plaintiff of the burden of bringing the case, but it also deprives her of the authority to decide whether and how the case should proceed.[36] Second, when a criminal defendant loses his case, he is convicted, and usually punished, for committing a wrong; a civil defendant who loses his case faces no such formal condemnation, and typically has to pay damages rather than undergo punishment.[37] We discuss the latter difference between civil and criminal procedures in § II.4, but should comment briefly on the first difference here.

---

[35] On the importance of this point, see von Hirsch and Simester, this volume: § III. 2.

[36] This analytically clear distinction is in practice blurred in various ways: by the possibility of bringing private prosecutions (which in England are still subject to state control in that the Attorney General can take them over and then drop them); by the fact that the police and prosecutors will often not proceed with a criminal case without the victim's consent (though they could legally do so, and might in practice at least try to persuade the victim to consent and co-operate); by the fact that a civil case, in particular a request for an injunction, might be brought by a local authority rather than by an individual or group.

[37] This tidy analytical distinction is also in practice often blurred, both by the way in which a verdict for the plaintiff might in fact be understood, and by the way in which damages can be, formally or informally, 'punitive'.

A civil procedure is suitable for offensive conduct whose impact is limited to an identifiable individual or small group, and whose offensiveness is reasonable rather than necessary (thus it will usually be wrongfully offensive, rather than offensively wrongful—morally mediated offensiveness leaves less room for the judgment that it is reasonable not to be offended). Of course assistance and support should be available, so that lack of means or expertise does not prevent victim-plaintiffs from pursuing their case: but if what (reasonably) offends me is, for instance, conduct by my neighbour that affects no one else and that others might (reasonably) not find offensive, it could properly be left to me to bring, or not to bring, a case. We should, therefore, consider a criminal or quasi-criminal procedure when the offensiveness is 'public' either because it affects a community as a whole, rather than identifiable individuals within it; or because it is of such a kind that we should not impose the burden of bringing a case on the victim, but should see it as something to which 'we' must respond collectively—which will typically be the case when the conduct is seriously offensively wrongful, as with a campaign of racist insults. We return to this second reason for a criminal response in § II.5.

An illustrative example is provided by the problem of 'high hedges'—a persistent source of neighbourly conflict at least in England, where hedge disputes can lead to murder.[38] I may dislike my neighbour's hedge—its height, the type of tree, its shape (or shapelessness). Such (mere) dislike is not yet a ground for claiming that the hedge, or my neighbour's conduct in letting it grow thus, is offensive. But suppose that he lets it grow so high that it becomes reasonably offensive: it keeps the sunlight off my garden; it blocks my view; it 'adversely affect[s my] reasonable enjoyment' of my property.[39] Perhaps this does not offend me—or not enough to do anything about it beyond an oral request to trim it; I realise that others would (reasonably) find such a hedge offensive or intrusive, but I do not care that much about it myself. If no one else is affected by it, it would be odd to insist that the law ought nonetheless to intervene. It should, surely, be for those affected by it to decide whether to take any further steps or not; that is, it should be a matter for a civil rather than for a criminal or quasi-criminal process.

If, however, I do find the hedge offensive, if it has a serious impact on my enjoyment of my property, the law can provide me with some recourse, should attempts at informal persuasion and negotiation fail: it can allow me to seek a legal order requiring my neighbour to cut the hedge back to a

---

[38] See http://news.bbc.co.uk/1/hi/england/lincolnshire/3032854.stm.
[39] Anti-Social Behaviour Act 2003, s 68(3)(a). There is room for argument about whether this is a matter of offence, or harm, or some other kind of impact on my interests; but what interest us here are the kinds of remedy that the law might provide.

reasonable height. It could provide a straightforward civil remedy—a civil suit that seeks such an order: it would be up to me to bring the case, and to return to court if the order was not obeyed. English law in fact now offers a somewhat hybrid remedy. The complainant need not take the case to court herself, but may complain to the local authority. If the authority is satisfied that she took 'all reasonable steps' to resolve the issue before making her complaint, that her complaint is not 'frivolous or vexatious', and that the hedge's height 'is adversely affecting [her] reasonable enjoyment' of her property, it can issue a 'remedial notice'. Failure to comply with that notice is an offence.[40]

Such provisions can be justified if certain conditions are satisfied. First, the relevant conduct is capable of being reasonably and seriously offensive, by interfering with a significant, albeit non-essential, human good—this is an issue for legislatures to decide. Second, whilst citizens who are offended by such conduct should try to resolve the problem by informal means (they should take 'all reasonable steps' before turning to the law), the offensiveness of the conduct is potentially serious enough to warrant a legal remedy if such informal steps fail. Third, the mere fact that someone persists, despite such informal steps, with seriously offensive conduct does not yet justify any legal remedy: the conduct must impinge on the complainant seriously (her complaint must not be 'frivolous or vexatious'), so 'adversely affecting [her] reasonable enjoyment' of the relevant good that, even considering whatever interest the other person has in engaging in the conduct, it is reasonable to demand that he desist. Fourth, the first formal, legal intervention is not to penalise the agent, but to require him to desist from the offensive conduct, or so to modify it that it ceases to cause reasonable offence; only if he refuses to do so does the possibility of a penalty arise.

Suppose, however, that the offensiveness of someone's conduct is too general, or too serious, for it to be practicable or reasonable to expect individual victims to pursue a civil law route. We might still hope to avoid mobilising the coercive apparatus of the criminal law, especially when the offensive conduct does not seem serious or threatening enough to class as ('really') criminal, by opting for a regime of non-criminal or administrative regulation.

4. Non-Criminal Regulation

A regime of non-criminal or administrative regulation is a regime of conduct rules that are administered and enforced by legally authorised bodies,

---

[40] Anti-Social Behaviour Act 2003, ss 65–78 (the phrases quoted are from s 68(2)–(3)); see Padfield, 2004: 724–5.

and breaches of which attract non-criminal penalties, typically fines.[41] We should distinguish two ways in which such a regime is 'non-criminal'.

First, it is formally non-criminal in that its penalties are not imposed by criminal courts, and a finding that a person has breached a regulation does not give him a criminal record. Second, it is substantively non-criminal in that a finding that someone has breached a regulation is not a conviction that condemns him as a wrongdoer, and its penalties are not punishments that censure the offender: they aim to discourage the prohibited conduct, not to condemn it.[42] A university's provisions for penalising plagiarisers are formally non-criminal, in that whatever committee decides on cases and their disposal is not a criminal court administering a criminal law; but they are probably substantively criminal, in that their aim is to determine whether the 'defendant' is guilty of the wrong of plagiarism (a wrong that counts, within that community, as a serious public wrong against its essential values), and to condemn and punish those who are proved to have committed that wrong. The substantive, rather than the formal, distinction between criminal and non-criminal modes of regulation is what interests us here.

The attractions of a regime of non-criminal regulation are obvious. We can hope that threats of administrative fines will significantly reduce kinds of conduct that 'materially affect the reasonable comfort and convenience' of others;[43] and we can achieve such a reduction in offensive nuisances whilst avoiding the costs involved in their criminalisation (the material costs of the criminal process, for prosecutors, defendants, and witnesses; the symbolic and possibly material costs of stigmatic conviction for defendants), and without exaggerating the importance of such conduct by labelling it as 'criminal'. Those very attractions should, however, make us pause.

First, although a breach of such regulations cannot lead to imprisonment, it can lead to heavy fines (up to £5,000 under German law, for instance), and under some regimes to other kinds of 'civil' penalty, such as disqualification,[44] all of which can be very burdensome. Second, if such breaches do not count as 'crimes', legislatures might be tempted to deprive 'defendants' of some of the protections they enjoy under the criminal law: to weaken or remove any *mens rea* requirement, for instance,[45] or to

---

[41] See Hörnle, 2001, on the German category of *Ordnungswidrigkeiten*; the Model Penal Code § 1.04, distinguishing 'crimes' from 'violations' as a 'noncriminal class of offenses'.

[42] See Feinberg, 1970, on the difference between 'penalties' and 'punishments'.

[43] *Attorney-General v PYA Quarries Ltd* [1957] QB 169, at 184 (Romer LJ); see n 70 below.

[44] See Model Penal Code, Commentary to § 1.04, 72.

[45] Thus the Commentary to the Model Penal Code suggests that offences of 'strict' liability should count only as 'violations'—that this is 'the appropriate means for dealing with the problem of strict liability' (Commentary to § 1.04, 72). But if the category of 'violations' were not available, it would be easier to argue that strict liability should simply be ruled out.

require a lower standard of proof. Finally, we should not be too quick to abandon the focus on proved wrongdoing that characterises the criminal law. This is partly because 'offensive behaviour' includes genuine wrongdoing that merits public recognition and condemnation as such: someone who subjects his neighbours to persistent, intrusively unpleasant noise, or defaces their environment with odorous rubbish or graffiti, might or might not be 'harming' them, but surely does them wrong; so too does someone who subjects members of some vulnerable ethnic group to a campaign of racist abuse. In addition, however, to insist on a focus on wrongdoing provides citizens with some protection against the state: for to justify making citizens liable to what could be heavy penalties, it would now need to be shown not just that the behaviour being penalised is in some way inconvenient or unwanted, but that it is wrong—and wrong in a way that merits the public condemnation that criminalisation involves.

It is indeed tempting to argue that we should eschew such non-criminal modes of regulation: partly for the reasons given above, and partly because they function as a system of deterrence—which is arguably inconsistent with the respect that we owe each other as responsible moral agents.[46] However, such regulatory regimes can play a useful role in contexts in which what matters is not so much the (fairly minor) wrongfulness of the conduct, as the disruption to the smooth functioning of social or institutional activities that it causes; so long as the penalties are modest, the moral objection to their use as deterrents is weakened—and is weakened still further insofar as the penalties can be justified as a contribution to the costs caused by the prohibited conduct (fines for the late or non-return of library books would be an example). Nonetheless, we do not see much scope for such regimes in the contexts in which worries about offensive conduct typically arise. What justifies the formal prohibition of such conduct, and formal attempts to dissuade people from engaging in it, must be in crucial part that it is wrong—that it is either wrongfully offensive or offensively wrongful: for if it is not wrong, it is not clear what good reason we could have to prohibit or to try formally to prevent it. But if its wrongfulness is crucial to justifying its prohibition, it should also be salient in any formal response to it: which is to say that that response, if it goes beyond the possibilities discussed so far, should be criminal.

5. Criminalisation as a 'Last Resort'

Is this then to suggest that we should criminalise all those kinds of 'offensive' conduct that others would treat as merely administrative 'violations'?

---

[46] See Duff, 1986: 178–86, 238–9; also von Hirsch, 1993: 10–12.

It is not, because we take seriously the slogan that the criminal law should only be used as a 'last resort'. By this we mean two things (although perhaps only the second strictly involves the idea of a 'last resort').

First, the criminal law should not be used against *every* kind of conduct that a polity could legitimately seek to dissuade: it must be reserved for those kinds of conduct that we should seek to dissuade because they are wrong in a way that properly counts as 'public', in other words as something that should concern the whole polity. Wrongs are 'public' in this sense either if they affect 'the public', rather than identifiable individuals who could be expected to pursue the matter via a civil procedure for themselves;[47] or if the wrong is of such a kind or is so serious that the victims' fellow citizens owe it to them to treat it as a public rather than as a private wrong—as a wrong that they share, which requires a public response from the whole community (Marshall and Duff, 1998). Once we have a system of criminal law, it is tempting for a legislature to broaden its reach to cover more and more kinds of conduct that it wants to reduce or dissuade; but that temptation should be resisted, to reserve the criminal law for its proper purpose.

Second, conduct that is in this sense a public wrong passes through the first of the three filters that Schonsheck (1994) argues should structure a decision procedure for criminalisation: it is in principle criminalisable. But that leaves many questions to be decided before we conclude of any particular species of publicly wrongful conduct that it should be criminalised: we must attend to the costs, both material and moral, of criminalisation; we must ask whether there are other, less coercive and intrusive, ways of discouraging or responding to such conduct. There is an important role here for the kinds of 'mediating principle' that von Hirsch and Simester (this volume) have begun to work out: they create further hurdles that must be crossed on the path from the initial determination that a certain type of conduct is in principle criminalisable to the conclusion that it should be criminalised. We might say here that the state should tolerate what private individuals or groups should not be required to tolerate:[48] we should recognise that there are types of wrongful conduct that are in principle apt for criminalisation but which we should refrain from criminalising, on the grounds that the moral cost of doing so (the cost to the freedom and privacy of citizens, for instance) would be too high. Individuals or groups can make their own informal efforts to dissuade such conduct (within the constraints of law—this is not a licence for vigilantism); the state might facilitate mediation processes of the kind sketched earlier. But it should not wield the bluntly coercive weapon of the criminal law.

---

[47] See *Attorney-General v PYA Quarries Ltd* [1957] QB 169, at 191 (Lord Denning on the idea of a 'public' nuisance); Smith, 2002: 774–5.

[48] See text at notes 26–27 above.

We offer no recipe to determine which kinds of wrongfully offensive or offensively wrongful conduct should be criminalised; ultimately, a 'balancing' is required of the considerations in favour of criminalisation that flow from the initial in-principle argument, against the counter-considerations that might flow from the mediating principles or from practical considerations of cost and efficacy. But we suspect that there will in the end be good reasons to criminalise some types of offensive conduct, whose wrongfulness merits formal, public recognition and condemnation.

First, there are types of offensively wrongful conduct, the clearest example being serious insults aimed against a vulnerable group, that merit criminalisation because they flout what should be the polity's central values, and constitute attacks whose victims should be able to look to their fellow citizens for support and protection; their offensiveness is both necessary and morally mediated.[49] Such wrongs might be a source of what certainly counts as harm, as when a campaign of racist insults incites racist attacks (or provokes violent retaliation); but we should not make harm a necessary condition of criminalisation. What matters about such insults is that they constitute a serious civic wrong, since they violate their victims' interest in being accorded even the minimal respect or recognition due to them as citizens.[50]

It might be objected that such insults, unless they encourage racist violence, merely 'outrage people's sensibilities', as contrasted with incitement to racial hatred, which 'endangers their material and physical well-being';[51] and that the criminal law should not be mobilised against mere 'outrage'. Now our claim is that such insults constitute serious enough 'public' wrongs, as flagrant denials of the human and civic standing of those who are insulted, that they ought to be publicly and formally condemned. However, first, this leaves open the question of how, and how severely, such conduct should be punished—it does not imply, for instance, that it should lead to imprisonment. Second, whilst the definition of the offence should not require that the insults be uttered in the presence of members of the insulted group, it should require that they be uttered in public: not because they are inoffensive when uttered in private, but because the offensive

---

[49] Chris Bennett and Andrea Baumeister objected (in discussion) that the justificatory work in such cases is done by the wrongfulness of the conduct—that its offensiveness becomes irrelevant. But the offensiveness is what characterises the wrong (the wrong involved not in the mere holding of racist views, but in their public expression in racist insults) as the particular kind of public wrong it is.

[50] Are there other types of offensively wrongful conduct that are in principle criminalisable, and that are not already criminalisable by virtue of their wrongfulness (or their wrongful harmfulness)? This question would lead into a discussion of pornography and obscenity, and of Feinberg's examples of 'profound offense'—a discussion that we cannot embark on here: see Feinberg, 1985: chs 9–16.

[51] The quote is from an unnamed Labour MP, contrasting blasphemy, as an offence that we should abolish, with incitement to religious hatred, as something that should be criminal: *The Guardian*, 18 October 2004, p 1: but we think it captures a common objection to the criminalisation of other kinds of insult.

wrongfulness that makes them apt for criminalisation partly consists in a public attack on their victims' moral standing. Third, there would clearly be real problems in defining the offence, especially since what is in principle worth criminalising is not every kind of serious racist insult, but only insults directed against vulnerable groups, for whom the denial of human and civic standing that the insult expresses will be all too real: but we are by no means confident that it will be possible to produce a practicable definition.

There are also types of wrongfully offensive conduct, and in particular persistent wrongfully offensive conduct, that might merit criminalisation because, whether or not they are strictly harmful, they seriously impair the quality of life of those affected by them. Examples include persistent, loud, intrusive noise in residential areas; ugly graffiti that deface the community's public spaces; littering that, even when it is not a health hazard, makes it hard or impossible to take pleasure in public spaces. Such conduct is wrongful when it subjects others to offence, annoyance, or distress that they should not have to put up with: but to make that judgment, we may need to inquire carefully not only into the nature and degree of its offensiveness, but into the extent to which it is reasonable to demand that those who engage in it should desist—an inquiry that might need to take into account the role that such conduct plays in their lives, and the costs to them of eschewing it. Such wrongful conduct is culpable, in a way that could properly attract criminal liability, when engaging in it displays a lack of the minimal respect for others' interests that we can properly demand of all citizens.[52]

We are not urging a rush to criminalise every species of offensive conduct. Our claim is more modest (and so, no doubt, less interesting): that we must be willing to criminalise serious kinds of offensively wrongful or wrongfully offensive conduct, without showing that they cause or threaten harm, if (as is sometimes the case) this is necessary in order to mark and condemn them as public wrongs. To put the point in slightly different terms that make clear where the persuasive burden as to criminalisation must lie, we should criminalise offensive conduct if and only if we are reasonably persuaded that for the state to do nothing, or to do no more than facilitate

---

[52] Compare von Hirsch and Simester, this volume, on '*treating other persons with a gross lack of respect or consideration*' as the 'element of wrongdoing' in offensive behaviour. This is true of many kinds of mediated offence: what makes an insult wrong and offensive is the disrespect it displays. However, it is not true of immediate (or of non-morally mediated) offence. When I play loud music every night (not to annoy my neighbours, but because that is what I enjoy), the primary offensiveness of my conduct does not depend on the lack of respect or consideration that I show, but on its continuing, intrusive and upsetting impact on my neighbours; I show a lack of respect or consideration by persisting with it only if and because I ought not to subject them to such offensive noise every night—ie only if and because such conduct is wrong. The lack of respect I show might compound the wrong, or my culpability in committing it: but the basic wrong, which gives us reason in principle to criminalise my conduct and only given which does my persistence display lack of respect, is the persistent making of such offensive noise.

attempts at mediation between those who find themselves in such 'conflict', would be to fail to take seriously enough the wrongdoing that it involves: for the central function of criminalisation is to define and condemn 'public' wrongs as wrongs.

There is, however, a further set of issues that we must discuss here—an issue foreshadowed by the example of high hedges that we mentioned in § II.3.

III. HYBRID RESPONSES: ASBOs, INJUNCTIONS, AND ABCs

The kinds of 'anti-social' behaviour that have provoked such panic among British politicians and commentators include many types of conduct that are and should be criminal without any need to appeal to an Offence Principle; they include such familiar and uncontroversial crimes as criminal damage, assault, and taking and driving away.[53] But our concern here is with conduct whose offensiveness (offensive wrongfulness or wrongful offensiveness) is the primary ground for suggestions that it should be criminalised, and with the legitimacy of two recent devices that seek to control such conduct without directly or immediately criminalising it, although in ways that ultimately rely on the power of the criminal law. The two devices are Anti-Social Behaviour Orders and Acceptable Behaviour Contracts: we will argue that whilst the familiar objections to ASBOs are overwhelming, an enriched form of ABC could provide a useful response to many kinds of wrongfully offensive behaviour; we will also comment briefly on injunctions, as an older hybrid device that avoids at least some of the objections to ASBOs.

1. Anti-Social Behaviour Orders[54]

An Anti-Social Behaviour Order is an order made by a court, on the application of a local authority or chief police officer: it imposes specified

---

[53] The important House of Lords cases on ASBOs, *R (on the application of McCann) v Manchester Crown Court* and *Clingham v Kensington and Chelsea RLBC* [2003] 1 AC 787, provide usefully illustrative fact situations.

[54] See Crime and Disorder Act 1998, ss 1–4; Anti-Social Behaviour Act 2003, s 85. The 2003 Act also provides for the closure of premises where drugs are used unlawfully (ss 1–11); measures against anti-social tenants (ss 12–17), and against parents of misbehaving children (ss 18–29); the dispersal of groups (ss 30–36) if their presence or conduct 'has resulted or is likely to result in any members of the public being intimidated, harassed, alarmed or distressed; and measures to deal with noise (ss 40–42), with graffiti and fly-posting, including a prohibition on selling aerosol paint to children (ss 43–54), and with high hedges (ss 65–84). All of these could be seen as matters of 'offensive' conduct; many have something in common with ASBOs (see also the Anti-Social Behaviour etc (Scotland) Act 2004, and the provisions of the Football Spectators Act 1989, ss 14A–J, inserted by the Football (Disorder) Act 2000, Sch 1, para 2), but we cannot discuss them here: for a useful critical discussion, see Padfield, 2004.

restrictions on someone who is proved to have acted 'in an anti-social manner'; the point of those restrictions is to prevent the future repetition of such anti-social behaviour. There are three central objections to ASBOs in their present form (see von Hirsch *et al*, 1995; Gardner *et al*, 1998; Ashworth, 2004; Simester, and von Hirsch this volume).

First, they do not depend on conviction for a criminal offence, and so cannot be justified as punishments for any such offence.[55] It must admittedly be proved that the person on whom the ASBO is to be made 'has acted ... in an anti-social manner, that is to say, in a manner that caused or was likely to cause harassment, alarm or distress' to others outside his household,[56] in other words that he acted in a way that constituted the conduct element of an offence under ss 4A–5 of the Public Order Act 1986. But no *mens rea* need be proved;[57] and though *McCann* held that the conduct must be proved effectively to the criminal standard, that is, 'beyond reasonable doubt', we must wonder whether this will be robust enough to resist erosion, given the court's insistence that the proceedings are civil, not criminal.

Second, an ASBO can impose dramatic restrictions on a person's life (including exclusion from the offender's own housing estate)—restrictions that look and are perceived as being harshly punitive; but (quite apart from the lack of a criminal conviction) they are not subject to the kind of constraint that could legitimise them as punishments. The conduct prohibited by the ASBO need not itself be criminal or even anti-social: what justifies the prohibitions is that they are 'necessary for the purpose of protecting [others] from further anti-social acts by the defendant',[58] and they can 'cover acts that are anti-social in themselves and those that are precursors to a criminal act'—not merely shoplifting itself, but entering the shopping mall.[59] Now we do not deny that prohibitions and exclusions of the kind involved in ASBOs might be justifiable as punishments for proven crimes: depending on the seriousness of the offence, and on the sentence's predictable impact, a temporary exclusion from a shopping mall could be part of an apt sentence for a shoplifter, and exclusion from football matches an appropriate sentence for a convicted football hooligan.[60] But such sentences

---

[55] The Crime and Disorder Act 1998, s 1C (inserted by the Police Reform Act 2002, s 64) provides for the making of an ASBO (in addition to any sentence) after conviction of 'a relevant offence'. The conditions for making such an ASBO are substantially the same as for those that do not follow a conviction; such ASBOs are not vulnerable to this first objection, but are vulnerable to the other two objections.

[56] Crime and Disorder Act 1998, s 1(1)(a).

[57] As the court emphasised in *McCann* [2003] 1 AC 787, at 808 (n 53 above), as part of the basis for the decision that ASBO proceedings are civil, not criminal.

[58] Crime and Disorder Act 1998, s 1(6).

[59] Home Office, 2002: 34.

[60] Under s 14A of the Football Spectators Act 1989 (n 54 above), a court can impose a banning order after conviction for a relevant offence, just as (n 55 above) ASBOs can be imposed after a conviction. In both cases, however, the order is supposed to be preventive rather than punitive, so that such provisions are also open to this objection.

are justified as punishments only if their severity is proportionate to the seriousness of the crime: the only proportionality requirement that applies to ASBOs, by contrast, is that they be proportionate to the mischief that is to be prevented, not to such wrongs as the person might have committed in the past.[61] As punishments (which is how they are perceived), ASBOs are liable to be disproportionately harsh, and are not subject to the proportionality constraints that should apply to punishments; as civil orders, such drastic preventive restrictions on citizens' movements and conduct based on predictions about the anti-social behaviour that they might engage in are inconsistent with the basic liberal principle that the state should treat its citizens as responsible agents.[62]

Third, although ASBOs formally count as civil orders, breaches of them are criminal and can attract a prison sentence of up to five years.[63] Perhaps courts will in fact proportion sentences to the criminally anti-social behaviour that they suppose (without adequate public proof) that the person has engaged in. But what is formally punished is not any such already-criminal behaviour (for no such behaviour need be proved), but the mere breach of the conditions of the ASBO: unless we are to attach to mere breach or defiance of the law an importance that sits uneasily with a liberal conception of the relations between state and citizen, such punishments are unacceptable.

ASBOs seek to evade the protections that a decent criminal law provides for all its citizens (notably the protections against hasty or unjust convictions and over-harsh punishments), by creating a hybrid civil-criminal procedure that allows courts to make criminals of individuals for conduct that is in itself neither harmful nor offensive. They are not an appropriate method of dealing with the admittedly serious problems posed by anti-social behaviour that can be so destructive of the peace and amenity of those who suffer it. If the behaviour that grounds an application for an ASBO is already criminal, it should be prosecuted and punished through the ordinary criminal process. If that is not practicable, because of the difficulties of gathering evidence and of persuading frightened witnesses to testify, and if such problems cannot be overcome by legitimate types of police surveillance (though it is unclear why that should not suffice), we should at least tackle the problem head on by proposing appropriate changes to the rules of evidence—not by this back door device.[64]

---

[61] Even this forward-looking requirement of proportionality (perhaps 'informal expectation' would describe it better) has no statutory authority; it appears in Home Office, 2002: 34. See Lord Hope's remarks in *McCann* [2003] 1 AC 787, at 824 (n 53 above).

[62] See Duff, 1986: 172–8.

[63] Crime and Disorder Act 1998, s 1(10).

[64] It might again be suggested that we need a category of 'violations', dealt with through simpler procedures, to cover less serious kinds of anti-social behaviour that should still attract a formal penalty: see above, n 41; also Ashworth, 2000: 253–6. We have already commented on this idea: see § II.4 above.

Suppose, however, that it seems hasty, oppressive, or excessive to mobilise the full weight of the criminal law straight away: we cannot be confident that it must have been clear to those engaged in some wrongfully offensive type of conduct that it constituted the kind of public wrong that merits formal condemnation and punishment; or we cannot be confident that, in its context and given its background, that conduct did constitute an unequivocal instance of what should be categorically condemned as a criminal wrong, though we are confident that we should take formal steps to dissuade its continuance. We might have such doubts about various lower level kinds of anti-social behaviour, for instance persistently offensive noise; and this might lead us to consider another hybrid device, that of the injunction.

2. Injunctions

An injunction, as we use the notion here, is an order made by a court, prohibiting a specified individual or group or organisation from engaging in some specified type of conduct, in order to prevent some type of wrongful conduct. It is a hybrid device in that, like an ASBO, it does not directly penalise the conduct with which it deals: it prohibits the conduct, and penalties become possible only if the injunction is breached.

Injunctions vary in several important ways. They vary, first, as to what kind of prior conduct, if any, must be proved before they are granted—in particular whether it must be proved that the injunctee has engaged in the wrongful conduct against which the injunction is directed, or only that he is likely to engage in it. They vary, secondly, as to the standard and rules of proof that are to apply. To what standard—a criminal 'beyond reasonable doubt' standard, or a civil 'on the balance of probabilities' standard—must the past conduct or future danger be proved? How far do evidential rules or constraints that apply to criminal trials apply here? They vary, thirdly, as to whether what they prohibit is just the wrongful conduct that is to be prevented, or conduct that is likely to facilitate or lead to that wrongful conduct. They vary, fourthly, as to what sanctions are available for breaches, in particular whether a breach should attract a criminal, an administrative, or a civil sanction. We cannot discuss the first two issues, about what kind of proof of what kind of prior conduct should be required, further here, although they raise important issues, but we will say something about the other two issues.

What kind of conduct could injunctions properly be used to prohibit? They are not plausibly used to prohibit conduct that is already and obviously wrong in a way that concerns the law—obviously criminal conduct, for instance; it would be bizarre to seek an injunction prohibiting someone from committing rape or theft. They are sometimes in fact used to prohibit conduct that is not itself wrongful, but that is seen as being preparatory to or a potential source of the wrongful conduct against which the injunction is really aimed: a local council could obtain an injunction prohibiting an alleged drug dealer from entering the council housing estate where he allegedly plies his trade.[65] When used in this way, injunctions are functionally equivalent to ASBOs, and are open to the objections discussed in § III.1 above.

A more clearly legitimate use for injunctions is to specify more precisely, and thus to prohibit more determinately, conduct that falls under an existing criminal offence definition; they are then in principle justified if the creation of such an offence was justified. The clearest actual examples of this use are not in fact injunctions issued by courts, but formal notices issued by local authorities. When a local authority issues an 'abatement notice' to deal with a 'statutory nuisance', it warns the person that what he is doing constitutes such a nuisance, and that he will commit an offence if he disobeys the notice;[66] when a local authority officer issues a 'warning notice' under sections 1–4 of the Noise Act 1996, she warns the offender that the noise he is making is excessive, and that he will be guilty of an offence if he does not desist.[67] Such notices provide both a clearer specification of the kind of conduct that is legally wrongful, and a warning that to persist with it will attract legal sanctions: they are appropriate when, as is quite often the case with various types of offensive behaviour, there might be uncertainty about just what kind of conduct is not merely extra-legally offensive, but legally wrong and sanctionable. They do not invite a negotiation about what kinds of conduct are or are not to be allowed, but declare authoritatively that this conduct falls within the legal definition of the relevant offence: this can be appropriate precisely when that definition, given the context in which it is to be applied, leaves real room for doubt about what it covers; the injunction constitutes a more precise determination of the law, and thus also gives fair warning of the law's demands to those who might infringe them.

The same rationale could be offered for some existing provisions for injunctions. Thus, for instance, landlords may seek injunctions prohibiting specified kinds of anti-social conduct by tenants,[68] whilst someone who fears (further) harassment can obtain an injunction that prohibits the injunctee from engaging in conduct that constitutes harassment.[69] If what

---

[65] Local Government Act 1972, s 222; *Nottingham City Council v Zain* 2001 WL 825283 (CA); see Paradine, 2001.

[66] Environmental Protection Act 1990, ss 79–80.

[67] See also the new provisions in the Anti-Social Behaviour Act 2003, ss 40–42; on which see Parpworth, 2004.

[68] Anti-Social Behaviour Act 2003, s 13, inserting a new s 153A into the Housing Act 1996.

[69] The Protection from Harassment Act 1997, s 3(3)(a), provides for injunctions 'for the purpose of restraining the defendant from pursuing any conduct which amounts to harassment [which is defined as criminal by s 1]'; s 3(6) makes it a criminal offence to breach such an injunction. This could be taken to permit an injunction not just against behaviour that actually constitutes harassment, but also against behaviour that might lead to harassing conduct, in which case it also exemplifies the first kind of ASBO-resembling injunction that we discuss; but what interests us here is the use of such injunctions to specify and prohibit conduct that would itself constitute criminal harassment.

the law counts as 'anti-social behaviour' or as 'harassment' is justifiably criminalised, such injunctions make it possible both to provide authoritative determinations of the relevant types of wrongful conduct, and to issue formal warnings to those who might engage in them; they could be appropriate when it might not be entirely clear just what conduct the law requires us to eschew. It might be hard to imagine that any tenant against whom an injunction prohibiting some specified type of anti-social behaviour could properly be sought and granted would not realise at least that he was behaving badly, but there might be real room for doubt about how far it was clear, or clear to him, just what kinds of conduct are prohibited: the injunction makes this clear to him, and warns him of the consequences of engaging in such conduct in future.

This is one way in which vague definitions of criminal conduct can be made more tolerable. To define a 'public nuisance' simply as a nuisance 'which materially affects the reasonable comfort and convenience of a class of her Majesty's subjects',[70] or simply to prohibit 'anti-social behaviour', will leave citizens in serious doubt about what they may or may not do; injunctions prohibiting specified types of nuisance can remedy that uncertainty and give potential offenders fair warning. We should, of course, be cautious about providing for injunctions to serve this purpose: their availability should not become an excuse for legislatures to define offences in unreasonably broad and vague terms, thus leaving the courts an inadequately constrained discretion to decide what types of conduct should count as 'anti-social' or as 'offensive'. But when, as will probably be the case with at least some kinds of wrongfully offensive conduct that is properly criminalised, there is real room for those engaged in such conduct to be unsure not so much about whether it is wrong, but about whether it counts as a 'public', criminal wrong; and when it is not practicable to provide offence definitions that would remove such uncertainty: there is room for this type of injunction or notice.

What kinds of sanction should attach to breaches of such injunctions? The first question is whether what is sanctioned should be the disobedience to the injunction, as an act of defiance of the law, the court, or the authority in whose name it was issued, or the commission of the wrongful conduct that the injunction declared to be wrong. A liberal system of law should not be in the business of punishing mere defiance: that would be more appropriate for subjects than for citizens. What should rather be sanctioned is

---

[70] Romer LJ, in *Attorney-General v PYA Quarries Ltd* [1957] QB 169, at 184; quoted as authoritative by Lord Schiemann, in *Nottingham City Council v Zain* 2001 WL 825283, para 8; for other definitions see Smith, 2002: 772–5.

persistence in the wrongful conduct, despite such an authoritative warning of its wrongfulness.[71]

The second question is whether the sanction should be a civil sanction (such as damages sought by the injured party), or an administrative sanction (such as a fine imposed by an authorised body, but without a criminal conviction), or a criminal sanction (a punishment for conduct that was—at least given the injunction—criminally wrongful). Civil remedies will sometimes be appropriate, when the matter can properly be seen as a private dispute about a private wrong. But when the wrong committed is 'public', either because it affects the public rather than an identifiable individual or because the victim's fellow citizens should share in it,[72] and when the sanction should mark the wrongfulness of the conduct, a criminal sanction is appropriate. These conditions are likely to be met by various types of offensive behaviour: for instance by wrongfully offensive conduct that disturbs the whole neighbourhood without being focused on particular individuals; and by offensively wrongful conduct that attacks its victim's civic status (as with a campaign of racist insults against a vulnerable minority).

Injunctions, like ASBOs, simply prohibit conduct, on pain of a sanction. We might, however, want to look for a more constructive response to antisocial and offensive behaviour: one that does not shy away from declaring wrongfully offensive or offensively wrongful conduct to be wrongful, but that also seeks to engage more productively with the offender. This leads us to a third type of hybrid response, based on the idea of an Acceptable Behaviour Contract.

3. Acceptable Behaviour Contracts[73]

An Acceptable Behaviour Contract (ABC) 'is a written agreement between a person who has been involved in anti-social behaviour and one or more local agencies whose role it is to prevent such behaviour.... The contract specifies a list of anti-social acts in which the person has been involved and which they agree not to continue'.[74]

---

[71] But the fact that an injunction was issued and disobeyed is still relevant: the offending agent will have engaged in the offending conduct *despite* such a clear and fair warning that he should not. Compare von Hirsch, 1998, on the way in which a criminal record can properly affect sentencing.

[72] See text following n 47 above.

[73] ABCs have no statutory basis. They were introduced as an informal provision in Islington, at first for young people but later for adults too, as an arrangement to be tried before seeking ASBOs; the failure of an ABC could lead to a formal application for an ASBO. See Home Office, 2002.

[74] *Ibid*: 52.

As currently used, ABCs are one-sided affairs that scarcely deserve to be called 'contracts'. First, there is no room for negotiation about what kinds of conduct the putative offender is to eschew: although only 'anti-social' conduct is relevant (unlike an ASBO, which can prohibit conduct that is in itself quite innocent), and although the individual should where possible 'be involved in drawing up the contract',[75] what is to count as anti-social behaviour is not open to negotiation. Second, whereas the putative offender must agree to refrain from the specified kinds of offensive conduct, all that the other party to the 'contract' has to agree is that he will not face further action (such as an ASBO or a prosecution) if he does refrain.[76] But we could imagine a system of ABCs that took the idea of a contract more seriously.

We can again take wrongfully offensive noise as our example. Noise, however intrusive, becomes potentially wrongful in a way that will concern the criminal law only if it becomes persistent, and even then there might be room for doubt about whether those making the noise would or must have realised how disturbing it was, and that this was the kind of conduct that constitutes a public wrong, as well as about what kinds, levels, and persistence of noise others should be expected to bear. Given the serious impact of persistent noise on people's lives, we might want to allow the criminal law to be used against those who make it. Given the doubts noted here, however, we might not want simply to criminalise the making of 'excessive noise', or of noise exceeding a specified level for a specified time or with a specified frequency: that would be too draconian (and either disturbingly vague if the offence is defined as 'excessive noise', or seriously over- or under-inclusive, and hard for citizens to apply, if it is defined in terms of decibel levels). So we make provision for ABCs—a provision that combines features of mediation and of injunction.

The first stage would, ideally, involve a discussion between the alleged offender and the complainants or their representatives—a discussion at which the complainants would explain how the alleged offender's behaviour affects them, whilst he would have a chance to explain his view of the affair. One aim of this would be mutual understanding, which might itself lead to some informal accommodation; the further aim, if no such informal agreement is possible or adequate, would be to agree the terms of a contract. The contract would specify what kinds of noise, at what times or places, the offender agrees not to make—a specification which might properly reflect some acceptable compromise between others' demands for peace and the noise-maker's own interests; in return, the complainants would agree not to

---

[75] *Ibid.*

[76] The Home Office guidance advises that '[s]upport to address the underlying causes of the behaviour should be offered in parallel to the contract' (*ibid*)—but this is clearly not to be part of the 'contract'.

complain so long as the noise did not exceed those limits. But the contract could also involve some further commitments by the complainants, especially if the offender has counter-complaints against them about conduct of theirs that seriously offends him,[77] or if he can show that his offending behaviour is at least in part attributable to problems with which he should receive some help: if, for instance, he is a youth who makes such a noise in the streets because he and his friends have nowhere else to go, and if the local community should provide more social facilities for their youth, the contract could properly include a commitment to provide such facilities.

Since the process could ultimately lead to a criminal charge, it should be conducted under the aegis of a criminal court: a court-approved mediator leads the meeting (and ensures that only reasonable complaints are discussed); whatever contract is agreed requires the approval of the court. If the alleged offender breaches such a court-sanctioned agreement, he could face a criminal charge (unless he can show that the other party has failed to fulfil its own part of the contract). The focus of that charge will be the particular offensive conduct: the noise-making that was defined as 'excessive' by the ABC. The contract will have put him on notice that such conduct would be criminal: assuming that its terms were fair, it constitutes fair warning; so he cannot complain if he is convicted for continuing to engage in such conduct.

We should emphasise two crucial differences between such ABCs and ASBOs. First, what the ABC requires of the alleged offender is simply that he refrain from conduct that has been agreed to be wrongfully offensive—whereas an ASBO can prohibit utterly inoffensive conduct. Second, what is punished if an ABC is breached is the offending behaviour itself, not the disobedience to the ABC: the punishment should be proportionate to the substantive wrong, the offensive behaviour, for which the person has now been convicted.[78]

Much more would need to be said about the operations of this expanded kind of ABC; all that we hope to have done here is to suggest that it provides a possible way of responding to at least some of the kinds of wrongfully offensive behaviour that reasonably worry so many people—a way that gives a legitimate but limited role to the criminal law.

IV. CONCLUDING REMARKS

It was not our aim in this chapter to take a firm view about what kinds of 'offensive' conduct could legitimately be criminalised—either directly, or

---

[77] There would, however, need to be some constraints on what counter-complaints can be brought up; without such constraints the process could spiral into an unproductive series of complaints and counter-complaints.

[78] But see n 71 above.

through such hybrid devices as ABCs or injunctions. Rather, our aim has been, more modestly, to clarify some of the issues, and to sketch some of the ways in which a liberal state and its citizens could properly respond to offensive conduct. This involved discussing (in § I) some different forms and structures that offensive conduct can display: of particular importance were, first, the point that offensiveness is not simply a matter of whether people are offended, but of whether it is reasonable, or necessary, to be offended—the point that offensiveness is a strongly normative notion; and, second, the distinction between wrongfully offensive and offensively wrongful conduct. In § II, we then explored some ways of responding to offensive behaviour: we hoped to show how various kinds of response that fall well short of the drastically coercive force of the criminal law can be appropriate, but also to sketch the kinds of reason that could legitimately lead us towards criminalisation. Finally, in § III, we looked at three kinds of hybrid response,[79] which involve an initial order or agreement that specified persons refrain from specified types of offensive conduct, and allow for criminal (or any other) sanctions only if the order is disobeyed or the agreement broken. We agree with many other critics that ASBOs are morally unacceptable, but can see a modest role for injunctions, and a possibly more fruitful role for a version of ABCs that takes much more seriously the idea that they are contracts.

REFERENCES

ASHWORTH, AJ (2000) 'Is the Criminal Law a Lost Cause?' *Law Quarterly Review* 16: 225.
—— (2004) 'Social Control and "Anti-Social Behaviour": The Subversion of Human Rights?' *Law Quarterly Review* 120: 263.
CHRISTIE, N (1977) 'Conflicts as Property' *British Journal of Criminology* 1: 1.
DUFF, RA (1986) *Trials and Punishments*. Cambridge: Cambridge University Press.
—— (2002) 'Crime, Prohibition and Punishment' *Journal of Applied Philosophy* 19: 97.
—— (2003) 'Restoration and Retribution', in A VON HIRSCH *et al* (eds), *Restorative Justice and Criminal Justice: Competing or Reconcilable Paradigms?* Oxford: Hart Publishing, 43.
FEINBERG, J (1970) 'The Expressive Function of Punishment', in *Doing and Deserving*. Princeton, NJ: Princeton University Press, 95.
—— (1984) *Harm to Others*. New York: Oxford University Press.
—— (1985) *Offense to Others*. New York: Oxford University Press.
GARDNER, J *et al* (1998) 'Neighbouring on the Oppressive' *Criminal Justice* 16: 7.

---

[79] See also Simester and von Hirsch, this volume, on 'two step' prohibitions.

GOODIN, RE (1991) 'Theories of Compensation', in R FREY and C MORRIS (eds), *Liability and Responsibility*. Cambridge: Cambridge University Press, 257.

HAMPTON, J (1989) 'The Nature of Immorality' *Social Philosophy and Policy* 7. 1: 22.

—— (1990) 'Mens Rea' *Social Philosophy and Policy* 7.2: 1.

Home Office (2002) *A Guide to Anti-Social Behaviour Orders and Acceptable Behaviour Contracts*. London: Home Office.

HÖRNLE, T (2001) 'Offensive Behaviour and German Penal Law' *Buffalo Criminal Law Review* 5: 255.

HULSMAN, L (1986) 'Critical Criminology and the Concept of Crime' *Contemporary Crises* 10: 63.

HUSAK, D (2004) 'The Criminal Law as Last Resort' *Oxford Journal of Legal Studies* 24: 207.

JAREBORG, N (2005) 'Criminalization as Last Resort' *Ohio State Journal of Criminal Law* 2: 521.

JOHNSTONE, G (2002) *Restorative Justice: Ideas, Values, Debates*. Cullompton, Devon: Willan.

MAGNET, J (2004) 'Spliffs Give off the Whiff of Decline and Fall' *The Times*, 30 January.

MARSHALL, SE and DUFF, RA (1998) 'Criminalization and Sharing Wrongs' *Canadian Journal of Law and Jurisprudence* 11: 7.

MENDUS, S (ed) (1988) *Justifying Toleration: Conceptual and Historical Perspectives*. Cambridge: Cambridge University Press.

MILL, JS (1998 [1861]) *Utilitarianism,* R CRISP (ed). Oxford: Oxford University Press.

MURPHY, JG (1988) 'Forgiveness and Resentment', in JG MURPHY and J HAMPTON, *Forgiveness and Mercy*. Cambridge: Cambridge University Press, 14.

—— (1998) 'Jean Hampton on Immorality, Self-Hatred, and Self-Forgiveness' *Philosophical Studies* 89: 215.

PADFIELD, N (2004) 'The Anti-Social Behaviour Act 2003: the Ultimate Nanny-State Act?' *Criminal Law Review*: 712.

PARADINE, K (2001) 'Using Civil Law to Tackle Crime and Disorder' *New Law Journal* 151: 1614.

PARPWORTH, N (2004) 'The Anti-Social Behaviour Act 2003: the Provisions Relating to Noise' *Journal of Planning and Environment Law*: 541.

RAPHAEL, DD (1988) 'The Intolerable', in S MENDUS (ed) *Justifying Toleration: Conceptual and Historical Perspectives*. Cambridge: Cambridge University Press, 139.

SCHONSHECK, J (1994) *On Criminalization: An Essay in the Philosophy of the Criminal Law*. Dordrecht: Kluwer.

SIMESTER, AP and SULLIVAN, GR (2003) *Criminal Law: Theory and Doctrine* (2nd ed). Oxford: Hart Publishing.

SIMESTER, AP and VON HIRSCH, A (2002) 'Rethinking the Offense Principle' *Legal Theory* 8: 269.

SMITH, JC (2002) *Smith and Hogan on Criminal Law* (10th edn). London: Butterworths.

VON HIRSCH, A (1993) *Censure and Sanctions*. Oxford: Oxford University Press.

—— (1998) 'Desert and Previous Convictions', in A VON HIRSCH and AJ ASHWORTH (eds), *Principled Sentencing* (2nd edn). Oxford: Hart Publishing, 192.

VON HIRSCH, A *et al* (1995) 'Overtaking on the Right' *New Law Journal* 145: 933.

VON HIRSCH, A *et al* (eds) (2000) *Ethical and Social Perspectives on Situational Crime Prevention*. Oxford: Hart Publishing.

VON HIRSCH, A *et al* (eds) (2003) *Restorative Justice and Criminal Justice: Competing or Reconcilable Paradigms?* Oxford: Hart Publishing.

3

Disgust: Metaphysical and Empirical Speculations

DOUGLAS HUSAK[*]

I. INTRODUCTION

WE KNOW THAT many Anglo-American jurisdictions have recently increased the severity of their legal responses to offensive behaviour. The introduction of the Anti-Social Behaviour Order (ASBO), the subject of several chapters in this volume, is the obvious example of this trend in the United Kingdom. In the United States, many municipalities vigorously enforce newly minted 'quality of life' offences.[1] What we do not know, however, is whether offensive behaviour *itself* has increased—nor, if so, why.[2] These latter issues are important. Assessing the extent of a problem is crucial in helping to decide whether we need new strategies to combat it. Moreover, our remedies are likely to be ineffective unless we understand the causal processes that have created the problem. If offensive behaviour itself is no more frequent than in previous eras, we might wonder why the law should resort to novel and controversial devices to deal with it.

We should be sceptical of the idea that offensive conduct is becoming more pervasive. Why would this trend take place at the present time? It is plausible to suppose that people simply *perceive* an increase in offensive behaviour, without any substantial change in behaviour itself. Perhaps people have thinner skins, or are quicker to complain. Persons in every era believe that the standards of civility and decency have deteriorated, and most of us regard the mores of the next generation as inferior to those of

[*] I would like to thank Christopher Knapp, whose work on disgust has been a major influence on my thought. He also provided me with detailed comments that were extremely valuable. Paul Roberts, Andrew Simester and Andrew von Hirsch also offered many very helpful criticisms, suggestions, and clarifications.

[1] This trend is especially prevalent in New York City. In the fiscal year that ended on 30 June 2003, the New York City Police Department issued 532,817 summonses for quality-of-life offences like graffiti and noise. This ticket blitz is widely perceived as a device to raise revenue without increasing taxes. See 'New Data Show Surge in Summonses', *New York Times* B1 (28 January 2004).

[2] We have much to learn about offence. As Paul Roberts (this volume: 31) laments, 'There is little concrete information about what actually offends people in Britain today, with what frequency, and how seriously'. Roberts need not have confined his observation to Britain.

our own (Neuberger, 1993). What *is* distinctive about contemporary society, however, is the readiness to demand legal solutions for such problems. But if perceptions rather than reality account for the supposition that offensive conduct is increasing, there is little justification for widening the scope of criminal prohibitions to address the situation.

Empirically-minded criminologists will almost certainly agree with my claim about the importance of determining whether and why offensive behaviour is more or less widespread, but are likely to despair about the prospects of finding out. Offensiveness itself, they are sure to say, is exceedingly difficult to measure. Even if we *could* gauge its incidence today, we lack reliable data about its frequency in the past, and thus have no basis to decide whether it is increasing or decreasing. Neither do we know *why* the amount of offensive behaviour might change in one direction or the other.

In light of these uncertainties, what insights might a legal philosopher hope to contribute? My chapter has three parts. In the first, I offer some introductory remarks about the scope of my project, and argue for its importance. I briefly defend my decision to focus on *disgust*—a particular *kind* of offence—rather than on offence itself. In the second part, I hazard some speculative claims about the *metaphysical* status of the property of disgustingness (or the property of being disgusting). I conclude that (what I will call) *disgust realism* is highly problematic. If my suspicions are warranted, the prospects for measuring the incidence of offensive behaviour are even more dismal than criminologists may have thought. When offence consists in disgust, there may be nothing in the world to measure other than the responses of people who report being disgusted. In the final part, I discuss the possible relevance of some *empirical* studies about disgust. Social scientists have made many important findings about disgust that are potentially significant for legal policy. Better data are needed. But my tentative observations suggest alternative explanations of why some people might call for more severe penalties for offensive behaviour—explanations that do not assume that offensive behaviour itself is more common.

I will conclude that these metaphysical and empirical speculations provide good reasons to be cautious before devising novel or additional legal remedies to curb offensive behaviour. Clearly, caution is advisable. Most legal philosophers, I trust, recognise a presumption in favour of personal liberty and thus against the legitimacy of legal interference. This presumption is especially strong when *criminal* intervention is proposed.[3] Almost certainly we have too much criminal legislation already, and calls to extend further the reach of the criminal sanction should be greeted with scepticism and scrutinised carefully.[4] William Stuntz (2001: 511) points out that 'anyone

---

[3] For further thoughts, see Husak, 2004: 207.

[4] William Stuntz (2001: 515) maintains that we are coming 'ever closer to a world in which the law on the books makes everyone a felon'.

who studies contemporary state or federal codes is likely to be struck by their scope, by the sheer amount of conduct they render punishable'. Proposals to expand the criminalisation of offensive behaviour would represent a further step in this direction. In addition, the imposition of criminal penalties for offensive behaviour is bound to be controversial and divisive. Thus we should be receptive to ideas that address the problem without inflicting legal penalties. The general thrust of my investigations is that at least *some* progress in reducing offence might be achieved without resorting to the heavy hand of the criminal sanction. Admittedly, I might be mistaken; perhaps no such progress is possible. But we cannot know unless we try, and we will not know *how* to try without immersing ourselves in some of the issues I explore here. My metaphysical and empirical speculations may have applications that I do not foresee or anticipate. At the very least, I am confident that legal policy can only benefit from being informed by the kinds of observations I hazard here.

Progress might be achieved in any of three ways. First, we might reduce the likelihood that people will become offended. Some individuals, we all know, are more susceptible to offence than others.[5] Perhaps we can learn why the former are more easily offended in the hope of decreasing their vulnerability. Second, we might lessen the magnitude of the offence that people experience. We also know that some individuals become offended more deeply and for a longer period of time than others. Perhaps we can learn why the degree of offence varies so widely. Finally, we might lower the probability that some people will perceive offensive conduct as wrongful. Some individuals are less inclined than others to segregate their moral judgments from their emotional reactions. Perhaps we can retard the readiness to believe that others have behaved wrongfully when their conduct is deemed to be offensive.

My strategy may seem to have a conservative tone which I am anxious to dispel. I might appear to 'blame the victim' when I propose to resolve a conflict by altering the reaction of the offended party rather than by changing the conduct of the offender. I offer several quick replies. First, I do not conceptualise my project as assigning 'blame' for offence to anyone. Instead, I merely explore the opportunities for lawmakers that arise from gaining a better understanding of the causal processes that give rise to offence. In addition, my approach is designed to supplement rather than to replace our efforts to reduce offensive behaviour. I do not pretend that legal means to retard offensive behaviour will no longer be needed. Finally, I concede that my strategy would be unacceptable if the conflict in question involved harm

---

[5] Judith Jarvis Thomson (1990: 254–5) believes it follows from this truism that we have no *rights* against others that they not offend us.

rather than offence. But offence is different from harm. For present purposes, the central difference is that the former, unlike the latter, necessarily involves a psychological state. We can be harmed without our knowledge, but we cannot be offended without having the appropriate mental experience. I harm you the moment I steal your property or infect you with a virus—even though you are unaware of my behaviour. But if my conduct does not place you in the relevant psychological state, I simply have not offended you. Suppose, then, that it is possible to reduce the incidence, magnitude, or perceived wrongfulness of offence without intervening in the conduct of the offending party. If so, lawmakers have a viable option that is unavailable in the case of harm.

We must begin our inquiry by asking: what exactly *is* offence? Most commentators who pose this question are requesting a *definition* of offence. This task is daunting.[6] In his seminal work, Joel Feinberg offers an extraordinarily broad answer. He proposes to 'use the word "offense" to cover the whole miscellany of disliked mental states' such as 'passing annoyance, disappointment, disgust, embarrassment, and various other disliked conditions such as fear, anxiety, and minor ("harmless") aches and pains'.[7] This collection of mental states appears to have little in common apart from the fact that they are all unwanted and generally are too trivial or fleeting to qualify as genuine harms. If we hope to find answers to metaphysical and empirical questions about offence, we cannot possibly employ so inclusive a definition. In fact, it is hard to see how progress on *any* important philosophical or jurisprudential problem should be anticipated as long as the central term in the inquiry remains so vague and ill-defined. Too much legal commentary purports to evaluate something called 'the offence principle' without first clarifying the nature of offence itself.

Hence our topic must be narrowed. For many reasons, I propose to focus on *disgust*—a particular *kind* of offence. First, disgust is a good candidate for being *paradigmatic* of the state of mind elicited by offence. The claim that I am offended by whatever disgusts me seems plausible as a matter of ordinary English—far more plausible, I submit, than the parallel claim about any number of other mental states listed by Feinberg, such as fear. Clearly, many legal philosophers had disgust in mind when they wrote about the legal significance of offence. Most of the fantastic stories on Feinberg's (1985: 10–11) imaginative 'ride on the bus' involve disgust. Second, there is a wealth of conceptual and empirical research on disgust from which to draw. Philosophers and social scientists have made many important findings that might be brought to bear on legal policy. In addition,

---

[6] Robert C Roberts (2003: 253) maintains that 'the defining proposition for disgust is this: X *is repulsive and worthy to be shunned; may it depart from me*' (italics in original).

[7] Feinberg, 1985: 1. I am aware that Feinberg uses the word 'offense' in a different sense from that of other contributors to this volume.

disgust has played a central role in the substantive criminal law. Two examples from the United States will suffice. Lord Devlin famously argued that disgust provides a compelling rationale for making some acts (for example homosexual sodomy) illegal.[8] Moreover, disgust figures prominently in the definition of obscenity (or pornography) formulated by the Supreme Court.[9] For these reasons alone, attention to disgust is warranted.

Legal philosophers have additional reasons to concentrate on disgust. Many contemporary theorists defend *expressive* theories of punishment.[10] Admittedly, enormous disagreement surrounds the questions of *what* punishment expresses or *how* its expressive dimension contributes to its justification (Adler, 2000). According to William Miller (1997), disgust is an essential component in a healthy society's aversion to crime. Building on Miller's scholarship, Dan Kahan (1998) contends that 'an expressively effective punishment must make clear that we are in fact disgusted with what the offender has done'. Since he believes that punishments should express disgust, Kahan (1996) rejects types of sanctions (such as fines or community service) that are not conventional means by which strong condemnation is conveyed. Kahan concludes that sanctions that express disgust are desirable because they increase the cost of lawbreaking, reinforce the norms that are broken, satisfy our retributive urges, and (as a bonus) save money for taxpayers. If these allegations are correct, disgust plays a central and indispensable role in the rationale of punishment as well as in the substantive criminal law itself.

Despite the advantages of focusing on disgust, I am unsure and noncommittal about whether or to what extent my conclusions can be extended to any of the other psychological states mentioned by Feinberg. I am fairly certain that they cannot be generalised to racial slurs and epithets. The main *point* of these behaviours is to cause offence. Neither do I envisage their straightforward application to such phenomena as noisy neighbours—perhaps a better example of the kind of problem that ASBOs are designed to address (Burney, this volume). In fact, most of the behaviours covered by ASBOs seem to have little to do with offence—and certainly nothing to do with disgust. Still, I suspect that a few of my observations about disgust can be applied to several other modes of offensive behaviour. But no general

---

[8] Devlin, 1965. Admittedly, Devlin's case for criminalisation depends on reactions of 'intolerance, indignation, and disgust' (p 17); he does not explicitly indicate to what extent his rationale rests on disgust alone. Indignation, I concede, provides a far more plausible basis for legal intervention. See § III *infra*.

[9] *Miller v California*, 413 US 15 (1973). At p 18, n 2, the majority cites the definition of 'obscene' in Webster's *Third New International Dictionary* (unabridged 1969) as: '1a: disgusting to the senses ... b: grossly repugnant to the generally accepted notions of what is appropriate ... 2: offensive or revolting as countering or violating some ideal or principle.' The *Oxford English Dictionary* (1933 ed) gives a similar definition: 'Offensive to the senses, or to taste or refinement; disgusting, repulsive, filthy, foul, abominable, loathsome.'

[10] The inspiration is Feinberg (1965).

argument for this conclusion can be given; a separate analysis is required for each of the miscellany of disliked mental states that fall under the umbrella of offence. If my suspicions are warranted, some kinds of offence might provide a justification for legal intervention while others will not. Blanket statements about *offence* or *the offence principle* are best avoided. I urge philosophers to resist categorical statements about the legal significance of offence without further specifying the *kind* of offence in question.

II. THE METAPHYSICS OF DISGUSTINGNESS

As I have indicated, my interest is somewhat different from those who propose a *definition* of offence. I am concerned with the *metaphysical* status of offence—the question of whether and in what sense the *property* of offensiveness exists. Rather than tackle the whole of this unmanageable problem, I will hazard some observations about the metaphysical status of disgust, a particular kind of response to offence. In particular, I am interested in whether it is sensible to say that some things *really are* disgusting—whether the property of disgustingness (or the property of being disgusting) can be predicated of things in the external world. For present purposes, I will express no worries about the metaphysical status of being disgusted. This latter phrase refers to a psychological state, and I have nothing novel to say about the ontology of our mental life. But *disgustingness* is altogether different. Is disgustingness itself somehow 'out there in the world'? Can we provide an adequate metaphysical analysis of it? What are the possible consequences for legal policy if we come to doubt that disgustingness is a property of things in the world?

Consider a phenomenon that should be familiar to all of us. Suppose I am disgusted by a given kind of behaviour, but you are not. What am I entitled to say to you (or you to me)? I cannot say: 'You claim not to be disgusted by the conduct in question, but you are mistaken; you *are* disgusted whether you know it or not'. As many commentators have noted, you, not I, are the better judge of whether or not you are in the psychological state of being disgusted. But may I say: 'Admittedly, you are not disgusted by the conduct in question, but so much the worse for you, because the conduct *really is* disgusting'. If such propositions are sensible and coherent, there must be some *fact of the matter* about whether conduct *really is* (or is not) disgusting—some fact of the matter over and above whether you or I happen to be disgusted by it. If no fact of the matter exists, it is hard to see how you could be mistaken in (honestly) reporting that you find nothing in the conduct to be disgusted by.[11]

---

[11] Admittedly, some meta-ethicists have tried to find a place for moral truth or falsity despite rejecting a realist account of moral properties. See, eg, Blackburn, 1993.

Let us understand *disgust realism* as including two distinct but related components.[12] First, judgments of the form 'X is disgusting' (or 'X really is disgusting') are capable of being true or false. If this first element of disgust realism were correct, those who do not concur with my judgment that X is disgusting would be capable of being mistaken. Of course, I, not you, might be wrong. The point is that mistakes are possible; there is a fact of the matter to be right or wrong about. My account of disgust realism includes a second component. Disgust realism must allow the property of disgustingness to *explain* our responses. When someone is (or is not) disgusted by X, and is asked to explain why he is in this psychological state, is he ever correct in replying that the reason he is (or is not) disgusted by X is because X is (or is not) disgusting? If we cannot provide a realist account of disgustingness, these purported explanations will fail; alternative explanations of why I am or am not disgusted by X will have to be provided. Ultimately, I will conclude that disgust realism as I have defined it is probably untenable, and the best account of the metaphysical status of disgustingness is more complex.

What are the probable implications for the law if disgust realism turns out to be indefensible? The truth of realism is not *necessary* to justify the legal doctrines I mentioned earlier. But it would certainly help. If given behaviours are not *really* disgusting, what could be the rationale for using our own reactions of disgust as a basis for depriving others of liberty? Might the imposition of criminal penalties be justified by the existence of a broad social consensus that given kinds of conduct disgust us? Some theorists have thought so.[13] But positions on these matters must await my subsequent discussion of our *disgust mechanism*—the causal processes that lead us to experience disgust. As we will see, some empirical facts about this mechanism should make us reluctant to cite our reactions of disgust as the rationale for legal intervention.

How should we assess disgust realism? Is anything in the world *really* disgusting? Few of us believe that things are (or are not) *inherently* disgusting. Presumably, disgustingness is a *relational* property. The relata are the object (or conduct) itself and the person(s) who react to it. Disgustingness, then, should be conceptualised as a *response-dependent* property: whether a thing X is or is not disgusting depends in some way on how people react to it. Other response-dependent properties are familiar to us.[14] Funniness, for example, cannot be conceptualised as an inherent property of a joke. Whether a story is or is not funny depends in some way on the response of

---

[12] Obviously, several competing accounts of realism exist. See Smith, 1994.

[13] 'Disgust when sufficiently widespread is as solid a basis for legal regulation as tangible harm.' Posner, 1999: 318.

[14] Some examples are controversial. Contemporary metaphysicians have struggled to provide a response-dependent analysis of colours. See Boghossian and Vellaman, 1989.

people to it. Fearsomeness is amenable to a similar analysis. Whether an object is or is not fearsome depends in some way on how people react to it.

Among the central questions in meta-ethics is whether *moral* properties like good are response-dependent. Inspired by Hume, a number of contemporary philosophers contend that the nature of value depends in some way on the composition of beings to whom things matter.[15] Moral values, it seems plausible to suppose, require human valuing, which somehow depend on our emotional constitution. The main challenge in defending a response-dependent analysis of moral properties—a problem that will resurface in the context of response-dependent analyses of emotions like disgust—is to find a suitable place for a cognitive or rational dimension in our moral judgments.

I have said that the existence of response-dependent properties like disgust depends *in some way* on how people respond to the object in question. But exactly how or in what way does the existence of these properties depend on human responses? Among the contested issues—with respect to both moral properties like goodness and non-moral properties like disgustingness—is whether the correct account of response-dependence will ground a version of metaphysical realism that includes both of the components I have described. *Subjectivism*, perhaps the simplest and most straightforward account of the relation between objects and reactions of disgust, fails to qualify as a coherent version of realism as I construe it here. According to disgust-subjectivists, 'X is disgusting' just means 'I am disgusted by X'. This analysis of disgustingness is analogous to subjectivism in meta-ethics. According to ethical subjectivists, 'X is morally good' just means 'I approve of X'.[16] Notice that both of these response-dependent analyses may *seem* to be versions of realism about the properties of disgustingness and goodness respectively. The proposition 'X is disgusting' (or 'X is bad') appears to have a truth-value; it is true if and only if I am disgusted by X (or disapprove of X). Unfortunately, as I have said, judgments about which things are disgusting (or good) are far from universal among human beings. Thus this same judgment might also be false, since different people are disgusted by (or disapprove of) different things. If you are not disgusted by X, it follows that X is not disgusting.[17] When two people disagree, subjectivism does not allow

---

[15] 'When you pronounce any action or character to be vicious, you mean nothing, but that from the constitution of your nature you have a feeling or sentiment of blame from the contemplation of it'. Hume, 1888: 469.

[16] For a discussion of varieties of subjectivism, see Rachels, 1994. I do not deny that some more sophisticated versions of what their proponents call subjectivism might be immune to many of the difficulties I raise here.

[17] Notice that disgust-subjectivists propose 'I am disgusted by X' as the analysis of 'X is disgusting', *not* as the analysis of the undefined locution 'X is disgusting-for-me'. The task is to provide a metaphysical account of disgustingness itself, not an account of disgust-for-me. Of course, it may be that we *cannot* provide a coherent analysis of the former, but only of the latter. If so, we should reject disgust realism.

us to say that what they disagree about is whether the thing in question *really is* disgusting.[18] Since both can be correct, neither ethical subjectivism nor disgust-subjectivism can account for the possibility of genuine disagreement between two people who make different judgments about whether X is disgusting (or good).[19]

Neither should subjectivism be regarded as a version of realism according to the second component of my definition. The disgustingness of X does not *explain* why someone is or is not disgusted by X.[20] If you and I appear to disagree about whether X is disgusting—if I am disgusted by X but you are not—it is hard to see how both you and I could point to X to *explain* our discrepant reactions. How can X simultaneously explain both my disgust as well as your lack of it? If I am correct, neither ethical subjectivism nor its analogue about disgust qualify as coherent versions of realism as I have defined it here. I conclude that subjectivism about disgust (and its meta-ethical counterpart about moral properties) is inadequate if we hope to provide a realist analysis of disgust by construing it as a response-dependent property. A satisfactory realist account of the metaphysical status of disgust must be more sophisticated.

In addition, disgust-subjectivism (as well as ethical subjectivism) renders the concept of disgust almost totally useless to the law. No one should believe that legal intervention in the conduct of another is justified simply because you or I happen to be disgusted by it. Any account of the legal significance of disgust—or, more generally, of offence—must deal with the problem of the *idiosyncratic* or *unusual respondent*.[21] Imagine that Smith is an anorexic who is disgusted by the sight of eating. The fact that eating causes Smith to be disgusted provides no reason to take legal action against persons who eat.[22] What would help to support legal interference (but obviously is not forthcoming in this case) is disgust realism as I have defined it—some reason to think that eating *really is* disgusting.

---

[18] Admittedly, some kinds of mistakes (and thus genuine disagreements) are still possible. If Sue believes that the stuff (X) on her plate is human flesh while Jane believes it to be beef, they might well disagree about whether X is disgusting. I assume that two persons concur about the referent of X when I say that subjectivism precludes genuine disagreement.

[19] An additional problem with ethical subjectivism is that much of our disapproval is not *moral* in nature; the analysis fails to distinguish moral badness from properties like ugly, shameful, repulsive, and the like.

[20] Subjectivism seems indifferent to whether the explanatory relation is the other way around; my psychological state of being disgusted by X explains why X is disgusting.

[21] Consider the various alternatives Feinberg (1985: 27–32) explores to try to solve this problem.

[22] Ultimately, Feinberg (1985: 35) seems to allow that even idiosyncratic and unusual judgments about disgust provide *a reason* to intervene. In other words, Feinberg holds that there is a reason to proscribe conduct that disgusts only those individuals with abnormal susceptibilities. I am unpersuaded. But even if this reason exists, its weight is miniscule—far too small to outweigh the presumption of liberty that attaches to the party whose conduct is alleged to be disgusting.

Can a better realist account be defended? Although I am sceptical, we should not give up so quickly. The most promising device to overcome the foregoing difficulties with subjectivism, while simultaneously preserving the possible significance of disgust to the law, is to inject a *rational* dimension into our analysis of judgments about disgust (Shoemaker, 2000). A rational component will block us from supposing that something (like eating) is disgusting whenever idiosyncratic and unusual respondents (like Smith) happen to be disgusted by it. The easiest way to inject a rational dimension into our analysis is by including constraints in the description of the respondents themselves, as well as in the nature of the conditions under which they respond. Let us stipulate that the respondents in question are *reasonable* and the circumstances in question are *ideal*. According to this suggestion, 'X is disgusting' just means 'A reasonable person P under ideal conditions C would be disgusted by X'. Unlike subjectivism, this analysis seems likely to qualify as a coherent version of realism. It specifies not only the truth conditions for judgments about disgust, but also explains how the property of disgustingness might account for our reactions. Those things that possess the property of disgustingness—that *really are* disgusting—are those things that will disgust reasonable persons under ideal conditions. If I am disgusted by X but you are not, my allegation that you are mistaken now begins to make some sense. You might not be reasonable, or the conditions under which you react to X may be less than ideal.

The foregoing analysis is potentially useful to the law. Only *some* judgments that I am disgusted by X will support legal intervention—namely, those in which X *really is* disgusting, as identified by the reactions of reasonable persons under ideal conditions. Those who (like Devlin) refer to disgust in their arguments for criminalisation, or (like the Supreme Court) incorporate disgust in their definitions of what materials can be censured, can overcome the problem of the idiosyncratic or unusual respondent by requiring that judgments of disgust be made by reasonable persons—typically, those who serve as legislators or as jurors.

Although this response-dependent analysis of disgust may seem to be capable of grounding a version of realism that is useful for legal purposes, it suffers from several problems. I will mention four.[23] First and most obvious are the formidable difficulties that arise in attempts to explicate the two constraints just introduced. Which traits make observer P *reasonable*, and when are conditions C *ideal*? Comparable questions, of course, surround 'ideal observer' theories of goodness in ethics (Brandt, 1955). Although I doubt that even this first difficulty can be resolved satisfactorily, additional problems plague response-dependent analyses of disgust.

---

[23] See also Feinberg's (1985: 35–37) grounds for failing to include a requirement of reasonableness in his test for when legal intervention is appropriate.

The second kind of problem is well known to philosophers who debate the adequacy of the parallel meta-ethical analysis of properties like goodness. GF Moore famously argued that each of these accounts is vulnerable to what came to be known as the *open-question argument*. If 'X is disgusting' means 'A reasonable person P under ideal conditions C would be disgusted by X', it follows that person P in conditions C must be correct about whether X is or is not disgusting. In other words, it becomes incoherent to deny that a given X is (or is not) disgusting while conceding that reasonable persons under ideal conditions would (or would not) be disgusted by it. A social reformer (or heretic), however, might contend that some of the things reasonable people are disgusted by (even under ideal circumstances) simply are not disgusting, or, conversely, that some of the things reasonable people are not disgusted by are disgusting after all.[24] Although few reformers may succeed in persuading others of their novel insights, their statements do not seem to be incoherent. Yet such statements are condemned to incoherence if judgments about disgust are analysed in the way I have indicated.

A third difficulty with this response-dependent analysis of disgust might be called the *conflation problem* (D'Arms and Jacobson, 1999: 732). Described abstractly, the problem is that some but not all of the reasons for which a reasonable person P under ideal conditions C will (or will not) be disgusted by X seem to bear on whether X is (or is not) disgusting. This response-dependent analysis of disgust cannot differentiate between these two kinds of reasons why P will (or will not) be disgusted by X. Unless there is some basis for separating these two kinds of reasons, this response-dependent analysis of disgust must be rejected.

Two examples of this latter difficulty may be helpful. The first example involves a threat; the second contains a promise. Suppose P, our reasonable person, is confronted by his boss, who threatens to withhold his bonus unless he somehow manages not to be disgusted by X. Or suppose P is approached by a philanthropist who promises to donate millions of dollars to prevent starvation in Africa if he can somehow manage to be disgusted by Y. The boss provides an excellent reason for P not to be disgusted by X, and the philanthropist provides an equally compelling reason for P to be disgusted by Y. Suppose that P manages to respond to these incentives by being disgusted by Y but not by X. It is doubtful that either of the reasons I have mentioned—the prudential reason in the first case, or the moral reason in the second case—undermines P's reasonableness or the quality of the conditions under which he responds.[25] At the same time, it is apparent that neither of these reasons bears on whether X or Y really is disgusting

---

[24] Some philosophers have offered the Big Mac as an example, but I think that hot dogs are an even better candidate. See D'Arms and Jacobson, 1999: 727.

[25] Of course, a defence of this conclusion must await an explication of the idealising conditions.

(D'Arms and Jacobson, 2000). Unless a response-dependent analysis can specify *which* of the good reasons to be disgusted by X or Y count in favour of predicating disgustingness to them, this response-dependent analysis of disgust should not be accepted.

As these examples indicate, some perfectly good reasons for P to be (or not to be) disgusted by X are irrelevant to whether X is (or is not) disgusting. Only those good reasons that are *appropriate* to P's judgment are relevant. So 'X is disgusting' must mean 'A reasonable person P under ideal conditions C would be disgusted by X *for appropriate reasons*'. Of course, stipulating that P must be influenced only by appropriate reasons does not *solve* the conflation problem; it merely states the test that proposed solutions must satisfy. The conflation problem itself persists; we have named rather than resolved the difficulty of providing a substantive account of the distinction between the good reasons that do and do not bear on whether X is really disgusting.

A fourth and final problem arises by drawing a contrast with the intuitive appeal of ideal observer theories in ethics. When two persons disagree about the morality of a war, for example, it is probable that one (or both) of their judgments were made under less than ideal conditions. Were they to agree about the relevant facts—about whether the invaded country actually possessed weapons banned under international law, for instance—their disagreement might be resolved. It is here (and undoubtedly elsewhere) that response-dependent theories about disgust diverge from those in ethics. When two people disagree about whether something is disgusting, it is far less plausible to suppose that one or both of their judgments were made under non-ideal conditions.[26] Imagine that I find spiders disgusting but you do not. How might I try to convince you that you are wrong and I am right (or vice versa)? You and I might agree about all of the relevant facts about spiders, and might have encountered spiders in similar situations. It seems unlikely that I could persuade you to share my reaction by identifying something about your circumstances that renders your judgment suspect.

Without a solution to each of these problems, we are left without an adequate analysis of the judgment 'X is disgusting' that can support a coherent version of disgust realism that includes the two components I have described—that is, a version that assigns a truth-value to these claims and allows X to explain our reactions. Although I presume that most philosophers would concur that an adequate analysis must be response-dependent, the details have yet to be supplied. Of course, I have barely scratched the

---

[26] I do not deny that differing conditions *may* explain our divergent reactions in the case of disgust. The object X may have been examined in an art gallery or on a street corner, for example. I claim that such divergent conditions are less likely to explain disagreements about disgust than disagreements about morality.

surface in discussing the different response-dependent analyses that qualify as versions of realism. Clearly it is premature to conclude that no realist analysis will prove defensible. Still, I think we are entitled to question disgust realism itself—and to ponder the implications for legal policy.

Before proceeding, however, I hasten to admit that numerous examples make disgust realism seem plausible. At least *some* propositions about disgust *do* seem to be false, and the absence of disgustingness in the object in question seems capable of explaining why. Suppose White believes that chairs are disgusting, but Black does not. Realism allows us to say that White and Black genuinely disagree, that both cannot be correct, that White is wrong and that Black is right. If someone found chairs to be disgusting, we would almost certainly conclude that his judgment was mistaken, not that chairs really are disgusting after all. The fact that chairs lack the property of being disgusting seems to explain why Black is right and White is wrong. We should not reject disgust realism unless we can say why such examples appear to count so heavily in its favour.

I believe that this challenge can be met. To do so, however, we must turn to empirical studies about disgust. These empirical findings, I hope to show, inform our unresolved inquiry about the metaphysical status of disgustingness. They provide some reason to think that disgust realism is mistaken, despite its undeniable appeal in the foregoing example. Perhaps the metaphysical conclusion I will defend should be called *qualified anti-realism*. Some but not all judgments about disgust will turn out to be amenable to a realist analysis, and empirical research on disgust will help to provide a principled account of the distinction.

Where have we come thus far? I began by asking whether disgusting behaviour *itself* has increased, and expressed sympathy with those criminologists who despair about whether we will ever find out. In the absence of a solution to the foregoing problems, however, the prospects for measuring the incidence of disgusting behaviour itself are even more dismal than we might have feared. We have yet to provide an adequate account of what disgustingness is, and thus can hardly be expected to decide whether the world contains more or less of it. Again, I should not be understood to insist that this difficulty cannot be overcome; disgust-realism may yet be salvaged.[27] Or it may not. Arguably, all there is to measure is whether people are in the psychological state of being disgusted more or less frequently. Respondents may truthfully report feeling more disgust, even though we cannot explain this trend by positing an increase in the incidence of conduct that really is disgusting. The incidence of conduct that really is disgusting cannot have increased if it does not exist.

---

[27] Alternatively, one can attempt to meet the challenge of providing an account of the truth or falsity of judgments like 'X is offensive' that does not require realism. See Blackburn, 1993.

III. DISGUST MECHANISMS

I have questioned whether (apart from a few kinds of cases to which I will return) we can explain our reaction of being (or not being) disgusted by X by claiming that X really is (or is not) disgusting. If my suspicions are well founded, we must look elsewhere if we hope to understand why we experience disgust. If the fact that X is disgusting rarely explains why we are disgusted by it, what does? How does an answer to this question bear on the justifiability of using legal sanctions to prevent behaviour regarded as disgusting?

It should be apparent that this inquiry *must* be important for legal policy. Most of us are reluctant to apply legal sanctions. In the case of Anti-Social Behaviour Orders (ASBOs), persons are given a chance to desist from specified offensive behaviours before incurring legal penalties—an opportunity that would almost never be extended if *harm* were inflicted. If possible, we should prefer to reduce the undesired experience of disgust without changing the behaviour that allegedly gives rise to it. Although this objective may seem utopian, even marginal progress would be welcome. And even if we could not reduce the *incidence* of disgust, we may be able to decrease its *magnitude*. This would represent a major achievement as well, inasmuch as a plausible case for legal intervention requires a balancing of several factors. Among these factors is the magnitude of disgust, construed by Feinberg to include its intensity, duration, and extent.[28] If people could be brought to feel a lesser degree of disgust, the case for legal prohibitions would be weakened. Finally, we may have some success diminishing the likelihood that persons will believe that they have been wronged or affronted when they experience disgust. This accomplishment would be valuable too, since it is hard to see how criminal punishment can be justified unless it is imposed for conduct that is regarded as wrongful (Simester and von Hirsch, 2002).

Are any of these goals attainable? Frankly, I am unsure. I *am* sure, however, that good empirical evidence is needed before we have any realistic prospects of finding out. No *a priori* considerations can tell us why, whether, or to what extent something will disgust someone. To understand this phenomenon, we must study the human *disgust mechanism*. Cognitive and experimental psychologists have undertaken most of the work of potential interest to legal philosophers. Unfortunately, my efforts will only scratch the surface. We still have a great deal to learn about our disgust mechanisms; the bulk of empirical research comes from the English-speaking world. The relevance of this research is not always clear, and my observations

---

[28] Feinberg, 1985: 35. Feinberg's balancing test is explicitly applied to offence, not to disgust. If disgust is indeed paradigmatic of offence, however, it should be amenable to the same general analysis.

are highly programmatic and undeveloped. The point of my investigations is to indicate how these empirical data might be useful to legal policy. Once we have a better understanding of the disgust mechanism, we may be able to reduce the incidence, magnitude, or moral significance of this unwanted psychological state—without changing the behaviour of others. If we reject disgust-realism—and conclude that the psychological state of being disgusted is not explained by the fact that objects really are disgusting—we should be especially receptive to these suggestions.

Despite our relative ignorance, there is much that cognitive and experimental psychologists *do* profess to know about disgust. First, disgust is generally included among the *basic* emotions.[29] In other words, the disgust mechanism is part of our inherited cognitive endowment, characteristically manifested by distinctive facial expressions. Each of us has the capacity to feel disgust, regardless of our historical or cultural circumstances. Unlike many other basic emotions, however, disgust is absent in nonhuman primates.[30] Moreover, we know that cultures differ, sometimes radically, in the stimuli (sometimes called triggers or elicitors) that give rise to disgust.[31] Some examples are familiar to us all. Kissing is thought to be disgusting in some places, as is eating dogs or touching corpses during mourning. Similar examples of cross-cultural differences in the specific behaviours regarded as disgusting could be multiplied indefinitely.

The significance of such cross-cultural diversity provides additional grounds for differentiating harm from offence. We need little empirical knowledge of psychology—and perhaps none that is controversial—in order to decide whether and under what circumstances conduct causes harm. Neither do we need anthropological surveys to confirm that given behaviours are harmful. When confronted with stories about cultures that condone infanticide, for example, none of us infers that the infants in these societies, unlike those in our own, are unharmed by the practice. Infanticide *does* harm infants, whether or not the culture allows it. Offence is different. We do not suppose that the sight of bare skin offends persons in cultures more accustomed to public nudity. In light of what we are likely to conclude from these cross-cultural studies, it is hard to see why we should expect an analysis to tell us whether public nudity *really is* (or is not) offensive.

Other empirical findings may be more surprising. We do not enter the world disgusted by the particular things we eventually come to regard as

---

[29] The concept of a basic emotion is explicated in Ekman, 1980.

[30] Most psychologists speculate that disgust has its evolutionary origin as a distaste response. Nausea is the most distinct physiological concomitant of disgust, and functions to inhibit ingestion. But this conjecture, however plausible, does not readily explain why disgust would have evolved only in humans.

[31] Some theorists contend that our reactions depend crucially on the *kind* of ethic—autonomy, community, or divinity—prevalent in a culture. See Shweder and Haidt, 2003.

disgusting; each of us must learn *which* stimuli in the external world will cause us to experience disgust. We are taught to be disgusted by given stimuli through *social referencing*—that is, by watching and mimicking the reactions of adults. Two kinds of evidence support this finding. First, children do not display even the most rudimentary kinds of disgust until a relatively advanced age. The rejection of decay odours in spoiled foods, for example, does not occur until somewhere between the ages of three and eight (Schmidt and Beauchamp, 1988). Young children tend to be attracted to faeces; enculturation eventually transforms their fascination into aversion. Studies of feral children provide the second source of evidence for the claim that persons need to learn which stimuli to be disgusted by. Lucien Malson (1972) found no evidence of disgust in any of the fifty feral children he examined, although several other emotional responses—such as anger, fear, and frustration—were clearly evident. These children could be taught to be disgusted by given stimuli, but displayed no indication that anything disgusted them at the time they were discovered.

Even though we must learn which stimuli disgust us, innate constraints limit the kinds of things we *can* find disgusting. Through social referencing, the disgust mechanism of young children is activated by a relatively small number of objects. Despite the fact that each culture has a somewhat different set of disgust stimuli, Paul Rozin suggests that 'there appears to be a "preparedness" to attach disgust to certain sorts of things (e.g. food) and not others (e.g. flowers, machines)'.[32] Rozin lists nine possible elicitors of disgust: food, body products, animals, sexual behaviours, contact with death or corpses, violations of the exterior envelope of the body (including gore and deformity), poor hygiene, interpersonal contamination (contact with unsavoury human beings), and certain morals offences (Rozin, Haidt and McCauley, 2000). Of course, immense cultural variation persists within these broad parameters.

Another empirical fact is of special relevance to our metaphysical and legal inquiries. We may be tempted to suppose that our reactions of disgust are wholly visceral, unmediated and unaffected by further facts we might learn about the objects that disgust us.[33] But this supposition is false; our disgust mechanism conforms to what some researchers have called *laws of sympathetic magic* (Rozin, Millman and Nemeroff, 1986). According to these laws, virtually all human beings regard given stimuli as disgusting

[32] Rozin, Haidt and McCauley, 2000: 637. At the same time, respondents were willing to say that just about anything—liberals or Republicans, for example—was capable of disgusting them (see at p 643). In a sense that is broader than that I adopt here, disgust is nearly synonymous with strong dislike.

[33] The useful distinction between mediate and immediate offence is explored in Duff and Marshall, this volume.

even when we know them to lack the properties that disgust us. One such law is *contagion*. Respondents are disgusted by objects that have come into contact with other objects they take to be disgusting. We often react with disgust to cleanly laundered clothes we know to have been worn by a person we find loathsome. Many people report that they would not drink from a glass that once held dog faeces no matter how many times the glass has been scrubbed and sterilised. A second such law is *similarity*. Most North American college students refuse to eat imitation vomit that they know to be made of chocolate fudge (*ibid*). In tandem, these two laws can produce some curious results. Many North Americans are unwilling to drink a glass of juice stirred with a new comb—even though they know the comb is clean and the juice is not actually infected. The general lesson is clear. Not all of the reasons that are relevant to whether an object disgusts us are reasons that bear on whether the object is disgusting.

These empirical findings should be compatible with a metaphysical account. The fact that we are generally disgusted by stimuli we know to lack disgusting properties complicates attempts to provide a response-dependent analysis that qualifies as a version of realism. Is our disgust mechanism somehow defective when we react with disgust to a meal served on a new and sterile bedpan? Should we deny that such objects would disgust reasonable persons under ideal conditions? If not, can these be among the kinds of things that *really are* disgusting? A realist analysis will have difficulty answering these questions.

In any event, the fact that not just any stimuli can trigger our disgust mechanism helps to explain some of the appeal of realism. Recall the case of White, who claimed that chairs were disgusting. We now have the resources to understand why his peculiar claim is false. Our disgust mechanism, when operating properly, does not react to chairs with disgust. But this case should not lead us to endorse a more robust realism—a realism that assigns a truth-value to *every* claim that things are (or are not) disgusting.[34] Thus I propose to coin the term *qualified anti-realism* to describe what I take to be the most plausible metaphysical view about the nature of disgustingness. *Some* statements of the form 'X really is disgusting' are false, even though many such statements are neither true nor false.

On the basis of these empirical findings, Christopher Knapp (2003) concludes that disgust is best conceptualised as a *relative* property. Perhaps no given stimulus disgusts all persons with properly functioning disgust mechanisms. Within the above constraints, we can say only that a thing X is disgusting *to* a person P, not that X is disgusting *simpliciter*. If I am disgusted by X but you are not, both of our disgust mechanisms may be working

---

[34] Even what I call a robust realism will allow for vagueness. Depending on our account of vagueness, *some* claims that X is (or is not) really disgusting might lack a truth-value.

exactly as they were designed to do. Knapp goes on to posit a close structural similarity between our language and disgust mechanisms. The universal grammar that is hardwired into all human speakers limits the kinds of syntactic systems we can learn. Universal grammar constrains but does not determine the content of the particular language we are taught to speak. Knapp contends (2003: 266–7):

> It makes sense to say that the language mechanisms in two individuals can both be in perfect working order and yet be configured to produce very different judgments and intuitions about the grammaticality of sentences. All this seems to be true of the disgust mechanism as well. The innate structure of the mechanism is not designed to determine the class of actual disgust triggers—the mechanism is designed to construct this set only upon receiving input from the social environment. And given this inclusion of a social learning process, it makes sense to say that two disgust mechanisms might be in perfect working order but nevertheless respond to very different things.

Despite the intriguing similarities noted by Knapp, there are obvious differences between our language and disgust mechanisms. Exposure to adult speakers is the only significant variable affecting the particular language we ultimately learn. Individual susceptibility to disgust, however, varies enormously *within* given communities.

These individual differences in susceptibility to disgust are correlated with given demographic variables that should greatly interest legal theorists. For example, women are far more sensitive to disgust than men. Intensity of disgust peaks during teen years, and declines thereafter. Disgust is linked to various kinds of psychopathology, most notably with obsessive-compulsive and eating disorders. Individuals who profess a fear of death are more easily disgusted than those who seek thrills. Perhaps most importantly, middle-class managers are more impervious to disgust than blue-collar workers.[35] Further studies can be expected to identify additional demographic variables that predict susceptibility to disgust.

Some of these results are potentially useful for legal purposes. No one advocates sex-change operations or devices to accelerate the aging process in order to reduce the incidence of disgust. But state policies might help to alter a few of the other correlates of disgust. Socioeconomic factors are the most obvious candidate. Social class predicts not only to what extent individuals are sensitive to disgust, but also whether they are likely to moralise their reactions. In one influential study, researchers monitored the responses of North Americans and Brazilians of higher and lower socioeconomic classes about a number of potentially disgusting but harmless actions,

---

[35] Evidence for these propositions is found in Rozin *et al*, 1999: 330.

including incestuous kissing, consuming one's dead pets, and eating a chicken after having sex with it. Respondents of higher socioeconomic status managed to separate their emotional feelings from their moral judgments, while other groups were quicker to condemn morally the behaviours that disgusted them—even when they admitted these behaviours to be harmless (Haidt, Koller and Dias, 1993). Lower-class respondents were more prepared than their privileged counterparts to insist that the disgusting actions should be stopped and punished, and to deny that they would be permissible just because they were customary in a given culture (Haidt, Koller and Dias, 1993: 618–19). This fact is enormously significant, since criminal sanctions should not be applied unless behaviour is wrongful. If disgusting conduct must be wrongful to qualify for criminal intervention, an obvious solution is to take steps to *de-moralise* disgust.[36] This goal is not wholly unrealistic. Research suggests that people with egalitarian ideals are less inclined to moralise their disgust (Miller, 1997). If so, better education and a decrease in socioeconomic disparity should help to reduce the incidence of disgust as well as the tendency to believe we have been wronged when we experience it. Of course, there are countless advantages in improving education or reducing deprivation; we have an additional reason to implement these measures if they also lessen the need for legal sanctions to combat disgust.

A final empirical result is also significant for legal policy. Individuals are far more likely to condemn disgusting behaviours performed by members of stigmatised, marginalised, or minority groups (Rozin, 1997: 392–3). In general, we are more easily disgusted by the behaviour of *the other*—of persons we regard as different from ourselves. This tendency is exacerbated when we perceive the other to be inferior to us. Let me cite just two examples. First, many respondents report disgust at the sight of other people's babies' diapers, but not those of their own children (Roberts, 2003: 255). In addition, researchers consistently find strong aversion to contact with objects previously possessed by persons believed to be strange or otherwise undesirable (Rozin, Nemeroff, Wayne and Sherrod, 1989). In light of these findings, it is not surprising that Anglo-Americans would report more offence generally and disgust in particular. Ethnic diversity has increased; we have more contact with *others* (Putnam, 2000). This contact facilitates opportunities for contagion that might explain the prevalence of disgust. Additional empirical research is needed to confirm the hypothesis that a perceived increase in offensive behaviour is caused partly by greater exposure to persons of different cultural and ethnic backgrounds we regard as

---

[36] I borrow this phrase from Christopher Knapp (2003), although he uses it for very different purposes.

inferior. To the extent that this diagnosis is accurate, however, it is none-theless clear that, in the long run, efforts to integrate social communities and facilitate understanding of diverse peoples are preferable to legal intervention.

Recall that many theorists appear to believe that disgust realism is not needed to justify legal intervention; all that is required is a broad social con-sensus that given stimuli are disgusting (Posner, 1999). I hope the foregoing empirical findings will give us pause before we impose legal sanctions sim-ply because disgust is sufficiently widespread. If our disgust mechanism indeed conforms to the laws of sympathetic magic described by cognitive and experimental psychologists, we should be reluctant to turn to law to combat disgusting behaviours. As most commentators recognise, we need reason to believe the conduct we would prohibit—whether harmful or dis-gusting—is wrongful. The offensive practices Simester and von Hirsch (2002: 275) would prohibit—such as insult and exhibitionism—are said to be wrongful because they exhibit a lack of respect or consideration. Although this allegation may be correct in relation to many modes of offensive con-duct, it cannot be true of all the behaviours we find disgusting. It is hard to see how conduct that triggers our disgust mechanism through contagion or similarity could be wrongful; it certainly need not show a lack of respect or consideration. We should not pretend to have a sound rationale for taking action against stigmatised and marginalised groups who frequently engage in behaviours we regard as disgusting. Apart from the principled difficulties I have discussed, criminal penalties against disgusting behaviour are objec-tionable in practice. Legal sanctions might cause further damage to social bonds, compounding rather than alleviating the problem they are designed to solve.

Thus the rationale for using disgust as a basis for criminalisation is dubi-ous. But what should be said about Kahan's argument that disgust is cru-cial to a justification of punishment? Among other difficulties,[37] this argu-ment appears to confuse disgust with indignation. This distinction is not a mere quibble. Unlike disgust, indignation provides us with a *reason* that can be used to defend legal intervention; it requires a belief that a wrong or harm has been perpetrated. We have a solid basis for being indignant about many crimes, but we typically are unable to provide a *reason* to be disgust-ed by anything.[38] Thus Martha Nussbaum (1999: 32) maintains that a just society makes moral progress when it separates disgust from indigna-tion. She concludes that 'while the law may rightly admit the relevance of

---

[37] For a rejoinder, see Massaro, 1999.

[38] In cases in which our disgust results from contagion or similarity, we *can* give reasons to explain our reaction. These reasons, however, will not warrant legal intervention.

indignation ... it will do well to cast disgust onto the garbage heap'.[39] This verdict may be too sweeping; my own position is a bit more cautious. Whatever may be the case with other modes of offensive conduct, I contend that the basis for using legal remedies against behaviours deemed to be disgusting is highly problematic.

IV. CONCLUSION

Legal philosophers may be too hasty in allowing legal intervention to protect persons from offensive behaviour in general and disgusting behaviour in particular. Perhaps this haste reflects the failure to appreciate some important differences between various kinds of offensive behaviour, as well as between offence and harm. Once these differences are recognised, other avenues to defuse social conflicts should be explored. The case for a wide scope of legal intervention is weakened, I think, if we reject disgust realism and conclude that things do not disgust us because they really are disgusting. To understand whether and to what extent various objects or behaviours disgust us—and why we sometimes believe we have been wronged when we become disgusted—we must examine empirical data about our disgust mechanisms. These data should make us sceptical that legal interventions in disgusting behaviour are justifiable. My metaphysical and empirical speculations offer hope that some small progress in reducing the unwanted experience of disgust can be achieved without resorting to the heavy hand of the criminal sanction.

REFERENCES

ADLER, MD (2000) 'Expressive Theories of Law: A Skeptical Overview' *University of Pennsylvania Law Review* 148: 1363.

BLACKBURN, S (1993) *Essays in Quasi-Realism.* New York: Oxford University Press.

BOGHOSSIAN, P and VELLAMAN, D (1989) 'Colour as a Secondary Quality' *Mind* 98: 81.

BRANDT, R (1955) 'The Definition of an "Ideal Observer" Theory in Ethics' *Philosophy and Phenomenological Research* 15: 407.

D'ARMS, J and JACOBSON, D (1999) 'Sentiment and Value' *Ethics* 110: 722.

—— (2000) 'The Moralistic Fallacy: On the "Appropriateness" of Emotion' *Philosophy and Phenomenological Research* 61: 65.

DEVLIN, P (1965) *The Enforcement of Morals.* Oxford: Oxford University Press.

EKMAN, P (1980) *The Face of Man.* New York: Garland Pub Co.

---

[39] Nussbaum, 1999: 22. Disgust, she adds, is among those emotions (jealousy is another) that are 'always of dubious reliability in social life, but especially in the life of the law'.

FEINBERG, J (1965) 'The Expressive Function of Punishment' *Monist* 49: 397.

—— (1985) *Offense to Others*. New York: Oxford University Press.

HAIDT, J, KOLLER, S and DIAS, M (1993) 'Affect, Culture, and Morality, Or Is it Wrong to Eat Your Dog?' *Journal of Personality and Social Psychology* 65: 613.

HUME, D (1888) *A Treatise of Human Nature* (Selby-Biggs ed).

HUSAK, D (2004) 'The Criminal Law as Last Resort' *Oxford Journal of Legal Studies* 24: 207.

KAHAN, DM (1996) 'What Do Alternative Sanctions Mean?' *University of Chicago Law Review* 63: 591.

—— (1998) 'The Anatomy of Disgust in Criminal Law' *Michigan Law Review* 96: 1621.

KNAPP, C (2003) 'De-moralizing Disgustingness' *Philosophy and Phenomenological Research* CXVI: 253.

MALSON, L (1972) *Wolf Children*. London: NLB.

MASSARO, TM (1999) 'Show (Some) Emotion', in SA BANDES (ed), *The Passions of Law*. New York: New York University Press, 80.

MILLER, WI (1997) *The Anatomy of Disgust*. Cambridge: Cambridge University Press.

NEUBERGER, J (1993) *Hooliganism*. Berkeley: University of California Press.

NUSSBAUM, MC (1999) 'Secret Sewers of Vice', in SA BANDES (ed), *The Passions of Law*. New York: New York University Press, 19.

POSNER, RA (1999) 'Emotion versus Emotionalism in Law', in SA BANDES (ed), *The Passions of Law*. New York: New York University Press, 309.

PUTNAM, RD (2000) *Bowling Alone: The Collapse and Revival of American Community*. New York: Simon and Schuster.

RACHELS, J (1994) 'Subjectivism', in P SINGER (ed), *A Companion to Ethics*. Oxford: Basil Blackwell, 432.

ROBERTS, RC (2003) *Emotions: An Essay in Aid of Moral Psychology*. Cambridge: Cambridge University Press.

ROZIN, P (1997) 'Moralization', in AM BRANDT and P ROZIN (eds), *Morality and Health*. New York: Routledge, 379.

ROZIN, P *et al* (1999) 'Individual Differences in Disgust Sensitivity: Comparisons and Evaluations of Pencil-and-Paper versus Behavioral Measures' *Journal of Research in Personality* 33: 330.

ROZIN, P, HAIDT, J and McCAULEY, CR (2000) 'Disgust', in M LEWIS and JM HAVILAND-JONES (eds), *Handbook of Emotions* (2nd edn). New York: Guilford Press, 637.

ROZIN, P, MILLMAN, L and NEMEROFF, C (1986) 'Operation of the Laws of Sympathetic Magic in Disgust and Other Domains' *Journal of Personality and Social Psychology* 50: 703.

ROZIN, P, NEMEROFF, C, WAYNE, M and SHERROD, A (1989) 'Operation of the Sympathetic Magical Law of Contagion in Interpersonal Attitudes Among Americans' *Bulletin of the Psychonomic Society* 27: 367.

SCHMIDT, H and BEAUCHAMP, G (1988) 'Adult-like Odor Preferences and Aversions in Three-Year-Old Children' *Child Development* 59: 1136.

SHOEMAKER, DW (2000) '"Dirty Words" and the Offense Principle' *Law and Philosophy* 19: 545.

SHWEDER, R and HAIDT, J (2003) 'Cultural Psychology of Emotions: Ancient and New', in R SHWEDER (ed), *Why Do Men Barbecue? Recipes for Cultural Psychology*. Cambridge, MA: Harvard University Press, 134.

SIMESTER, AP and VON HIRSCH, A (2002) 'Rethinking the Offense Principle' *Legal Theory* 8: 269.

SMITH, M (1994) 'Realism', in P SINGER (ed), *A Companion to Ethics*. Oxford: Basil Blackwell, 399.

STUNTZ, W (2001) 'The Pathological Politics of Criminal Law' *Michigan Law Review* 100: 505.

THOMSON, JJ (1990) *The Realm of Rights*. Cambridge, MA: Harvard University Press.

4

Penalising Offensive Behaviour: Constitutive and Mediating Principles

ANDREW VON HIRSCH AND AP SIMESTER

I. EMERGENCE OF THE 'OFFENSIVE CONDUCT' ISSUE

ENGLISH CRIMINAL LAW prohibits various kinds of offensive behaviour, often under general public-order legislation. Classic instances are prohibitions regarding public nudity, public sexual acts, and exhibitionism. Two decades ago, when there was extensive interest in decriminalisation, there appeared to be a trend toward diminishing the scope of such prohibitions. More recently, however, there has been a growing emphasis on 'quality of life crimes'—and, in a less tolerant political atmosphere, measures against incivilities are on the increase. It is claimed that a strongly interventionist policy of dealing with offensive behaviour will improve the quality of public environments. Hence, for example, English legislation enacted in 1998 has authorised courts to issue 'civil' orders against 'anti-social behaviour' with severe criminal penalties for breach.[1] The Government has also adopted proposals to make begging a recordable (hence imprisonable) crime.[2] Similarly, in France, recently enacted legislation imposes criminal penalties for a wide variety of 'uncivil' behaviour.[3] Because the scope of such quality-of-life prohibitions is potentially so broad, it is essential to develop criminalisation principles that limit their scope. This chapter aims to sketch some of those principles.

---

[1] Crime and Disorder Act 1998, ss 1–4; Anti-Social Behaviour Act 2003. For fuller discussion, see Burney, and Simester and von Hirsch, both this volume.

[2] See Home Office, 2003, para 3.43. Begging has been treated as a minor offence since 1814, but making it a recordable crime means that the judge's sentencing discretion includes imposing a term of imprisonment.

[3] See *Loi pour la sécurité intérieure*, No 2003–239, 18 March 2003.

The chapter has two main parts. The first (§§ II and III) surveys what rationale for criminalisation, if any, might provide a *prima facie* basis for proscribing at least some kinds of offensive behaviour. Is offensive conduct harmful, and thus subject to proscription under the Harm Principle? Would it be preferable, instead, to develop a separate Offence Principle, and what should its content be? The second part (§ IV) concerns mediating principles governing the criminalisation of offence. Suppose that certain obnoxious conduct was covered by the Offence Principle, and thus was potentially subject to prohibition. What intermediary principles, then, might further restrain the proscription of such conduct?

II. PREVIOUS ACCOUNTS OF 'OFFENSIVENESS'

A number of accounts have been proposed to explain when and why offensive behaviour may legitimately be criminalised. These do not seem adequate, however, for a variety of reasons.

1. Offence as 'Harmful' Conduct?

In Anglo-American criminal-law theory, the Harm Principle is the principal basis for criminalisation: to be proscribed, the conduct needs ordinarily to do or risk harm to other persons (Feinberg, 1984). Could offence prohibitions be rationalised in terms of their potential harmful consequences to others? The Harm Principle serves as a safeguard of personal freedom: to justify interfering with the actor's liberty through criminal prohibition, it must be shown why his conduct is injurious or potentially injurious to others. Offensive behaviour—for example, exhibitionism—is not in any obvious way injurious. Might one, however, adopt a broader understanding of 'harm' that would permit offensive behaviour to be subsumed under the Harm Principle?

One possible line of argument would be to treat offence as itself a kind of harm. Louis B Schwartz (1963) takes this approach, arguing that offensive behaviour (or more precisely, the state of being offended) is psychologically harmful. When a person sees someone exposing himself, for example, the dismay, distress and shock the person feels constitutes psychological harm.

Harm, however, should involve more than generating distress: it involves a set-back to something more substantial—the impairment of a person's interests (Feinberg, 1984: chs 1–6). Characteristically, this occurs through the infringement of some resource (physical, proprietary, or otherwise) over which that person has a legitimate claim (von Hirsch, 2003: 16–17). A resource, in turn, might then be understood as referring to the longer-term means or capabilities that someone possesses.[4] If harm is so understood, this can help to explain the link between harming and wrongdoing· when D invades a resource of P's over which P has a legitimate claim, and D does so with the requisite intent (or, perhaps, negligence), this is *prima facie* a culpable wrong—and, thus, legitimately a potential object for the censuring response of the criminal law. In this case, D's conduct is wrong in virtue of the consequential harm. By contrast, consider the case where E causes momentary affront to Q. His conduct involves no impairment of Q's resources. Moreover, were the idea of harm extended to include such cases, it is not clear why any comparable form of wrongdoing is involved. In essence, E has displeased Q; but no one has the generalised obligation to refrain from displeasing others.[5] Hence E's conduct cannot be wrong simply because it causes affront. In turn, absent wrongdoing, the censuring response of the criminal sanction seems inappropriate.

The concept of psychological harm, as actually used in ordinary language, reflects this understanding: it consists of more than the state of being affronted. The psychologically-harmed person's personal resources or coping mechanisms need to be impaired in various ways—for example, through his having been traumatised, or his having difficulty in concentrating on work or in conducting normal social relations. These are not the standard effects of offensive behaviour. Mere affront is not a species of psychological harm.

2. Offence as Leading to Eventual Harm?

An alternative version of the offence-as-harm thesis concerns the harms that *remotely* may result from the conduct. This view concedes that harm involves the invasion of a resource, so that offensive conduct is not in itself harmful. Offensive behaviour, on this view, may nevertheless be criminalised because of the chain of consequences it generates, which eventually risks producing actual harm. An example of this perspective is the so-called 'broken windows' thesis: that incivilities left unchecked can lead to the deterioration of neighbourhoods and subsequently to higher rates of injurious behaviour, such as thefts or assaults.[6] But here, the resulting harm depends

---

[4] A resource may have either instrumental value, as a means to other ends, or constitutive value, as something desired for its own sake. Some resources may be both: good health, for example, is valued both because it facilitates other pursuits and because it may be enjoyed in itself.

[5] Cf Thomson, 1990: 254–5, emphasising the variable and subjective nature of individual sensibilities.

[6] See Wilson and Kelling, 1982; but doubt is cast on their thesis by Sampson and Raudenbush, 2001 and Taylor, 2001.

upon other intervening choices. The indecent exposer, for example, directly injures no one; his conduct merely might help to induce respectable people to leave the neighbourhood, creating the potential for a 'criminal element' to move in—and it is the latter who may decide to hurt people.

These intervening-choice scenarios raise problems of fair imputation: it is questionable whether the harmful choices of actors later in the causal chain should fairly be attributed as being, even in part, the moral responsibility of the initial actor. Unless the initial actor, through his conduct, gives implicit support or endorsement to others' subsequent harmful choices,[7] or becomes in some other way responsible for those choices,[8] holding him criminally answerable infringes basic ideas of *Eigenverantwortung*: of the separateness of persons as choosing moral agents.

3. A Separate Offence Principle?—The Feinberg Version

Perhaps it is a mistake to try to stretch the Harm Principle to accommodate offensive behaviour, as that would make the principle altogether too permissive. An alternative strategy would be to adopt a more narrowly drawn Harm Principle (one that continues to treat harm as involving the infringement of someone's longer-term resources), and deal with offensive behaviour through a separate Offence Principle. This is the approach of Joel Feinberg (1985).

On Feinberg's formulation of the Offence Principle, offence consists in the causing of affront to other persons' sensibilities (notwithstanding that their interests are not affected in such a manner as to constitute harm). That affront to sensibility, Feinberg argues, constitutes a *prima facie* basis for invoking the criminal law, provided a sufficient number of people are sufficiently affronted. The decision to criminalise should then depend on the intensity and pervasiveness of the affront, on whether the conduct occurs in settings where others cannot readily avoid being confronted by the conduct, and on the social value of the behaviour.

---

[7] We cannot pursue this issue in detail here. However, the problems of intervening choice and fair imputation are addressed more fully, in the context of the Harm Principle, by von Hirsch, 1996 and von Hirsch and Wohlers, 2003.

[8] For instance, there may be cases of *accumulative* harm or offence (von Hirsch, 1996: 265), in which any one person's conduct is not by itself so harmful or offensive as to justify criminalisation, but where, if enough others did the same, there would be sufficient harm or offence. (Environmental harms, such as pollution, are often accumulative in this way.) A version of this reasoning figured in *Chief Constable of Lancashire v Potter* [2003] EWHC 2272 (Admin), *The Times*, 10 November 2003: in deciding whether there were grounds to make an Anti-Social Behaviour Order against a prostitute, a court may consider the anti-social effects of her behaviour not merely alone, but in conjunction with that of other prostitutes in the area.

Feinberg's analysis has the strength of recognising that offence is distinct from harm, in that it does not necessarily set back the interests of a person. However, his purely subjective view of what counts as offence creates two kinds of difficulties. The first of these lies in the potential over-breadth of his account: whereas only certain things I do may harm you, almost anything I do might conceivably affront you. Feinberg meant his formulation to keep the scope of offence prohibitions narrow and, in a tolerant social environment, that would no doubt be the result: relatively seldom would the affront to sensibility be sufficiently extensive and intense to pass his proposed tests for criminalisation. But in an atmosphere of reduced tolerance, the opposite might well occur: a great variety of conduct could elicit widespread and intense affront, and thus become eligible for prohibition.

The second and more fundamental difficulty with Feinberg's approach is that merely affronting or displeasing others does not constitute wrongdoing.[9] If I smoke cigars in a train compartment, that is a wrong in virtue of the serious inconvenience caused to others present (aside from any possible health risk from passive smoke inhalation). But if I smoke my cigar in the street I do others no wrong—even if viewers happen to disapprove of smoking and thus have their sensibilities affronted. Unless a case can be made why the conduct is reprehensible, it is not an appropriate subject for the censuring response of the criminal law.

III. OFFENCE AS WRONGDOING: DISRESPECTFUL OR INCONSIDERATE TREATMENT OF OTHERS

From our proposed perspective, offence would be treated (as in Feinberg's view) as involving affront to people's sensibilities, and as being distinct from harm. Our theory of offence differs from Feinberg's, however, in that we treat offence as not *merely* involving affront to others' sensibilities; an element of *wrongdoing* is also required.

This requirement of wrongdoing is integral to the idea of conduct's being offensive. Consider a simple example of offensive behaviour: young men playing large portable radios ('boom-boxes') at top volume on public transport facilities. Here, the bare fact that other passengers are affronted

---

[9] While Feinberg does suggest that the affront caused must be wrongful, he appears to require by this only that the conduct must involve a requisite criminal intent and that there be no defence of justification or excuse for the offending conduct (1985: ch 7; compare Feinberg, 1984: 105–9). Moreover, he asserts that there is no requirement that the affront be reasonably taken (1985: 36). For discussion, see Simester and von Hirsch, 2002: 270–5. Certainly, our point does not merely concern the offender's *mens rea*. If I intentionally cause affront to someone, that still does not suffice to satisfy the Offence Principle, unless reasons can be given why the affront treats that person in a manner that constitutes a *wrong*.

or irritated does not capture why or how such behaviour is offensive. What makes it so is that it is profoundly inconsiderate of those others, because the loud radio-playing is so intrusive (for reasons we discuss below). Absent this ingredient, there is nothing reprehensible about the behaviour and, we think, there is not even a *prima facie* case for its criminal prohibition.

Can any general standard be formulated concerning what counts as wrongdoing for the purposes of the Offence Principle? In a recent article (Simester and von Hirsch, 2002), we have proposed such a standard: that the element of wrongdoing consists in treating other persons with a gross lack of respect or consideration. It is this lack of respect or consideration, rather than the affront to sensibility in itself, that establishes the wrongfulness of the conduct—without which element the censuring sanction of the criminal law should not be invoked.

Including this requirement of wrongdoing would help to restrict the scope of the Offence Principle. To illustrate, consider public begging. Since begging can generate much public resentment, a purely subjective standard of offensiveness could support a broad prohibition of begging, such as England has adopted.[10] Our proposed analysis, however, would not support a prohibition that included peaceable, non-aggressive solicitation—because of the lack of convincing reasons why this treats others disrespectfully or inconsiderately. It is only aggressive begging that is thus intrusive and which falls within the ambit of the Offence Principle, for reasons we set forth later.

The wrongdoing requirement calls upon the proponent of criminalisation to put forward reasons *why* the conduct is a wrong—namely, under our proposed account, why the conduct treats others with a gross lack of consideration or respect. Indeed, providing adequate reasons is crucial to our model, in order to avoid circularity. Suppose that a given species of conduct is widely disliked. It should not be permissible to argue simply that the conduct makes public spaces less enjoyable for others, and is (for that sole reason) inconsiderate. Were this mode of argument permissible, our suggested model would collapse into Feinberg's subjective standard. Hence we need independent normative arguments why certain kinds of conduct are inconsiderate or disrespectful, and hence potentially offensive. It should be possible to generate such arguments, as the following types of cases illustrate.

1. Insulting Conduct

Insult involves, by its very nature, disrespectful treatment. It is social convention, of course, that gives various words, gestures, or acts an insulting

---

[10] See text at n 2. For advocacy of a sweeping prohibition of peaceable begging, see Ellickson, 1996; contrast von Hirsch and Shearing, 2000.

meaning. But expressions of contempt are wrongful for reasons that go beyond mere convention: people have a claim, grounded in human dignity, against intentionally demeaning treatment. Conduct is insulting not simply by virtue of the effect (of causing affront) that it may have on its audience, but rather because of what it expresses—for example, because it is intentionally derogatory. The conduct thus becomes offensive even if the discomfort it produces is relatively fleeting, and no longer-term interests of the person are compromised.[11]

2. Infringements of Anonymity in Public Spaces

People are entitled, when moving about in public space, to be left essentially alone. That entitlement of anonymity—which is based on notions of privacy and autonomy—involves being free to go about one's business with no more than momentary and casual scrutiny by others, and no more than fleeting unsolicited requests from others for one's attention or assistance.[12] One might briefly be asked for directions by a stranger, but if one does wish to respond, he or she is not entitled to pursue the matter insistently. Being asked by a stranger for monetary assistance is similar: a brief, polite request is not intrusive, but insistently or aggressively demanding funds offends against one's entitlement to anonymity in public places—one's right to be left alone.

3. Pre-emptive Public Behaviour

Consider conduct in public places which is sufficiently obtrusive that it pre-empts others' normal use of space—as in our example of playing portable radios loudly on public transport. Here, the reason why the conduct is wrongful is that the actor makes use of the space for his preferred activity

---

[11] In our analysis, insult is offensive rather than harmful conduct—indeed, it is a paradigm of such conduct. However, the German commentator, Knut Amelung (2002), has argued that insulting behaviour actually sets back an important interest, namely the interest in being treated as a being worthy of equal respect *qua* citizen. This view might be arguable for racist insults, because such expressions typically treat their objects as inferior beings unworthy of equal status with other citizens. However, it seems less plausible for everyday insults. If another driver becomes irritated with my driving style and makes a rude gesture or calls me a moron, doubtless this is disrespectful and hence offensive under our definition of offence (although our first mediating principle, concerning tolerance for varying styles of self-presentation, would militate against criminalisation). Such minor insulting conduct does not, however, seem to call my status as an equal citizen seriously into question.

[12] See, more fully, von Hirsch, 2000, considering how public CCTV surveillance may infringe this entitlement to be 'left alone'.

in a manner that leaves reduced scope for others there to pursue their preferences in peace. It is difficult to concentrate on reading one's newspaper, or to carry on a normal conversation with a friend, if someone else is making a terrific din nearby on his 'boom-box'. The relevant norm here is that of mutual consideration in shared public space. Someone wishing to play his radio ought to show consideration to the newspaper reader, by not playing it too loudly. The newspaper reader, on the other hand, may not insist on complete silence, as he could in a library; this leaves others (including the radio-player) sufficient scope for their preferred activities. What makes the loud playing of the boom-box offensive is the infringement of such norms of mutual consideration.[13]

4. Exhibitionism

Suppose that someone is sitting peaceably in the park and cannot concentrate on his newspaper, this time because another person is exposing himself nearby. This seems also to be inconsiderate conduct, which denies others the peaceable use of public space. But here, the explanation of the behaviour's inconsiderateness is not quite so straightforward as in the preceding case, since the conduct does not pre-empt common space in the same direct fashion as loud radio-playing. Something needs to be added concerning why the conduct is objectionable. A possible explanation might be drawn from Thomas Nagel's (1998) conception of 'reticence', regarding obligations of mutual restraint concerning persons' private (and especially their intimate) sphere. Notions of reticence include an entitlement to privacy—to exclude others from one's personal domain. But the obverse should also obtain: we are entitled not to be involuntarily *included* in the personal domain of others—particularly, to be spared certain intimate revelations. It is the wrongfulness of that involuntary inclusion that, arguably, makes exhibitionism a matter of treating others without consideration.

5. Sensory Affront?

In their chapter for this volume, Duff and Marshall distinguish between 'mediated' and 'immediate' offence. Whereas mediately offensive conduct is offensive only when it violates some convention or standard, the wrongness

---

[13] In this situation, unlike that of insult, the offence involves a direct affront to the senses: the unpleasant sound of the boom-box directly interferes with the newspaper reader's concentration. However, the judgment of offensiveness remains in important part a normative one. The operating norm is that in shared public space, people should be considerate of each other's use and enjoyment. That is why, on one hand, the radio-player may not play his radio too loudly, and on the other, the newspaper-reader may not demand library-like silence. See further below, § III.5.

of *immediately* offensive conduct derives, they say, from the sensory affront it causes (at 59):

> We can take noise as a good example of this: noise that offends not because of its meaning (as racist hate speech offends), but simply by virtue of its character as noise—its particular sound (as when a finger scratches a slate), or its volume or intrusiveness.

Suppose that my cesspit makes a pungent assault on my neighbour's senses. The smell, Duff and Marshall would say, is 'offensive' by virtue of its immediate sensory unpleasantness and the visceral response it elicits, not by virtue of any disrespect it may (or may not) manifest: any lack of respect I show by maintaining the cesspit may be a further derivative wrong, and may bear on my culpability, but the case for criminalisation arises from the noxiousness of the cesspit itself. Similarly, where I disturb my neighbours by playing loud music regularly, they assert that the wrong rests in the noise *per se*: 'the basic wrong, which gives us reason in principle to criminalise my conduct and only given which does my persistence display a lack of respect, is the persistent making of such offensive noise' (this volume: n 52).

It is certainly true that affront may sometimes be caused via the senses rather than, as on other occasions, via our normative sensibilities. But even here, more is required to establish a wrong.[14] First, as Husak points out in this volume, disgust is not a natural category; it is, rather, an acculturated, learned, response. Conversely, one can develop a tolerance even to immediately offensive phenomena. In turn, whether a given sensory experience causes affront is likely to depend on time and place: on whether exposed sewers, for instance, are a feature of the main streets.[15] Secondly, even where a smell or noise is typically experienced as disgusting or affronting, it does not follow that it is wrongful. Gangrene may smell worse than flatulence, but only the latter is capable of being wrongfully offensive—and even that case depends on how and why it occurs. If I am woken at midnight by my neighbours' (intentionally) causing loud bangs and flashes on their premises, this does not establish offensiveness without further specification concerning whether their conduct is inconsiderate in the circumstances: is it, for example, Guy Fawkes Night?

---

[14] See above, n 13. Duff and Marshall accept that not all immediately offensive events need be wrongful: the offensiveness must impose a burden on its audience that they should not be expected to tolerate. Nonetheless, on their analysis such events are wrongful *by virtue of* their offensiveness.

[15] This need not be to reject the distinction drawn by Duff and Marshall. But it is to suggest that even immediate offence is normatively sensitive and, as such, is not the negative of mediated offence. Given that responses of immediate affront are acculturated, the affront itself depends upon embedded normative standards and beliefs. We may say, therefore, that there *are* reasons—reasons, moreover, that are amenable to normative review—why a person is immediately offended. (Compare Duff and Marshall, this volume: n 7.)

Sometimes, as the law of nuisance recognises, unpleasant stimuli may interfere with the quiet enjoyment of our homes or other resources. A glue factory, like the cesspit, might (in modern contexts) seriously affect the habitability and quality of life in nearby houses. But these are cases where the reason why we—rightly—complain is because of the *effect* such things have on our lives; because they set back our interests and make our lives worse. In other words, the wrongfulness of such cases is grounded in their harmful consequences. They fall within the scope of the Harm Principle.

6. The Multifarious Grounds for Offence

It may be concluded from the preceding examples that there is no single explanation why conduct may be offensive. Moreover, the explanations differ in type: insult directly expresses disrespect and tends to be targeted at individual victims or groups; pre-emptive and exhibitionist conduct is frequently not targeted at all, and its wrongfulness depends in part on the violation of negotiated social conventions. Certain cases, especially of pre-emption and infringement of anonymity, may sometimes become offensive only by virtue of repetition. These variations suggest that different types of offensive conduct may warrant different forms of legal and non-legal regulation. But, certainly before criminalisation is legitimate, specific reasons why each type of putatively 'offensive' conduct is inconsiderate or disrespectful need to be generated. Some of these reasons will need further elucidation (for example, our account of 'reticence' and its relation to exhibitionism); and some are likely to be controversial. But the very demand for reasons limits the scope of offence significantly. It is not enough that the conduct displeases; grounds must be provided as to why that conduct is wrongful, in the sense of being grossly inconsiderate or disrespectful.

IV. MEDIATING PRINCIPLES REGARDING CRIMINALISATION OF OFFENSIVE CONDUCT

Although the version of the Offence Principle proposed here narrows the potential scope for criminalising behaviour that affronts others' sensibilities, we do not believe that this suffices. Not all conduct that is 'offensive' (in our suggested sense of treating others without consideration or respect) should be criminalised. There should be a series of mediating principles that further restrict the scope of criminalisation. Feinberg does mention certain mediating principles,[16] but these were designed for his broad subjectivist

---

[16] For example, that the affront to sensibility must be serious and widespread, albeit not universal: see Feinberg, 1985: 27–36.

definition of offence (as something constituted by affront to sensibility). Given our narrower conception of offence, what limitations should there be? We suggest the following mediating principles.

1. Social Tolerance

Whereas the Harm Principle concerns infringements on the identifiable interests of others, offence tends to have much more to do with presentation of self in public space. (The young man playing his 'boom-box' on a public transport facility may have no desire to trouble others; he just likes to have his music with him and to hear it played loud.) Hence, regulating offence tends to be considerably more restrictive of personal self-expression. Styles of self-presentation may also conflict: behaviour that you consider routine matters constituting your personal style may be intrusive upon my peace and quiet, as the radio-playing example again indicates. But a plural society is not just a present social fact (that people have different lifestyles) which needs to be 'managed'. It is also a normative matter: we *ought* to encourage varying and sometimes even conflicting lifestyles.[17] Two lifestyles can be valuable even if they contain elements that conflict. If we take the idea of a plural society seriously, therefore, we should be especially concerned about the effects of prohibiting unconventional behaviour on the liberty and self-expression of those regulated. As such, this argument suggests the desirability of sparing use of offence prohibitions.

The case for sparing use is reinforced by the character of offensive behaviour: that it does not, in itself, affect others' longer-term resources, in the manner that harmful behaviour does. Granted, offended persons suffer a wrong, by virtue of the disrespectful or inconsiderate manner in which they are treated. But the absence of setbacks to their interests tends to give the wrongdoing a less serious character—and thus leaves more scope for countervailing concerns such as the importance of self-presentation.

This approach of sparing use can be given effect through a principle of *social tolerance*: that a significant margin of tolerance should be granted even to conduct that is disrespectful or inconsiderate. So far as offence prohibitions are concerned, it is legitimate to call upon citizens to be reasonably thick skinned: only the more egregious forms of offensive behaviour should be prohibited. This principle of social tolerance should, for example, significantly curtail the criminalisation of insult (Simester and von Hirsch, 2000: 276): in a lively, plural society, it does not seem appropriate to criminalise routine insults, such as the use of certain well-known words

---

[17] For fuller development of this perspective, see Raz, 1995: 162ff.

or gestures, even though these certainly involve disrespectful treatment.[18] It should only be certain grave forms of insult—for example, demeaning references to minority groups—that should be candidates for criminalisation.

It remains for us to ask how such a social tolerance principle might be implemented. Feinberg (1985: ch 9) provides a hint in his discussion of 'profound' offence; perhaps it is profound offence that primarily should be criminalised. Even so, however, what should matter under our conception of offence is not only the extensiveness and intensity of affront caused but also the degree of lack of consideration or respect shown by the conduct. In our proposed formulation of the Offence Principle, we have thus required that there be a *gross* lack of consideration or respect. On this view, for example, merely calling someone a rude name or making an unpleasant gesture at him would not suffice, because the disrespect involved is insufficiently serious.

A further reason for withdrawing social tolerance and criminalising the behaviour would be that the behaviour in question is potentially conducive to significant adverse social side-effects. Consider the case of racial insult. This kind of behaviour tends to engender an atmosphere of bigotry that may lead to a variety of eventual harms, ranging from unfair job discrimination to actual violence. Nevertheless, the mere risk of such harms would not by itself justify proscribing the behaviour *directly* under the Harm Principle, because of concerns about fair imputation: the causal chain leading to the ill consequences is mediated through choices of numerous independent actors.[19]

In situations such as these, the offensiveness of the conduct could properly be combined with an assessment of its remote consequences in order to justify criminalisation. Racial insult is manifestly offensive. Should it nonetheless be tolerated? One reason why not is supplied by the conduct's social side-effects—its potential for exclusionary social consequences. Invoking such side-effects would not be subject to the objection concerning fair imputation, because the justificatory work in establishing wrongdoing is done by the immediate offensiveness (in our sense) of the behaviour. The adverse social side-effects are being invoked as a supplemental ground in order to help overcome our reluctance, for the sake of permitting varying styles of self-presentation, to criminalise even disrespectful or inconsiderate conduct.

In gauging the conduct's adverse side-effects, their frequency, severity, and pervasiveness may be considered. In deciding whether to criminalise intrusive begging, for example, it would be proper to take into account the

---

[18] Indeed, English criminal law, unlike the German Penal Law (§ 185), contains no general criminal prohibition of insult. Compare the provisions of the Public Order Act 1986, ss 4A and 5, which prohibit a restricted range of insulting conduct.

[19] See above, § II.2; Simester and von Hirsch, 2002: 285–7.

extent of its adverse impact on the use of public space. This is another respect in which the Offence Principle differs from the Harm Principle. Under the latter principle, conduct that does substantial harm to its victims may be prohibited even if the conduct occurs relatively infrequently, because the protection of the person's vital interests is so important. With the Offence Principle, the impact on individuals who are affronted plays a smaller role, as we have seen—because there is no immediate intrusion into such persons' longer-term interests. Concerns about the pervasiveness and scale of its side-effects may, therefore, have a more significant role to play.

If we may thus consider eventual harmful consequences, what is gained through the adoption of an Offence Principle? Why not base penalising the behaviour directly on the conduct's (indirectly) injurious effects, as would advocates of the 'Broken Windows' thesis, discussed earlier? The answer is that the conduct's being immediately offensive, in our suggested sense, remains essential for its criminalisation. Conduct that does not qualify as grossly inconsiderate or disrespectful, such as peaceable begging, should not be criminalised, even if it were to have adverse indirect effects on others' use of public space.

2. A 'Ready Avoidability' Principle

Feinberg suggests a mediating principle that is of considerable interest, although he does not spell out its rationale. This is his notion of 'avoidability': that it speaks against criminalising offensive conduct that others could readily avoid witnessing or being confronted by it.[20] On this view, showing pornographic images would not be sufficiently offensive for prohibition if available only on video cassettes or DVDs which those who object need not view.

Notice, however, that this example is a polar case of avoidability, since it characteristically involves conduct done in private that occurs unwitnessed from the public domain, and which no one is compelled to witness. As such, it is hard to see how, under our analysis, it is offensive behaviour at all. The reason for not criminalising 'offensive' conduct that is wholly segregated from public view is not that it is avoidable, but that, since offence is a communicative wrong, there is no wrongdoing.

Conversely, were someone to show pornography in a park or marketplace, the case is straightforward and its avoidability has no practical role

---

[20] In this respect, the Offence Principle operates differently from the Harm Principle, where no avoidance principle would ordinarily apply. It is no reason for tolerating assaultive conduct on 14th Street that those wishing not to be assaulted may use 15th Street instead; see Simester and von Hirsch, 2002: 295.

to play; the pornography is, in effect, unavoidable. It is between these extremes, where conduct is at least partially in the public domain, that avoidability has a place as a mediating principle.

An illustration of this role is provided by the well-established practice of nude bathing in certain continental European countries. In Germany, for instance, the public display of genitalia is legally permissible, provided it occurs in specified public bathing areas. Here, the segregation from view may be only partial: the nude bathing area may be simply a portion of the riverbank, which is visible to others from the opposite side of the river. What appears to be at work here is some sort of notion of reciprocity: certain areas are segregated, albeit partially, from general public view. This gives those wishing to bathe nude more scope to engage in that conduct, while providing clues to others that if they do not wish to witness it, they might direct their attention elsewhere. Such reciprocal arrangements give greater scope to varying, and otherwise possibly colliding, lifestyles.[21] Thus it may be helpful—for conduct in public spaces deemed potentially offensive—to have an explicit 'avoidability' requirement: that the conduct is to be deemed offensive only if others could not *readily* (i.e. without undue restriction of their own liberty) avoid being confronted by the behaviour. Doing so would, in effect, introduce a threshold standard of avoidability as a side-constraint, rather than a mediating principle, such that potentially offensive conduct is not a candidate for criminalisation unless it is insufficiently easy to avoid. Even then, however, where potentially offensive conduct cannot *readily* be avoided (so that the side-constraint is not engaged), the *degree* to which it is avoidable, and the extent to which its avoidance intrudes upon the liberties of others, remains operative as a weighting factor when assessing the case of prohibition.

3. An 'Immediacy' Requirement

Another principle restricting criminalisation should concern 'immediacy': the prohibited conduct should be offensive in itself, and not merely make it possible or likely that the actor (or someone else) will engage in *further* behaviour that is offensive.[22] An instance of this problem is Singapore's former chewing gum prohibition. Gum-chewing was prohibited, not because there was anything objectionable about the behaviour itself, but because it could lead gum-chewers to engage in further conduct that is offensive in the

---

[21] In the case of nude bathing areas, such arrangements might be established by local regulation, but that need not be a prerequisite: an established common practice should suffice.

[22] As stated here, the requirement of immediacy would bar intervening-choice liability entirely. It may be, however, that there are some cases where the requirement of immediacy can be overridden, so that it operates instead as a strong presumption.

sense of being inconsiderate: especially, depositing chewed gum on seats or pavements.

What is the rationale for this immediacy principle? The concern about immediacy derives, in the first instance, from the idea that there must be wrongdoing involved in the offence; there is nothing wrong with conduct, such as chewing gum or entering a park, that *might* induce an intervening choice (by the actor or someone else) to engage in subsequent conduct that is offensive.[23]

But might there be grounds for overcoming the intervening-choice objection, as there are for the Harm Principle, when the initial actor's conduct implicitly endorses the subsequent offensive choices?[24] It is not so easy, in the context of offensive conduct, to think of instances where this might be the case; in part because of significant structural differences between the Harm and Offence Principles. In the Harm Principle, the wrongdoing is typically focused on the ill consequences or risks of the conduct, since it is generally *prima facie* wrong to cause harm to others. Thus, where the fair-imputation issue can be overcome, it may be permissible to criminalise conduct that creates a risk of remote harms without itself being harmful. In the Offence Principle, however, the wrongdoing is constituted by the disrespectful, or inconsiderate, expressive character of the conduct itself. As such, it is less straightforward to overcome imputation concerns and justify the criminalisation of conduct that—even though it may raise the likelihood that others, or the actor himself, will commit further acts that are offensive—in itself lacks any characteristic of wrongfulness.[25]

Beyond these difficulties concerning the structure of the Offence Principle, there is an important additional consideration: the effect of a prohibition on liberty and, particularly, on freedom of movement. An immediacy requirement is of particular importance for the criminalisation of offence because of the implications for access to public space. If the requirement is not insisted upon, so that conduct may be proscribed merely because it may lead to subsequent offensive choices, this will tend to permit the exclusion of people from public space because of a wide variety of concerns about what they may subsequently do when there. Examples might include barring beggars from public spaces altogether, on the grounds that they may engage in intrusive begging; and prohibiting youths from congregating in certain public spaces, because they may then behave offensively

---

[23] This point about intervening-actor liability is noted earlier, in the context of the Harm Principle: see above, § II.2.

[24] For discussion of such grounds, see von Hirsch and Wohlers, 2003: 204–7.

[25] Many cases of aggregative offence, discussed earlier in n 8, will survive the requirement of immediacy since they typically involve conduct that is immediately and wrongfully offensive, albeit sufficiently so for criminalisation only when part of a similar pattern of behaviour by others.

toward passers-by. Prohibitions of this kind, were they to become extensive, would tend to create a two-class scheme of access to public facilities: unrestricted access to a preferred class of conventional citizens; and restricted access for individuals deemed to have the potential for engaging in offensive conduct if permitted to enter. This contravenes a fundamental principle of modern free society: namely, that its public spaces should be available for unrestricted access by all.[26]

V. CONCLUDING THOUGHTS

In this chapter, we have suggested that the concept of offensive behaviour can better be elucidated through an Offence Principle that is distinct from the Harm Principle. That Offence Principle, moreover, should not concern itself merely with the affront that a person's conduct causes to others' sensibilities; it should also provide an account of when, and why, causing that affront constitutes a wrong. We have suggested a general standard of when the offence becomes a wrong, one that relates to the conduct's showing a gross lack of respect or consideration for others, and we have suggested, through a number of illustrative cases, when and why that may be the case. Additionally, we have sketched a number of mediating principles that would restrain criminalisation even of conduct qualifying as offensive under our definition. These principles concern, first, a degree of tolerance for offensiveness, based on values of tolerance for varying styles of self-presentation; secondly, a principle of 'ready avoidability', which would restrict criminalisation of conduct that others readily can avoid witnessing or being confronted with; and thirdly, an 'immediacy' requirement that requires that the conduct be offensive (on our definition) in itself, and not merely make it possible or likely that further behaviour would occur that would qualify as offensive. Our proposed wrongfulness requirement for offence, and our suggested mediating principles, are aimed at keeping criminal offence prohibitions suitably constrained in scope.

These two bases for criminalisation, harm and offence, nevertheless have certain important elements in common. Both are concerned with the protection of other persons, and both seek to ground the wrongfulness of the conduct in normative claims that persons have not to be treated badly. Thus, ultimately, both conceptions broadly depend upon the imperative to treat other persons with respect for their dignity and humanity. Nevertheless, we think the analysis can be undertaken in a more differentiated fashion if a distinction is observed between conduct that sets back

---

[26] For fuller discussion of this issue of free access to public spaces, and of the legitimacy of criminal-justice measures that restrict it, see von Hirsch and Shearing, 2000.

persons' interests and resources, where the Harm Principle comes into play, and offensive conduct that does not diminish the person's resources but nevertheless treats them, in certain ways, without the consideration and respect that should be due to them as fellow citizens.

REFERENCES

AMELUNG, K (2002) *Die Ehre als Kommunikationsvoraussetzung.* Baden Baden: Nomos Verlagsgesellschaft.

ELLICKSON, R (1996) 'Controlling Chronic Misconduct in Public Spaces: of Panhandlers, Skid Rows and Public Zoning' *Yale Law Journal* 105: 1165.

FEINBERG, J (1984) *Harm to Others.* New York: Oxford University Press.

—— (1985) *Offense to Others.* New York: Oxford University Press.

Home Office (2003) *Respect and Responsibility: Taking a Stand against Anti-Social Behaviour.* London: HMSO.

NAGEL, T. (1998) 'Concealment and Exposure' *Philosophy and Public Affairs* 27: 3.

RAZ, J (1995) 'Free Expression and Personal Identification', in J RAZ, *Ethics in the Public Domain* (rev edn). Oxford: Oxford University Press.

SAMPSON, R and RAUDENBUSH, S (2001) *Disorder in Urban Neighborhoods: Does it Lead to Crime?* Washington, DC: National Institute of Justice.

SCHWARTZ, LB (1963) 'Morals Offenses and the Model Penal Code' *Columbia Law Review* 63: 669.

SIMESTER, AP and VON HIRSCH, A (2002) 'Rethinking the Offense Principle' *Legal Theory* 8: 269.

TAYLOR, R (2001) *Breaking Away from Broken Windows.* Boulder, CO: Westview Press.

THOMSON, JJ (1990) *The Realm of Rights.* Cambridge, MA: Harvard University Press.

VON HIRSCH, A (1996) 'Extending the Harm Principle: Remote Harms and Fair Imputation', in AP SIMESTER and ATH SMITH (eds), *Harm and Culpability.* Oxford: Oxford University Press.

—— (2000) 'The Ethics of Public Television Surveillance', in A VON HIRSCH, D GARLAND and A WAKEFIELD (eds), *Ethical and Social Perspectives on Situational Crime Prevention.* Oxford: Hart Publishing.

—— (2003) 'Das Rechtsgutsbegriff und das "Harm Principle"', in R HEFENDEHL, A VON HIRSCH and W WOHLERS (eds), *Die Rechtsgutstheorie: Legitimationsbasis des Strafrechts oder dogmatisches Glasperlenspiel?* Baden Baden: Nomos Verlagsgesellschaft.

VON HIRSCH, A and SHEARING, C (2000) 'Exclusion from Public Space', in A VON HIRSCH, D GARLAND and A WAKEFIELD (eds), *Ethical and Social Perspectives on Situational Crime Prevention.* Oxford: Hart Publishing.

VON HIRSCH, A and WOHLERS, W (2003) 'Rechtsgutstheorie und Deliktstruktur: Zu den Kriterien fairer Zurechnung', in R HEFENDEHL, A VON HIRSCH and W WOHLERS (eds), *Die Rechtsgutstheorie: Legitimationsbasis des Strafrechts oder dogmatisches Glasperlenspiel?* Baden Baden: Nomos Verlagsgesellschaft.

WILSON, JQ and KELLING, G (1982) 'Broken Windows: The Police and Neighbourhood Safety' *Atlantic Monthly* (March).

5

Legal Regulation of Offence

TATJANA HÖRNLE

I. DIFFERENT WAYS TO THINK ABOUT CRIMINALISATION

WHAT KINDS OF conduct should be prohibited through the criminal law? Which justifications for such prohibitions are convincing, and which are not? Which goods and interests are important enough to warrant criminal punishment if someone's behaviour endangers them? Criminal law theorists coming from different legal cultures tend to take different approaches when answering these questions. This is apparent when one compares the literature in the UK and the USA with the work of German penal theorists. Although the issue of criminalisation has been somewhat neglected amongst those writing about criminal law (Roberts, this volume), there is some literature to draw upon.

Anglo-American writers evaluate the behaviour in question by asking in what way it encroaches upon the *interests of other persons*. Their way of tackling the issue of criminalisation typically starts with some kind of *descriptive account*. From that point of view, a necessary (although not sufficient) condition of criminalising certain behaviour is its negative impact on another person (or other persons). What is required is a narrative relating the relevant action to someone else's quality of life. For example, the first chapter of Joel Feinberg's book *Offense to Others* recounts a disastrous bus ride. Feinberg describes in vivid colours numerous unpleasant experiences endured by a passenger who is unable to avoid them or to leave the bus (Feinberg, 1985: 10–13). He relies on the imagination of the reader, who is called upon to put him or herself in the position of the unfortunate passenger, in order to demonstrate why such conduct should be suppressed. After arousing the reader's empathy as the unwilling witness of offensive conduct (ranging from affronts to the olfactory sense and aesthetic standards to bad bodily habits, gross table manners, public sexual acts, the showing of Nazi symbols, and insulting and racist remarks), Feinberg examines why and under what conditions such conduct should be penalised. Crucial for his argument are *hurt feelings* or other negative emotional states of mind experienced by those who are confronted with the offensive behaviour.

Andrew von Hirsch and Andrew Simester have shown in this volume and elsewhere that Feinberg's reliance on unpleasant feelings is not a sufficient argument in favour of criminalisation. They argue for a normative reformulation of the offence principle. The offended person should be required to give *valid reasons* why the conduct should be deemed objectionable. These reasons would be the foundation for penal prohibitions. Whether and how many other persons in fact feel affronted in their sensibilities would not be determinative. Without sound normative reasons, they argue, the conduct should not be punished—not even when a substantial number of people feel offended (Simester and von Hirsch, 2002; Narayan, 1990; von Hirsch, 2000). In spite of their critical remarks about Feinberg's theory of offence, von Hirsch and Simester do not challenge the basic structure underlying it. Also, according to them, one has to explain in what way the conduct affects *other persons*. They substitute Feinberg's reliance on emotions with a more refined and normative evaluation, but like him they rely on the same reference point: the (potential) 'victims' of the offence. One becomes a victim if one can plausibly claim to have been treated with a gross lack of respect or consideration (von Hirsch and Simester, this volume; Simester and von Hirsch, 2002). This requires, like Feinberg's analysis, a description of how the offender's action was blameworthy in relation to specific other persons.

There are remarkable conceptual differences between this approach and the prevailing views in the German literature about criminalisation. From the traditional German perspective, the question of criminalisation depends on whether the behaviour in question violates a *legal good* (ein Rechtsgut).[1] This notion of 'legal good' is characterised by a higher level of abstraction. What matters is the legislator's decision to protect goods that are generally rated valuable. German penal theorists see the abstraction of legal goods from specific human interests as an advantage (Neumann, 1986: 124–5; Seher, 2000: 71–72). The influence of the 'legal goods' doctrine explains why a more concrete, down-to-earth approach like Feinberg's has not been met with great interest in Germany.[2] A substantial body of academics even opposes the idea that individuals are to be the beneficiaries of the criminal law. Rather, they insist, it is the task of legal prohibitions to promote the *common* good and to prevent *social* harm. Individuals are only to be protected if this serves the public interest.[3] Many criminal prohibitions in the German Penal Code that would at first glance be obvious candidates for justifications relying on 'offence to others' are not seen this way. According

---

[1] See eg, Roxin, 1997: § 2; Jescheck and Weigend, 1996: 7–8.

[2] Until very recently, Feinberg's work was hardly discussed in the German literature. See now Seher, 2000; Wohlers, 2000.

[3] See Amelung, 1972; Jakobs, 1991: 2/7ff.

to the dominant explanation in the German literature and in court rulings, what in this volume is examined as 'offensive behaviour' should be prohibited because it endangers 'public peace' (öffentlicher Friede). For example, the Code's prohibition against racial insults (§ 130 I) is not explained in terms of the interests of those who are targets of such remarks. Rather, the prevailing opinion asserts that § 130 I protects a *collective good*, that is, public peace (Roxin, 1997: § 2/12; Lenckner, 2001: § 130/1a). From this perspective, it does not matter whether the persons who are verbally attacked could claim to be intentionally subjected to grossly disrespectful treatment. The offender is punished because he has threatened public peace, not because he has offended others.

It remains, however, unclear what 'public peace' is meant to be. According to a common definition cited by the courts and in the literature, it is 'the condition of general security as well as general trust in the further existence of safe conditions and the sense of security within the population' (Lenckner, 2001: § 126/1; Rudolphi, 1998: § 130/9). Pointing to 'general security' does not, however, yield a satisfying explanation: every crime violates 'general security'. To define the protected good as 'the absence of any crime' is pointless.[4] Instead, one could emphasise the dangers of public uproar, unrest or street fights provoked by racial insults. By taking this approach, it would not be necessary to construct 'public peace' as a genuine, independent public good. If there is indeed a risk of severe consequences such as violence among or between groups in society, the prohibition might be justified with a remote harm argument. It would be the health, lives, and property of those afflicted by violent actions that would be protected through criminal norms against racial insults. However, as with any remote harm argument, one would need to examine whether the remote harm could be legitimately attributed to the person who has uttered racial insults (fair imputation).[5] *Public trust* could be a separate phenomenon. Trust might be being preserved, one could argue, independent of public unrest (well before outbreaks of violence become likely), as a general precondition of leading a satisfying life in society. The psychological condition 'trust' might be measured with the instruments of social psychology. But such measurements are difficult, and are certainly not possible within the context of legal decision making. In reality, statements about 'public trust' and how it was damaged by particular actions are either mere guesses or mirror judges' subjective views of how reprehensible the action is. Talking of 'public trust' hides personal perceptions of the wrong done behind a pseudo-objective label. It is, I conclude, not convincing to justify penal prohibitions

---

[4] See Fischer, 1988: 161–2; Wohlers, 2000: 270.
[5] See for questions of fair imputation von Hirsch and Wohlers, 2003: 196ff; Hörnle, 2005: § 8.

with the notion of 'public peace', despite the popularity of this argument in the German literature.

German penal theory could profit from a change of perspective. Instead of legitimising criminal prohibitions with vague notions like 'legal good' or 'public peace', it is preferable to examine a victim's perspective as von Hirsch and Simester do. 'A victim's perspective' does not refer to subjective sensibilities; how actual victims of the conduct in question perceive their situation is not relevant. Rather, it is crucial what interests people *typically* have, whether these are worthy of protection, and how these interests are set back by particular actions. The starting point for any theory about criminalisation should be that conduct might be criminalised if it has some kind of *negative impact on another person* or other persons (if there are not mediating principles disfavouring criminal prohibitions). How this notion of 'negative impact' is to be operationalised needs further discussion, which I will do in the following paragraphs. Such details aside, it is worth emphasising what the main usefulness of the Anglo-American approach would be from a German perspective: to provide a clear analysis differentiating conduct affecting others and conduct affecting only the actor himself or no identifiable person at all. The arguments against paternalist and moralist justifications (which Feinberg addressed in the third and fourth volumes of *The Moral Limits of the Criminal Law*) depend on the premise that the criminal law's aim is to prevent people from seriously intruding upon the lives of others.

In order to set aside moralistic and paternalistic reasoning, examining offence from a victim's perspective is important. It is more difficult to argue against moralistic reasoning when criminal norms in general are seen to protect or promote some vague public good. In some cases, an obscure public good is mentioned while the true nature of a criminal prohibition is to prevent conduct perceived as immoral. For instance, the German Penal Code contains a norm prohibiting Holocaust denial (§ 130 III). It is not easy to explain whose interests are violated by such denials. If a Holocaust survivor's personal history and personal suffering are challenged as being invented, this person's interests are affected. But, such specific circumstances aside, false representations of historical facts do not affect the personal interests of those taking notice of such statements. With Feinberg's approach, one might point to negative feelings, mostly anger, which many people will feel after hearing Holocaust deniers' utterings. But if one requires normative reasons to apply the category 'offence to others', such reasons are hard to find. The most straightforward explanation for § 130 III of the German Penal Code is as follows: to deny the existence of the Holocaust violates a strong taboo and is perceived as highly immoral. Pointing to the immorality of certain acts is, however, not seen as an adequate justification for criminal prohibitions among contemporary German writers. Thus, again, the widespread solution is to claim that § 130 III of the German Penal Code protects public peace (Lenckner, 2001: § 130/1a; Rudolphi, 1998: § 130/1a). With respect to prohibitions like this, German tradition legitimises penal norms with rather vague public goods and omits any more specific analysis of human interests. This way of approaching questions of criminalisation is not very helpful. Often, it obscures the true reasons (moralistic, sometimes also paternalistic considerations) why certain behaviour is punished.

II. INCONSIDERATE BEHAVIOUR OR BEHAVIOUR VIOLATING THE RIGHTS OF OTHERS?

My starting point for the following sections is that issues of criminalisation cannot be discussed adequately by referring to vague concepts like 'legal goods'. The German 'Rechtsgut' doctrine obscures the crucial question of whether conduct is prohibited for paternalistic or moralistic reasons or because it affects other human beings. The question then is how this notion of 'behaviour affecting others' can be developed in a more detailed way to be useful as an instrument of critical evaluation. Obviously, 'affecting others' cannot be a sufficient criterion, as many acts have negative consequences for others without being proper candidates for criminalisation.

Von Hirsch and Simester, in their contribution to this volume and other publications, follow Feinberg's lead insofar as they *distinguish between harmful conduct and offensive conduct*. According to this concept, there are two separate reasons for criminalisation: harm and offence. Harm, they argue, consists of an infringement of certain long term interests, that is, *resources* to which someone has a legitimate claim. Momentary affronts, passing emotions, etc, do not qualify as harm because they do not directly involve people's resources ('longer term means or capabilities they possess') and because merely displeasing another person does not constitute wrongdoing (von Hirsch and Simester, this volume). Although they argue against Feinberg's concept of offence, for whom the affront to other persons' sensibilities is sufficient, they also recognise an offence principle as a distinct principle for criminalisation.

Their critique of Feinberg's approach is convincing. It would be problematic to rely simply on hurt feelings and other negative emotions when considering penal norms. Moralistic considerations could be disguised as liberal claims because strong opinions about moral issues and unpleasant emotions after incidents contrary to moral beliefs are usually involved (Papageorgiou, 1994: 263ff; Dalton, 1987: 906ff). If somebody judges certain behaviour to be obnoxious, he is likely also to react emotionally if he witnesses it. Thus, in the end, moralistic reasoning would determine the scope of the criminal law, while negative feelings are only intermediate stages.

To a certain degree, doubts about the relevance of emotions with respect to moral beliefs could be soothed by Feinberg's mediating principles. His process of carefully balancing opposing interests helps to avoid the collapse of 'offence to others' into pure legal moralism. If certain conduct is a source of distress for only a minority of abnormal susceptible persons, their emotions will normally be outweighed by reasons against prohibitions.[6] In practice, Feinberg's weighing principles restrict criminalisation mainly to public conduct that is unavoidable for others. Feinberg's safeguards could be reinforced by also limiting the behaviour warranting criminal sanctions strictly (without any exceptions) to public behaviour.[7] But, even with an 'only public offensive behaviour' restriction, a psychological offence theory might be too extensive. With a theory based on emotional responses, the issue of criminal sanctions would depend on *how many people* are upset. One could punish even relatively innocuous acts if a sufficiently large number of persons feel offended. On the other hand, a quantitative weighing of interests complicates the protection of minorities. If a racist slur is aimed at a very small and unpopular minority, probably not many people will be distressed.[8] A theory of offence based on the *factual* occurrence of negative feelings is thus indeed not satisfying.

The alternative, according to Simester and von Hirsch, is to add normative reasons to the construction of a separate category called 'offence to others'. They see that specific wrongdoing in treating others with a *gross lack of respect or consideration*. Even if many people feel considerable resentment after witnessing certain behaviour (they refer to public begging as an example), it may only be prohibited by the criminal law if the actor treats such persons with a gross lack of respect or consideration (e.g., only if the begging is aggressive). Von Hirsch and Simester continue by describing four types of offensive conduct: insults, infringement of anonymity in public spaces through intrusive behaviour, pre-emptive public behaviour, and exhibitionist behaviour.[9]

In my view, the distinction between harm and offence is not necessary. The strength of an interests-centred approach can be retained without being divided into two separate categories.[10] Both the harm principle and the offence principle are based, in the mode Simester and von Hirsch have developed them, on primarily descriptive concepts. They are not merely descriptive, as they presuppose that one can claim the resources in question as one's own, and assert that the disrespect shown constitutes wrongdoing; these are normative claims.[11] But first they have to describe what resources

---

[6] Feinberg, 1985: 33ff; critically Dalton, 1987: 894.
[7] See Dalton, 1987: 910.
[8] See for this problem Narayan, 1990: 130.
[9] In this volume: § III.
[10] See also Hörnle (2001), where I have briefly outlined a few of the following arguments.
[11] See von Hirsch, 2002: 6; Simester and von Hirsch, 2002: 280ff.

are (longer term means or capabilities someone possesses) and how the conduct affects such resources. In addition, which kinds of conduct are seen as treating others with a gross lack of respect and consideration is a matter of social convention (for example, what kind of gestures are seen as very rude in a certain context). My doubts relate to two concepts that are of central importance in von Hirsch and Simester's analysis: *resources* and *a gross lack of respect or consideration*. Of course, there is an obvious 'hard core' for both concepts where Simester and von Hirsch's arguments are entirely convincing. Uttering grave insults against a person in her presence constitutes treating the victim with a gross lack of respect. Property offences, arson, and bodily injuries leaving the person sick or handicapped diminish the victim's resources. A lasting negative impact on important means (property) or capabilities (the use of one's bodily functions) permits putting such crimes easily in the category 'harm to others'. However, the usefulness of 'diminished resources' and 'gross lack of respect or consideration' to give *prima facie* reasons for criminal prohibition is less obvious in other cases. I will argue that the notion of resources is somewhat too narrow to cover the more serious kinds of wrongdoing, whereas 'gross lack of respect or consideration' is too wide even for mere *prima facie* considerations in favour of criminalisation.

Harm, according to von Hirsch and Simester, has to be determined in a *prospective way*, with a view to *the victim's future*: conduct is harmful if it diminishes his or her opportunity of having a good life. The impairment of personal or proprietary resources which people typically (not, as I have already mentioned above, individually) need to pursue their plans and to ensure their well-being constitutes harm. Causing such harm with the required *mens rea* means that (mediating principles notwithstanding) there are reasons to prohibit the conduct under a 'harm to others' principle.[12] For a great number of crimes, this is an adequate account of when and why the offender harms others. But a few questions remain concerning intangible conditions as 'resources'. It seems possible to extend the notion of 'resource' beyond tangible objects (such as bodies or those physical objects constituting a person's property) to include intangible conditions. Being able to determine who enters one's private home, or to control one's sexual contacts, could be called resources upon which one has a legitimate claim. These are conditions that are important for the future life of the persons who become victims. However, these intangible conditions cannot be impaired by human actions. Somebody entering my apartment without my permission while I was not there did not diminish the resources I have. The same is true of sexual intercourse without consent. The fact that in the past one's sexual autonomy or privacy was disregarded has no consequences for

---

[12] Simester and von Hirsch, 2002: 281.

future claims to have them respected. Such incidents do not diminish conditions necessary for one's well-being—not because luck caused a fortunate outcome (that would be the case if bodily injuries healed surprisingly fast), but because there is *typically* no impact on means and conditions necessary for the victim's future life. The incident certainly affects the victim emotionally; they will suffer anger or fear after they have realised what has happened. In terms of future well-being, the emotional side would need to be stressed. However, if 'resource' is the key word to mark a boundary between harm and mere emotional distress, it would be more convincing to exclude the examples I have just mentioned from the category 'harm'—but this would not be a satisfying solution because to categorise them as 'no harm' understates their seriousness.

Such problems can be avoided if one omits the term 'resources' and abandons attempts to distinguish between 'harm' and 'offence'. Rather, I propose to draw the crucial line somewhere else and to differentiate between *conduct that violates the rights of others* and conduct that does not (and thus could only be prohibited on moralistic or paternalistic grounds). If it violates the right of another person, there is no need to ask whether it is harmful or offensive. The crucial question then is: Did the conduct violate a *legal right* of the person afflicted by the action?[13] Asking whether the victim can refer to a right in that sense (a legal right, not to be confused with moral claims) means substituting the term 'resource' with a straightforward normative concept.

Relying on a normative concept such as 'rights of others' is, of course, not a panacea. My approach obviously leads to the next question: How should the notion of 'rights' be defined? What constitutes a right in the sense that its violation is a *prima facie* reason for criminal punishment? The concept of right, if it is used for purposes of criminalisation, cannot simply be derived from rights acknowledged in civil law or constitutional law. Criminal law with its highly intrusive measures cannot simply point to the recognition of rights in other areas, but has to be more attentive to the importance of human interests to justify penal consequences. Therefore, it is necessary to identify people's *most important interests*. However one develops the argument, at some point one has to relate normative concepts to important interests that people have. Thus, in the end, there are no substantial differences between the ways Simester/von Hirsch and I argue. However, for some instances (like the right to sexual autonomy or to privacy), arguments are more convincing if one omits the phrase 'resources'. Entering another person's private home without their permission violates the right to privacy. Sexual contact without the other person's consent violates her right to sexual autonomy. This is a retrospective assessment—it

---

[13] See for the concepts of rights and interests Hörnle, 2005: § 3.

suffices that the right has existed in the past. Conditions like 'deciding for oneself', 'keeping a private side of life', and similar important interests are not of a permanent nature like tangible objects. They have to be re-affirmed in every new situation where they are questioned by a potential intruder. There is no link between past conduct and future well-being beyond the emotions of the victims. The notion of a 'resource' that could be impaired is not helpful. Of course, the person whose right has been violated has been harmed—but that harm has occurred can be better explained by referring to rights than by referring to resources.

In addition, for some of the actions classified by von Hirsch and Simester as 'merely offensive', it is not clear why they do not constitute 'harm' if one opts for a wide concept of resources beyond tangible objects. If sexual autonomy is a resource to which someone has a legitimate claim, why is exhibitionism not harmful to those persons whom the offender consciously targets? If the exhibitionist takes pleasure in exposing himself to others and thus intentionally makes them unwilling participants in his personal sexual game, he violates their right to choose sexual role-play for themselves. The fact that no bodily contact occurred would only exclude the label 'harm to another person' if pain or humiliation through physical acts were necessary. If, however, 'sexual autonomy' is the key, exhibitionism falls into the category 'harm to others'.

That the retrospective concept 'violating rights of others' is preferable to a resource-based approach to harm can also be shown with other examples. Imagine that a patient in a hospital declares that (for religious or other reasons) she opposes autopsies and transplantation of organs and that her body after her death must remain untouched. Against her explicit wishes, after her death all her organs are removed and her body destroyed (as she has no surviving relatives or friends, nobody protests against this treatment). One could hardly say that a resource was diminished, as the person once relying on this body is dead. However, it is possible to argue that a living person has the *right* to make arrangements that remain valid after her death and that this right has to be respected even when she has died.[14] Autopsies and transplantations of organs against a patient's orders violate his or her surviving rights: they harm this person.

The theory that distinguishes a separate offence category from harmful conduct also raises doubts when one turns to the notion of 'gross lack of respect or consideration'. Von Hirsch and Simester assume that with these keywords one can at least make a preliminary choice for criminalisation according to the principle 'offence to others' which then needs further 'fine tuning' by applying mediating principles. They stipulate that 'specific reasons

---

[14] See for this discussion Müller, 1996; Hörnle, 2005: § 7; Hoerster, 1997.

why each type of putatively "offensive" conduct is inconsiderate or disrespectful need to be generated'.[15] However, the concept 'gross lack of respect or consideration' is extremely broad. The mere fact that someone treats his unfortunate fellow beings grossly disrespectfully or inconsiderately can hardly provide even a *prima facie* justification for criminal punishment. There are many instances of conduct deserving of reproach because it is highly inconsiderate: someone might knowingly or even intentionally let people with whom he has an appointment wait for hours on several occasions. Or he or she might spoil an important social occasion like a wedding with highly tactless remarks about the bride's or bridegroom's past. Some people can be very disrespectful and inconsiderate. It is, however, hard to imagine addressing such problems by means of the criminal law.

Von Hirsch and Simester do not offer abstract principles why *some* instances of gross lack of respect or consideration should be candidates for criminal prohibition. They name four groups in which one can come to an agreement that criminal sanctions could be appropriate (provided the mediating principles do not restrict the scope of criminalisation). But more interesting, it seems to me, is the question: Why do we *not* consider criminal punishment for many other examples of highly disrespectful treatment? Why do we not impose a penal sanction on the woman who is always late for her appointments and who has, without excuse, annoyed those waiting for hours for the third time this week? Or the tactless joke-teller at the wedding party? Or someone who attends a funeral in highly inappropriate attire?[16] Here, again, it seems useful to approach these questions examining 'rights of others'. There are large segments of social life where we get angry at people who treat others with a gross lack of respect or consideration and where we have reasons to be angry—but where we cannot claim a legal right not to be treated this way.

It is necessary to distinguish between *moral and social obligations* and *legal rights*. This distinction *cannot* be drawn by simply pointing to 'important interests'. The criterion of importance excludes the more trivial cases, that is, minor deviations from traditions, manners, and good taste. One might be slightly irritated for a moment if, for example, someone does not respond to a friendly greeting. However, having the rules for social contact always obeyed meticulously is not an important interest. But, minor digressions from the requirement of politeness aside, one can claim an *important* interest to have others respect crucial rules for considerate relations with their fellow beings. From the perspective of the person concerned, of the 'victim', another's blatant disregard for social and moral obligations can be as blameworthy as disregard for one's rights. The consequences of gross

---

[15] In this volume, at 24.

[16] See Narayan (1990: 13, 40, 175), who frequently cites this as an example of offensive behaviour.

disrespect in a social context can be even more disastrous than disrespect for one's rights. What would be the lesser evil: to be treated with severe lack of respect in a formal social setting like one's wedding or the funeral of a parent, or to be prevented from enjoying a quiet lunch hour in the park by someone playing his boom-box nearby? One can assume with confidence that having one's lunch break spoiled is less serious than the gross disrespect shown at occasions of high personal importance.

The notion of importance can sometimes be misleading when we talk about criminalisation. In *Harm to Others* Feinberg lists various welfare interests, that is, interests needed to pursue a personal, autonomous way of life. Among these welfare interests he includes emotional stability and stable interpersonal relationships (Feinberg, 1984: 37). It is indeed plausible that emotional and social conditions are a central means to achieve one's goals in life; probably, one might argue, more important than most material goods. Still, despite their importance, there are no offence descriptions in our modern legal codes protecting, for example, the continuation of friendships and marriages against mischief done by others. Obviously, the existence of penal norms is not *merely* a function of the *importance* certain interests have. Interests related to private or social networks cannot be protected by legal rights just as are other interests. The reasons for this are, however, not related to the importance of these interests. The same is true for offensive behaviour: identifying *prima facie* reasons for criminalisation is not possible by simply pointing to the *degree* of disrespect and lack of consideration.

Sometimes, it is a matter of *social tolerance* whether criminal punishment should be an option when considering behaviour grossly lacking in respect or consideration. There are, as Simester and von Hirsch point out, some examples of offensive conduct that can be seen as expressions of personal lifestyle.[17] Conflicts resulting from different ways of presenting one's chosen identity may be solved by requiring social tolerance from the party who is annoyed by the other.[18] In some instances where participants in a social setting perceive others to be disrespectful (where, for example, a brightly coloured dress is worn at a funeral), the actor can claim this to be an expression of his unconventional lifestyle. But not every instance of rude behaviour can be justified as a matter of self-presentation. To ask for tolerance requires that the actor can come up with a certain kind of statement in order to defend her behaviour. She must make plausible that her conduct is rooted in different moral values or different aesthetic preferences. Under this condition, she can point to the classical liberal notion that it is valuable for a plurality of lifestyles and values to exist in society.[19] However, some-

---

[17] In this volume: § IV.1.
[18] See Duff and Marshall, this volume.
[19] See von Hirsch and Simester, this volume.

one displaying a gross lack of respect or consideration for others often will not be in a position to explain her conduct using coherent moral values or aesthetic ideas. Rather, she would understand the wrongfulness and point to forgetfulness, sloppiness, or other personality traits not even seen by her as values to be protected.

If neither 'important interests' nor 'tolerance' are the key concepts for deciding which instances of severely disrespectful acts might be dealt with by the criminal law, what *is* crucial? Of the four examples of offensive conduct mentioned by Simester and von Hirsch, three involve interactions with strangers in public places. This is no coincidence. Rights against others are important in those social interactions where self-regulation does not work. To have a 'legal right against others' means not only to be able to *demand* something from those others, but also to demand it in a way that includes *support by the state's legal system*. Interaction with people in a social or private context very often does not include such a right against the other participants. Perhaps one reason for this is that one can choose with whom one wishes to interact. The freedom to lead an autonomous life comprises free personal choices about social interactions. Exercising this freedom, however, entails an obligation not to complain about disappointments. Avoidance of even grossly disrespectful or inconsiderate treatment becomes one's own responsibility—for example, by carefully selecting the guests attending important social occasions such as one's wedding reception. The threshold for state intervention is thus higher in private and social relationships. Someone treating others grossly inconsiderately in a social or private setting can be criticised as doing something morally wrong and as breaching social obligations. But a 'right' of the other person implies that this right could be enforced beyond informal reactions. Such a legal right to ward off disrespectful actions begins, for example, with serious defamations that circulate beyond the narrow privately controlled sphere.

The situation is different with respect to *interactions with strangers* in *public*. Here, it is not possible to make conscious choices about those one wishes to interact with. Strangers who are not bound together in a social network cannot, where necessary, be directed by 'soft tools' to behave in respectful or considerate ways. Therefore, conflicts about the proper use of public space can be decided by resorting to legal rights—provided that important interests concerning one's own plans within the public space are reasons enough to evoke a right against the perpetrator. Furthermore, mediating principles such as the concept of social tolerance become important in relation to the inevitable conflicts resulting from shared spaces and commodities. The list of examples concerning the issue 'conflicts in the public sphere' can be extended beyond those given by von Hirsch and Simester. For example, this explains why false threats and announcements of serious crimes may be prohibited by the criminal law. Someone who calls a journalist or a police station and declares that a bomb has been placed in an airport or train station does not pose a danger if the statement is false. However, he acts in a way grossly inconsiderate to the needs of others. The caller knowingly prevents others from making use of important public commodities like air or railway transport. In doing so, he violates the rights of others (and harms them).

Von Hirsch and Simester concede that 'gross lack of respect and consideration' is not sufficient to require criminal prohibitions. They address the issue of *mediating principles,* which preclude criminalisation although the conduct is offensive.[20] My argument that many instances of grossly disrespectful behaviour do not call for penal sanctions could be turned into arguments about mediating principles. Not to punish disrespectful behaviour that occurred in private could be explained by pointing to privacy as a mediating principle. But it seems less helpful to have a very extensive standard like gross lack of respect as a 'wide entrance' for debates about criminalisation and then to require a set of principles to 'keep the ghost one has called in the bottle'.[21] Why start with an extensive standard in favour of criminal prohibitions if the majority of cases in the end have to be sorted out by resorting to mediating principles? Under such conditions, the opening argument does not deserve the description '*prima facie* reason'.

In my view, it would be preferable to give up the notion of offence as a separate principle of criminalisation. Rather than defining what offence is in contrast to harm, all potential candidates for criminalisation would need to pass the test of whether the rights of others are at stake. If one opens the discussion with the question: 'Has the other person a legal right not to be treated this way?', much conduct that is perceived by many as offensive could be exempt from criminalisation before even mentioning mediating principles. It is possible to develop a concept of rights that is *narrower* than the notion of gross disrespect. For example, consider statements that are disrespectful of ideas important to others. Such statements could be permitted because of the freedom of speech principle as a mediating principle. A prohibition against offensive speech about religions and religious organisations[22] could be challenged because it conflicts with the right to speak freely about controversial religious issues. But it is also possible to argue differently, if 'rights of others' is treated as necessary for justifying penal sanctions (as a necessary, although not sufficient condition; mediating principles also can count against using the criminal law if rights are at stake). For a liberal penal theory pointing to rights, it is important to keep the scope of rights limited to a core of typical human interests. It is easier to achieve a narrow 'entrance' for debates about criminalisation with a normative concept like rights than

---

[20] In this volume: § IV.

[21] See Dalton, 1987: 890.

[22] This is a crime in Germany, § 166 Penal Code. Again, the standard explanation is a 'public peace' argument: see, eg, Lenckner, 2001: § 166/1; Lackner and Kühl, 2004: § 166/1.

with a descriptive concept like 'gross disrespect'. Rights to be protected by the criminal law have to be traced back not only to important interests, but also to interests which are of importance to (almost) everybody *independent of individual lifestyles*. Interests connected to individual choices about a 'good life', which are very important for some, but not for many others who do not opt for this specific way of life, should not count as 'rights' for the purpose of criminalisation. Coming back to my example, this means that blasphemy and similar conduct may hurt people's feelings and treat religious persons with a gross lack of consideration, but it does not violate their rights. Adherence to religious beliefs, which is necessary to be afflicted by blasphemy, is not a general precondition for a good life but is based upon the personal choices of some people. Thus, with a rights-centred theory, there is not even a *prima facie* reason to penalise offensive remarks against religions.

III. CONCLUDING REMARKS

Opening discussions about criminalisation with the questions 'What interests do human beings typically have? Are important interests impaired by the conduct in question?' is a convincing starting point. It is superior to the usual approach in German doctrine, which uses the concept of 'Rechtsgut' (legal good). Therefore, in most central premises I agree with the theses von Hirsch and Simester have proposed in this volume and elsewhere. Specifically, it is important to substitute Feinberg's emphasis on negative emotions with the question whether those who feel offended can point to valid reasons for being offended. However, I would go one step further towards a largely normative rather than a partly descriptive approach. Relying on the crucial criterion of whether the legal rights of others are violated to determine *prima facie* reasons in favour of criminalisation, there would be no need to define what the differences between harmful and offensive conduct are. Efforts to distinguish a separate category called 'offence to others' could be abandoned in favour of *one* necessary condition for criminalisation (in contrast to paternalistic and moralistic reasoning), that is, the violation of another's rights. The issue of 'rights' seems useful for several reasons. For some wrongful acts, the notion of 'harm due to impaired resources' is too narrow. If one stretches the category 'resource' beyond tangible objects to intangible conditions, the offender cannot diminish something. Past conduct does not influence conditions for future wellbeing if one leaves the victim's emotions aside. It harms the victim, but this evaluation has to be retrospective and point to the violation of rights. Additionally, the concept of grossly disrespectful and inconsiderate behaviour is overly broad. Within private and social relations, one has to cope with such incidents. To differentiate the few punishable incidents from the many that are not, it is preferable also to ask whether one has a right to be protected against such conduct. Sometimes, decisions about the acknowl edgement of rights run parallel to the mediating principles von Hirsch and Simester have to apply extensively in their concept of offence.

To rely on the notion of rights is not a panacea, as one still has to debate what constitutes a right in the context of criminalisation (it is not possible to point simply to rights acknowledged in constitutional or civil law). A liberal concept of rights to be protected by the criminal law not only has to identify important interests, but must also single out those that cannot be protected by the persons concerned themselves. Another crucial requirement is that the interests have to be general in character, that is, shared by (almost) everybody as a pre-condition for life plans (but not as part of individual plans for a good life). Interests of high personal importance that are based on personal choices, personal beliefs, etc cannot be reasons to extend the scope of the criminal law. With such a concept of rights adequately tailored to the issue of criminalisation, the scope of *prima facie* reasons is narrower than the concept of 'gross lack of respect or consideration'.

REFERENCES

AMELUNG, K (1972) *Rechtsgüterschutz und Schutz der Gesellschaft.* Frankfurt/ Main: Anthenäum Verlag.

DALTON, H (1987) '"Disgust" and Punishment' *Yale Law Journal* 96: 881–913.

FEINBERG, J (1984) *Harm to Others.* Oxford: Oxford University Press.

—— (1985) *Offense to Others.* Oxford: Oxford University Press.

FISCHER, T (1988) 'Die Eignung, den öffentlichen Frieden zu stören' *Neue Zeitschrift für Strafrecht* 8: 159-65.

HÖRNLE, T (2001) 'Offensive Behavior and German Penal Law' *Buffalo Criminal Law Review* 5: 255–78.

—— (2005) *Grob anstößiges Verhalten. Strafrechtlicher zum Schutz von Moral, Gefühlen und Tabus.* Frankfurt/Main: Klostermann Verlag.

HOERSTER, N (1997) 'Definition des Todes und Organtransplantation' *Universitas:* 42–55.

JAKOBS, G (1991) *Strafrecht Allgemeiner Teil* (2nd edn). Berlin: de Gruyter Verlag.

JESCHECK, H-H and WEIGEND, T (1996) *Strafrecht Allgemeiner Teil* (5th edn). Berlin: Duncker & Humblot Verlag.

LACKNER, K and KÜHL, K (2004) *Kommentar zum StGB* (25th edn). Munich: CH Beck Verlag.

LENCKNER, T (2001) §§ 126, 130, in A SCHÖNKE and H SCHRÖDER (eds), *Kommentar zum StGB* (26th edn). Munich: CH Beck Verlag.

MÜLLER, K (1996) *Postmortaler Rechtsschutz—Überlegungen zur Rechtssubjektivität Verstorbener.* Frankfurt/Main: Verlag Lang.

NARAYAN, U (1990) *Offensive Conduct: What is it and When may we Legally Regulate it?* (PhD Dissertation, Rutgers State University of New Jersey, New Brunswick).

NEUMANN, U (1986) 'Moralische Grenzen des Strafrechts. Zu Joel Feinberg, The Moral Limits of the Criminal Law' *Archiv für Rechts- und Sozialphilosophie* 72: 118–25.

PAGAGEORGIOU, K (1994) *Schaden und Strafe,* Baden Baden: Nomos Verlag.

ROXIN, C (1997) *Strafrecht Allgemeiner Teil 1* (3rd edn). Munich: CH Beck Verlag.

RUDOLPHI, H-J (1998) § 130, in H-J RUDOLPHI, *et al* (eds), *Systematischer Kommentar zum Strafgesetzbuch.* Neuwied: Luchterhand Verlag.

SEHER, G (2000) *Liberalismus und Strafe.* Berlin: Duncker & Humblot Verlag.

SIMESTER, A and VON HIRSCH, A (2002) 'Rethinking the Offense Principle' *Legal Theory* 8: 269–95.

VON HIRSCH, A (2000) 'The Offence Principle in Criminal Law: Affront to Sensibility or Wrongdoing?' *King's College Law Journal* 11: 78–89.

—— (2002) 'Der Rechtsgutsbegriff und das 'Harm Principle'' *Goltdammer's Archiv* 149: 2–14.

VON HIRSCH, A and WOHLERS, W (2003) 'Rechtsgutstheorie und Deliktsstruktur—zu den Kriterien fairer Zurechnung', in R HEFENDEHL, A VON HIRSCH and W WOHLERS (eds), *Die Rechtsgutstheorie,* Baden Baden: Nomos Verlag, 196–214.

WOHLERS, W (2000) *Deliktstypen des Präventionsstrafrechts.* Berlin: Duncker & Humblot Verlag.

6

Crimes of Offence

JOHN TASIOULAS

IN THIS CHAPTER I address, in an exploratory way, certain philosophical issues bearing on the criminalisation of offensive behaviour. Section I introduces the notion of offensive behaviour and, in the course of drawing various distinctions, makes some proposals about the conditions under which such behaviour may be legitimately criminalised. Section II touches on metaphysical questions that arise in trying to make sense of the claim that behaviour can be objectively offensive—specifically, whether the property of disgustingness admits of a realist analysis—and poses a challenge to anyone who would invest the answers to those questions with practical significance. Finally, in section III, I express doubts about the utility of framing the debate in terms of the question whether offensive, yet inherently harmless, behaviour should be criminalised.

I

Only offensive behaviour that is wrongful is eligible for criminalisation: there must be a moral reason, typically an obligation-generating one, against engaging in such behaviour. This follows from the requirement that crimes should be a sub-set of all moral wrongs, that is, those that the community as a whole has a legitimate interest in publicly identifying, preventing, and condemning through punishment. But how can the category of wrongful offensive behaviour be isolated within the broader class of moral wrongs or even the narrower class that attracts this public interest? The problem arises because all wrongful behaviour is offensive, at least on a suitably relaxed construal of 'offensive'. This is due to the conceptual link between an act's being morally wrong and its perpetrator being blameworthy in virtue of his wrong-doing. Thus, all wrongful behaviour is offensive insofar as blameworthiness is a form of offensiveness. However, when lawyers, criminologists, philosophers and others debate the criminal prohibition of offensive behaviour, they do not take the entire class of moral wrongs as their subject-matter. Instead, they are concerned with a familiar sub-set thereof that includes public drunkenness, racist abuse, the making of loud and persistent noise, indecent exposure, the ostentatious display of Nazi symbols, and so on, but excludes paradigmatic crimes such as murder, rape and assault.

What, if anything, unifies this open-ended list of wrongs into a coherent group? The most important shared feature is that their wrongfulness—or, more accurately, their wrongfulness so far as the case for criminalising them is concerned—is mainly attributable to the offence they are liable to cause others. The link between offensiveness and wrong-doing here is not conceptual but constitutive: what *makes* certain acts wrong is, to some significant degree, the fact that they are apt to offend others. A brutal murder justifiably outrages and horrifies those who witness it, but what makes murder wrong is not its tendency to elicit these responses; instead, it is the fact that the murderer grossly violates his victim's right to life. By contrast, one might propose to criminalise public copulation or the utterance of racist taunts precisely because of the wrongful affront they cause to others' sensibilities. Subtract this dimension—for example, consider the same behaviour taking place unobserved and in private—and the wrongfulness essential to the original case for criminalisation evaporates. This is so even if the behaviour would still be wrong for other reasons.

Now, being offended does not only, or even necessarily, refer to manifesting a blaming response. Rather, it encompasses a variety of aversive responses including anger, distress, disgust, horror, indignation and so on. Blaming may be integral to some of these responses, but it is not exhaustive of them. Thus, I can be offended by something, such as a terrible stench, in this broader sense without holding anyone blameworthy or even responsible for causing the stench or failing to prevent or terminate it. It is the failure to distinguish 'offence', understood as the blaming response, from 'offence' as an aversive response more generally that leads Roberts to make the awkward and unnecessary linguistic stipulation that something can be found offensive only if it is presented as someone's responsibility (Roberts, this volume: n 23). An imputation of responsibility is certainly a necessary condition for holding someone blameworthy, but not for finding something offensive.

If a species of offensive behaviour is to have the kind of wrongful character necessary to justify its criminalisation, two further conditions must normally be satisfied. The first is an experiential condition: the offence (whether actual or threatened) must be the upshot of directly perceiving the behaviour in question or some relevant product of it. It will not suffice to be offended by the bare knowledge that the behaviour has taken place. One justification for this condition is that its satisfaction is generally required to hold the perpetrator criminally responsible for the offence caused or threatened. One can more readily be held accountable for offence caused to others where this is mediated by direct experience of one's behaviour rather than where it is not. Moreover, being offended through directly experiencing the offensive conduct is typically a more significant detriment to one's interests than offence prompted by the bare knowledge that the conduct is taking place, which is either not a set-back to one's interests or only a trivial one. But perhaps the most important justification is that a robust conception of liberty leaves very little room for criminalising wrong-doing *primarily* on the basis of the offence that bare knowledge of its occurrence is liable to produce (Hart, 1963: 46).

The second, related condition is that the space in which the offending behaviour is experienced must be public rather than private, that is, a domain in which the community as a whole has a substantial interest in regulating, whether through laws or social conventions, the nature of what might be experienced. For, as Nagel has stressed, the private/public divide operates not only as a shield against invasions of privacy, but also as a filter on the private material that may be properly admitted into the public sphere (Nagel, 2002: 15). Hence the tendency to characterise crimes of offence as outlawing certain kinds of 'anti-social' or 'uncivil' behaviour. Clearly, this second condition helps to define the context in which the first condition operates and ministers to the general requirement that criminalisable wrongs are those that attract the requisite public interest. Of course, the public domain is very heterogeneous in character. Interaction within its various segments—schools, high streets, football stadia, shopping centres, churches—is properly subject to quite diverse expectations and conventions. An important consequence of this is that whether behaviour is offensive, or wrongful in such a way as to generate a *pro tanto* reason for criminalising it, will often depend upon the segment of public space in which the behaviour takes place.

We can draw various distinctions among wrongs whose wrongfulness (at least for the purposes of criminalisation) is primarily attributable to their offensiveness. Sometimes offence is a primitive response that exhibits little or no responsiveness to reasons. Examples include the disgust induced by the sight and smell of a decomposing, maggot-infested carcass or the oppressiveness of insufferably loud and persistent noise. Even if such primitive responses are to be ascribed a propositional content, for example, 'This is disgusting/insufferable and to be avoided', in addition to a characteristic affect and behavioural response, the content itself directly refers to the relevant affect. Thus, the 'disgusting' character of the carcass consists in the fact that it is apt to arouse disgust. Let us call cases of this sort instances of *primitive offence*. This does not mean, of course, that one cannot—often, for perfectly good reasons—train oneself to overcome or inhibit such responses, for instance if one is a sanitation or health care worker. Neither does it rule out the possibility that something that might otherwise cause offence ceases to do so when perceived against the background of a certain kind of relationship or attitude. It is a familiar experience that one is not disgusted by the dirty nappies of one's own infant, even if they nonetheless remain disgusting. If we could imagine our relations to the world profoundly transformed by the love of God, then perhaps nothing would occasion primitive offence.[1]

By contrast, some things we find offensive, like public indecency or racist speech, are experienced as possessing some property by virtue of which a response of offence is properly *merited*. If, on reflection, the object of offence is found not to possess the relevant offence-meriting property, or if the property to which offence is taken is judged not to merit offence, then the persistence of offence will seem unjustified. This property, where it exists, will consist in the object's falling foul of some relevant standard of assessment, the nature of which will vary from case to case. In the examples of public indecency and racist speech, they are moral norms of sexual propriety and respect for others. But the standards in play need not always be moral in character: for example, one's aesthetic or religious sensibilities can be offended by garish clothing or sacrilegious utterances. Let us call these cases of *norm-governed offence*.

Note that I am not suggesting that anyone undergoing a response of the second kind must actually *judge* that an offence-meriting property characterises the object of their disgust. This differentiates my view from that defended by Duff and Marshall. They draw a distinction between immediate and mediate offence that is akin to that which I have drawn between primitive and norm-governed offence. However, they conceive of mediate offence as involving a *judgment* on the part of the offended person that an authoritative standard has been breached by the object of his offence, a violation that he takes to justify his offended response.[2] Unlike this essentially Stoicist view, my more Aristotelian characterisation of norm-governed offence does not entail the presence of any such judgment. This is because I want to preserve the evidently heteronomous character that the experience of offence can assume: the way in which responses of offence can present their objects in ways that run athwart the offended person's considered judgments. In particular, I want to leave open the possibility of cases where someone experiences norm-governed offence, but cannot plausibly be said to judge, even temporarily, that the object of his offence merits that response.

Here is one such case. N is a middle-aged man who, although the recipient of a fundamentalist religious upbringing, has over the course of his life fought his way to a deep and sincere commitment to liberal values. While dining at a restaurant one evening, he finds himself intensely disgusted by a

---

[1] See the instructive discussion of Werfel's poem *Jesus and the Carrion Way* in Kolnai, 2004: 80–81, 88–90.

[2] 'Intrinsic to mediated offence ... is a normative judgment, that what I find offensive violates some standard or value that I take seriously, and that I can cite in explaining my reason for finding X offensive': Duff and Marshall, this volume: 60.

display of affection (e.g. hand-holding) between a gay couple at the next table. One can easily imagine N being shocked and dismayed at his own disgust. The reason he is dismayed, I suggest, is that he judges his reaction to be completely unwarranted—in other words, that nothing about the gay couple's behaviour merits his disgust. But if so, we should understand the offended response as having a propositional content, that is, as presenting the behaviour as having certain disgust-meriting qualities (e.g. it is experienced as 'dirty'), but one which N need not endorse for this response to count as disgust. Should we say, instead, that he is making conflicting judgments: the judgment embodied in his disgust and the contradictory judgment that gives rise to his dismay? It seems to me that convicting him of irrationality in this way is an excessive price to pay in order to preserve the idea of offence as judgment-involving.

One further distinction: that between what is objectively offensive and what is subjectively offensive. The latter is simply a matter of empirical fact about the aversive mental state(s) that perception of something induces or is likely to induce in a given observer. The former is determined by some independent standard according to which the object in question properly counts as offensive. For X to be objectively offensive it will not be enough that any particular individual, or group of individuals, happens to be offended by X. Instead, X must meet a standard for being offensive that is independent of the responses of the individual or group in question. This distinction cuts across that between primitive and norm-governed offence. Some things are objectively primitively offensive and others objectively offensive in a norm-governed way. However, the nature of the standard operative in each case differs. The standard for objective primitive offensiveness refers to a causal relationship. Something is objectively primitively offensive if perception of it by ordinary human agents in standard conditions is liable to cause them offence. The objectively disgusting character of a rotting carcass just is its tendency to induce—in normal human beings and in standard circumstances—a reaction of disgust. The relevant standard in the case of norm-governed offence refers not merely to a causal relationship but to a normative, or reason-giving, one. Something is objectively offensive in a norm-governed way if it has properties that constitute a *reason* for anyone perceiving it to be offended. Again, public copulation or racist speech are plausibly treated as proper objects of norm-governed offence, whereas the prospect of sharing a room with someone of a different race is not.

Now, it is the category of the objectively offensive that is the primary candidate for criminalisation, rather than the merely subjectively offensive. Almost anything can be subjectively offensive, so subjective offensiveness *per se* generates no reason to desist from the behaviour in question or to prevent it. But such reasons typically do obtain in the case of objectively offensive behaviour. They are reasons grounded in the fact that the behaviour has qualities that make it offensive independently of any particular individual or group's judgment or reaction to it: for example the fact that it causes a stench or expresses disrespect (see also Duff and Marshall, this volume). Moreover, if the reasons against the behaviour invoke a moral standard— and in particular if they possess a certain stringency, that is, if they impose an obligation not to subject others to the offensive behaviour—then engaging in such behaviour will be wrongful. Finally, where the sort of wrong in question is one that the community has a legitimate interest in identifying and condemning by means of the criminal law (and here the experiential and public space conditions mentioned previously will be relevant), there will be a *pro tanto* case in favour of its criminalisation. This *pro tanto* case might be outweighed by considerations relating to the cost of prohibiting the offensive behaviour, including costs in liberty, or considerations relating to toleration or the rule of law, among various others.

The foregoing set of conditions explains why public indecency is a plausible candidate for criminalisation (objectively offensive in a norm-governed way) but public hand-holding by homosexual couples is not (only subjectively offensive to some in a norm-governed way). It is not that in the second case reasons of liberty, the rule of law or toleration defeat the reasons for condemning or criminalising the behaviour in question whereas in the first case they do not. Instead, in the second case, but not the first, there are no reasons for condemning or criminalising the behaviour to begin with because it is not objectively offensive and, partly in consequence, not wrongfully offensive. So, in addition to appealing to mediating principles of the sort elaborated by Feinberg (1985: ch 8) and by von Hirsch and Simester (this volume), we also need to address a crucial prior issue: whether the relevant behaviour is objectively offensive. Of course, nothing I have said is intended to preclude entirely the legitimacy of criminalising subjectively offensive behaviour. But, in cases where this is appropriate, the argument for criminalisation assumes a significantly different character. For instance, in order to establish the wrongfulness of merely subjectively offensive behaviour, one would typically have to show that the perpetrator knew, or reasonably ought to have known, of the victim's susceptibility to being offended by this sort of behaviour. In addition, some traditional 'harm condition' for criminalisation, over and above the fact of offence, has greater plausibility in this sort of case (e.g. some requirement that the conduct constitutes harassment that restricts the victim's liberty or invades his privacy).

Of course, Feinberg strenuously resists the idea that the 'reasonableness' of the offence it causes is relevant in determining whether it is legitimate to criminalise any form of behaviour. Whether norm-governed offence is objective or not is, for him, beside the point. He gives two reasons for rejecting a reasonableness criterion: it is both redundant and dangerous. First, such a criterion is rendered practically otiose by the 'extent of offence standard', a mediating principle according to which the more widespread the susceptibility to a given kind of offence, the more serious is a given instance of that offence. It is highly unlikely, he suggests, that virtually everyone would have an unreasonable disposition to take offence at a given kind of behaviour. This means that, even on a subjectivist construal of norm-governed offence, it is unlikely that there will be a compelling case for criminalising behaviour that causes manifestly unreasonable offence. More generally, it is mediating principles such as the extent of offence principle that, Feinberg believes, prevent his reason-insensitive conception of offence from legitimating 'wholesale invasions of liberty that are contrary to common sense and liberal conviction' (Feinberg, 1985: 49). Second, by relying on the extent of offence standard, rather than a reasonableness criterion, 'legislators need not themselves assume the prerogative of determining the reasonableness of emotional reactions, a dangerous power indeed in a democracy' (*ibid*: 35).

Both reasons seem to me inadequate to deprive the objectivity of norm-governed offence of the sort of significance I have claimed for it. There are three main problems with reliance on the extent of offence standard. First, one might be justifiably less sanguine than Feinberg that this standard will almost invariably result in outcomes congruent with the reasonableness criterion. Isn't the tendency of people to take offence unreasonably often very widespread, especially with respect to the behaviour of minority groups? Second, even if one shared Feinberg's optimism on the first point, one should be worried that the case against criminalising public hand-holding by interracial couples turns partly on the brutely contingent fact that revulsion at this sort of behaviour is confined to a tiny racist minority (*ibid*: 27–29). Third, and most fundamentally, Feinberg's position commits him to the view that, for example, in a deeply racist society there is a *pro tanto* reason to prohibit public hand-holding by interracial couples simply because of the offence that witnessing such displays of affection would cause to most onlookers. But given the unreasonableness of the offence caused, how can such behaviour even be classified as wrongful?[3] Of course, Feinberg believes that any reason in favour of criminalisation is bound to be decisively defeated once other relevant considerations are factored in, such as the evident value of affection between couples irrespective of their race (*ibid*: 29). But there is still something undeniably grotesque in the idea that anything counts in favour of criminalisation in this case.

What about the argument from legislative over-reach? The supposed danger here cannot depend on the risks of authorising legislators to apply reasonableness criteria in general. After all, one of the countervailing

---

[3] As Simester and von Hirsch point out (2002: 274), Feinberg announces early on (1985: 1–2) that criminalisable offensive behaviour must be *wrongful*, but largely disregards this requirement in the rest of the book.

considerations on which Feinberg places great weight in the interracial hand-holding case is the perfect reasonableness of the offending behaviour. Instead, the problem must be one that arises in assessing the reasonableness of 'emotional reactions'. But why isn't it the case that, in deciding that interracial hand-holding is reasonable, one is also judging the emotional responses of those who engage in such behaviour (i.e. the love or affection for a member of another race which the behaviour manifests) to be reasonable? More generally, it is not clear why the rational assessment of emotional reactions poses a special problem here. It is not as if the proposal is to *punish* people for unreasonable emotional reactions; instead, the assessment is advanced as part of a *constraint* on the use of coercive state power. Finally, even if there is a special problem, surely there are less drastic remedies than the one Feinberg recommends, especially given the difficulties with relying on the alternative extent of offence standard.

We might note, in passing, that the significance of the objectively offensive reveals the inadequacy of the following argument from parsimony directed against crimes of offence by Braithwaite and Pettit:[4]

> The more offensive the conduct, the greater the power of informal social control and the more susceptible is criminalization to rejection on grounds of parsimony. The less offensive the conduct, on the other hand, the more persuasive is the argument that criminalization is needed if the conduct is to be stopped; but in that case, of course, it ceases to be clear why the promotion of dominion requires that the conduct cease.

Apart from anything else, this argument is undermined by its tendency to equate how offensive certain behaviour is with how much offence it actually generates or is likely to generate in society as a whole. The category of the objectively offensive stands in the way of any such facile equation. Behaviour that intensely offends many others might not be objectively offensive at all (e.g. public displays of interracial affection) and, in consequence, is not appropriately prevented on the grounds of its offensiveness either through the criminal law or through informal social sanctions. Conversely, in a racist society, especially one in which the racially vilified group has absorbed a subordinate self-image, publicly expressed racist abuse might cause serious offence to very few. Such abuse remains, however, objectively offensive. Indeed, the fact that very few are even mildly offended by the public utterance of racist abuse, *contra* the argument quoted above, gives us an additional reason for criminalising it. This is the shared reason we have, as a political community, to give unequivocal and public expression to our condemnation of such behaviour as wrongful.

---

[4] Braithwaite and Pettit, 1990: 97; see also Feinberg, 1985: 31, for a more guarded version of this point.

It is perhaps also worth noting an asymmetry between primitive and norm-governed offensiveness with respect to the significance of actually causing or risking offence. I have just suggested that a strong case may exist for criminalising behaviour that is objectively offensive in a norm-governed way, even if the likelihood of anyone actually being offended by it is negligible. Where behaviour is objectively offensive in a primitive way, the fact that offence is highly unlikely to be caused may very well undermine the case for criminalisation. One way in which it may do so is by preventing the behaviour from being wrongful in the first place. Imagine, for example, that the peculiar atmospheric conditions in a certain locality are such as to prevent hydrogen sulphide from having its characteristic 'rotten egg' smell. In that context, anyone aware of this fact who released hydrogen sulphide in a public place would not be committing any wrong (assuming that exposure to the gas has no other deleterious effects). The reason, presumably, is that the wrongfulness of primitively offensive behaviour turns on the fact that it is apt to *cause* a certain response, whereas the wrongfulness of norm-governed offensive behaviour turns on the fact that such a response is *merited*, even if it does not occur. Of course, this is not to deny that the case for criminalising norm-governed offensive behaviour may be strengthened if the likelihood of people manifesting the offended response is higher rather than lower.

II

The line of criticism just deployed against Braithwaite and Pettit can be redeployed against Husaks (chapter in this volume). He advocates a strategy for diminishing the need to criminalise offensive behaviour that involves taking steps to reduce the likelihood that people will be offended, or will perceive offensive behaviour as wrongful, and reducing also the magnitude of the offence they are liable to experience. This strategy is seriously undermined if the chief focus of criminalisation is objectively offensive behaviour, especially of the norm-governed variety. Now, of course, Husak expresses scepticism about the very idea that some things are 'objectively offensive'. This is because one way—but by no means the only way—of cashing in on the notion of that which is 'objectively' offensive is by adopting some form of realism about the property of offensiveness. Husak's discussion gains in richness and interest by taking as its subject-matter one particular mode of offence, i.e. disgust, concerning which he defends two broad theses: (a) that we should adopt a (qualified) anti-realism regarding the property of disgustingness, and (b) that this anti-realism renders 'highly problematic' the use of 'legal remedies against behaviour deemed to be disgusting' (Husak, this volume).

Of course, the notion of 'realism' is itself a heavily contested one. Nevertheless, Husak's twin-pronged interpretation of it seems acceptable.

To be a realist about a certain kind of entity or property, one must hold (1) that statements asserting the existence of that entity or attributing that property admit of truth, and (2) that facts non-redundantly involving this entity property have explanatory power. I would elaborate the explanatory power test along the lines proposed by David Wiggins, in his discussion of moral objectivity (Wiggins, 1998: chs III–V). The question is whether vindicatory explanations are possible such that the best full explanation of why someone finds something disgusting or believes it to be disgusting appeals to—or leaves no room to deny—the fact that it really is disgusting. It is entirely consistent with this thesis that many instances of being disgusted or believing something to be disgusting are best explained in a non-vindicatory manner, for example as the upshot not of the disgustingness of the object in question but rather of the social conditioning or peculiar psychological make-up of the individual experiencing disgust. Many defenders of disgust realism would insist that such a non-vindicatory explanation can be constructed in N's case: nothing the gay couple did warranted his disgust.

I find Husak's case for (a) inconclusive, but before explaining why, I should register a cautionary note about (b). Husak does not contend that establishing disgust realism is necessary to justify legal intervention on the grounds of the disgustingness of certain wrongful acts, but he does believe that it would 'certainly help' (Husak, this volume).[5] However, the enterprise of drawing normative implications from metaphysical theses is fraught with difficulties. Even if anti-realism about disgust were correct, it is hardly obvious that this would in any way impinge upon, let alone undermine, the case for criminalising behaviour that was found disgusting. Consider here the parallel with those philosophers who defend anti-realism about ethics. In *A Treatise of Human Nature*, David Hume famously wrote:

> Take any action allow'd to be vicious: Wilful murder, for instance. Examine it in all lights, and see if you can find that matter of fact, or real existence, which you call *vice*. In which-ever way you take it, you find only certain passions, motives, volitions and thoughts. There is no other matter of fact in the case. The vice entirely escapes you, as long as you consider the object. You never can find it, till you turn your reflexion into your own breast, and find a sentiment of disapprobation, which arises in you, towards this action. Here is a matter of fact; but 'tis the object of feeling not of reason. It lies in yourself, not in the object. (Hume, 1976: 468–9)

This is an apparently unambiguous endorsement of anti-realism regarding the wrongfulness of murder and, by extension, moral properties as a whole.

---

[5] How this formulation of what is at stake squares with Husak's previously-noted claim that disgust anti-realism renders the use of legal remedies against behaviour deemed disgusting 'highly problematic' is a little unclear.

A murder's wrongful character is a property not of the act itself, but rather of the sentiment of disapprobation elicited in us by observing or contemplating that act. But no sooner has he made this claim than Hume goes on to downplay heavily, if not deny completely, its practical significance:

> [T]his discovery in morals ... is to be regarded as a considerable advancement of the speculative sciences; tho' ... it has little or no influence on practice. Nothing can be more real, or concern us more, than our own sentiments of pleasure and uneasiness; and if these be favourable to virtue, and unfavourable to vice, no more can be requisite to the regulation of our conduct and behaviour. (*Ibid*: 469)

Nor is Hume unique in minimising the practical significance of ethical anti-realism; many contemporary philosophers of a broadly Humean persuasion, such as JL Mackie, Bernard Williams, Richard Rorty, Simon Blackburn, and Jeremy Waldron, follow him on this point. So too, interestingly enough, does that archetypal moral rationalist, Kant. Although the latter advances the decidedly anti-Humean thesis that morality is grounded in pure practical reason rather than sentiment, Kant denies that the notion of practical reason in play here can be given a straightforwardly realist construal. Morality, for Kant, is not a matter of responsiveness to evaluative features of the world; instead, it is constructed through the process of conforming one's principles of action to the purely formal constraints of practical reason.

Philosophers of a Humean and Kantian bent combine a denial of ethical realism with a preparedness to make all kinds of ethical arguments, including arguments for the criminalisation of behaviour on the ground of its wrongfulness. Is this conjunction also 'highly problematic' by Husak's lights? Would he claim that ethical anti-realism, if true, throws into question the use of legal remedies against moral wrongs such as murder, rape and assault? If not, why should things be different with disgust anti-realism? Of course, I do not mean to exclude the possibility that both Humeans and Kantians are mistaken about the practical irrelevance of their anti-realism. Moreover, even if they are not mistaken, this may be for reasons that are not available to a disgust anti-realist who wishes to maintain a comparable quietism about the normative implications of his doctrine. In particular, it may be that there are ways of making sense of the objectivity of ethics that do not involve any form of realism. Thus, the Kantian can take heart from his alternative grounding of morality in pure practical reason, whereas the Humean would appeal to a standard of correctness founded in the sentiments of a supposedly homogeneous human nature. Perhaps neither sort of move is available to the disgust anti-realist. Nevertheless, there is an onus of proof on anyone who asserts the practical significance of anti-realism, or any metaphysical doctrine, and it is not obvious that Husak has discharged it.[6]

---

[6] I have explored this issue at a general level in Tasioulas, 2002.

Let me now turn to Husak's defence of (a). When he comes to assess the prospects of disgust realism, he takes as the object of his critique an analogue of the ideal-observer theory of ethics. There are at least two reasons why this is an unhappy choice. First, the theory is defined by Husak as one about the meaning of statements predicating the quality of being disgusting. But realism about disgust is not essentially a doctrine about the meaning of statements ascribing disgustingness; instead, it is a metaphysical thesis about the status of the property of disgustingness. With this interpretation of the thesis, one can avoid the 'open question' objection Husak derives from GE Moore, since this objection specifically targets doctrines that seek to define evaluative terms purely naturalistically. Second, it is doubtful that this theory—even re-interpreted as a metaphysical theory—would amount to a genuine form of realism. This is because it presupposes that being fully informed about an object does not involve knowing that the object is disgusting. Instead, that property can be attributed to the object only if a reasonable person in the right conditions would be disgusted by it. But then, it seems, the property of disgustingness is not invoked to explain the response; instead, disgust is understood as a response to a world that does not include the feature of disgustingness, the latter feature being a projection of the independently characterised response.

In light of the questionable suitability of his target theory, it would have been helpful had Husak considered the prospects of perhaps the most compelling model for disgust realism, that developed by McDowell and Wiggins in connection with their respective defences of a variety of ethical realism. The central idea in the McDowell/Wiggins theory is that a form of realism can be maintained in which worldly property and subjective response form a reciprocally related pair (see e.g. McDowell, 1998: 151ff; Wiggins, 1998: 195f).[7] On the one hand, this contrasts with standard forms of anti-realism, theories that explain attributions of the property in terms of the projection of a response that can be understood independently of the property that is supposed to result from the process of projection. On the other hand, a contrast is also intended with heavy-duty forms of realism, which claim that the nature of the property can be elucidated entirely independently of any reference to its relation to a human (or other) subjectivity. Instead, a third possibility is envisaged, one that accords priority to neither the property nor the subjective response:

> What about a position that says the extra features are neither parents nor children of our sentiments, but—if we must find an apt metaphor from the field of kinship relations—siblings? ... Denying that the extra features are prior to the relevant sentiments, such a view distances itself from the idea that they belong,

[7] It should be said that both McDowell and Wiggins are uneasy about the label 'realism' for this third position; but the label is acceptable provided we keep in mind the position for which it stands.

mysteriously, in a reality that is wholly independent of our subjectivity and set over against it. It does not follow that the sentiments have a priority. If there is no comprehending the right sentiments independently of the concepts of the relevant extra features, a no-priority view is surely indicated. (McDowell, 1998: 159–60)

Of course, merely gesturing in the direction of this third possibility is not the same as establishing a form of disgust realism under its auspices. Indeed, as it turns out, McDowell believes that in contrast to certain ethical qualities like justice and cruelty, or even qualities like the amusing or the comical, disgustingness fails to qualify as real even on a no-priority interpretation of realism. This is because, he conjectures, we can plausibly regard disgust as a 'self-contained psychological item, conceptualizable without any need to appeal to any projected property of disgustingness' (McDowell, 1998: 157).[8] But there seems to me to be a strong case for accepting McDowell's model while resisting his wholesale anti-realist verdict on disgust.

How might realism about the disgusting be vindicated? To begin with, any such vindication would presumably have to be restricted in scope. This is because there do seem to be attributions of disgustingness that conform to the anti-realist analysis. When a small child finds boiled vegetables disgusting, is his response best explained by the disgustingness of the vegetables? Here, disgust really does plausibly operate as a 'self-contained psychological item' that happens, for certain individuals, to be aroused by boiled vegetables, without any quality of disgustingness having to be invoked to make sense of that response. Cases like this are comparable to differences in people's favourite colour; the colour blue has no choice-justifying property that renders it superior to the colour red. But not all cases of disgust, I think, are amenable to this sort of treatment. The matter turns on whether we are entitled to the thought that, in some cases, there are reasons to be disgusted—reasons that reflect a sensitivity to the disgustingness of the object in question—and to rank different sensibilities as better or worse according to their level of attunement to those reasons. [9]

The morally disgusting seems an especially promising domain for vindicating this possibility. What is at issue here are the prospects for developing a critical phenomenology of disgust, one that gives substance to the thought that disgust can be a response that is merited in light of the moral qualities of its objects. One of the most illuminating contributions to this project is Aurel Kolnai's *On Disgust*, according to which moral disgust—analogously to physical disgust—alerts us to 'the presence of a particular quality of

[8] Wiggins, by contrast, impliedly favours a form of disgust realism, see Wiggins (1998: 199–200).

[9] This would amount to a norm-governed form of objectivity. I leave aside the question whether primitive disgustingness can be given a realist interpretation, perhaps by exploiting a comparison with the perception of secondary qualities. See eg, McDowell, 1998: 131–50.

the unethical, namely, the morally "putrid" or "putrescent"' (Kolnai, 2004: 81). Kolnai elaborates on the types of personality and the sorts of conditions and actions—certain forms of satiety, excessive (or misplaced) vitality, mendacity, falsehood and various kinds of moral softness—that properly elicit moral disgust (Kolnai, 2004: 62–72, 80–90). As one might expect, sex is a central concern:

> [I]n general one should think here of perverse, polygamic sexuality, of an order which is inimical to life or which is overwhelming. There is here a vast realm of objects of disgust ... The disgust reaction will be directed against the immoral to the extent that the latter is experienced as a 'soiling', a 'sullying' of life and its values, and, to a somewhat lesser degree, perhaps, against a 'satanic' or mechanical and superficial sexuality ... But further, even the presentation of sexual behaviour that is not strictly sinful can arouse disgust, either through accidental proximity or for its harmless lack of taste, as more sensitive persons can be affected by public references to the wedding night at a wedding banquet. (Kolnai, 2004: 66)

Given the rich network of concepts, standards and beliefs—all, of course, subject to ongoing amendment and refinement in the light of critical scrutiny—that bear on the meaning and value of sexual intercourse and the moral constraints that structure it, aren't there good reasons to be disgusted by public copulation or bestiality, for example? Aren't there good reasons, figuratively speaking, for one's moral stomach to turn upon being exposed to such practices? And would we not rank a sensibility that did not regard them as at least eligible objects of moral disgust as inferior to one that does?

Of course, this is just a suggestion. But it is already open to various challenges. First, one might seize on the reference to *moral* disgust in order to argue that what is actually being described here is vehement moral condemnation or indignation, rather than disgust. Intuitively, this seems implausible. As Kolnai insists, disgust can be experienced at exposure to sexual conduct without the person experiencing the disgust going on to judge the conduct to be immoral (recall N's case). More positively, we can speak of *disgust* in the case just mentioned because, *inter alia*, there is an emphasis on the perceptual quality of the object found disgusting as distinct from any of its other causal consequences, because the visceral reaction it arouses bears a sufficiently close resemblance to primitive forms of disgust, and because the behavioural response associated with it is the removal of the object from one's perceptual vicinity and resistance to any contact with it. Its *moral* character turns on the fact that what is presented violates specifically moral standards of conduct.[10] A disgust realist, of course, would owe us a much fuller account of those qualities that are properly found disgusting in the sexual domain and elsewhere.

---

[10] Here I draw partly on the characterisation of disgust in Kolnai, 1988: 586–7, 589–90.

Second, a version of Husak's *conflation* problem has to be confronted. Can we adequately discriminate—from among the reasons for finding something disgusting—between those that really show it to be disgusting and those that do not? There are two points to make here. First, on a no-priority view, the standpoint from within which any such demand can be legitimately issued and satisfied is one *internal* to the type of sensibility in question. There is no question of prescinding entirely from a sensibility prone to disgust in order to identify genuinely disgusting features of the world. Second, thus stated the issue is not so much metaphysical as one hostage to the everyday, contested, and piecemeal process of distinguishing between what is and what is not disgusting. Ultimately, the question is whether this process can sustain the thought that some sensibilities are better attuned than others to what really is disgusting—whether debate, criticism, and refinement of one's sensibility is possible in this domain—or whether the idea of such discrimination among sensibilities runs into the sand, as in the case of differences in people's favourite colour. If it is capable of sustaining a realist interpretation, the fact that responses of disgust are empirically subserved by a 'disgust mechanism', such as that described by Husak, will not trouble the disgust realist. After all, these empirical explanations do not compete with the realist's explanation of the disgusted response, but join with it in comprising a full explanation of its occurrence in any given instance. Realism about a property x requires that the fact that A is x can *figure in* the best full explanation of why someone believes A is x or experiences A as x; there is no need to show that the fact that A is x *exhausts* any such explanation.

Third, in addressing the preceding question, the disgust realist must give an account of divergence in what is found disgusting, a phenomenon which Husak quite rightly sees as putting disgust realism under pressure. Isn't he right to suggest that such variation is always best explained by upbringing, individual psychological make-up, and related factors, rather than by the hypothesis that some are detecting what is really disgusting and others are not? Well, not obviously so. First, appeals to the responses of those unformed by culture, for example Husak's discussion of feral children, have limited force in this context. Such examples show that a developed sensitivity to what is morally disgusting depends upon mastery of a conceptual repertoire that only initiation into a culture can bestow. But the same is true of cognitive sensitivity to features of the world described by physics, without impugning the realist credentials of the latter. Now, once we are within the realm of the cultural, we should notice that realism is perfectly compatible with considerable *cross-cultural* pluralism in what is found disgusting. Here are two reasons for the compatibility. First, that something is disgusting is often a matter of disgust being a rationally eligible response to it, rather than a mandatory one.[11]

---

[11] See the instructive discussion by Duff and Marshall (this volume: I.3) of the contrast between reasonable and necessary offence.

So, the non-criticisable failure by some sensibilities to be disgusted by it need not undermine the claim that such a response is rationally eligible. Second, what is genuinely disgusting is often partly determined by local convention. The moral realist should readily admit that whether behaviour is dishonest depends in part upon the conventions, for example regarding commercial bargaining, that prevail at a particular time and place. Similarly, what counts as disgusting may partly depend upon the precise content of conventions that determine the meaning and value of various activities, that give content to norms of respect or that regulate what may appropriately be disclosed in public spaces of different kinds (see e.g., Simester and von Hirsch, 2002: 277–9). The key point is that not just any action could be disgusting—just as not any action could be dishonest—for that would undermine the fundamental realist idea that there are constraints, grounded in the properties of things, regarding what is a fitting object of disgust.

III

According to a standard approach to our topic, the philosophically interesting issue in this area is whether intrinsically harmless, yet wrongful, offensive behaviour constitutes a legitimate object of criminalisation (e.g. Feinberg, 1985: 10; Simester and von Hirsch, 2002: 280–90). Endorsing this approach, Roberts offers public copulation and Holocaust denial as 'good examples' of this sort of conduct (Roberts, this volume: 14; see also the many examples in Feinberg's famous 'ride on the bus' discussion: Feinberg, 1985: 10–13). By contrast, I prefer Duff and Marshall's suggestion that we should focus on the kind of wrongful set-back to interests that offensive behaviour might involve in any given case, eschewing reliance on a quasi-technical concept of 'harm' that is supposed to contrast in this way with 'offence' (Duff and Marshall, this volume). Duff and Marshall advocate this approach on the grounds of simplicity. But this consideration can be supplemented by reflection on the problems confronted by those who treat the harm/offence distinction as pivotal.

Consider Roberts' examples of supposedly harmless yet offensive behaviour. These are certainly among the forms of offensive behaviour that are serious candidates for criminalisation. But it's not at all clear that they are intrinsically harmless. If 'harm' is interpreted in composite terms (as Roberts following in the footsteps of Feinberg interprets it), in other words as a *wrongful* set-back to another's *interests*, then why should the offence that both of these activities involve, considered in itself and irrespective of further knock-on effects, never amount to harm? Now, arguing for the criminalisation of Holocaust denial is a rather complicated undertaking, since it might be thought that it is a form of expression that attracts protection under the right to free speech. So let me instead consider the less problematic example of public sex. Now, one central prudential value or human interest is enjoyment. This qualifies as a prudential value on most theories of well-being: hedonism (which reduces all prudential value to pleasure), informed desire theories (according to which certain forms of enjoyment would be the object of our informed desires), and objective list theories (according to which enjoyment features along with certain other goods as a prudential value). Conversely, various forms of displeasure, upset, and disgust plausibly constitute prudential disvalues, ways in which a person's life typically gets worse for him by virtue of undergoing these experiences. Isn't it eminently plausible that some of our most enjoyable activities in public places— for example, walking in a public park—would be thoroughly spoiled by the prospect of stumbling upon copulating couples? The verdict of the Williams Report on this topic will strike many as plain common sense:

> Laws against public sex would generally be thought to be consistent with the harm condition, in the sense that if members of the public are upset, disgusted, outraged or put out by witnessing some class of acts, then that constitutes a respect in which the public performance of the acts harms their interests and gives them a reason to object.[12]

At this point the standard riposte is to invoke a *de minimis* condition. Even if public copulation involves a wrongful impairment of others' interests, it is usually too insignificant to count as harm; this is because the criminal law 'should not concern itself, even *prima facie*, with very trivial annoyance or disappointments' (Roberts, this volume: 14). But this smacks of stipulation, not argument. Of course, it is true that there are innumerable examples of fairly trivial forms of wrongfully offensive behaviour which cannot be said to impinge upon others in such a way as to generate even a *prima facie* case for criminalising them, for example various commonly encountered forms of crude or impolite behaviour. But this isn't the class of conduct that any reasonable person would propose to criminalise on the grounds of its offensiveness. Instead, what is really at issue are examples such as those invoked by Roberts. But if so, why should we think that exposure to public copulation, racist abuse, etc are all less serious set-backs to our interests than minor assaults or pick-pocketing? The fact that consequential detriments to interests will also usually be present shouldn't obscure the potentially important independent contribution to the case for criminalisation that is made by the wrongful detriment to interests constituted by the offensiveness of the behaviour *per se*. One need only conduct a thought-experiment. What would make your day worse: if the person opposite you on the bus indecently exposed himself or if he stole five pounds from you? However one answers, if the latter is sufficiently detrimental to one's interests to be in principle criminalisable, why not also the former?

---

[12] Williams, 1981: 99. I assume, of course, that the position is advanced on the basis that public nudity is objectively offensive in a norm-governed way.

In response to this line of thought, defenders of the harm/offence distinction often surreptitiously resort to a double standard: they set a significantly more demanding requirement for 'harm' in the case of offensive behaviour than that which they are prepared to invoke elsewhere. So, for example, Simester and von Hirsch contend that '[p]sychological harm is something that does exist, and on occasion it may be caused by offensive conduct, but it consists of more than the state of being affronted. Diminution of one's cognitive or evaluative powers, and so on, is not the standard effect of offensive conduct. The normal person may be irritated or disgusted when seeing someone disrobing on the bus, but he or she is unlikely to suffer such impairments' (Simester and von Hirsch, 2002: 288). But must the profound affront to one's sensibilities caused by public copulation, or the public exhibition of synthesised images of violence and sexual degradation, really lead to the 'diminution of one's cognitive or evaluative powers' in order to count as a set-back to interests that is cognisable as such by the criminal law? In the case of minor assault, wouldn't a comparable demand, for example 'diminution of one's physical powers', rightly be found overly demanding? Certainly, all manner of assaults on my person can leave my physical capabilities perfectly intact, yet this is compatible with the existence of a powerful case for criminalising them on the grounds that they wrongfully transgress my interests (e.g. my interest in not experiencing gratuitously inflicted pain, etc).

On a more charitable interpretation, defenders of the harm/offence distinction do not appeal to a double standard, but instead invoke a specially restricted interpretation of 'harm'. On this view, the notion of harm ascribes key significance to one interest above all others—our interest in living an autonomous life (see Raz, 1986: 413). So understood, harm involves '[t]he impairment of a person's opportunity to engage in worthwhile activities and relationships and to pursue valuable, self-chosen goals' (Simester and von Hirsch, 2002: 288). Of course, given the plausibility of a pluralist account of well-being, in which autonomy is one among various other prudential values, there is a serious question why harm is to be defined primarily by reference to this one value. Moreover, even if this characterisation of harm could be motivated, it seems implausible that wrongful set-backs to other interests that do not constitute 'harm', in this strict sense, cannot be proscribed by the criminal law. Indeed, Raz seemingly admits that the prevention of severe pain, even if it does not amount to autonomy-based harm, is a legitimate basis for state coercion (Raz, 1984: 414n).[13]

If the preceding line of argument is correct, then what is really at issue is whether offensive behaviour ever involves the kind of wrongful set-back to interests that generates a *pro tanto* reason in favour of its criminalisation.

---

[13] In this context, he contrasts the 'narrow' harm principle with a 'broad' version that would allow 'coercion for the prevention of pain, offence and perhaps some other injuries to a person as well' (1986: 414). By contrast, he is apparently not receptive to the idea of offence being in itself a basis for criminalisation.

This is precisely the question that Duff and Marshall suggest is the proper focus of deliberation. Imagine someone who grants this, but then proceeds to contend that there is an important difference between harm (= wrongful set back to interests) and a certain species of offence, that is, norm-governed offence, especially where the norm in question is moral in character. This view expresses the understandable reluctance felt by some to admit that whether people's interests are damaged can turn on the moral norms that are correct or that people accept or to which their sensibilities are attuned. But this reluctance makes most sense in response to the thesis that there is a *pro tanto* case for criminalising behaviour that is merely subjectively offensive in a norm-governed way (where the norm in question is moral), for example the offence the racist experiences on being confronted with the interracial couple. But, as I have already argued, the primary candidate for criminalisation *qua* offensive is behaviour that is *objectively* offensive, whether primitively or in a norm-governed fashion. So, the relevant moral norm is not hostage to vagaries of individual temperament. Even leaving this point aside, the aspiration which the new distinction reflects, that of keeping the notion of harm free of any moral taint, is not obviously well-founded. To begin with, on a composite interpretation such as Feinberg's, harm involves a component of wrongfulness, as well as a set-back to interests, and the former is clearly a moral matter. On this view, in order for the impairment of another's interests to constitute harm it must be the causal product of a wrongful action.

Still, one might imagine a partisan of the revised offence/harm distinction insisting that clarity is to be achieved by interpreting that second component—set-back to interests—in morally-neutral terms. Even if the set-back has to be *caused* by wrongful conduct to constitute harm, its own *intrinsic nature* can be characterised without any reference to morality. Yet there are two objections here. The first stems from the thought that wrongfulness and the relevant sense of set-back to interests cannot always be so neatly picked apart. As Antony Duff has argued, some set-backs to interests cannot be adequately understood as the set-backs they are except by reference to their character as wrongful (compare damage to one's property by act of God with the same material damage caused by vandals) while, in other cases, the set-back to interests cannot even be identified except in terms that include the wrongfulness of the action that produced it (e.g. the sense of violation of one's privacy and autonomy is an important aspect of the damage to interests that burglary involves) (Duff, 2001: 16–26).

The second objection is that, even if wrongfulness and impairment of interests could always be disentangled, there are strong reasons to deny that an adequate specification can always be given of human interests independently of any reference to moral concerns generally. One of the most important prudential values is deep personal relations. But it is impossible to characterise such relations without invoking moral values. For instance, any prudentially valuable form of friendship will involve some form of moral respect between the friends.[14] Similarly, a broadly Aristotelian tradition holds that the value of the object or activity in which pleasure is taken affects the prudential value of that pleasure. If pleasure is taken in something tawdry or base, for example, then the person's interests will be diminished, rather than enhanced, by experiencing it. Consider, in this light, the interest that is impaired when one is offended by the sight of two fellow passengers copulating on a bus. Surely, the operative interest here is one in not being involuntarily subjected to graphic displays of morally shameless or degraded behaviour. It would grossly distort the situation to speak instead of an interest in not being shocked or upset by unfamiliar and unexpected practices, for example. The moral quality of the conduct to which one takes offence can be essential to understanding what is so nasty about being exposed to it.[15]

Rather than pursue these admittedly speculative reflections further, let me turn to a passage in Mill's *On Liberty*—the main philosophical source of the contemporary preoccupation with the nature and scope of 'harm' in the theory of criminalisation. In the passage, Mill directly addresses the prohibition of offensive conduct:

> [T]here are many acts which, being directly injurious only to the agents themselves, ought not to be legally interdicted, but which, if done publicly, are a violation of good manners, and coming thus within the category of offences against others, may rightly be prohibited. Of this kind are offences against decency; on which it is unnecessary to dwell, the rather as they are only connected indirectly with our subject, the objection to publicity being equally strong in the case of many actions not in themselves condemnable, nor supposed to be so. (Mill, 1972: 153)

Here Mill seems to endorse the permissibility of criminalising, or at least socially sanctioning, some forms of offensive behaviour. And he must be doing so on the grounds that such conduct is harmful, since for him (unlike, for example, Feinberg), *only* harmful conduct may be criminalised. But surely the indecent behaviour he refers to ordinarily causes no 'harm', if the latter notion is understood in a pre-moral sense. Presumably, it is for this reason that Jeremy Waldron—a defender of a version of the revised harm/offence division, one that he also attributes to Mill—suggests that this passage should 'charitably be overlooked' as aberrant (Waldron, 1993: 130).

---

[14] See the discussion of deep personal relations, and the inter-penetration of the moral and the prudential in Griffin, 1996.

[15] At some point, we shall also need to ask to what extent the desire to keep prudential 'interests' free of moral taint embodies the doctrine, essential to utilitarianism as classically conceived, that the 'good' is prior to the 'right'. For it is arguable that this doctrine, rather than being something to be affirmed, is the ultimate source of many of utilitarianism's difficulties, eg various familiar problems of alienation and obligation 'overload'.

In any case, Waldron says, the final sentence of the passage quoted above indicates that Mill believed that the behaviour in question, and the offence it causes, can be characterised independently of any moral assessment:

> He does ... make it clear that it is not the deviance or the perceived or actual immorality of the action in question which makes their public performance so indecent; rather, it is a matter of the type of action that it is. For example, on this view, all forms of public copulation might be regarded as indecent, including marital sex in the missionary position for the sole and only purpose of procreation, not just sodomy, fellatio, masturbation, etc. So if the spectacle of indecency is to be regarded as harmful, the harm involved is not (straightforwardly) moral distress, in the sense with which we are concerned. (*Ibid*: 130)

But, whatever its merits as Millian scholarship, this second line of argument is rather strained (notwithstanding the parenthetical qualification). It is dubious to attribute the offensiveness of indecent conduct exclusively to the *type* of behaviour in question, without any moral assessment figuring in the latter's specification. Such an attribution might seem half-way plausible with respect to the various sexual activities listed by Waldron, but it is much less plausible in the case of public nudity. Need one think that there is always something offensive about nudity as such, independently of any issue of morality, in order to oppose public nudity on the grounds of indecency? And even if there were, why should this be the only kind of offensiveness that matters when it comes to deciding whether to criminalise public nudity?

However one might answer these questions, there is a further problem with Waldron's argument. It unhelpfully abstracts the 'type' of action in question from the moral significance of the context in which it is performed But, as Waldron himself observes, the category of actions at issue are mainly sexual acts *performed in a public context*. Now, what could possibly motivate the inclusion of that italicised clause, if not the thought that their public performance entails the violation of authoritative moral standards regarding what may properly be presented to public view without being offensive? The offensiveness of the acts in question is not fixed exclusively by the nature of the acts considered 'in themselves', but also by the context in which they occur. This is why the Williams Committee correctly observed that the idea that 'indecent displays' are a legitimate object of criminal prohibition is apt to mislead. The case for criminalisation turns on the *context* in which the display takes place, and context is important because it is partly determinative of the display's moral character, for example as one that is properly found morally offensive (Williams, 1981: 98–99).

The failure of the second line of argument throws us back to Waldron's first suggestion, that the passage should be treated as aberrant. But we should follow this advice only if we wish to saddle Mill with a morality-free conception of interests. I have indicated some reasons for resisting that conception. Moreover, there are grounds for thinking that Mill would have been sympathetic to those reasons. Certainly, he regarded utility as 'the ulti-mate appeal on all ethical questions'. But, as he immediately went on to stress, 'it must be utility in the largest sense, grounded on the permanent interests of a man as a progressive being' (Mill, 1972: 74). Indeed, on clos-er inspection, it turns out that Mill subscribed to a broadly Aristotelian con-ception of well-being of the kind mentioned earlier. For even if we think of him as, strictly speaking, a hedonist in the theory of prudential value, his insistence on the qualitative dimension of pleasurable experiences means that the prudential value of such experiences is partly determined by, among other qualities, their moral character. It is that more expansive conception of our interests, I think, that will allow us to treat at least some serious forms of offensive behaviour as wrongfully impairing our interests in such a way as to render them eligible for criminal prohibition.

Let me conclude with two disclaimers. First, it has not been my inten-tion in this section to argue that, in the theory of criminalisation, we need only appeal to a Harm Principle,[16] even when we are dealing with the prohibition of offensive behaviour. The tendency of my argument has been, instead, that criminalisable wrongs (including criminalisable offensive behaviour) will ordinarily involve a set-back to interests. This is what mat-ters, not whether such conduct satisfies a technical standard of 'harm' that contrasts with offence. Quite apart from that, I am sceptical about the util-ity of appealing to any such master principle in ethical deliberation. What is required, instead, is that the bearing of a variety of salient considerations should be registered in any given case; placing all these considerations under the umbrella of a single principle doesn't obviate that fact and may even obscure it. Second, nothing I have said is inconsistent with thinking that there are important reasons for treating crimes of offence as a special category of criminal wrong-doing. But I doubt that these reasons are of the philosophically deep kind suggested by proponents of the harm/offence dis-tinction. The distinctiveness of the category of crimes of offence does not consist in the fact that some forms of wrongful offensive behaviour are properly criminalisable—*mirabile dictu*—despite not inherently involving any detriment to human interests significant enough to count as 'harm'. Instead, the most important reasons for treating crimes of offence as a distinct category are far more likely to reflect the ethical salience of certain historical and instutional facts, such as the lamentable propensity of leg-islatures to invoke 'offensiveness' as a justification for enacting criminal laws that oppress and further marginalise unpopular minority groups. But

---

[16] 'It is always a good reason in support of penal legislation that it would probably be effec-tive in preventing (eliminating, reducing) harm to persons other than the actor (the one pro-hibited from acting) and there is probably no other means that is equally effective at no greater cost to other values.' Feinberg, 1984: 26.

these considerations, although of unquestionable significance, take us beyond the more abstract themes that have been my concern in this chapter.[17]

REFERENCES

BRAITHWAITE, J and PETTIT, P (1990) *Not Just Deserts: A Republican Theory of Criminal Justice*. Oxford: Oxford University Press.

DUFF, RA (2001) 'Harms and Wrongs' *Buffalo Criminal Law Review* 5: 13.

FEINBERG, J (1984) *Harm to Others*. Oxford: Oxford University Press.

—— (1985) *Offence to Others*. Oxford: Oxford University Press.

GRIFFIN, J (1996) *Value Judgment: Improving our Ethical Beliefs*. Oxford: Oxford University Press.

HART, HLA (1963) *Law, Liberty, and Morality*. Oxford: Oxford University Press.

HUME, D (1976) *A Treatise of Human Nature* (2nd edn). Oxford: Oxford University Press.

KOLNAI, A (1998) 'The Standard Modes of Aversion: Fear, Disgust and Hatred' *Mind* 107: 581.

—— (2004) *On Disgust*. Chicago and La Salle, IL: Open Court.

MCDOWELL, J (1998) *Mind, Value, and Reality*. Cambridge, MA: Harvard University Press.

MILL, JS (1972) 'On Liberty', in MILL, JS *Utilitarianism, On Liberty, and Considerations on Representative Government*. London: JM Dent & Sons.

NAGEL, T (2002) *Concealment and Exposure & Other Essays*. Oxford: Oxford University Press.

RAZ, J (1986) *The Morality of Freedom*. Oxford: Oxford University Press.

SIMESTER, AP and VON HIRSCH, A (2002) 'Rethinking the Offense Principle' *Legal Theory* 8: 269.

TASIOULAS, J (2002) 'The Legal Relevance of Ethical Objectivity' *American Journal of Jurisprudence* 47: 211.

WALDRON, J (1993) 'Mill and the Value of Moral Distress', in *Liberal Rights: Collected Papers 1981–1991*. Cambridge: CUP.

WIGGINS, D (1998) *Needs, Values, Truth* (3rd edn). Oxford: Oxford University Press.

WILLIAMS, B (1981) *Obscenity and Film Censorship: An Abridgement of the Williams Report* (abridged ed). Cambridge: CUP.

---

[17] My thanks are owed to Roger Crisp, David Wiggins Dorothea Debus, and Andrew Simester for helpful comments on a previous draft.

7

Regulating Offensive Conduct through Two-Step Prohibitions

AP SIMESTER AND ANDREW VON HIRSCH

I. CONSTRAINING THE CRIMINAL LAW

I<small>N CONTRAST WITH</small> much of the rest of the legal system, the criminal law has a distinctively moral voice. Criminal prohibitions and sanctions convey censure: both *ex ante* of the proscribed activity, which is marked out as something that ought (as well as must) not be done, and *ex post*, through conviction and punishment of any individual who is found nonetheless to have perpetrated that activity. As such, the criminal law should, and generally does,[1] couch its prohibitions in a manner designed to engage with agents capable of moral deliberation.[2] It does not merely coerce; it also makes a moral appeal to citizens to desist. Its sanctions are not merely instrumental; they also express disapproval of the offender's wrongful conduct.

Given the criminal law's censuring character, and the potential severity of its sanctions, it is appropriate for the creation and implementation of criminal prohibitions to be subject to important safeguards. Some of these safeguards have constitutional status, and constrain the legislatures of particular jurisdictions. But all are, at the very least, norms to which any decent state should aspire. They include, without being limited to, the following:

(1) *Representative authority.* Prohibitions should be deliberated upon and adopted by a representative body. Where potentially significant sanctions are involved, this should be a high-level representative body, such as Parliament. Where the particular content of a prohibition is delegated to some lower-level body, any determination of that content should be directed and closely guided by the terms of the delegation.

(2) *Generality.* Prohibitions should be general in character: they may not single out the behaviour of particular persons for proscription.

(3) *Wrongful conduct.* The scope of prohibitions should be limited to certain kinds of wrongful conduct; for example, those activities satisfying

---

[1] But not always, for example in some cases of strict liability. See Simester, 2005.

[2] For discussion, see, eg, Duff, 2002; von Hirsch and Ashworth, 2005, ch 2.

a properly defined Harm Principle or Offence Principle (Feinberg, 1984, 1985; Simester and von Hirsch, 2002).

(4) *Culpability*. Further, the specification of prohibitions should include an appropriate culpability requirement. Usually, this criterion is addressed by specifying a need for *mens rea* and making the offence subject to an adequate range of exculpatory defences (e.g. Simester and Sullivan, 2003: chs 5, 16).

(5) *Fair warning*. Prohibitions should be specified in terms that are sufficiently clear and unambiguous, so that citizens have suitable advance guidance about the law's requirements (Simester and Sullivan, 2003: § 2.3).

(6) *Fair trial*. When a person is accused of violating criminal prohibitions, stringent procedural and evidential limitations must be observed, including high standards of proof, in order to ensure the integrity and fairness of the criminal justice process (e.g. Roberts and Zuckerman, 2004).

(7) *Proportionality*. Upon a finding of guilt, the determination of the resulting sanction should observe proportionality requirements regarding the relation between crime-seriousness and sanction-severity (von Hirsch and Ashworth, 2005: ch 9).

The foregoing demands play a crucial role in safeguarding the liberty of citizens, both in preserving freedom of lawful action and in ensuring that people are not undeservingly convicted and punished. But because they can make it difficult to impose sanctions on supposed wrongdoers, there has been a recent temptation to resort to *two-step prohibitions* (TSPs). These involve the issuance of (nominally) civil prohibitory orders against persons who have been found engaged in, or are expected to engage in, undesired conduct; where a breach of the order becomes a criminal offence. The content of the order can vary considerably: it may require the actor to cease and desist from further conduct of the same kind, or it may contain other substantive content, including access prohibitions designed to prevent him from entering certain places where he might engage in that kind of conduct or other conduct that is deemed undesirable. So, for example, the United Kingdom legislature has introduced the device of an Anti-Social Behaviour Order (ASBO).[3] In short, where D has been committing 'anti-social' acts, the local council or chief of police may apply to court for an ASBO regulating D's future behaviour. If D then contravenes the order, he commits an offence for which he may be imprisoned for up to five years.

II. THE NATURE OF TSPS

We shall consider the appropriate preconditions and content of TSPs in § III. But perhaps their most important feature is their structure. A standard instance of criminal wrongdoing has only one temporal location:

---

[3] Crime and Disorder Act 1998, s 1; Anti-Social Behaviour Act 2003.

t_{Std}: proscribed behaviour by D occurs, leading to criminal prosecution (predicated on proof of conduct at t_{Std}).

By contrast, the TSP mechanism operates on a three-incident timeline:

t_0: qualifying behaviour by D occurs;

t_1: TSP Order issued (predicated on proof of D's behaviour at t_0, but forward-looking);

t_2: conduct by D occurs in contravention of the TSP, leading to criminal prosecution for violation of the order (predicated on proof of conduct at t_2).

The order made at t_1 is, formally, a civil mechanism, but it is backed up by criminal sanctions. As such, the TSP supplies a means of bringing the criminal law into play (at t_2) in circumstances where obtaining a criminal conviction is difficult at t_1, either because prosecution is impractical, or because the anti-social behaviour at t_0 was not by itself an offence. Effectively, the TSP order (TSPO) supplies a criminal law bridge between t_0 and t_2. It connects the underlying behaviour at t_0, which supplies the original impetus for the state's intervention, to the possibility of prosecution at t_2.

1. Why the Desire for TSPs?

The temptation to deploy TSPs arises from two main practical problems relating to the use of traditional criminal-law prohibitions to regulate some varieties of offensive conduct. The first concerns difficulties of proof, especially in cases of harassment and intimidation. The rules of evidence pertaining to civil processes are less stringent than those governing criminal procedure—for example, they permit the adducing of hearsay. By introducing a system of civil regulatory orders, the legislature evades the procedural and evidential obstacles of using existing criminal law mechanisms to regulate certain forms of offensive conduct by individuals that can sometimes have the effect of intimidating into silence the victims who are potential witnesses.[4] Even where the conduct complained of at t_0 itself constitutes a criminal offence, the evidential constraints upon criminal trials may mean that, in practice, it cannot be prosecuted effectively. In such circumstances, the TSP mechanism means that the court can nonetheless

---

[4] See e.g., *Clingham* [2002] UKHL 39, paras 16–17 (Lord Steyn): 'Often people in the neighbourhood are in fear of such young culprits. In many cases, and probably in most, people will only report matters to the police anonymously or on the strict understanding that they will not directly or indirectly be identified.... Unfortunately, by intimidating people the culprits, usually small in number, sometimes effectively silenced communities. Fear of the consequences of complaining to the police dominated the thoughts of people: reporting incidents to the police entailed a serious risk of reprisals.'

make a civil order against D. In turn, D may be convicted if, at t_2, he breaches the terms of that order (where proof of that breach is subject to rules of criminal procedure and evidence in the normal way). The advantage to prosecutors is that the conduct prohibited by the personal order granted at t_1 may be different, and easier to observe and prove, than was the conduct originally complained of at t_0.

(We note, in passing, a partial response to this argument: that, if the difficulty is procedural, a better and less dramatic approach would be to look for a procedural solution, for example by rectifying difficulties in the laws of evidence concerning hearsay.[5] It may also be worthwhile to develop and improve community-based witness protection programmes, and to direct greater resources toward fostering a more vocal community, one better placed collectively to resist intimidation.[6] To the extent that these solutions are effective, they seem preferable to the much more radical and problematic device of the TSP.)

The second perceived difficulty is that the criminal law will obviously be unavailable where the initial conduct at t_0 is not itself a criminal offence. In this case, the impediment is not procedural but substantive. Moreover, it may not always be appropriate to criminalise the initial type of conduct directly. Sometimes, it is only repeated instances of an act (which is by itself lawful) that warrant prohibition where, in isolation, the act itself does not deserve to be criminalised. *In aggregate*, a series of minor evils may generate a significant harm to the quality of others' lives.

This possibility finds acknowledgement already in English criminal law. The Protection from Harassment Act 1997, for example, prohibits 'a course of conduct' that is calculated to harass or annoy others. Isolated wrongs, not by themselves crimes, will not do. In a different context, the common law offence of conspiracy to defraud proscribes conduct by two persons that, when done alone, is not illegal (Simester and Sullivan, 2003: § 15.3). Both of these offences are controversial, and it is no surprise to find that the ambit of criminal harassment lacks satisfactory definition.[7] It verges on the impossible to specify, in general terms, the factors in such cases that turn merely irritating conduct into a serious wrong. The TSP offers an alternative means to regulate such conduct. It can be used to bring within the criminal ambit a course of conduct where single instances thereof are not suitable for criminalisation; either because they are insufficiently serious wrongs in isolation, or because they are not by themselves wrongs at all,

---

[5] Described by Lord Steyn as 'inflexible and absurdly technical' in *Clingham, ibid*, para 18.

[6] It is also worth mentioning that there are specific offences of witness intimidation, in s 51 of the Criminal Justice and Public Order Act 1994 and ss 39–41 of the Criminal Justice and Police Act 2001 (the latter pertaining to civil cases).

[7] See e.g., Wells, 1997; Simester and Sullivan, 2003: § 11.8.

and become wrongs only when done repeatedly and for certain motives. Here, the TSPO offers a flexible—one might say, tailored—means to regulate ongoing courses of conduct without the need to prohibit every instance of that conduct, performed by anyone, *tout court*. As such, its use could even help to avoid overcriminalisation—provided it is used legitimately, and not in abrogation of the objections and limitations to be set out in § III.

2. The Dual Character of TSPs

The TSPO is designed to be, and is formally, a civil order—it is this very feature that allows TSPs to bypass constitutional limitations such as those governing standards of proof in criminal trials. But what sort of order is the TSPO *in substance*? Is it civil or criminal? This question affects not only the moral debates raised by the TSP mechanism, but also the extent to which the protections of the European Convention on Human Rights (ECHR) are available against TSPOs since, from the point of view of the protections contained in the ECHR, domestic law's designation of the proceedings as 'civil' is not dispositive of the matter.

It seems clear that the issuance of a TSPO at t_1 is not *formally* a finding of criminality or a criminal disposal. There is no conviction or formal condemnation of the sort that the criminal law involves.[8] Neither is there anything of the criminal-record consequences that a conviction imports. As the House of Lords observed of one such order in *Clingham*, 'the purpose of the procedure is to impose a prohibition, not a penalty'.[9] The possibility of criminal sanctions such as conviction and imprisonment arises only in respect of *future* conduct, not in respect of the conduct that gave rise to the TSPO. By way of elucidating this point, their Lordships drew a distinction between the making of a TSPO and the disposition, considered in *Steel v UK*,[10] of imprisonment for refusing to be bound over. Of the latter mechanism, Lord Steyn noted that 'there was an immediate and obvious criminal consequence'—imprisonment—to be imposed in respect of a past wrong, not (unlike the TSPO) for a future wrong. Thus the disposition complained of in *Steel* is, in substance, punitive and criminal rather than civil. At t_1, the TSPO is not the same.

To this extent, then, making a TSPO is not intrinsically a criminal process or disposal. It lacks most, if not all, of the core features of the

---

[8] Compare, in *Clingham* [2002] UKHL 39, paras 28ff, the discussion of the three categorising criteria laid down in *Engels v The Netherlands (No 1)* (1976) 1 EHRR 647, 678–9, para 82: (a) domestic classification; (b) nature of the offence; (c) the severity of the potential penalty.

[9] *Clingham* [2002] UKHL 39, para 68.

[10] (1998) 28 EHRR 603, 636, paras 48–49. See *Clingham* [2002] UKHL 39, paras 32 (Lord Steyn), 107f (Lord Hutton).

criminal verdict. Rather, it is a form of *criminalisation*: an *ex ante* criminal prohibition, not an *ex post* criminal verdict. The TSPO makes it a crime to do Y in the future (at t_2), not a crime to have done X in the past (at t_0). Hence, as we shall see, many of the fundamental concerns about the TSPO arise over its operation as a technique of criminalisation.

That having been said, the issuance of a TSPO may itself have a quasi-punitive effect.[11] The personal order at t_1 is capable of operating as a sanction that is *effectively* like penal hard treatment, even if it lacks the formal element of censure associated with a criminal sentence. The form of a TSPO may be not merely a cease-and-desist order (indeed, it is often not of that form) but rather may be an exclusion order or the like. Hence, in *Clingham* itself, one set of appellants had been barred from the suburb that, until recently, had been their home. Being expelled is a very serious matter: the purpose is preventative, but the State's act is both backward-looking, in that it responds to conduct at t_0, and a significant restriction of D's liberty. It is an unwelcome imposition—something akin to penal hard treatment—that sets back D's interests. Lord Hope may have been right to state that 'the *purpose* of the procedure is to impose a prohibition, not a penalty'.[12] But one *effect* of the TSPO can be, and frequently is, to inflict something as onerous as a penalty.

There are, then, two core functions of the two-step mechanism. First, it criminalises *ex ante* at t_1 the conduct specified in the personal order. Secondly, it may have the effect of imposing a deprivation upon D at t_1, predicated *ex post* on D's conduct at t_0. As we shall see, those deprivations may be severe and may not be constrained by requirements of proportionality. The restrictions imposed at t_1 can effectively be, and frequently are, sanctions for the underlying conduct at t_0 to which it responds.

III. BYPASSING CONSTRAINTS, AND THE POTENTIAL FOR MISUSE

We turn now to consider the safeguards that may be lost through the use of TSPOs. As a penalising sanction for conduct at t_0, the personal order potentially sacrifices such in-principle constraints as the requirement to give fair warning and the need for proportionality. As an act of criminalisation at t_1

---

[11] This point is raised by Ashworth *et al* (1998). On reflection, however, it may be not be entirely accurate to assert (*ibid*, n 4), that 'an ASBO effectively criminalises those against whom it is issued'.

[12] *Clingham* [2002] UKHL 39, para 68. Contrast the phrasing by Lord Steyn (*ibid*, para 30): 'Here the position is that the order itself *involves* no penalty.' (Emphasis added in both quotations.)

(via the content of the TSPO), it ought to be subject to constitutional and other rule of law constraints that govern the legitimate criminal prohibition of behaviour by citizens. These constraints should set tight limits on the legitimacy of any two-step mechanism—limits that are, in practice, bypassed.

1. Fair Trial

Because TSPOs are designed to be civil orders, they are said to be exempt from many of the rules applicable to criminal processes. For example, there may be no requirement of a personal appearance, by either the defendant or a complainant. Moreover, the evidential rules governing proceedings at t_1 are those of the civil law—hence, as we noted earlier, hearsay becomes acceptable.[13] Indeed, this is part of the point.

Why is this potentially problematic? Most of us agree that deprivations and sanctions in the civil law may justifiably be imposed without always demanding the procedural safeguards found in the criminal law. In what way, then, does the TSPO go beyond the ordinary realm of civil law judgments?

The difficulty lies in the range of rights and liberties of which the defendant can be deprived. Even though TSPOs lack the safeguards to which criminal prohibitions are subject, the restrictions imposed by such orders may be no less severe than the sanctions applicable to ordinary criminal prohibitions. In a civil case, following proof under civil rules, a defendant may face deprivation of property rights and, on occasion, an injunction not to commit a specific legal wrong or to perform a specific obligation. But the range of the TSPO may be much greater, including exclusionary orders that deprive D of access to geographical areas and public space. In such cases, as we suggested in § II.2, the substance of the order, which is driven by retrospective considerations, can be comparable in onerousness to a criminal punishment. At least where the order involves a substantial curtailment of liberty, it seems to us that the civil methods of proof required for issuance of the order at t_1 are inadequate.

2. Representative Authority

Being the product of a civil hearing, the prohibition contained in the TSPO is generally issued by a first-instance judge, such as a magistrate, rather than

---

[13] *Clingham* [2002] UKHL 39 (ASBO proceedings at t_1 subject to civil rules of evidence and procedure, notwithstanding that the *standard* of proof required was, in effect, the higher standard required in the criminal law); above, § II.1.

by a legislative body such as Parliament. Since the TSPO operates as an act of criminalisation,[14] this raises a separation of powers issue: it is no longer appropriate in modern law for the judiciary to create offences.

Admittedly, the TSP process must be initiated by an *applicant*, typically a lower-level administrative official.[15] But even then, the concern remains that this effectively delegates powers of criminalisation too far, unless the legislation includes detailed guidance and constraints concerning the appropriate content of TSPO orders. To some extent, this is a straightforward rule-of-law objection: the lives of individual citizens are not governed by promulgated general law, but rather are exposed to the discretionary initiatives of local officials. While it is an inevitable feature of law that its rules must on occasion be given a more particular content, for example through detailed court orders, the rule of law requires that those orders be shaped and guided, as closely as possible, by more general legislation (Raz, 1977: 199–200). Only then can citizens plan their lives in reliance upon stable, promulgated, and predictable law.

Beyond these considerations, however, a requirement of representative authority more directly implicates norms of democracy. A delegated criminalisation technique such as the TSP leaves citizens with reduced opportunities to voice objections, through their representatives, concerning the losses of liberty involved. Because they involve decisions that very significantly affect the personal freedoms of citizens, criminal prohibitions ought to be imposed by a representative body—a body that is directly answerable to the citizens it regulates—rather than (say) by administrative or judicial officials. Not only does this ensure that important decision are appropriately vested in the democratic polity, it also helps to keep them visible, thereby maximising the opportunities for public debate about the merit or otherwise of each prohibition.

It is true that regulatory powers are often delegated in other contexts, for example to health and safety regulatory agencies, and the like. But the operation of those agencies is itself under the rule of law: typically, those agencies are fettered by regulatory frameworks and administrative law rules. No such constraints apply to the TSPO. This difficulty is compounded because, unlike the enforcement activities of regulatory bodies—which are confined to particular, directed and specialised activities—the TSPO framework need not be confined to any specific context or type of activity. Hence, individuals do not have the option of taking themselves outside the scope of the criminalisation process by refraining from the relevant specialist activity, an option that they normally have in other regulatory contexts.

---

[14] Above, § II.2.
[15] Under the English ASBO legislation, the initiator is normally a local authority official or the local chief of police.

One incidental upshot of all this is that it can become possible to use the TSPO to derogate from the decisions of Parliament by prohibiting specific, personal instances of activities that are otherwise generally permitted: for example, insulting behaviour, or sexual promiscuity not amounting to criminally proscribed prostitution. Potentially, the TSPOS could even prohibit Xing by D where a criminal prohibition of Xing had actually been considered but not implemented by Parliament.[16]

3. Generality

Another objection to criminalisation through TSPs is that the prohibition is *in personam*, rather than being couched in general terms. This might loosely be termed a Bill-of-Attainder objection: criminalisation should not be personal. Convictions are personal: prohibitions are not. They are, and should be, rules of general application, that govern everyone—or, as a minimum, everyone falling within the relevant class affected by the rationale behind the rule. It is a constitutional, rule-of-law value that everyone is equal before the law. But the TSPO is a form of *ad hominem* criminalisation: it declares, in effect, that everyone else may do X, but D in particular may not.

Bills of Attainder are rightly declared illegitimate by the US Constitution.[17] This is for a complex variety of reasons—very often, Bills of Attainder impose penalties that bypass the need for a trial and conviction, something the TSP process does not do. Nonetheless, the TSPO shares with Bills of Attainder the repugnant feature that it singles out individuals and restricts their liberties, thereby differentiating them from the rest of society *ex ante*. In effect, it creates one rule for D, and another for everyone else.

The point is one of equality. Apart from certain categorical exceptions, such as children,[18] the members of a modern democracy are—and have a right to be—treated as having equal standing in the community. We no longer segregate citizens into distinct legal and political classes (women, serfs, slaves, etc), but recognise that everyone is equal before the law. This means both that each person has an equal right to participate in the democratic process and, conversely, that the law does not discriminate between individuals. Citizens thereby have a shared responsibility for the law: they are both its authors, through representatives answerable to them, and the joint subjects of its governance. The TSP, by contrast, abandons reciprocity in favour of burdening individual targets.

---

[16] This has in fact occurred: below, § V.

[17] Article 1, Section 9, Paragraph 3; together with retrospective laws.

[18] Even then, the distinction is drawn contextually and not for all purposes; and members of such categories are to be treated even-handedly within the category.

At a practical level, this technique also means that otherwise unwelcome prohibitions can more easily be targeted at the unpopular (the so-called 'anti-social') within a society. Thus conduct which many persons are free to do may become prohibited for such 'undesirable' persons, with all the discriminatory potential that this involves. Doing so tends, moreover, to make such prohibitions easier to adopt, since limiting prohibitions to unpopular individuals or groups can render it more difficult to generate effective opposition to their adoption.[19]

4. Criminalisation

Once the making of an TSPO at t_1 is understood as (*inter alia*) an act of delegated criminalisation, certain related constraints become apparent, constraints that are misleadingly obscured by its status as a civil order. Criminalisation restricts liberties—it is meant to. I am not free to discharge my shotgun in your direction, because doing so might interfere with your health. No doubt that is an acceptable restriction. But because it restricts liberty, there are good reasons why legislators should be parsimonious about criminalising conduct.[20] These reasons are in play whenever a freedom is withdrawn. They are especially powerful considerations with TSPs because, in effect, TSPOs can—and frequently do—operate as a form of pre-emptive regulation, for example by excluding D from a public space.

One difficulty with a pre-emptive prohibition is its remoteness from the prospective behaviour by which it is motivated. Depending on its content, a TSPO might prohibit behaviour that is legitimate in itself, such as entering a certain area, merely by virtue of an ostensible risk that the actor might subsequently choose while there to perpetrate undesired conduct. As von Hirsch (1996) has argued, pre-emptive prohibitions raise concerns of fair imputation, about the extent to which that prospective further wrongdoing provides a reason why D's current conduct, which is itself innocent, should be the subject of a proscription backed up by criminal sanctions.

The concerns about pre-emptive regulation are particularly strong when the technique used is one of exclusion. Prohibitions of this sort deny the moral agency of the defendant, by refusing to recognise her as a morally

---

[19] Compare the well-known commentary upon the Holocaust by Martin Niemöller: 'First they came for the Communists, and I didn't speak up because I wasn't a Communist. Then they came for the Jews, and I didn't speak up because I wasn't a Jew. Then they came for the trade unionists, and I didn't speak up because I wasn't a trade unionist. Then they came for the Catholics, and I didn't speak up because I was a Protestant. Then they came for me—and by that time no one was left to speak up.'

[20] Cf the liberal commitment to the Harm Principle, e.g. in Feinberg, 1984.

responsible human being and participant in society—D is not given the opportunity to behave responsibly in public. Once D is found to have engaged in the conduct at t_0, triggering issuance of the order, she no longer has free access to public spaces. Thenceforth, her decision to refrain from committing criminal offences—and even to refrain from committing conduct of the type that gave rise to the order (if that was non-criminal)—becomes immaterial. She is simply excluded from those spaces, irrespective of what her choices would have been had she been permitted access.[21]

This denial of access to public space also raises problems of identity and self-definition. For most of us, our lives involve, and are in part defined by, the interaction and relationships we have with other members of our society. It is through such interaction that a person's membership of her society is affirmed, in the eyes both of the person herself and of the rest of society.[22] The ability to interact depends, in turn, on access to public space; thus exclusion tends not only to preclude the particular undesired conduct that lies behind the TSPO, and the way of life to which that act gives expression, but also to undermine D's participation in the society itself; and, ultimately, to undermine D's identity as a human being.

5. Quasi-Criminalisation at t_0

It may seem plausible to respond to the foregoing concern (in § III.4) by highlighting the fact that D becomes subject to a TSPO only if she has perpetrated the qualifying conduct at t_0. In England, for example, the TSP mechanism is engaged only if it is shown that D has done something 'anti-social'.[23] But to the extent that D's conduct at t_0 is relied upon to justify the imposition of onerous and quasi-punitive sanctions such as an exclusion order, the specification of qualifying conduct itself counts as a form of quasi-criminalisation. (And, as we suggested in § III.1, proving that conduct at trial should be governed by criminal rules.) Suppose that øing is prescribed as qualifying conduct, proof of which makes it legitimate to issue a TSPO. In effect, while persons who ø will not immediately receive a criminal conviction, the State announces *ex ante* that such persons will be directly subject to sanctions (at t_1), and will thereafter become liable to criminal dispositions.

As such, the specification of øing itself should be constrained by principles such as the Offence Principle. But, because TSPs are frequently designed to regulate conduct that is problematic only when repeated or

---

[21] A fuller discussion of this argument is found in von Hirsch and Shearing, 2000.

[22] See generally Raz, 1995.

[23] Crime and Disorder Act 1998, s 1.

sustained,[24] the criteria under which a TSPO is available will tend to include behaviour at t_0 that is not by itself either wrong or offensive or harmful, and which need not be a criminal offence. The use of a TSPO in such contexts is reminiscent of Ellickson's proposal (1996: 1185) that 'chronic street nuisances' may be excluded from areas of a city's public space, through techniques of property-law zoning; where persons are regarded as chronic street nuisances if they:

> Persistently act in a public space in a manner that violates prevailing community standards of behavior, to the significant cumulative annoyance of persons of ordinary sensibility who use the same spaces.

Indeed, in England the ASBO criteria go further than Ellickson's, in that the behaviour complained of need not in fact cause any distress; it is sufficient that it be 'likely' so to do.[25] They go further, too, than Feinberg's (1985) criteria for the criminalisation of offence.[26] Feinberg required that the affront caused to others by D's behaviour be both grave and predictably widespread across the community; whereas the criteria laid down in the ASBO legislation are satisfied if affront is caused merely to one individual.

This concern must be dissected. It is not inherently objectionable that the qualifying behaviour at t_0 need not actually cause harm or offence. The criminal law frequently prohibits behaviour (e.g. drunk driving, speeding, and the like) without requiring that the behaviour must be harmful *per se*. Indeed, this is generally true of what might be termed 'inchoate' offences; speeding, for example, is rightly proscribed on the ground of its characteristic riskiness: that it is generally *likely* to cause harm. *Per se* harmless or offensive actions may come within the scope of the Harm or Offence Principles where they *standardly* create a risk of harm or offence, even if not in every instance. The justification for criminalising these cases is, in part, practical—it is simply uneconomic to frame and administer laws other than with regard to the standard cases. Even exceptionally able drivers must drive at a speed set with reference to their less competent counterparts.

Further, there may also be nothing intrinsically wrong in using TSPOs to prohibit behaviour that, when viewed in isolation, is not a criminal offence. *Ongoing* anti-social behaviour, at its worst, can significantly affect the lives of other persons—even where any one instance is, by itself, a lawful and relatively trivial matter—because it can degrade the quality of life in common public space. It may be that such harm is not a 'direct' and immediate consequence of the anti-social behaviour, but that is not a requirement of the

---

[24] Above, § II.1.
[25] Below, § V.
[26] For discussion, see von Hirsch and Simester, this volume.

Harm Principle—which is quite capable, in appropriate cases, of extending to indirect harms.

Rather, the deeper concern about the preconditions for issuing an TSPO is the requirement that D's behaviour at t_0 be a wrong—again, something obscured by the fact that the TSPO is formally civil. In practice, this requirement is characteristically abrogated by TSP legislation. In England, for instance, the definition of qualifying 'anti-social' behaviour is expressed purely in terms of the reactions of the audience: conduct done 'in a manner that caused or was likely to cause harassment, alarm or distress to one or more persons not of the same household'.[27] As such, it exposes D to the risk that his unconventional behaviour, which wrongs no-one, may lead to a personal order purely because it causes, or is likely to cause, distress or alarm in others—whether or not that distress is appropriate or justified. Suppose, for example, that there were a convention in some locality that persons of different races should not have any physical contact in public.[28] If an interracial couple hold hands in the park, they may cause widespread distress amongst others in the park; but it does not follow that behaviour such as this should be prohibited.

In our view, to the extent that the order made at t_1 has the effect of a sanction, by imposing deprivations on D, that order ought as a minimum to be predicated on a wrong. Indeed, this requirement very often applies to civil as well as criminal law. Sanctions in tort ordinarily are imposed only upon proof of a wrong by D—there must be an infliction of personal or property damage, in violation of P's rights, or a failure by D to perform as promised. Like remedies in tort, the personal order mechanism singles D out for *in personam* deprivations. While it need not, as a conceptual requirement, do so on the basis of a criminal offence, the civil order that it constitutes should nonetheless be predicated on a wrong.[29]

---

[27] Crime and Disorder Act 1998, s 1(1)(a).

[28] Cf the discussion in Simester and von Hirsch, 2002: 278–9.

[29] In the particular case of the English ASBO legislation, the possibility of an order being issued following behaviour that is not wrongful is somewhat ameliorated by s 1(5) of the Crime And Disorder Act 1998: 'For the purpose of determining whether the condition mentioned in subsection (1)(a) above is fulfilled, the court shall disregard any act of the defendant which he shows was reasonable in the circumstances.' The objection is therefore weakened in respect of the ASBO itself, in so far as s 1(5) introduces a normative element into the criteria for anti-social behaviour established in s 1(1)(a). Nonetheless, it retains considerable force, in that behaviour may be unreasonable (for example, in virtue of being immoral) without it following that the behaviour wrongs anyone. Suppose that D decides to harm himself. His behaviour, in principle, may be unreasonable and distressing to others; but it is not therefore a wrong to anyone else. Still less does it follow that behaviour is a wrong from D's failure to show that it is reasonable: it is not clear why the onus of proof should rest on D to establish the reasonableness of his behaviour. Yet a woman who repeatedly attempted suicide by throwing herself into the River Avon was served with an ASBO prohibiting her from jumping into rivers or canals: 'A Triumph of Hearsay and Hysteria', *The Guardian*, 5 April 2005, 20.

6. Fair Warning

Like any sanction, as well as being predicated on a wrong, the potential for hard treatment at t_1 should be notified clearly in advance. This constraint demands that the qualifying conduct at t_0 be defined in terms that are sufficiently specific to give citizens an adequate opportunity of shaping their behaviour to avoid running foul of the law and incurring a TSPO. However, the use of TSP mechanisms to regulate conduct that is not in isolation suitable for criminalisation (above, § II.1) tends to lead to the legislative description of qualifying conduct being vague and unspecific. In England, for example, the criteria for issuing an ASBO are defined in very loose and sweeping terms. Anti-social behaviour is conduct performed 'in a manner that caused or was likely to cause harassment, alarm or distress to one or more persons not of the same household'. This open-endedness is intended as a positive feature, since it allows for flexibility in the availability of an order; but it is also a serious drawback, in so far as very little is offered by way of guidance to defendants about what behaviour may incur an order. As such, the statute gives inadequate advance warning to D about the potential legal consequences of her behaviour.

Strictly speaking, the objection here is not that the preconditions of the TSPO violate the principle of *legality*, since that principle applies paradigmatically to criminal rather than civil law; and the issuance of a TSPO does not itself constitute a criminal conviction. Moreover, once criminal processes are invoked at t_2, *ex post* the order, there typically *is* good guidance: the terms of the order itself are usually clear and unequivocal.

Rather, the objection is that citizens are also entitled to adequate advance notice before their behaviour incurs substantial civil sanctions. People need to know the legal consequences of their actions, civil as well as criminal, if they are to be able to plan their lives with confidence. It may be that this is a less pressing requirement than it is in the criminal law, where sanctions are accompanied by convictions and official censure that the personal order mechanism lacks. Nonetheless, to the extent that the terms of a TSPO go beyond a mere cease-and-desist order enjoining behaviour that is already a criminal wrong, the personal order imposes a deprivation on the defendant that he ought to have a prior opportunity to avoid. The more serious the deprivation, of course, the more important it becomes that this opportunity is made available. Since deprivations of any sort can have a considerable impact upon the well-being of and choices available to individuals, the power to impose them always raises issues of the rule of law. If the rule of law is to be observed, persons subject to State deprivations should be dealt with in accordance with determinate and knowable law (Hayek, 1944: 72; compare Fallon, 1997: 8):

> Stripped of all its technicalities, [the rule of law] means that government in all its
> actions is bound by rules fixed and announced beforehand—rules which make it

possible to foresee with fair certainty how the authority will use its coercive powers in given circumstances and to plan one's individual affairs on the basis of this knowledge.

This means not only that the content of a personal order should be determined in accordance with law, but that the basis of one's exposure to that order should be knowable in advance and not *ex post*. Knowing where we stand augments the ability of citizens to live autonomous lives—indeed, the possibility of being guided by the State's rules is foundational to our capacity as individuals to make decisions. As Raz (1979: 214) puts it, '[t]his is the basic intuition from which the doctrine of the rule of law derives: the law must be capable of guiding the behaviour of its subjects' (cf Schauer, 1991: 137–8.) It may be that more precise specification of the criteria at t_0 will allow certain forms of miscreancy. But incomplete regulation is sometimes the right price to pay for the rule of law.

7. Culpability

There is no reason why *mens rea* safeguards should be diluted in TSPOs. However, by virtue of the formally civil character of the prohibition, there is a tendency to neglect this essential aspect of criminal liability. By contrast with the criminal law, civil prohibitions lack an expectation of *mens rea*, and there need be nothing problematic about no-fault liability in tort for products or high-risk activities.[30] As such, the TSP framework seemingly eliminates the need for *mens rea*—thus the criminal sanctions for violating an ASBO, for example, do not presuppose knowing infringement of the order.[31] *Mens rea* should, however, remain a requirement of any TSPO; moreover, criminal-law defences such as self-defence and necessity should be available, in the normal way, for their breach.

8. Proportionality at t_1

Requirements of proportionality tend to be attenuated by the TSP process in two ways. First, understood as a response to conduct at t_0, the hardships imposed at t_1 by the TSPO are not limited by significant proportionality constraints, because of its nominal status as a civil rather than criminal order.[32] Secondly, even the criminal disposal following conduct at t_2 may become disproportionate, since the criminal conviction at that point is

---

[30] As in *Rylands v Fletcher* (1868) LR 3 HL 330.
[31] Crime and Disorder Act 1998, s 1(10).

driven by the fact of D's violating the TSPO, rather than by the wrongness of D's conduct *per se*.

Beginning with the first concern, it seems to us that the scope and intrusiveness of the order at t_1 should bear a reasonable relationship to the seriousness of the wrongdoing that D is proved to have done at t_0. It should, in other words, be deserved as well as useful.[33] Otherwise, the intermediate use of TSPOs to enforce existing criminal laws opens up the possibility, for example, that the constraints imposed in the order may run for a very lengthy period (say, ten years) in circumstances where the maximum permissible penalty under the criminal law for D's underlying behaviour at t_0 is much less (say, a few months' imprisonment or even a fine).

Additionally, the harshness of the burden imposed by the order ought to be subject to a ceiling, if the order is to be made pursuant to civil procedures. Suppose that D is alleged to have committed a serious criminal wrong, justifying a sentence that imposes substantial restrictions on D's freedom of movement.[34] Such a sentence ought to be imposed only upon proof, to a criminal standard, of D's wrongdoing. Moreover, we take it that this standard should not be evaded by the device of removing the formal element of the criminal conviction from the process; by establishing a non-criminal exclusions regime within the civil law. An imposition of this gravity is a significant deprivation. Its very onerousness demands that it be imposed only subject to adequate fairness constraints, including those of proportionality. In our view, lengthy exclusion orders from suburbs and town centres in which D resides are sufficiently onerous penalties to warrant similar demands.

Also problematic is the possibility, seen in the English legislation, that the content of the order at t_1 need only be necessary to prevent 'further' anti-social acts;[35] it need not be confined to preventing the same variety of acts that are alleged already to have occurred. This strikes us as problematic: it exposes D to deprivations that in no way respond to past wrongdoing.

9. Proportionality at t_2

The second proportionality concern arises in respect of the criminal sanction that is imposed ultimately for violating the TSPO. Like the sanctions for contempt of court, criminal dispositions in such cases are *prima facie*

---

[32] The importance of proportionality in civil law is further discussed in von Hirsch and Wasik, 1997: esp 612–15.

[33] Or, in the language of the ASBO, 'necessary': below, § V.

[34] Such restrictions need not involve imprisonment: they include, for example, lengthy probation terms with strict conditions that restrict access to public space.

[35] Crime and Disorder Act 1998, s 1(6).

concerned with the fact of breach of the order at t_2, and purportedly unconcerned with the actual nature of the contravening behaviour. Punishment is therefore, at least potentially, underpinned by an authoritarian defiance-rationale, and not by a desert rationale. (Hence punishment for violating an ASBO in English law may involve a prison sentence of up to five years' duration, even where the underlying criminal wrong is not imprisonable, or is imprisonable for a lesser maximum.) This also seems wrong to us. Punishment ought, in principle, to be determined primarily by reference to the gravity and wrongfulness of D's actual conduct at t_2, not by reference to the fact *per se* that it is has been prohibited by the order. Otherwise, the TSPO will be operating *in terrorem*: D is directed to desist from certain behaviour, wrongful or not; and is threatened with unpleasant consequences whose severity depends merely on the fact of disobedience. The scheme becomes, in Hegel's terms, a stick raised to a dog.[36]

IV. USING TSPS IN SPECIALIST CONTEXTS: THE ACP

The constraints described in § III militate strongly against a wide use of two-step TSPs to help prevent harmful or offensive conduct. More generally, the use of civil mechanisms to enforce criminal law also risks undermining the moral authority of the criminal law as an institution, through weakening the paradigm distinction between criminal and civil laws, and the association of the former with condemnation of culpable wrongdoing. Blurring the difference between criminal and civil laws risks loss of clarity of the criminal law's distinctively moral voice.

Despite this, certain more limited two-step schemes do seem to be permissible as ancillary civil prohibitions (ACPs). These schemes operate in aid of particular regulatory or licencing schemes, or as a means for enforcing certain civil causes of action. Examples are disqualifications from certain professions following conviction or determination of professional misconduct; anti-molestation orders; and tree-preservation orders.

ACPs also tend to lack the safeguards of the criminal law listed in § 1. For example, the prohibitory order may normally be imposed by a lower-level administrative or judicial official, rather than a representative body, and it may be aimed at a particular individual without being general in application. Why, then, are ACPs generally regarded as acceptable? The answer seems to lie in the limited and ancillary character of the regulatory scheme. There is no generalised discretion to issue prohibitory orders. Legitimate ACPs are curtailed in two important respects.

---

[36] For discussion of why defiance of authority *per se* should not be a basis for measuring the severity of criminal punishment, see von Hirsch and Ashworth, 2005: 149–50.

The first limitation concerns the narrowing of the range of behaviour that may trigger an ACP. ACP schemes operate only within specifically delimited areas of behaviour. A professional disqualification, for example, may issue only for persons engaged in certain regulated and licensed professions, who have engaged in particular kinds of malpractice (cf von Hirsch and Wasik, 1997). If one does not wish to be exposed to this kind of disqualification risk, one can engage in other, less regulated kinds of work. An anti-molestation order may issue only if the actor repeatedly harasses a particular person. A tree preservation order may affect only those who own land on which certain kinds of trees grow. If I choose to live in a flat—or live in a house but have no such trees in my garden—I need not worry about being affected.

The second limitation concerns the restricted variety of conduct that may be barred by an ACP order. In ACPs, the prohibitory order should relate only to specified limited types of activity, such as continuing to practice as a solicitor after disbarment; approaching a particular individual whom the actor has harassed before; or sawing off the limb of a tree that is protected by a preservation order. No general good-conduct requirement may justify issuance of an ACP; and the order may involve no general diminution of civil rights.

Provided these limitations are observed, the ancillary character of ACP regimes is crucial to their acceptability: they operate specifically in aid of particular regulatory or licensing schemes (in which case their content and form tends to be tightly confined); or as means of enforcing certain civil causes of action; or they enjoin instances of conduct that is already (and more generally) a legal wrong. It is essential, we think, that administrative and judicial officials do not have a generalised discretion to issue orders prohibiting citizens from engaging in conduct at large, and which is not already a legal wrong. No country respecting personal liberty ought to enact a scheme that gives officials a generalised discretion to prohibit conduct.

V. ASSESSING THE ENGLISH ASBO LEGISLATION

The foregoing analysis permits us to deal with the ASBO legislation straightforwardly.[37] The ASBO is not sustainable as a legitimate ACP, because of the wide ambit of the kinds of conduct that may trigger issuance of an order, and because of the broad range of conduct that may be prohibited by the order itself. Indeed, the ASBO confers an enormous discretion

---

[37] For recent concerns expressed by the European Commissioner for Human Rights, see Gil-Robles, 2005: paras 108ff.

to prohibit undesired behaviour, since the triggering conduct includes anything causing, or likely to cause, 'distress' to another,[38] and the order itself may contain prohibitions of almost unlimited scope, constrained only by the requirement that they be 'necessary for the purpose of protecting other persons from further anti-social acts by the defendant'.[39] There is no legislative requirement of proportionality.[40] The order at t_1 can include, for example, a curfew or an exclusion from an area (estate, suburb, shopping mall; even one's home). Moreover, the order can be for an indefinite period and in any event must last for a minimum of two years.

The legislation thus creates the power to issue prohibitions at t_1 of behaviour that is not otherwise criminally proscribed, and which may be harmless (or which, in the case of access prohibitions, merely provides an occasion for subsequent criminal or offensive conduct). Neither the triggering conduct, nor the prohibitory response, need satisfy the Harm Principle or Offence Principle. Moreover, the prohibition shares other problematic features of TSPOs generally, in that it operates *in personam* rather than as a generally applicable prohibition and is issued by low-level officials rather than a representative legislative body. As such, the ASBO bypasses public deliberative processes.

The practical import of this last point is illustrated in three areas of criminal law reform: decriminalisation of self-destructive behaviour such as attempted suicide; exemption from criminal liability of mentally disabled individuals; and the partial decriminalisation of prostitution, including elimination of imprisonment for offences of solicitation. Each of these reforms was achieved after extended public discussion and parliamentary debate. The ASBO device, however, has permitted *de facto* disregard of these reforms, with virtually no discussion. ASBOs have been issued against individuals attempting suicide;[41] against autistic youths;[42] and against prostitutes.[43] Infringement of ASBO directives in these cases will expose the defendant to criminal conviction and imprisonment. No doubt, had comparable proscriptions been proposed as general amendments to the criminal

---

[38] *Per* Crime and Disorder Act 1998, s.1(1)(a), the triggering conduct ('anti-social behaviour') is anything done 'in a manner that caused or was likely to cause harassment, alarm or distress to one or more persons not of the same household'. This extremely broad test is ameliorated somewhat, but only somewhat, by the enactment of a defence in s 1(5): 'For the purpose of determining whether the condition mentioned in subsection (1)(a) above is fulfilled, the court shall disregard any act of the defendant which he shows was reasonable in the circumstances.' See also n 29 above.

[39] Crime and Disorder Act 1998, s 1(6).

[40] Home Office guidance on the form of the order nonetheless suggests that proposed prohibitions should be 'reasonable and proportionate'. Home Office, 2000: § 13.5.

[41] Above, n 29.

[42] 'Children with Autism the Target of ASBOs', *Observer*, 22 May 2005, 7.

[43] 'ASBOs "are bringing back jail for prostitutes"', *The Guardian*, 25 May 2005, 7.

law, strong objections of principle would have been raised—and the chances of their approval would be far from clear.

Might the ASBO scheme fare better if the triggering conduct were limited to behaviour proscribed by the criminal law? This would still not make it a legitimate ACP scheme. Granted, the triggering behaviour would then have to be behaviour that has been adjudged wrongful by a representative body. But the scope of the order's prohibitions would still remain virtually unlimited. This would mean that a very wide swathe of conduct—including access to much public space—could be proscribed *in personam* by unelected decision-makers, without any of the other essential safeguards described in § I being in place. Moreover, the sanctions for violation need not observe proportionality constraints with respect to the underlying wrong. While this might be tolerable for legitimate ACPs of limited scope, it should not occur in broader TSP schemes. For example, the scheme might still result in the issuing of an order prohibiting someone from soliciting (or entering any area where he or she might be inclined to solicit), a minor form of offence, and yet lead to a long period of confinement for violations.

By contrast with legitimate ACP regimes, the ASBO exposes citizens to a general discretion of officials. The potential area of coverage of the ASBO is unduly wide, both because the initial conduct requirement at t_0 is sweepingly defined and because the constraints on the content of the prohibition at t_1 are so minimal.

VI. CONCLUSION

In this chapter we have identified a variety of problems with the two-step personal order mechanism. Our concerns include, *inter alia*, the breadth and imprecision of the triggering criteria at t_0; the untrammelled range of the order that may be made at t_1, with its potential effectively to impose substantial restrictions of liberty; the requirement only for civil process at t_1, bypassing criminal standards of protection for the defendant's rights; and the potential for punishment at t_2 based on rationales of defiance rather than the wrongfulness of the underlying conduct.

At a generic level, the problem with TSPs is their intermediate character. The TSPO falls between criminal and civil stools and, as such, imports inadequate safeguards. The main problems are twofold. The first difficulty is that a TSPO has the potential to visit significant deprivations without adequate notice and procedural protections. The issuing of a TSPO at t_1 can, without more, impose severe deprivations without observing the protections that are and should be demanded by criminal law. The second difficulty is one of criminalisation; especially, in violation of the rule of law. TSPOs are an inappropriate means of delegating and personalising the legislative powers to prohibit behaviour by citizens. In our view, the TSPO poses foundational challenges to the preservation of rights and freedoms within a free society.

Some of these objections apply even if the TSPO is deployed only to regulate conduct that is already an offence under existing criminal law. But the personal order comes into its own, and becomes a more dangerous threat to the rights of citizens, when used to regulate more nondescript unwelcome behaviour that is not itself prohibited as an offence.

What alternative versions of a two-step scheme might, nonetheless, be legitimate? Our thoughts on this are tentative, but some implications might be drawn for such schemes from the discussions in §§ III and IV. First, two-step schemes cannot be sustainable as proper forms of criminal prohibition—because the order issued is not made by a representative body and is targeted at particular persons. If sustainable at all, therefore, they would have to be akin to ancillary civil prohibitions. But in that case, their scope must be substantially restricted, with respect to both the kind of conduct that may trigger an order, and the scope of that order. Moreover, the schemes need also to observe the various constraints, such as proportionality and fair warning, that were noted in § III.

REFERENCES

ASHWORTH, A *et al* (1998) 'Neighbouring on the Oppressive: The Government's "Anti-Social Behaviour Order" Proposals' *Criminal Justice* 16(1):7.

DUFF, RA (2002) 'Rule-violations and Wrongdoings', in SC SHUTE and AP SIMESTER (eds), *Criminal Law Theory: Doctrines of the General Part*. Oxford: Oxford University Press.

ELLICKSON, RC (1996) 'Controlling Chronic Misconduct in City Spaces: of Panhandlers, Skid Rows, and Public Space Zoning' *Yale Law Review* 105: 1165.

FALLON, RH (1997) 'The "Rule of Law" as a Concept in Constitutional Discourse' *Columbia Law Review* 97: 1.

FEINBERG, J (1984) *Harm to Others*. New York: Oxford University Press.

_____ (1985) *Offense to Others*. New York: Oxford University Press.

GIL-ROBLES, A (2005) *Report on the Visit to the United Kingdom 4-12/11/2004*. Strasbourg: Council of Europe, CommDH(2005)6.

HAYEK, FA (1944) *The Road to Serfdom*. London: Routledge.

Home Office (2000) *Anti-Social Behaviour Orders—Guidance on drawing up local ASBO protocols*. London: HMSO.

RAZ, J (1977) 'The Rule of Law and its Virtue' *Law Quarterly Review* 93: 195.

—— (1979) *The Authority of Law*. Oxford: Oxford University Press.

—— (1995) 'Free Expression and Personal Identification', in RAZ J, *Ethics in the Public Domain* (rev ed). Oxford: Oxford University Press.

ROBERTS, P and ZUCKERMAN, A (2004) *Criminal Evidence*. Oxford: Oxford University Press.

SCHAUER, F (1991) *Playing by the Rules: A Philosophical Examination of Rule-Based Decision-Making in Law and in Life*. New York: Oxford University Press.

SIMESTER, AP (2005) *Appraising Strict Liability*. Oxford: Oxford University Press.

SIMESTER, AP and VON HIRSCH, A (2002) 'Rethinking the Offense Principle' *Legal Theory* 8: 269.

SIMESTER, AP and SULLIVAN, GR (2003) *Criminal Law: Theory and Doctrine*. Oxford: Hart Publishing.

VON HIRSCH, A (1996) 'Extending the Harm Principle: Remote Harms and Fair Imputation', in AP SIMESTER and ATH SMITH (eds), *Harm and Culpability*. Oxford: Oxford University Press.

—— (2000) 'The Ethics of Public Television Surveillance', in A VON HIRSCH, D GARLAND and A WAKEFIELD (eds), *Ethical and Social Perspectives on Situational Crime Prevention*. Oxford: Hart Publishing.

VON HIRSCH, A and ASHWORTH, A (2005) *Proportionate Sentencing: Exploring the Principles*. Oxford: Oxford University Press.

VON HIRSCH, A and SHEARING, C (2000) 'Exclusion from Public Space', in VON A HIRSCH, D GARLAND and A WAKEFIELD (eds), *Ethical and Social Perspectives on Situational Crime Prevention*. Oxford: Hart Publishing.

VON HIRSCH, A and WASIK, M (1997) 'Civil Disqualifications Attending Conviction' *Cambridge Law Journal* 56: 599.

WELLS, C (1997) 'Stalking: The Criminal Law Response' *Criminal Law Review* 463.

8

'No Spitting': Regulation of Offensive Behaviour in England and Wales

ELIZABETH BURNEY

THERE ARE PLAINS, foothills, and peaks in the landscape of regulation of offensive behaviour. The primary regulation is through norms of social acceptability—informal, parochial, and shifting over time and place. These plains and swamps can trap the unfamiliar visitor but, by and large, people conform out of habit. Secondary regulation includes formal rules and regulations imposed in particular places (concerning noise levels, for example) or by organisations with control in their particular sphere (such as clubs, or professional and sporting authorities). Thirdly, above these foothills stand the requirements of the law, both civil and criminal, which according to context may become the arbiters of what is or what is not offensive and what the sanctions should be.

Spitting provides a simple illustration. There was a time when pub floors were covered in sawdust and spittoons were in regular use. Eventually, tobacco was smoked rather than chewed, manners changed, and notices exhorting 'no spitting' appeared. Nowadays, spitting on the floor is so widely accepted as offensive that such notices are unnecessary. In polite circles in England spitting is only acceptable—indeed expected—at wine-tastings, and even there anyone spitting on the floor would be unlikely to receive another invitation.

But spitting does not merely contravene polite mores. For example, it can be a health hazard and as such might be singled out for regulation in certain contexts. Indeed, public health concerns underlaid the ban on spitting in pubs. Since the SARS outbreak, the Chinese government has introduced severe punishment for spitting. Some health workers in East London have expressed support for the idea of outlawing spitting in view of the marked increase in tuberculosis in the area.

Spitting has a language of its own, and deliberate offensiveness is part of it. Football players may spit on the ground to clear their throats but to use the same action insultingly can be punished through club discipline or by criminal charges, as several recent examples have shown. Arsenal's Patrick Viera received a six-game suspension and a £45,000 fine for spitting at another player, and the Liverpool player El Hadji Diouf was fined £58,000 by his club for spitting at Celtic supporters. Sometimes the police step in. A Glaswegian was convicted of assault by spitting—so plainly in this case the action attracted the censure of the criminal law. Less severely, when photography recorded the spray of spittle directed at rival fans by Wayne Rooney, the 17-year-old Everton player was given a police warning.[1]

Internationally, attitudes to spitting vary. But any perceived increase in Britain cannot simply be blamed on 'foreigners'. In London, staff on the Underground have been issued with DNA kits to help identify irate passengers who spit on them. Spitting is often prohibited in the conditions attached to Anti-Social Behaviour Orders (see below).

What all this anecdotal evidence demonstrates is twofold: context and cultural norms determine whether any particular action is considered offensive; and the sanction varies greatly according to both the context and the authority wielding the sanction.

There are obviously many kinds of proscribed conduct where either criminal or civil action may arise from the same event, and offensive behaviour is only one category. This discussion is concerned with the rather narrow but contentious issue of criminalising offensive behaviour. But the control and regulation of such behaviour, as these opening paragraphs demonstrate, is achieved by many different and sometimes overlapping means, of which the criminal law is only one, and not always the harshest.

This chapter will look at some of the main legal methods in operation in England and Wales today, and particularly at recent developments in statute law employing administrative, civil, and quasi-criminal law as well as overt criminalisation. A short historical review of the regulation of offensive behaviour in England and Wales is followed by an account of developments over the past twenty years, with a special focus on the origins and nature of legislation against 'anti-social behaviour'. A separate section looks at the regulation of sexual activity, with a focus on the overlap between moral attitudes, nuisance, and 'offence'. The final section sums up the main themes revealed in the whole survey.

I. HISTORICAL REVIEW

First, some sketched historical background. Breach of the peace, an instrument available to this day, was established in the fourteenth century at a time of particular unrest, but became a general procedure for dealing with

---

[1] *The Economist*, 26 April 2003.

the whole range of violent, threatening, or otherwise upsetting behaviour. Perpetrators (whether they admitted the conduct or not) could be bound over by justices to keep the peace—a constraint on future behaviour. Insults or other offensive conduct might be the trigger. Recognisances were sometimes used for quite serious crimes, but also for a raft of petty injuries. The restraint was needed because people reacted strongly to aspersions; indeed the high murder rate in the Middle Ages has been partially attributed to a strong sense of personal honour easily inflamed by perceived affront. But, as the name implies, what was at stake was the 'King's Peace', rather than any hurt or upset experienced by individual victims.

In the close-knit, but often quarrelsome, small communities of the late medieval and Tudor period, the law intervened to maintain harmony. Behaviour was then, in modern parlance, deemed 'anti-social' if it upset social relations, rather than offending individual sensibilities. Such behaviour might, but need not, include what nowadays would be classified as criminal: people could be indicted simply for 'causing dissension'. Indeed, sometimes litigants were seen as troublemakers. Taking someone to court for an alleged grievance could stir up the neighbours to take sides, and the regular condemnation of vexatious suits offers a stark contrast to our modern-day 'compensation culture'.

Slanderous gossip was seen as a direct attack upon community values and could result in crude physical punishment. The ducking stool was used for 'scolds'—almost invariably women, who would nowadays be deemed 'nasty neighbours'. Far worse, in the witch-hunting period of the early seventeenth century, irascible or eccentric women might be condemned to death for sorcery. These were 'outsiders' within their communities and, as such, vulnerable. More obvious outsiders, such as rootless strangers, were treated with fear and suspicion, something illustrated by the Tudor and early Stuart laws against vagabondage; which find their counterpart in twentieth and twenty-first century legislation directed at travellers, beggars, and the homeless.

Bawdy and drunken behaviour had always been disapproved of but this response took on a more state-directed character in the early seventeenth century, with statutes and directives against drunkenness and swearing, which village constables were expected to enforce. The intensive social control of the Puritan era slackened after the Restoration, creating a gap that legal regulation came to fill. A succession of royal decrees urged more zealous punishment of immorality and profanity. The cause was taken up with enthusiasm by groups of upright citizens who, towards the end of the seventeenth century, formed Societies for the Reformation of Manners, a kind of moral neighbourhood watch. But the growth of urban populations, working class poverty, and cheap liquor, particularly in London, soon overwhelmed such efforts—which came to be displaced by concerns about more serious crime.

The modern era, which for our purpose starts in the early nineteenth century, saw the development of forms of regulation of offensive behaviour which laid the foundations of present-day systems. The Vagrancy Act 1824, which still remains on the statute book, linked notions of offensive conduct and public order. Building on the common law offence of 'outraging public decency', indecent exposure of genitals by a male with intent to insult a female was made a statutory offence under this Act. By its nature, the Act perpetuated the notion of the threat to public order and morals being created by the existence of indigent people thought to have no stake in society. This readily evolved into the stereotypes of the 'undeserving poor' and the 'dangerous classes' that were to haunt respectable society during the Victorian era.

Rapid urbanisation and industrialisation eroded traditional social bonds and, at the same time, created physical conditions that presented considerable health hazards and a fear of moral as well as physical disorder. Environmental controls began to be seen as a safety measure in more senses than one. What are now sometimes termed 'incivilities' were addressed by a raft of public health and nuisance legislation. Housing was built and managed with a view to improving the behaviour as well as the health of the working classes, while the new police force maintained public order outside the home. The twin pillars of public order and nuisance remain the framework upon which state regulation of offensive behaviour is constructed. Both branches of law are to a large extent predicated upon reaction to particular behaviour, rather than the behaviour itself.

In the private sphere, the law and practice of tort supplies plentiful possibilities for redress against offensive behaviour. In particular, the law of nuisance has both a public and a private aspect. Private nuisance complaints have been around for centuries, connected with damage to or obstruction of property rights. Individuals are further protected against certain types of nuisance, such as noise, by modern environmental legislation (see below). Public nuisances occur when the rights of the public at large are affected—for example, by obstruction of the highway.[2] By extension, some types of offensive behaviour are classified as 'nuisance', including the old crime of begging with exposed wounds and, in a more modern version, display of obscene material. Present-day regulation of soliciting, begging, urinating, etc, has similar origins.

---

[2] The changing nature of perceptions of nuisance is nicely illustrated in the preface to the third edition of Garrett and Garrett (1908: v–vi): 'With the modern application of mechanical power to locomotion and traction, excessive traffic has taken new forms in excessive speed, smoke, noise etc, all of which come directly under the head of nuisance, as contributing an interference with the free and uninterrupted use of the highway, by causing danger or inconvenience to the public in an exercise of the common law right.'

It has been mentioned that what offends people (or may offend them) in one context may be quite acceptable in another. Likewise, regulation may take on very specific, contextual forms. Those faded, defaced notices at the entrance to public parks are entitled (if you can still read them) 'Byelaws'. Their current appearance betrays their marginal, insignificant status and the toothlessness of the local authority that imposed them perhaps 100 or more years ago. In 2003 the central government reminded councils of the potential of byelaws to control 'anti-social behaviour'. More of this later. The time has come to look at the political context and the policy initiatives relating to offence regulation in recent times and particularly under the Labour government from 1997 to the present.

II. OFFENCE REGULATION, 1986 TO 1997

In keeping with the Victorian past of such regulation, conduct or negligence that might cause offence to others is governed by both criminal law (mainly public order and related legislation, together with aspects of common law) and environmental regulation, together with a significant body of housing law. There is a growing tendency to create instruments that blend civil and criminal law, marrying a lower standard of proof and offender protection and more stringent sanctions.

The year of the Public Order Act 1986 is an appropriate baseline for discussion of contemporary offence regulation. Together with the Housing Act 1996 (both passed by Conservative governments), concepts and powers were introduced which have been developed and expanded in the on-going policies of New Labour directed against anti-social behaviour.

1. Public Order Regulation

Public order, the preservation of the peaceful co-existence of the general public, has, as described above, been a core concern of law enforcement since the Middle Ages. What constitutes infringement of public order is a wide and often contentious field and has had many statutory definitions, changing with the times.[3] The 1986 Act provided new ones. Promotion of racial hatred through promulgation of offensive material was covered in sections 18–23. (Racist incitement was already illegal under the 1965 and 1976 Race Relations Acts.) The generic public order offences were defined in sections 4 and 5. Section 4 is the more serious offence, covering

---

[3] For discussion and examples see Lacey and Wells, 1998.

threatening and abusive behaviour and conduct putting in fear of immediate violence, or provocative of violence. Section 5 is the lesser offence, but
one with a potentially very wide interpretation. Crucially, it relies upon the
idea of subjective victimisation: words, behaviour, or display in a public
place 'within hearing or sight of a person likely to be caused harassment
alarm or distress thereby' (intending thereby to include people who, even if
upset, would not be provoked into breaching the peace). It is a defence to
prove that the accused was unaware of anybody within sight or earshot
who might be affected. An additional offence (section 4A), in the context of
racial harassment, was introduced in the Criminal Justice and Public Order
Act 1994, specifying the intent to cause harassment, alarm, or distress.

Section 5 is most relevant to the discussion of offensive conduct. It has
attracted much debate, given its open-ended character. Prosecution depends
upon the evaluation by a constable of the presumed emotions of a putative
victim (a warning must have been given and ignored). The maximum penalty is a fine of £1,000. It has been argued that there was little need for a new
law to cover conduct more traditionally dealt with by means of arrest for
breach of the peace and a binding over by magistrates.[4] Section 5 was made
to look somewhat ridiculous when initially it was found to have been used
mainly by police officers against people who had been rude to them.[5]

Racially aggravated versions of such conduct dealt with by sections 4,
4A and 5 were introduced in the Crime and Disorder Act 1998, with significantly enhanced maximum sentences. These new offences are complement-
ed by six other racially aggravated offences covering assault, harassment,
and criminal damage. The bulk of prosecutions for the various racially
aggravated offences have been for public order, and in many cases the sole
evidence has been one racist word spoken in anger or insult.[6] This legislation has undoubtedly raised awareness, at least amongst criminal justice
practitioners, that the offensiveness of racist language and racially targeted
actions constitutes a social harm beyond that found in the same conduct
when done without the racist element. Similar thinking lay behind the creation of a specific offence of racist chanting, in the Football (Offences) Act
1991.

Religious aggravation was added to the Crime and Disorder Act 1998 in
the wake of the outrages of 11 September 2001, as a way of addressing ani-
mosity against Muslims. Previously, such incidents had been dealt with as

---

[4] Following criticism by the European Court ((1998) 28 EHRR 603 and (2000) 30 EHRR
241), bind-overs must be based on the criminal standard of proof and must specify more exactly the conduct to be avoided.

[5] Newburn, Brown and Crisp, 1990; see also *DPP v Orum* [1989] 1 WLR 88.

[6] Burney and Rose, 2002. For example, in *R v White* a man of Caribbean ethnicity was convicted of a racially aggravated public order offence against s 4 for calling a bus conductor who
had accused him of pick-pocketing a 'stupid African bitch'.

racial, although there was an anomaly regarding Jews and Sikhs—who, being defined legally as ethnic groups, were statutorily protected under the definition of racial hostility. Prior to this, the idea of specific protection against religious hostility had been viewed with great caution in official circles, as being too complex and liable to lead to all kinds of claims from people with obscure religious affiliations. More generally, in modern times, religion has been viewed as a private matter regarding which, although clearly the source of many affronts, it is not appropriate for the state to intervene. It is a matter of debate as to whether an increasingly multi-cultural society should reinforce this caution, or challenge it—this sometimes taking the form of arguments for abolishing or for extending the moribund law of blasphemy. However, the changed climate in the post-9/11 era led the government, under pressure from Muslims, to introduce legislation against stirring up religious hatred, a controversial measure which was going through Parliament during 2005. Opponents argued that freedom of expression was being sacrificed to potential sensibilities.

Such measures often arise from political overreaction. The Criminal Justice and Public Order Act 1994 was passed during a period of moral panic against people with unorthodox lifestyles—new age travellers, squatters, ravers, and gypsies (Smith, 1995). By criminalising trespass, it dealt a blow at the traditional habits of gypsies (Campbell, 1995) and, paradoxically, made it more likely that they would cause offence to the public by intruding on spaces close to residential areas, or by being forced into permanent housing where they might come into conflict with other residents (Burney, 1999).

The catch-all concept of 'harassment, alarm or distress' introduced in the Public Order Act 1986 was to have an influential legislative life and eventually became a justification for some of New Labour's most repressive policies. It first re-surfaced in the Protection From Harassment Act 1997, passed shortly before the Conservatives lost power in the spring of that year, in the wake of another moral panic, this time against 'stalking'. The conduct complained of must have occurred at least twice. The lesser version may be dealt with either as a summary offence with a maximum of six months in prison, or by means of a civil law injunction, which becomes a more serious crime—five years maximum—if breached. The more serious form of harassment, where the complainant is put in fear of violence, is an 'either way' offence also bearing a five year maximum sentence. It was commented at the time (Wells, 1997) that 'the Act underlines the increasingly blurred line between civil and criminal forms of redress'.

The Act is awkward to use, not least because of the time-limits involved in proving two distinct occasions. It has been applied in a variety of ways, not only against 'stalkers' but also against demonstrators, and against neighbour harassment, including in its racially aggravated form. As Celia Wells (1997) has pointed out, existing legal principles and interpretation of the concept of assault were already adequate to cover harassment. She comments (at 470) on:

> a strange unity between those who call for legislation on the grounds that the law is inadequate and those who decry what they see as judicial licence in extending the law. Both subscribe to a view of the criminal law which is difficult to match with its practice—a view which elevates minimal *mens rea* requirements to something more, which ignores the extensive use of public order offences to supplement assault and injury offences, and which assumes that the law solves social problems.

2. Housing Act 1996

The behaviour of social tenants is a highly regulated and politically charged concern. The social and economic marginalisation of the social housing sector which occurred during the Thatcher years produced management problems that were aggravated, in the eyes of the authorities, by the enhanced security of tenure granted to tenants and obligations towards the homeless. No longer could 'nasty neighbours' and 'problem families' be easily steered clear of council estates or swiftly ejected when they caused trouble.

Legislation in 1985 and 1996 addressed this problem through the civil law of landlord and tenant. The Housing Act 1996 gave local authorities power to control access to social housing through a housing register, enabling them to exclude anybody with a history of anti-social behaviour. They could apply a system of 'introductory tenancies', whereby new tenants had to prove in their first year that they could behave decently and not accumulate rent arrears before they gained full security. Refusal to grant this was a matter for the local authority alone. Grounds for eviction of secure tenants were extended to include not only the 1985 grounds of causing a nuisance to neighbours, and committing or permitting immoral or illegal activities on the property, but also for conduct 'likely to cause nuisance or annoyance', and for being convicted of an arrestable offence in the property or its locality. Moreover the same prohibitions extended to family and visitors, so that a tenant became at risk of eviction for the conduct of others of which she might not even be aware.

A sharper behaviour-oriented instrument was contained in sections 152 and 153, which gave local authority landlords (and to a more limited extent other social landlords) the right to seek an injunction against anybody using violence or threats against a tenant or anybody else going about their lawful business in or near the dwelling—a procedure aimed particularly at abuse of council staff. Power of arrest could be attached in certain circumstances, hearsay evidence was permissible, as were *ex parte* proceedings in urgent cases. Breach of an injunction can, of course, result in imprisonment.

This legislation has been applied with different degrees of enthusiasm in different local authority areas. It has provided a template for further offence regulation by the Labour government, as will be demonstrated.

3. Environmental Protection

The control of environmental 'incivilities' or nuisance—most commonly litter, graffiti, fly-tipping, dog mess, and noise—is in the historic tradition of public health regulation, administered through local councils by people now known as environmental health officers. These are all things that in different degrees cause offence, although at least the first two are features of local life often endured to the point of indifference. Noise, however, is the most universally complained of environmental irritant and, at its worst, is seriously destructive of well-being. The right to 'peaceful enjoyment' of the home is never so threatened as by persistent intrusive noise, although it is also something over which individual sensibilities vary widely. Between neighbours, amplified music is nowadays a frequent source of complaint; poor insulation makes people more vulnerable to this and to violent quarrelling and swearing next door, another common irritant. As a group of housing academics observed, 'neighbour disputes are inseparable from the wider issue of "nuisance" which appears to be a matter of growing concern'.[7]

While it is not really clear if, or how far, the noise problem is getting worse—people complain more, but so they do about everything—from time to time the legislators decide that 'something must be done'. The Environmental Protection Act 1990 laid a duty on local authorities to 'take such steps as were reasonably practicable' to investigate noise complaints (section 79(1)). It reinforced the conditions for serving an abatement notice (section 80) and speeded up summary proceedings for breach. Failure to comply with an abatement notice was a criminal offence attracting a maximum penalty of a level 5 fine (section 80(4) and (5)), and inspectors could seize the equipment of persisters. Some local authorities began to run night noise patrols, particularly at weekends. Others relied upon the 'reasonably practicable' provision and seldom investigated noise complaints—or in some areas sheltered behind the perception that complaints about noisy parties were racially inspired. A committee looking at the whole question of noise nuisance concluded that it might be too dangerous for environmental inspectors to intervene when a party was in full swing (Burney, 1999).

Around this time there was much debate about ways to reduce noise nuisance—including physical improvements, social education, and local consensus. One suggestion put forward by a group of environmental lawyers

---

[7] Karn *et al*, 1993.

was for Neighbourhood Noise Watch, along the lines of neighbourhood (crime) watch. But this was rejected as too divisive. As far as the law was concerned, it seemed to be a choice between strengthening the right to individual civil redress against noise nuisance, and making it a crime. Neither the inspectors nor the police were keen on the latter.

However, following another 'moral panic' during a hot summer where noise from neighbours inflamed tempers and even (it was alleged) led to several deaths, the Noise Act 1996 was passed. Excessive noise at night from domestic premises became a crime *if* local authorities so chose (in fact, few did, because it carried too many obligations). It set a decibel standard and made provision (section 10) for seizure and forfeiture of offending equipment by police. A £40 spot fine can be imposed and repeating the offence the same night attracts a level 3 fine. Thus stood domestic noise regulation as Labour came to power.

III. NEW LABOUR AND MODERN OFFENCE REGULATION

Media coverage of 'noisy neighbours' and 'neighbours from hell' chimed with complaints being received by local MPs, particularly in areas blighted by de-industrialisation. Pressure also came from an influential group of social landlords, who claimed that the powers granted under the Housing Act 1996 were not enough to curb nuisance and aggression on housing estates where they were already finding it hard to fill vacancies.

A popular cause was identified by the Labour party. In the summer of 1995 it published a paper entitled 'A Quiet Life: Tough Action on Criminal Neighbours', arguing for a new approach to 'persistent and anti-social criminal neighbours'. Although the talk was of criminals, and much of the conduct described was plainly criminal, the paper proposed that people suffered from serial offences and harassment which could not be dealt with adequately through case-by-case criminal prosecution (at this point, the Protection from Harassment Act 1997 had not been introduced). There was no attempt to assess prevalence or causation, although it was asserted that 'across Britain there are thousands of people whose lives are made a misery by people next door, down the street or on the floor above or below'. The paper relied heavily on anecdotal evidence and a couple of *causes célèbres* to support its argument for a new kind of injunctive control, called a 'community safety order'. This was a civil order, but would carry a criminal conviction with a seven year maximum sentence if breached.[8]

---

[8] The paper attracted heavy criticism, especially from lawyers, academics, and civil liberties groups. See Ashworth *et al* 1998. The critics were scorned by Home Secretary Jack Straw as 'detached metropolitan elites', with no experience of the real world. (Hansard HOC, 8 April 1998, col 370.)

Once in government, Labour introduced a revised version of this instrument, the Anti-Social Behaviour Order.[9] The focus therefore had widened to address not just 'anti-social crime', but 'anti-social behaviour'—a very elastic concept which was intended to embrace almost any kind of potentially upsetting conduct, including noise and other incivilities normally dealt with through environmental control and housing management. This all-embracing label was to be used to justify further censure, regulation and punishment for a continuing stream of new policies and legislation. The only definition supplied in the Crime and Disorder Act 1998 (*per* section 1(1)(a)) was somewhat similar to sixteenth century indictments for 'causing dissension':

> the person [accused] has acted ... in an anti-social manner, that is to say, in a manner that caused or was likely to cause harassment, alarm or distress to one or more persons not in the same household as himself.

Once more, the drafting of the Public Order Act 1986 was borrowed to justify legal intervention with a highly imprecise basis. Only this time, actions that might have qualified for public order prosecution were to be dealt with in a far more draconian way. The ASBO, as it is commonly called, is a civil order of an injunctive nature, lasting a minimum of two years and carrying such negative conditions as are deemed by magistrates to be warranted in the particular case. Breach of the conditions creates a criminal offence punishable for adults with a maximum of five years' imprisonment. Again, as in the Protection from Harassment Act 1997, civil and criminal sanctions are combined, so that the eventual sanction may be a criminal conviction for actions that are not criminal in themselves.

The ASBO therefore creates an individualised crime category, used as a form of situational crime prevention.[10] Here, the experience of its actual application will be summarised, and lessons drawn from (i) its generally minimal, but very localised, impact, and (ii) its use for purposes often outside the original concept as set out in government guidance.

Only 2,455 ASBOs had been imposed by 31 March 2004, at the end of the first five years of its availability. This compares with the estimate of 5,000 per annum produced when the measure was under discussion in Parliament. Some local authorities and police forces have been enthusiastic users, led by Greater Manchester with 422 ASBOs. Manchester is also the keenest authority when it comes to using Housing Act powers against people misbehaving on council estates, and the two types of sanction are closely connected, with specialist lawyers in certain authorities driving the process. Many other councils have used the power only once or twice— sometimes because they are put off by time and cost, sometimes because

---

[9] Crime and Disorder Act 1998, s 1.
[10] For further discussion see Simester and von Hirsch, this volume.

they prefer to use other means to deal with troublemakers. The usage has increased with the introduction of legislation to make ASBOs more widely available, particularly to criminal courts (see below).

A more favoured instrument is the so-called Acceptable Behaviour Contract (ABC), which involves an agreed set of rules brokered by police with young people and their parents. It has no legal force, and runs for only six months, but does produce measurable improvements in behaviour (Bullock and Jones, 2004). However it is seldom a 'contract' in the sense of offering a *quid pro quo*, although there have been examples of parental support, or leisure facilities for local youths, in response to behaviour agreements (Duff and Marshall, this volume). Breaking an ABC may lead on to an ASBO, or a possession order if the recipient's family are social tenants.

When the ASBO legislation was first passed, draft guidance circulated to local authorities discouraged the use of ASBOs for under 18s, especially because other strategies were being developed by the new multi-agency crime and disorder partnerships and youth justice teams. But strong objections were expressed, and the guidance was changed (except for 10 and 11-year-olds). The keenest authorities had argued for ASBOs as a response of first resort precisely because Housing Act powers were not enforceable against minors, although their parents could be evicted for their misbehaviour. In the event, ASBOs have become primarily used against children and young people, and are seen as a way of dealing with unruly teenagers. They have also been used to drive prostitutes and beggars out of town, two other groups not forming part of the original paradigm. The adult 'neighbour from hell', the original inspiration for the ASBO, has not featured prominently in the orders issued (Burney, 2002, 2005).

The two-year minimum length of an ASBO means that there is a high risk of breach. Court returns for the period 01/06/2000 to 31/12/2003 reveal a 42 per cent breach rate, of which 55 per cent led to a custodial sentence. The true breach rate is likely to be even higher, because orders which, for example, ban somebody from a wide urban area for many years are hard to police. One Manchester boy was banished from the district where his family lived for ten years. The London Borough of Camden has targeted nuisance drug users with a number of ASBOs banning individuals from the entire borough for similar periods. Enforcement has been used by several councils as the justification for publishing pictures of children subject to ASBOs. The Anti-Social Behaviour Act 2003 waives the usual youth court anonymity for ASBO breachers.

Individual ASBOs can be very detailed, as just one example, imposed by Haringey magistrates, shows. The individual subjected to an order was prohibited from doing the following for two years (Burney, 2002):

- shouting, spitting, using verbal/physical and/or racial abuse, swearing, drinking alcohol, smashing bottles, throwing eggs, stones or other

items at vehicles or property in any street in the LB of Haringey including inciting or encouraging others in the commission of any of the above,
- entering the Park Ward area of Tottenham (other than to remain at his home address) for one hour before and after the scheduled kick off time of any football match held at White Hart Lane football stadium, and
- leaving his home address between the hours of 8 pm and 7 am unless under the direct supervision of a youth worker for the LB of Haringey on an organised event

Shouting and spitting may be undesirable, but are not usually punishable. The other details of the order suggest that this teenager is not a pleasant character, but it is highly questionable whether he deserves, and is going to obey, a curfew imposed for two years that is four times as long as the maximum criminal curfew order. It is sometimes the case that breaches are anticipated, and welcomed, as an opportunity to bring a criminal charge against a persistent offender where there is insufficient evidence for a criminal prosecution based on the original conduct.

The House of Lords decided in *Clingham*[11] that the ASBO was not legally a punishment and that it did not count as a criminal charge for the purposes of section 6 of the Human Rights Act. Nevertheless, in a convoluted way it was held that proof of conduct to support an ASBO application should effectively be to a criminal standard, in spite of its being a civil order. Lord Hope stated that 'there are good reasons, in the interests of fairness, for applying the higher standard of proof when allegations are made of criminal or quasi-criminal conduct which, if proved, would have serious consequences for the person against whom they are made' (para 82). The consequences of an ASBO, despite the fact that it does not count as a criminal record, are indeed often far more serious in terms of restrictions on liberty than any likely criminal sentence arising from the same conduct.

Dissatisfied with the low usage of ASBOs, the government enacted a series of measures designed to encourage more extensive use. Amendments to the Police Reform Act 2002 during its passage through Parliament widened access to ASBOs and changed procedures. Section 61 of that Act extends the right to apply for an ASBO to transport police; and to social landlords other than local authorities (the latter are increasingly handing over their housing to non-profit associations). It also permits ASBOs to be enforceable nationwide, not just in the area of the original local or police authority (creating a mind-boggling enforcement problem).

The county court is for the first time given the power to impose the order, in conjunction with related proceedings (section 63)—a measure designed to assist social landlords, for example by restraining the future behaviour

---

[11] [2002] UKHL 39.

of a tenant who is being evicted. Likewise a criminal court (section 64) can impose an ASBO on proof of past anti-social behaviour, which need not be related to the current offence(s). Unlike other ASBOs, these can be imposed without any of the agency consultation built into the normal procedure. Post-conviction ASBOs have proved popular with the police, and account for most of the increase in orders that has occurred since the relevant section came into force in December 2002. Another boost has been given by section 65, which creates an interim order. In urgent cases this can be imposed *ex parte*, restraining the alleged perpetrator before the court has heard the full case, if magistrates consider it 'just' to do so. Breach of an interim order is punishable in the same way as a full order.

All this was not considered enough: subsequent legislation, the Criminal Justice Act 2003 and the Anti-Social Behaviour Act 2003, include further ASBO-enhancing clauses. Detailed provision is made in the Criminal Justice Act 2003 for increased intervention with youths who are subject to ASBOs: section 322 creates an Individual Support Order, available to the Youth Court, which is intended to address underlying problems (such as drug abuse) associated with the anti-social behaviour. Although it too is a civil order, breach becomes a criminal offence with a fine of up to £1,000 (£250 for under 14s). The thinking behind this provision is rehabilitative, but legally it moves the ASBO still nearer to a criminal offence, since the support programmes will mirror those being imposed through the youth court in its normal criminal capacity.

The Anti-Social Behaviour Act 2003, discussed in more detail below, gives councils the power to prosecute ASBO breaches themselves rather than waiting for the Crown Prosecution Service to do so—there had been complaints that these cases were often put at the back of the queue.

1. 'Respect and Responsibility' and the Anti-Social Behaviour Act 2003

A new onslaught against 'anti-social behaviour' was launched in March 2003 in the White Paper *Respect and Responsibility—Taking a Stand Against Anti-Social Behaviour*, and most of its proposals soon passed into legislation. The document relies upon the much-quoted but largely discredited 'broken windows' thesis: that incivilities cause community decline (research suggests that, if anything, it is the other way round).[12] While no-one could disagree with the idea that showing respect to others is an important principle of social life, and that lack of it gives offence, the authoritarian tone and the detailed proposals are both sweeping and discriminatory. Particular groups of people—parents of recalcitrant children,

---

[12] See, in particular, Sampson and Raudenbush, 2001 and Taylor, 2001.

social tenants, beggars—are singled out for new controls and sanctions. The listed examples of anti-social behaviour include both personal and environmental incivilities (paragraph 1.6):

Harassment and intimidating behaviour
Behaviour that causes alarm or fear
Noisy neighbours
Drunken and abusive behaviour
Vandalism, graffiti and other deliberate damage to property
Dumping rubbish or litter.

Paragraph 1.7 goes on to assert that '[a]nti-social behaviour is a problem manifested in hundreds of ways and locations, but the effects of each incident are immediate, real and personal. They can also be long-lasting, causing distress to individuals and sometimes scarring communities for years afterwards'. This rhetoric seeks to encompass in one frightening image what in fact amounts to a catalogue of disparate social problems and irritants, all of which already come under criminal or regulatory sanctions. It is true that certain neighbourhoods experience a concentration of such things, but there is little recognition of structural causes in the White Paper. The theme is of helping communities to 'take responsibility' for dealing with anti-social behaviour and the tools proposed are primarily repressive and punitive, spelled out in the legislation.

The main features of the Anti-Social Behaviour Act 2003 (ASBA 2003) are as follows. In Part 1, police are given strong powers to close down premises used for unlawful use or supply of Class A drugs, where 'disorder or serious nuisance to members of the public' has occurred. This provision is aimed at 'crack houses'.

Part 2 addresses housing, and is directed at anti-social behaviour by and among social tenants—a group already more strictly controlled than any other section of the public and, specifically, far more so than people living in other tenures. Social landlords must devise and publish policies and procedures for dealing with anti-social behaviour and are given sharper tools with which to do so. Section 13 abolishes sections 152 and 153 of the Housing Act 1996, concerning injunctions and powers of arrest, and replaces them with an 'anti-social behaviour injunction' which has an even wider focus. It applies to conduct that is merely 'capable of causing nuisance or annoyance to any person', which may be only 'threatened' rather than engaged in, and which 'directly or indirectly relates to or affects the housing management functions of a relevant landlord'. The conduct counts only if it is directed against a resident or visitor to the accommodation or its locality, or a landlord's employee. Yet it is immaterial where the conduct takes place, which seems a very elastic interpretation of a landlord's legal standing. Power of arrest (where violence is involved or threatened) is now supplemented by the power to exclude somebody for a specified period (no limit is set) from his normal place of residence.

Tenants with secure tenure may be 'demoted' to probationary status for anti-social conduct (section 14) by means of a county court 'demotion' order. Section 16 says that where proceedings are brought for possession on grounds of anti-social behaviour, consideration must be given by the court to the likely effect on others if the nuisance or annoyance continues.[13]

Parents are dealt with in Part 3. Parenting orders (also a civil order with a criminal sanction for breach) were already available for parents of offending children, but the Act permits them to be obtained by local education authorities when children have been excluded from school; and they must also normally be made when a child under 16 receives an ASBO. A parenting order may now include a residential element, but only if interference with family life is not disproportionate. Nevertheless, this provision makes these civil orders even more like a criminal sentence. Parents of children excluded from school or truanting may be invited to enter into a 'parenting contract', involving commitments designed to improve the child's behaviour and/or school attendance. Though voluntary, refusal to enter into or carry out the commitments may be taken into account if a parenting order is sought.

Serious misbehaviour or truanting by a child could also result in a fixed penalty notice being issued to the parent by the school or Local Education Authority (something seen as unhelpful by many teachers). The fixed penalty notice is a sanction made available for many misdemeanours throughout the Act, with the right to issue them available to accredited civilian functionaries. Previous legislation (the Criminal Justice and Police Act 2001) created fixed penalty notices for disorderly youths, and this Act extends that response to people as young as 16. A provable crime must have been committed before such notices may be issued.

The White Paper also announced heavier penalties for beggars. Begging has been made a notifiable offence (meaning that it will appear on a criminal record) and the ASBA 2003 provides community penalties for repeat offenders, so as to make drug treatment and testing orders available. (This does nothing to resolve the chronic lack of facilities to deliver such orders.) The beggars themselves need not have been aggressive or have attracted public complaints for the new rules to apply, which raises the question of

---

[13] These were not, as it happens, the most controversial measures contemplated by the government. An earlier private member's bill introduced by Frank Field, MP for Birkenhead and a leading doomsayer about anti-social behaviour, proposed depriving anti-social tenants of housing benefit. This was widely criticised, and not welcomed by housing authorities, but the government was minded to draft its own version. A consultation document was issued, but so strong were the ensuing objections, especially from landlords, that the policy was reluctantly abandoned—with the caveat that if other remedies proved insufficient, it might be revived.

why such measures are justified; perhaps it is deemed that the mere sight of a beggar is too upsetting to be borne.

Extraordinary provisions in Part 4 of the Act permit the police to declare zones where, because of significant or persistent anti-social behaviour, they believe that special powers are needed. These powers consist of the right to disperse groups of two or more people from public spaces where one or more members of the party are behaving in a way that has caused, or is likely to cause, someone to be intimidated, harassed, alarmed, or distressed. This means that individuals in the group who are behaving quite reasonably still have to leave, and if they do not live in the locality may be forbidden from returning for up to 24 hours (there is no mention of what happens if they work or go to school there). Inside these zones a night-time curfew may also be imposed on under-16s. The White Paper makes it clear that it sees these measures as the answer in places where people feel intimidated by groups of young people; the Paper cites in justification the British Crime Survey's finding that 32 per cent of people consider that youths 'hanging about' are a big problem in their area.

The 'relevant locality' must be designated in consultation with the local authority and publicised locally, while the order may last for up to six months—but is renewable. Anyone disobeying instructions under this head commits a summary offence subject to a £2,000 (level 4) fine and/or a maximum of three months in prison. If the police choose to exercise their powers under Part 4 with vigour, there could be areas of the country where normal rights are severely curtailed for long periods at a time, and young people especially are refused the right to foregather; all in the name of helping the community to overcome anti-social behaviour.

Environmental powers are extended in other parts of the Act. Local chief executives will have the power to close down noisy pubs temporarily; and the Noise Act now applies to all local authorities, not just those who choose to adopt it. Graffiti and fly-tipping can be dealt with (if the perpetrator is identified) by means of a fixed penalty notice from the local authority, which may keep the proceeds. Yet more local nuisance enforcement is detailed in the Clean Neighbourhoods and Environment Act 2005. Moreover, police powers to issue fixed fines for disorderly and nuisance street behaviour were greatly extended in the Criminal Justice and Police Act 2001, and are being used widely against offensive behaviour connected with binge drinking.

Over and above these new legislative measures, the government is doing all it can to encourage local councils to use existing powers. Guidance on byelaws reminds them that these are localised criminal offences which can be applied to local sources of nuisance behaviour, through powers granted by a series of Acts of Parliament going back to the nineteenth century. New byelaws can only be made against existing nuisances, and model byelaws provided by the Office of the Deputy Prime Minister show how these can include modern hazards such as skateboards and powered model aircraft. A number of councils introduced byelaws against public drinking in named areas, but this procedure has been overtaken by new crimes relating to public drinking created in the Criminal Justice and Police Act 2001. Fines for disobeying byelaws seldom range above level 3 (£1,000) and there is the small matter of enforcement: perhaps this will be undertaken by the new breed of neighbourhood wardens and the civilian Community Support Officers created by the Police Reform Act 2002. Fixed penalty notices for pensioners speeding along the pavement in their electric buggies may yet be on the way!

2. Regulation of Sexual Nuisances

The socially complex history of laws controlling sexual activity need only concern us where it relates to conduct that takes place in the public arena. This may be sexual behaviour that is deemed inappropriate according to the norms of the time, such as public displays of intimacy, especially of a homosexual nature. Or it may be sexually motivated conduct, short of violence, which causes nuisance, annoyance, or alarm—such as indecent exposure, kerb-crawling, and active soliciting. Indecent exposure, a male-only offence, formerly had to be consciously directed at a victim ('intent to insult'), but the Sexual Offences Act 2003 adds recklessness to the definition.

Lacey and Wells (1998: 353) comment that: '[n]on-conformity is threatening and displays of culturally inappropriate behaviour are often controlled through public order mechanisms, such as the power to bind a person over to be of good behaviour.' They go on to refer to 'the prevailing view that pornography and prostitution need be controlled only to the extent that they offend the public gaze, or have public order implications'. Since the enactment of the Sexual Offences Act 1967 the law has provided that prostitution is not an illegal activity but that advertising and touting for it is an offence.

Only recently have kerb-crawlers been targeted as a serious nuisance. They are now subject to increasing control through the criminal law[14] and have also been exposed to shaming mechanisms, such as sending identifiable summonses to their home address or naming them in local newspapers—tactics that arguably violate their rights to privacy and family life. Physical obstacles to deflect traffic have been used in areas where residents have complained of the activities of kerb-crawlers (and, by implication, of offence caused by the presence of prostitutes).

---

[14] Kerb crawling carries a maximum £1,000 fine and became an arrestable offence in the Criminal Justice and Police Act 2000. Under the Criminal Justice Act 2003, kerb-crawlers may lose their driving licence.

At draft stage, a clause in the 2003 Sexual Offences legislation criminalising sexual activity taking place anywhere open to public view got bogged down in definitions and was eventually confined to public lavatories (section 71). Genital exposure with intent to alarm or distress is proscribed in section 66. For good measure, the common law offence of 'offending public decency' is made a statutory either-way offence in the Criminal Justice Act 2003 (section 320).

The underlying right not to be pestered or deliberately insulted in a sexual manner is an enduring one, but definitions of what constitutes offensive public conduct can be slippery and easily overtaken by changing attitudes and counter-claims of individual freedom. As Fitzgerald (1962: 78) remarks, '[p]eople have a right to demand that certain behaviour which disgusts or nauseates them should not take place in public. With regard to nuisance and indecency, however, the offence to the person affronted has to be weighed against the hardship in preventing the person committing the offence from continuing the activity in question'. The occasional persistent nudist demonstrates this conflict.[15] It may be that restrictions are acceptable in order to protect the public from affront at violations of sexual and decency norms; but such restrictions must be amenable to variation with changing attitudes—as has happened with censorship of the arts over the past fifty years. In terms of definition, there has been a tendency to shift from the non-specific 'offending public decency' and the all-purpose binding-over into substantive offences and statutory penalties. This may facilitate challenge, but also risks unpredictable and unfair consequences.

IV. COMMENTARY

Much recent legislation is premised on the view that traditional ways of dealing with nuisance and intimidation are inadequate. 'Traditional' is taken to mean both the informal enforcement of social norms within communities, and formal controls exercised by public servants and the law. The stereotypical neighbourhood where these mechanisms have broken down is one of very low socio-economic status, where in an unstable population a large number of households are headed by single women, the youth population is high, and so are levels of mental illness and substance abuse. At the same time, support from public services has shrunk drastically. Police, and increasingly social landlords, are perceived as holding the line against 'anarchy'.

Current government policy seems to be based upon the view that the whole country is falling apart due to an onslaught of uncivil behaviour.

---

[15] See discussion in this volume by Duff and Marshall: 59, 64.

Complaints do come from far and wide, not just from the deprived neigh-bourhoods described above; indeed, if anything, the middle classes are more prone to make a fuss about loutish behaviour and other forms of nuisance (Loader *et al*, 1998). It is impossible to measure the extent to which manners have changed for the worse, or sensibilities increased; or how far we are sim-ply seeing a recycling of historic disapprovals. Many issues focused on par-enting and children's behaviour seem to require remedial, more than legal, action. At the same time, there is a strong connection of anti-social behav-iour with mental health and other types of special need (Hunter *et al*, 2000).

Nevertheless, coercive legal intervention has been the political response. The call for 'something to be done' has come from politicians and public service workers in the most deprived neighbourhoods, and pressure groups such as the Social Landlords Crime and Nuisance Group have been at the forefront of demands to deal with anti-social behaviour. The outcomes have been described in this chapter.

There are several recurrent features of this new wave of behaviour con-trol that call for comment.

- *Reliance on contingent and subjective effects and judgments in the definition of offensive behaviour.*
  The Public Order Act 1986 introduced the idea of conduct which, in the opinion of a constable, was likely to cause 'harassment, alarm or distress' to a bystander. The Protection from Harassment Act 1997 and the Crime and Disorder Act 1998 (section 1) took up the chorus of 'harassment, alarm or distress' and the ASBA 2003 has its own vari-ant in the Anti-Social Behaviour Injunction (section 13), referring to conduct which is 'capable of causing nuisance or annoyance', an even weaker test. Such standards involve serious problems of vagueness and suffer from a lack of adequate guidelines.
- *The use of civil remedies to control offensive behaviour of a criminal nature.*
  It is clear that, in practice, nearly all ASBOs are issued for conduct that constitutes a criminal offence. Likewise, the Housing Act 1996 provides grounds for eviction and injunctions against social tenants and their associates in circumstances where criminal prosecution would be just as valid. The Local Government Act 1972 also pro-vides councils with an injunctive power for the good of people in the area, which has been used against criminals. Civil remedies in gener-al have the merit of focusing on the victim, and they are favoured because of their relative swiftness—but also, by those who use them, for their lesser requirements of evidence and for permitting *ex parte* proceedings in certain circumstances. The consequences—eviction, for example—may be disproportionate and more severe than a crim-inal sentence.

- *Reliance on discretionary decisions by officials.*
  The housing procedures place great power in the hands of administrators, with sometimes—for example, refusal to grant a secure tenancy—no right of appeal to an outside tribunal, apart from judicial review. The whole ASBO process also relies excessively on officials' discretion in framing and seeking orders, and can result in unwarranted and disproportionate prohibitions.
- *The combination of a civil law sanction with a criminal offence for breach.*
  All the potential injustices associated with civil law as crime control are compounded when the breach of a civil order leads to a criminal punishment. The original conduct might not even have been criminal; and the breach may be purely technical, such as entering a forbidden zone. Breaches of ASBOs and (civil) sex offender orders carry maxima of five years' imprisonment; parenting orders when breached may attract fines of up to £1,000 (Level 3).
- *Vicarious punishment.*
  Normally eschewed in the criminal law, this occurs in the treatment of social tenants, who may be evicted on account of other people's bad conduct; and the punishment of parents whose children commit offences (even though, with the abolition of *doli incapax*, children are presumed to be fully responsible themselves). Part 4 of the ASBA 2003 gives police the power to restrict the movements of people who are in a group where somebody, other than themselves, is misbehaving.
- *The focus of control on unpopular groups.*
  People with unconventional lifestyles (travellers, squatters, ravers) were the focus in the Criminal Justice and Public Order Act 1994. Noisy neighbours joined sex offenders and the parents of offending children on the government's blacklist. Beggars are among those singled out in the 2003 White Paper, and ASBOs have been targeted at unruly youths. It is clear from the White Paper that some of the most restrictive elements in the ASBA 2003 have been drawn up with the aim of preventing youths from congregating—the justification being, it seems, merely that the sight of them makes many people feel uncomfortable.
- *Potential conflicts with the Human Rights Act.*
  Although *Clingham* ruled that the evidential rules for ASBOs were not in breach of section 6 of the Human Rights Act 1998, because it is a civil and not a criminal procedure, this judgment nonetheless laid down what was virtually a criminal standard of proof for an ASBO application. The restrictions available under the new interim ASBO, which like an injunction can be imposed *ex parte*, look ripe for a human rights challenge if they go beyond reasonable temporary restraint. The Individual Support Order certainly goes beyond the purely restraining nature of the ASBO, since it will impose positive

obligations, such as undergoing drug treatment. Individuals subject to specific ASBO prohibitions, or to a dispersal order under Part 4 of the ASBA 2003 may argue that their rights to family life and freedom of association have been violated. These are only some of the difficulties raised in recent legislation, despite the routine declaration by the Home Secretary that all is HRA compatible.

When David Blunkett continued the crusade launched by his predecessor Jack Straw (and developing themes introduced by previous Conservative governments) against an almost unlimited range of behaviour which, at worst, may be grossly offensive and often downright criminal, but at the opposite end might merely be annoying to somebody. Recently, and notably in the White Paper *Respect and Responsibility*, this has taken the form of a moral wake-up call to 'communities' to impose better standards of behaviour. The 'wake-up call' was not meant to be a call to vigilantism, though some might read it as such. Many worthy initiatives are referred to: targeting help at deprived neighbourhoods, problem families, unskilled parents, and substance abuse; and tackling environmental nuisances. But in the end, the new tools actually offered by the Home Office are the repressive new laws described in this chapter. The Anti-Social Behaviour Unit, set up in the Home Office in 2003, has adopted a crusading role, touring the country drumming up enthusiasm for enforcement.

Mediation is mentioned in passing but none of the legislation makes it, or any other form of conflict resolution, a required first step. Diversion or negotiated peace can work, for example, with troublesome youths. Moreover, there is little sign in current policies of the view that people who behave badly towards their neighbours are human too, and that their behaviour might arise from problematic circumstances.

Repression directed against demonised social groups is bound to be popular. There are votes to be gained by introducing laws which, directly or indirectly, criminalise potentially offensive behaviour. Enough people have experienced low-level unpleasantness for tough talk to resonate. Yet the lurid horror stories that lead the campaigns are almost certainly atypical, and usually involve palpable breaches of existing criminal law. Media attention ensures continued public consciousness of bad cases, creating a penumbra of insecurity which facilitates the introduction of yet more regulation, nearly always duplicating existing powers.

In a fragmented society, the perception that the government is stepping in to manage social relations may be reassuring, however illusory. In practice, the public seems to manage pretty well on its own. As indicated at the beginning of this chapter, the great majority of people behave according to accepted norms and do not spit in other people's beer or otherwise cause offence. The government wants the well-mannered majority to suppress the nasty neighbours and loutish youths by draconian means. It may underestimate ordinary people's common sense in adopting such a frenetic tone, and such repressive measures, and by taking so little notice of problem-solving approaches and structural deficits.

REFERENCES

ASHWORTH, A *et al* (1998) 'Neighbouring on the Oppressive' *Criminal Justice* 16(1): 7.

BULLOCK, K and JONES, B (2004) *Acceptable Behaviour Contracts: Addressing Antisocial Behaviour in the London Borough of Islington*, Home Office Online Report 02/04. London: Home Office.

BURNEY, E (1999) *Crime and Banishment: Nuisance and Exclusion in Social Housing*. Winchester: Waterside Press.

—— (2002) 'Talking Tough, Acting Coy: What Happened to the Anti-Social Behaviour Order?' *Howard Journal* 41: 469.

—— (2005) *Making People Behave: Antisocial Behaviour, Politics and Policy*. Cullompton: Willan Publishing.

BURNEY, E and ROSE, G (2002) *Racist Offences: How is the Law Working?* Home Office Research Study 244. London: Home Office.

CAMPBELL, S (1995) 'Gypsies: the Criminalisation of a Way of Life?' *Criminal Law Review* 28.

FITZGERALD, PJ (1962) *Criminal Law and Punishment*. Oxford: Oxford University Press.

GARRETT, EW and GARRETT, HG (1908) *The Law of Nuisance* (3rd edn). London: Butterworths.

HUNTER, C, NIXON, J and SHAYLER, S (2000) *Neighbour Nuisance, Social Landlords and the Law*. Coventry: Chartered Institute of Housing.

KARN, V, LICKISS, R, HUGHES, D and CRAWLEY, J (1993) *Neighbour Disputes: Responses by Social Landlords*. Coventry: Institute of Housing.

LACEY, N and WELLS, C (1998) *Reconstructing Criminal Law: Critical Perspectives on Crime and the Criminal Process* (2nd edn). London: Butterworths.

LOADER, I, GIRLING, E and SPARKS, R (1998) 'Narratives of Decline: Youth, Disorder and Community in an English "Middletown"' *British Journal of Criminology* 38: 388.

NEWBURN, T, BROWN, D and CRISP, D (1990) 'Policing the Streets' *HORS Bulletin* 29. London: Home Office.

SAMPSON, R and RAUDENBUSH, S (2001) *Disorder in Urban Neighbourhoods: Does it Lead to Crime?* Washington: National Institute of Justice.

SMITH, ATH (1995) 'The Criminal Justice and Public Order Act: the Public Order Elements' *Criminal Law Review* 19.

TAYLOR, R (2001) *Breaking Away from Broken Windows*. Boulder, CO: Westview Press.

WELLS, C (1997) 'Stalking: The Criminal Law Response' *Criminal Law Review* 463.

9

Social Capital, Trust and Offensive Behaviour

BRYAN S TURNER

THIS CHAPTER PROPOSES a theory of social capital to explain how declining trust in modern societies can explain individual fears about and public outrage against offensive behaviour. The argument is that low social capital in young men produces offensive behaviour, which I shall define as any action, and typically non-instrumental action, that is undertaken to cause symbolic affront to the community. By 'non-instrumental' I mean that such actions are not necessarily designed to satisfy the material interests of the young offenders, such as stealing cars or shoplifting, but to satisfy their psychological sense of frustration and alienation. Hence, offensive behaviour may involve vandalism rather than simple theft. Such behaviour is intimidating to members of social groups who themselves have low social capital, and feel marginalised and powerless, for example the isolated elderly in inner-city public housing. Because government policy is often driven by concerns expressed in focus groups, ministers responsible for the enforcement of law and order respond with policies that target offenders in an attempt to offer the public a sense of symbolic vindication—such as the use of Anti-Social Behaviour Orders. In turn, these governmental responses, which are often themselves quite severe, tend further to alienate and isolate youth groups, who may well respond by increasing their offensive behaviour. There is a well established theory in the sociology of deviance, namely labelling theory, which argues that policing and other forms of law enforcement can reinforce social stereotypes of young offenders, resulting in further social exclusion and the amplification of their deviant behaviour (Becker, 1963). My theory of social capital therefore describes a spiral of increasingly offensive non-instrumental activity in the community, the high level of fear among disadvantaged sections of the elderly population, and the further amplification of anti-social behaviour.

I. SOCIOLOGICAL EXPLANATIONS

Sociology as a discipline was a product of the nineteenth-century industrial revolution in which sociologists such as Emile Durkheim were concerned to provide distinctive explanations of emerging patterns of disorder. Sociology can be defined as the science of social institutions, that is, regular patterns of activity governed by social norms. Against a background of disorderly behaviour in urban spaces, sociologists sought to understand the conditions that produce normative order. The disorientation of values and beliefs in urban society resulted in *anomie*. In this respect, Durkheim (1951) constructed the classical form of sociological explanation in his *Suicide*. He associated high rates of suicide in France with the disruption of social norms brought about by urbanisation and rapid social change. What he called 'anomic suicide' was characteristic of a society exposed to new norms of utilitarian individualism and the erosion of the social bonds of traditional, rural society. Variations in the extent of social solidarity were significant in explaining differences in suicide rates between rural and urban, religious and non-religious social groups. As a result, young unmarried men in the city were, for example, more exposed to these 'suicidal currents' in modern society than women in rural communities with familial ties and domestic responsibilities. Durkheim's thesis has been subject to considerable criticism (Douglas, 1967), but his approach established the defining characteristics of a sociological, as opposed to psychological, approach to behaviour. There is ample empirical evidence to suggest that social isolation and low social integration are important causes of poor health, delinquency, crime, and depression (Turner, 2004). For example, the social isolation of elderly men in urban America is a significant factor in their high rates of mortality and morbidity (Klinenberg, 2002). Since offensive behaviour might be deemed a topic ripe for sociological interpretation, we should start by outlining the essential features of a sociological perspective.

The first characteristic of classical sociology is the quest to understand and define 'the social' as opposed to 'the natural'. Sociology has been consistently critical of attempts to understand social phenomena in terms of the natural endowments of human beings. It would thus be sceptical of any claim that offensive behaviour could be explained by a person's genetic legacy because, to offend, an action has to transgress some accepted norm of social behaviour. Sociological explanations substitute 'institutions' for 'instincts'. Sociology insists on the reality of the social world, but it also wants to distinguish itself from economic, political, and even cultural perspectives. What is offensive varies between social groups over time, and hence offensive behaviour is a product of social interpretation. Secondly, classical sociological explanations of the social assume a particular form— they typically eschew variables that are characteristic of individuals such as their motives, personalities, needs, or beliefs. Methodological individualism as an epistemology is not typical of classical sociology. Sociology does not necessarily deny the existence of psychological variables relating to human behaviour; it tends simply to be indifferent to psychological perspectives. Thirdly, sociological explanations tend to assume a critical form, because they challenge the taken-for-granted assumptions of the agents themselves. In western societies, where, as a result of the social and political influence of liberalism, people think of 'individuals' as having causal priority, sociological accounts are not part of 'common sense'. Classical sociology is counter-intuitive. It produces arguments that tend to defy or to deny common-sense assumptions. In this respect, Durkheim and classical sociology regarded psychological explanations as approximating common-sense understanding of human behaviour by incorporating everyday assumptions about 'human nature'. Sociologically speaking, the reason why offensive behaviour exists is not that there are offensive individuals. Sociology is not interested in research findings about the identifying characteristics of offensive individuals; its task is to understand the social conditions that tend to produce offence. What properties of the social structure evoke an environment that fosters offensive behaviour?

In order to clarify further what I mean by a *sociological* explanation of behaviour, it is important to establish a better understanding of the 'social'. Classical sociology involved not only the quest to understand and define the social as a field of special intellectual endeavour, but also to grasp the social as a moral phenomenon distinct from individualism. If the character of sovereignty defines the political, the social is defined by trust. Trust is the social dimension that underpins social relations, especially contractual relations in the social sphere. Just as money is the medium of exchange in the economy, trust is the medium of reciprocity in the social field.

The social, whatever else it entails, has two interrelated core elements. First, it is constituted by social interaction; secondly, these social actions must cohere in social institutions. Classical sociology is the study of the institutionalisation of relations of trust—the family, religion, the law, customs, and so forth. As one might expect, the social is in practice difficult to define. There were therefore various levels of analysis in the classical tradition. Because the debate with economics as a science was central to much of nineteenth-century social thought, it is hardly surprising that Karl Marx and Max Weber approached their task of analysing capitalist society in terms of a model of economic action. The economic model involved the idea of rational actors satisfying their wants in a competitive market. Social action was modelled on a similar set of notions, but sociologists sought to study social collectivities (such as social classes), questioned the rationality of economic behaviour (by including notions such as ideology), and questioned the idea of needs and wants (by demonstrating their cultural relativity). Whereas economics involved the study of the rational selection of means and ends in conditions of scarcity, sociology can be regarded as the study of the conditions of trust that underpin social institutions. In economics, money provides a measure of the distribution of rational choices, whereas trust is only an indirect or proximate measure of social solidarity. In short, sociology—in contrast to classical economics—developed much richer or thicker notions of behaviour and action, but at the cost of precision and predictability. The point of this extended commentary on early sociology is to indicate the development of an argument that anxieties about the increase in offensive behaviour are consequences of a decline in trust, and low trust is a function of the erosion of social capital. Offensiveness is an effect of low trustworthiness, not of individuals, but of social relationships.

II. SOCIAL CAPITAL, CIVIC PARTICIPATION, AND HEALTH

The contemporary notion of social capital has a number of somewhat disparate intellectual origins (Turner, 2003). The notion developed out of economics as a method of explaining investments in education, training, and welfare in order to produce human capital, and became associated with the sociological contribution of James Coleman to the study of education. Coleman (1988) showed how social capital facilitates social action through trust and trustworthiness. Trust makes social action more efficient, because it reduces transaction costs (Lin, 2001). In the sociology of education, Pierre Bourdieu identified different forms of capital—economic, social, cultural, and symbolic. He defined social capital as investment in social connections, namely those social relationships that are valuable (Bourdieu, 1993: 33). Accepting an invitation to an employer's home for afternoon tea is an investment in social capital in order to create influential connections. A different interpretation has been developed by Robert D Putnam. In his research of civic traditions in modern Italy, Putnam (1993) showed that civil society requires trust, and that trust arises from two sources, namely the norms of reciprocity and networks of civic engagement.

Putnam's work has been important in the context of debates about the decline of social capital in American public life, where his theory of civic engagement as a product of social capital can be related to the legacy of Alexis de Tocqueville, who had argued that voluntary associations were the bedrock of American democracy. Whereas in Europe people were dependent on the state to provide many essential services, in colonial America local communities would form voluntary groups to erect civic buildings, construct roads, build schools, or found hospitals. Writing in 1831, de Tocqueville (1959: 212) argued that the 'power of the association had reached its highest degree in America' where it served many purposes. Temperance societies were an example of an association of men who mutually agree to abstain from alcohol and other vices, and discover in this collective asset an aid in resisting a form of deviance that is intimate and personal to each man, that is to his own inclinations. Durkheim's argument followed this logic closely in his study of the social causes of acts of suicide.

The Tocquevillian tradition has been reinvigorated by the Putnam's research. In his inquiry into the civic traditions that support democratic processes, Putnam (1993: 167) concludes that social capital, as a feature of social organisation that includes trust, norms, and networks, 'can improve the efficiency of a society by facilitating co-ordinated actions'. Social trust is essential for building up civil society through norms of reciprocity and engagement, and it is the main antidote to the negative effects of individual competitiveness and egoism that are characteristic of free markets. Social capital represents the investments of people in communal activity.

Social capital theory suggests explanations of crime that are both rich and parsimonious. Putnam (2000: 310) showed that in the United States the higher levels of social violence in southern states (and variations between southern states) are best explained by low social capital. He also examined the results of a lifestyle survey in which respondents were asked whether they agreed or disagreed with the statement 'I'd do better than average in a fist fight'. The increase in pugnacity between the 1970s and 1980s is consistent with an overall decrease in social capital, but states with low social capital were more pugnacious than states with high social capital. Putnam's work also supports the theory of neighbourhood effects on crime and delinquency, namely that a decline in community associations creates an urban environment in which children more readily embrace delinquent activities. Neighbourhood areas of low social capital are characterised by the absence of positive norms, supportive associations, and informal adult friendships. In research on the flight of high income families from the inner city, William Julius Wilson (1987: 144) in *The Truly Disadvantaged* noted that 'the removal of these families made it more difficult to sustain the basic institutions of the inner city (including churches, stores, schools, recreational facilities, etc) in the face of prolonged joblessness'.

We can summarise these different approaches to social participation and trust by defining social capital as the social investments of individuals in social networks, such as their membership of formal and informal groups and associations. Social capital therefore provides us with a measure of the degree of social integration or social solidarity in any given society. The density of social membership in community groups, churches, voluntary associations, and neighbourhood groups is a measure of the extent of norms of reciprocity and in turn a measure of the vitality of trust. It is important to recognise that the social capital debate has emerged as a critical tool to analyse the negative effects of growing social inequality on what used to be called 'social pathology' (poor health, domestic violence, delinquency, and crime) in a period of 'neo-liberal' economic and social policies that involve privatisation, deregulation, and 'incentivisation'.

III. SOCIAL PATHOLOGY: HEALTH AND CRIME

In recent years, there has been a significant neo-Durkheimian revival in the quest for distinctive sociological explanations of both mental and physical health. There is an important parallel between sociological explanations of poor health and criminal behaviour. My intention is to explore the research on health as the basis for a theory of offensive behaviour. Durkheim's notion that social integration protected individuals from bouts of depression has been applied to community studies of mental health. Social psychologists have studied how community ties provided a protective social integration against the impact of negative life events (Dohrenwend and Dohrenwend, 1981). Further research has explored how social support might more directly act as a buffer against hurtful life events such as divorce or bereavement (Berkman and Syme, 1979). While psychologists have long been aware of the impact of stress on individual health, it has been difficult to find objective measures of stress to explain variance in health outcomes. Life events provide an alternative measure of episodes that attack an individual's composure and self-esteem. Stress and strain in social relations are obviously related to life cycle, and the decline of 'relational stress' with aging may compensate for the eventual decline in social participation that is a feature of ageing (Due *et al*, 1999).

The work of Brown and Harris (1978) provides a clear illustration of the use of Durkheimian sociology in the explanation of depression. These authors showed how social structures (primarily friendship networks) protected vulnerable individuals, typically young mothers, from the depressive effects of negative life events. Durkheim's idea of suicidal forces driving individuals 'irresistibly' towards suicide has been refined to demonstrate that individuals do not succumb to 'depressive forces' if they are socially integrated into primary social relationships, such as the family or neighbourhood group. Likewise there is reason to believe that high social capital means that individuals are better protected from episodes of mental illness and report higher levels of well-being (Kawachi and Kennedy, 2002: 180–5; Lin, 2001: 244–5). Does the same argument apply to crime and deviance, and what are the precise connections between social structures and individual behaviour?

There is considerable literature in the social sciences that demonstrates that voluntary association membership contributes to a decrease in psychological stress by providing a shield against its principal forms (Rietschlin, 1998). Membership of voluntary associations is also important in increasing satisfaction and reducing depression. It is additionally associated with improvements in physical well-being and lower mortality. The relationship between well-being (both physical and mental) and membership of voluntary associations is likely to be reciprocal, because healthy, confident, and satisfied individuals are more likely to join voluntary associations than depressed and alienated ones. A recent study by Thoits and Hewitt (2001) on volunteering and well-being confirms that there is a reciprocal relationship between satisfaction and voluntary association membership, but their study emphasises work in voluntary associations rather than simply membership.

These authors discovered that 'volunteer service is beneficial to personal well-being independent of other forms of religious and secular community participation' (*ibid*: 126). Voluntary work and membership enhance various aspects of well-being including satisfaction, physical health, and reduced incidence of depression.

Social capital theory has been a method of recasting existing theories relating income inequality to individual morbidity and mortality. There is a long tradition of social science research that has employed income inequality as a measure of social class to demonstrate that infantile mortality rates, for example, are highly correlated with parental income (Wilkinson, 1996). More recent versions of the theory have suggested that income inequality is causally connected with population health via a societal variable, namely social cohesion and trust, and that cohesion and trust are measures of social capital. In the United States, research has taken measurements of trust in individual states to show that trust has a direct effect on the relationship between income inequality and life expectancy (Kawachi and Kennedy, 1997). The underlying thesis is that high levels of income inequality in a society produce low trust, and low trust creates a poor social environment that in turn impacts on both health and crime.

Another feature of the social capital debate has been the political dimension of crime, health, and inequality; namely, the issue of power. At both the psychological and social levels, a sense of powerlessness and alienation has been closely implicated in poor health and social deviance. However, it is in the field of community development that the notion of social capital as power has had important consequences for social policy. Hawe and Shiell (2000: 879) draw an important distinction here between what they regard as Putnam's 'romantic essentially middle class view of social capital' and Bourdieu's idea of social capital as a field of social struggles over influential 'connections'. In talking about 'community' as a source of protection of individuals from risks, we must also recognise that communities are receptacles of power and that they are stratified by social and cultural capital. Social policy interventions to improve social capital in communities to reduce crime cannot afford to neglect this dimension of power relations within communities. Social capital can be both a bridge between communities and a barrier between them. It is for this among other reasons that crime, health, and citizenship become entwined politically and sociologically. Effective and empowered citizens are supported by communities that have effective, collective resources or social capacities, and this capacity for action is essentially what Coleman (1994: 304) meant by 'social capital' when he wrote, 'a group whose members manifest trustworthiness and place extensive trust in one another will be able to accomplish much more than a comparable group lacking that trustworthiness and trust'.

The impact of the 'neo-liberal' economic revolution of the 1970s has had the consequence of increasing health inequality between and within societies. Recent sociological research has returned to the issue of income inequality as an explanation for illness but has set these income inequalities within the broader context of social integration and cohesion. There appears to be an important connection between the level of aggregate inequality in society, social divisions, the decline of social involvement, low trust, low self-esteem and increasing morbidity, and declining life expectancy. High crime rates, social disorganisation, domestic violence, and civil disturbance also measure low social capital (Coburn, 2000). Social capital is a method of measuring social integration as social investments. Crudely speaking, the more people are involved in society, the better they are protected from poor mental and physical health. The more people are socially connected, the lower their propensity to engage in anti-social behaviour. In this causal argument, both sickness and crime are functions of high inequality and low social cohesion. The biological and psychological connections between individual health outcomes, social participation, and economic inequality remain obscure, but one can reasonably assume that a sense of self-worth is a consequence of supportive social environments that have beneficial consequences for members of communities. Similar arguments apply to the low self-esteem of young offenders in urban neighbourhoods of high unemployment and low incomes.

IV. SOCIAL CAPITAL AND TRUST

The basic premise of Durkheimian sociology was that shared social values are necessary for social existence. These general values are the foundation of the social norms that guide individual action (Parsons, 1951). The problem with modern complex societies is that these values are increasingly fragmented and complex, and social relations thus become more unstable. The conditions that underpin social reciprocity also become more fragile and precarious. Putnam (1993: 172) lists four reasons why general reciprocity has beneficial effects in terms of enhancing co-operation: it increases the costs of defection; it fosters norms of robust co-operation; it improves communication; and it embodies past successes of collaboration and provides a model of future co-operation. These theories of social capital have been criticised by Jack Knight (2001) because they, like the functional theory of social integration in American sociology in the 1950s, suffer from a functional circularity. Because the importance of reciprocity is explained by its effects, these theories do not provide an antecedent causal account of changes in reciprocity.

Knight's alternative is to note that value consensus in modern societies is unusual, because increasing social diversity destroys the cultural homogeneity of traditional societies. He then makes a distinction between sharing a common set of beliefs that are positively valued, and knowing about a set of beliefs that provides common expectations. In this cognitive sense of sharing, 'co-operative predictable behavior is guaranteed by the existence of mechanisms that converge expectations toward actions that satisfy the requirements of mutual benefit' (Knight, 2001: 358). Co-operation with social norms affects a person's attitudes towards how other people will co-operate, and in turn this expectation shapes assumptions about future behaviour. Knight develops this argument to make sense of Putnam's observation that social capital is a resource that increases with use. The growth of generalised trust is a function of everyday compliance with norms, and the more individuals co-operate with each other, the more they trust one another. Past experience of reliable co-operative interaction tend to increase our general sense of the trustworthiness of others in the community. In short, trustworthiness routinely generates trust (Hardin, 2001). Conversely, lack of reciprocity tends to deflate trust.

In the light of this analysis, what diminishes trust in modern society? Knight's argument, following that of Steven Lukes (1991), is that social diversity undermines community and the erosion of common values and shared sentiments undermines trust. Ethnic and multicultural diversity is an obvious feature of most advanced societies. Trust in culturally diverse societies is difficult to achieve because there are important differences of interest, of basic social ends, and of social beliefs and values. In culturally diverse societies, social groups will employ strategies of social closure to secure advantages over resources against outsiders who are seen to be competitors (Askonas and Stewart, 2000; Young, 1999). Informal forms of social regulation and normative regulation are unlikely to work effectively in social environments where social equality and fairness are manifestly absent. The greater the distributional bias in resource allocation, the greater the propensity of disprivileged groups to disrupt existing social arrangements. The greater the disadvantages, the greater the incentive of disprivileged groups to distance themselves from dominant groups. The greater the disadvantage, the lower the probability that marginalised groups will respond positively to normative (that is, non-instrumental) motivation to comply with existing social norms. The history of apartheid in South Africa would be an extreme instance of this system of social closure, but social conflict between groups on the basis of ethnic classification remains a common aspect of political violence in contemporary societies (Chirot and Seligman, 2001).

In societies that are culturally diverse, generalised trust cannot be sustained simply by reliance on informal mechanisms, like customs, to ensure compliance and co-operation. Max Weber's treatment of formal rules in *Economy and Society* (1978) suggests that the consequence of formal legal institutions is to increase dependence on impersonal formal mechanisms to secure productive, co-operative social interactions. In this sense, the growth of a litigious society is paradoxically a measure of the decline of trust. Knight (2001: 365) argues that the task is 'to construct a conception of the rule of law in a socially diverse society that satisfies the requirements of social order and co-operation and, as a *possible* by-product, creates the conditions for the emergence and maintenance of informal mechanisms like trust'.

While Knight is pessimistic about achieving such a desirable outcome, he supports a pragmatist interpretation of the rule of law as a mechanism for satisfying the interests of different social groups in a differentiated social order. To accommodate the different interests of culturally distinct social groups, law must develop a range of mechanisms that are not unduly conflictual and divisive. Legal proceduralism as a juridical principle underlines the importance of overt and predictable legal processes in the resolution of conflict (Sciulli, 1992). In this respect, the work of Lon Fuller (1969) has been important in developing legal procedures (adjudication, mediation, managerial discretion, contract, and legislation) that can contribute to social co-operation. Pragmatism suggests that legal decisions have to satisfy a condition of equal respect and treatment of members of different social groups.

While Knight provides a useful interpretation of how the rule of law might operate in a culturally diverse society, he remains pessimistic about the efficacy of such formal processes in generating generalised trust. In my view, we need to see the rule of law within a broader social and political framework, namely a framework of social citizenship. The institutions of modern citizenship have been the principal mechanisms of social inclusion in contemporary society, and citizenship has played a major role in mitigating the negative consequences of the market. In particular, social citizenship is important in containing and reducing the negative consequences of social class differences in capitalism.

According to TH Marshall (1950), citizenship expanded through three stages. In the seventeenth century, the growth of legal rights was inscribed in habeas corpus, the jury system, and the rule of law. Political rights in the nineteenth century were institutionalised in the parliamentary system, free elections, and the secret ballot box. Finally, social rights in the twentieth century were associated with social security and the welfare state. Citizenship is a status that compensates for or ameliorates the class inequalities that arise from a capitalist market. Marshall's view of the welfare state and citizenship can be regarded as the sociological dimension of social Keynesianism. Mass mobilisation of the population for warfare was an important condition for the growth of post-war social rights; the origins of the National Health Service can be traced to the medical inspections of the South African Boer War, when the British working class was deemed unfit for combat. The expansion of social rights in the twentieth century was connected with military discipline and combat requirements (Mann, 1987).

Marshall's account of British social citizenship helps us to identify important differences between the development of citizenship institutions in

Britain, the United States, and continental Europe. In British society, citizenship evolved through the nineteenth and twentieth centuries as an amelioration of the negative effects of social class and the capitalist market. Citizenship provided individuals and their families with social security. The tension in British citizenship is that it assumed significant state intervention in the regulation of the market, but also emphasised individualism, initiative, and personal responsibility. In the United States, where there has been political reluctance to support the growth of a universal welfare state, citizenship is associated with political membership, migration, and ethnicity rather than with welfare rights and social class. The citizenship debate is still dominated by de Tocqueville and the theory of associational democracy. For de Tocqueville, the lack of centralised, bureaucratic government in America had encouraged the flourishing of individual initiative and voluntary associations rather than state intervention to solve local community problems. Contemporary sociological research has found that Americans were alienated from politics at a formal level, but their social involvement was expressed through a multitude of local and informal associations. Both British and American traditions are distinguished from continental European traditions, where historically citizenship is connected with civility and the civilising process. The bourgeois European citizen was an educated and cultivated private person, who depended on the state to guarantee freedoms and to sustain a moral public order.

The entitlements of Marshallian citizenship were conditional upon work, war, and reproduction. A person became an effective citizen by contributions to the economy, wartime service and parenthood. The Marshallian citizen was a worker, a soldier, and a parent, whose contribution to society through taxation and service was rewarded by a range of social rights. These social conditions have been eroded by the casualisation of employment, the termination of conscription and compulsory military service, the transformation of family life through divorce, and the lone parent household. The economic foundations of traditional citizenship may be described as Fordist insofar as they were based on full employment, a dominant manufacturing sector, mass production, and the nuclear family as the principal site of consumption. The arrival of a post-Fordist economy based on the service sector, flexible employment, and the globalisation of production has disrupted the necessary relationships between national citizenship, employment, a career and the nuclear family. The economic revolution of the late 1970s created a political environment in which governments were no longer committed to the universalistic principles of the traditional welfare state. In this environment the principles of active citizenship were based on the norms of welfare for work, private insurance for health care, private education, flexible retirement, and healthy lifestyles. Thatcherism in Britain rolled back the 'Nanny State' and promoted private initiatives in an enterprise culture. New Labour adopted a Third Way strategy that encouraged joint ventures between public and private sectors in health care and education. Community enterprise was intended to replace the traditional voluntary association in delivering services in the third sector. In modern society, citizenship has become a contested category, because globalisation, migration, and an international labour market have destabilised the traditional relationships between the state, sovereignty and national territory. Political debates over 'the rights of others'—aliens, migrants, refugees and asylum seekers—have become an important dimension of the definition of national identity (Benhabib, 2004).

It is possible to argue that citizenship was eroded in the late twentieth century because the three pillars of Marshallian citizenship have been undermined by economic, social, and technical changes (Turner, 2001). Changes to the labour market—the casualisation of employment, the uncertainty of pensions after retirement, the growth of part-time work, and the development of flexible work-time—have destroyed the sense of career and loyalty to the work place (Sennett, 1998). In turn, the transformation of work in late capitalism—such as the growth of call centres, the increase in female employment, and the decline of industries that were dominated by a unionised male labour force—has undermined traditional notions of masculinity and respect (Sennett, 2003). The termination of military conscription has also weakened an important source of social identification through a common experience of national service. The foundations of national citizenship—universal taxation and military conscription—have been radically transformed. The erosion of the welfare state, the decline of a universal scheme of pension rights, and the growth of the professional army have diminished the sense of active participation in social institutions. Finally, marriage and family life have been transformed by changes in divorce laws, the aging of the population, and the curtailment of kinship obligations. These historical changes to citizenship are associated with the decline of social capital through formal institutions. It is important not to exaggerate the decline of membership of and involvement in voluntary associations in society generally (Marinetto, 2003). Nevertheless, low civic engagement is characteristic of deprived neighbourhoods, which are also characterised by poor health, crime, and delinquency (Brown, Kenny and Turner, 2000).

V. TRUST AND OFFENSIVE BEHAVIOUR

Offensive behaviour is a function of low social trust, and low social trust exists where the reciprocity between social groups is fragmented, infrequent, and spasmodic. Inadequate reciprocity emerges when social groups are segregated by either lack of spatial propinquity, social distance, or an absence of shared expectations. Ironically the use of Anti-Social Behaviour

Orders and modern policing tactics often prohibits young men from entering the inner city, thereby further isolating them from mainstream society.

Offensive behaviour is the behaviour of individuals or social groups that offends certain prevailing social norms. Offensive behaviour is typically the non-instrumental contravention of these norms. It offends where it appears to have no rational motive; it is behaviour that appears to be designed to cause an affront rather than behaviour that is designed to improve the material advantage of the criminal. For example, theft has the instrumental objective of increasing the material resources of the perpetrator, and the affront is the side effect of the theft. 'Laddism'—such as alcoholic displays of random violence against bystanders—offends especially because it appears to be meaningless and provocative. Offensive behaviour typically includes minor assaults, graffiti, damage to property, trespass, loutishness, and uncouthness. The essence of offensive behaviour is its symbolic character. Vandalism is typically a seemingly purposeless attack on property or person that entails a symbolic assault on the victim's status as a law-abiding citizen. Behaviour associated with louts and hooligans is typically associated with alcoholism and drug dependency, and thus with behaviour that is assumed to be irrational because it is out of control. Finally, it is overwhelmingly the deviant trademark of young men.

Offensive behaviour is likely to increase in modern society. Traditional working-class areas of cities often had well established norms of neighbourliness and respectability that have been disrupted by urban modernisation and geographical mobility. The reminiscences of Richard Hoggart (1988) of the back-to-back terraces of working-class Leeds in the inter-war period provide a vivid picture of the delicate balance between local neighbourliness, the need to 'keep yourself to yourself', and suspicion of police and other petty officials. The weight of sociological evidence points to the relative stability of the urban, working-class neighbourhood in the 1950s, where the majority were born and grew up in the same cluster of streets (Meacham, 1977: 47). Locality and kin were important ingredients of social control.

In the contemporary city, young men are often disconnected from mainstream society, because the modern labour market does not provide them with life-long careers and conventional objectives—marriage, reproduction, home-ownership, pensions, and retirement benefits. They cannot become effective citizens and their loutish behaviour is symbolic of this disconnection. Offensiveness will also increase in societies that are multicultural and diverse, and where there are basic disagreements about codes of appropriate behaviour. In this sense, Durkheim's concept of *anomie* is not entirely appropriate as a description of modern society. In a diverse and differentiated society, norms will be characterised not by their absence but by the shallowness of the support they receive. As Knight has pointed out, while there may be cognitive agreement about norms, there is unlikely to be an evaluative consensus. In a complex society, there will be extensive diversity and confusion about social norms.

The notion of normative confusion should not induce wholesale nostalgia for the past. Offensive behaviour has a long history. From a Durkheimian perspective, offence is the necessary product of the existence of a customary norm (Traugott, 1978). Throughout British history, crime has been associated with the 'meaner sorts' (Cannadine, 1999: 48). According to the *Oxford English Dictionary*, 'ruffian' was used in 1531 to describe persons of low character, given habitually to crime and violence. In seventeenth-century London, the apprentice boys alarmed the populace with their offensive behaviour. The word 'hooligan' came into the English language in 1898—apparently the name of an Irish family in south-east London who were noted for their ruffianly behaviour. In 1857, 'lout' came to mean, according to Rugby School slang, a common fellow or cad. Contemporary anxiety about offensive behaviour in Britain can be more precisely dated from youth protests against middle-class culture in the youth movements that were associated with the mods and rockers. These youth movements were harbingers of consumer society in Britain and a transition from a traditional society based on work, the Protestant Ethic and the dignity of labour to a society that promotes leisure and consumption through personal indebtedness. These youth movements were a symbolic threat to traditional values, but the Brighton riots involved relatively minor damage to property. The amplification by the British press of these deviant acts converted relatively minor instances of illegal conduct into offensive behaviour that was a symbolic challenge to the moral order. Through deviancy amplification, these youthful protesters became 'folk devils' (Cohen, 1972).

Jock Young (1999: 35) has argued that the rise in crime in the period 1960 to 1975 occurred at a time of full employment, rising living standards, and expanding welfare services. This crime wave contradicted the conventional sociological view that associated crime with poverty. Young is critical of sociological attempts to explain this increase in crime as merely a symbolic crisis in British society. What Young called the 'aetiological crisis' was partly solved in British sociology by the development of labelling theory, notions of moral panic, and social constructionism. The rise in crime was not thought to be a substantial increase in the underlying process of crime, but more the outcome of the amplification of deviance (Wilkins, 1964). However, the deviancy theory of the 1960s and 1970s now seems unfashionable. By contrast, social capital theory does not suffer from the problems identified by Young. Low social capital is not the same as low economic capital, because social capital theory is concerned with the quality of social life, particularly civic institutions. While low social capital is often related to low income, social, cultural, and economic capital can vary independently (Bourdieu, 1984). Social dislocation and isolation can occur in social groups that have considerable economic resources, and declining, ineffective civic institutions can exist in periods of economic prosperity.

Contemporary society is characterised by the social isolation and dislocation of youth groups. The social disconnectedness of young men is a function of the erosion of citizenship. In particular, the casualisation of work makes it difficult for young men to form households and provide adequate resources for reproduction. Because romance is closely associated with personal consumption, forming romantic attachments involves economic investments which many young men cannot afford (Illouz, 1997). This erosion of citizenship has serious implications for the status of young working-class males and constitutes a symbolic threat to masculinity. Offensive behaviour is in this regard a negative expression of traditional forms of masculine behaviour involving drunkenness, loutish behaviour, and random violence. The growth of a 'laddish culture' is a direct product of the erosion of effective participation in mainstream social life as a consequence of the decline of traditional working class occupations and activities. While football and football clubs traditionally provided occasions for the expression of working-class masculinity through aggressive behaviour, the modern football club, which is closely associated with profitability, has contained such offensive behaviour through the development of all-seater stadia, and the direct management of football clubs to attract high-spending, wealthy customers (Sandvoss, 2003: 114). Chanting, violence, abusive language, and the use of fireworks were typical manifestations of traditional forms of offensive behaviour, but these are alien to the culture of so-called new or respectable fans. Loutish behaviour by young fans is now confined to spaces outside the stadium.

A decrease in social capital is associated with increases in crime and social deviance. Post-communist Europe and Russia have experienced increases in prostitution, drug dependency, homicide, and suicide as a result of deregulation, the privatisation of services, and the collapse of state welfare. The current increase in HIV/AIDS is also associated with the decline of social capital in these societies. From empirical studies of social capital, we might infer that the growth in offensive behaviour is simply a function of the decline of social capital. One objection to this inference is that in Britain (and other western societies) there has been a steady decline in many forms of criminal behaviour including violent crimes such as homicide, burglary, and theft. It is important to make a distinction between actual increases in offensive behaviour and perceived or subjective definitions of such increases. These may vary independently, because an increase in perceived risk may not be the product of an actual rise in crime.

The decline of social capital that is evident in many deprived urban areas will explain the prevalence of crime among the urban underclass of modern society. Disconnected and dislocated urban youth make a disproportionate contribution to crime and offensive behaviour, despite the general decline in violent crime. Lack of trust produces a fear of crime and a heightened perception of offensive behaviour among vulnerable social groups, despite the actual decline in various types of violent crime in the 1990s. This atmosphere of fear and distrust is enhanced by periodic government campaigns against offensive behaviour. Determined intervention by the police against the anti-social behaviour of young people can often have a 'blow-back' effect, because such intervention can intensify the stereotyping of youth and further margin-alise them from mainstream society. The spiral of action and amplification has been analysed by 'social reaction theory', which has examined the problem of 'deviance amplification' with special reference to the consequences of the enforcement of prohibitions on the use of drugs among young men. These ideas were developed by sociologists such as Edwin Lemert (1967) who claimed that, where stereotypical labelling excludes people from normal social roles, they are often forced to resort to secondary deviance—such as shoplift-ing or car theft—because they cannot support themselves financially through legitimate forms of work. The use of restraining orders on young offenders can make it more difficult for them to interact in non-criminal social groups. The result is a drift towards criminal social roles—a process that sociologists have called 'delinquent drift' (Matza, 1969). The paradox of social control is that it can often increase the behaviour it is intended to diminish or to expunge.

In the last decade there has been a deliberate political manipulation of the fear of symbolically offensive acts. Since the Tory Conference of 1993, when Michael Howard coined the expression 'If you don't want the time, don't do the crime', Conservative and Labour leaders have competed with each other to be regarded by the electorate as parties of law and order. In the summer of 2004, Howard returned to the issue of crime by arguing that human rights and political correctness worked against victims and made it difficult for the law to prosecute offenders efficiently. There has been an attempt to argue that human rights legislation is an aspect of a compensa-tion culture that has been economically problematic for public authorities. Howard was also critical of Labour's attempt to cap prison numbers, and committed the Tories to between ten and twenty-two new prisons. Further, he argued that crime had increased substantially, thereby dismissing the British Crime Survey, which shows that crime has actually fallen. However, Labour Party leaders have also been keen to embrace this political posture and David Blunkett has won the reputation in the British press for being a Minister who is 'tough' on crime. In seeking to counter Conservative Party policy objectives, in August 2004 Blunkett announced measures to give police extra powers to levy duties on publicans and to provide community support officers to detain people for anti-social behaviour. In a modern de-mocracy, electoral politics employing focus groups to identify popular fears and anxieties can have the unfortunate effect of reducing trustworthiness and creating an atmosphere of panic and fear, because there is an amplifi-cation of public concern that in turn fuels the use of police measures that may further alienate marginalised social groups.

VI. CONCLUSION

Much of the discussion of social capital has assumed that trust will emerge informally from the everyday network of social relationships that are associated, for example, with church attendance, club membership, or participation in neighbourhood groups. Underprivileged neighbourhoods are urban areas in which the informal wellsprings of trust have run dry. This analysis of trust is parallel to conventional views about how money functions. It is argued that money can only function where there is confidence (informal trust) in money. However, as Geoffrey Ingham (2004: 187) argues in *The Nature of Money*, any 'extension of monetary relations across time and space requires *impersonal trust and legitimacy*. Historically, this has been the work of states'. In a large and complex social environment, informal trust requires the backing of the rule of law and state institutions. The disorderly character of modern cities requires a legal framework that is fair and transparent. In western democracies, there has been a secular trend of declining trust in governments. This deflation of trust has been aggravated by the role of public relations and the media in managing the relationships between government and electorate. In Britain during the 1980s and 1990s, there was a significant increase in political strategies that employed focus groups and 'spin doctors' to identify political issues among the electorate. In Britain, more than ninety percent of PR professionals work for government or business, and less than ten percent work for non-profit organisations (Schudson, 2003: 149). Paradoxically, the increasing importance of spin appears to be closely associated with declining trust in governments.

Political manipulation of public anxieties about offensive behaviour is therefore likely to have a 'blow-back' effect, because informal trust needs the larger framework of legal and political backing. The competition between the major political parties in Britain and America to be parties of 'law and order', and the frequent claims by ministers of the Crown that they will 'get tough' with offenders, are likely to be counter-productive strategies resulting in further erosion of confidence in government. Uncertainty about the trustworthiness of politicians feeds into a general social environment of lack of confidence in strangers. The decline in electoral participation in many western democracies and increasing tax evasion are general measures of alienation from formal political processes. Declining social capital rather than declining prosperity is the underlying cause of the offensiveness within modern society.

REFERENCES

ASKONAS, P and STEWART, A (eds) (2000) *Social Inclusion. Possibilities and Tensions.* Basingstoke: Macmillan.

BECKER, HS (1963) *Outsiders. Studies in the Sociology of Deviance.* Glencoe, IL: Free Press.

BENHABIB, S (2004) *The Rights of Others. Aliens, Residents and Citizens.* Cambridge: Cambridge University Press.

BERKMAN, SL and SYME, SL (1979) 'Social Networks, Host Resistance and Mortality: a nine year follow-up study of Alameda County residents' *American Journal of Epidemiology* 109: 186–204.

BOURDIEU, P (1984) *Distinction. A Social Critique of the Judgement of Taste.* London: Routledge and Kegan Paul.

—— (1993) *Sociology in Question.* London: Sage.

BROWN, G and HARRIS, T (1978) *Social Origins of Depression.* London: Tavistock.

BROWN, KM, KENNY, S and TURNER, BS (2000) *Rhetorics of Welfare. Uncertainty, Choice and Voluntary Associations.* Basingstoke: Macmillan.

CANNADINE, D (1999) *The Rise & Fall of Class in Britain.* New York: Columbia University Press.

CHIROT, D and SELIGMAN, MEP (eds) (2001) *Ethnopolitical Warfare. Causes, Consequences and Possible Solutions.* Washington, DC: American Psychological Association.

COBURN, D (2000) 'Income Inequality, Social Cohesion and the Health Status of Populations: the role of neo-liberalism' *Social Science & Medicine* 51(1): 139–50.

COHEN, S (1972) *Folk Devils and Moral Panics. The Creation of the Mods and Rockers.* Oxford: Martin Robertson.

COLEMAN, JS (1988) 'Social Capital in the Creation of Human Capital' *American Journal of Sociology* 94: 95–120.

—— (1994) *Foundations of Social Theory.* Cambridge, MA: The Belknap Press.

DOHRENWEND, BS and DOHRENWEND, BP (eds) (1981) *Stressful Life Events.* New York: Prodist.

DOUGLAS, J (1967) *The Social Meaning of Suicide,* Princeton: Princeton University Press.

DUE, P, HOLSTEIN, B, LUND, R, MODVIG, J and AVLUND, K (1999) 'Social Relations, Network, Support and Relational Strain' *Social Science & Medicine* 48(5): 661–73.

DURKHEIM, E (1951) *Suicide. A Study in Sociology,* Glencoe, IL: Free Press.

FULLER, L (1969) *The Meaning of Law.* New Haven: Yale University Press.

HARDIN, R (2001) 'Conceptions and Explanations of Trust', in KS Cook (ed), *Trust in Society.* New York: Russell Sage Foundation, 3–39.

HAWE, P and SHIELL, A (2000) 'Social Capital and Health Promotion: a Review' *Social Science & Medicine* 51(6): 871–85.

HOGGART, R (1988) *A Local Habitation. Life and Times: 1918–1940.* London: Chatto & Windus.

ILLOUZ, E (1997) *Consuming the Romantic Utopia. Love and the Cultural Contradictions of Capitalism.* Berkeley: University of California Press.

INGHAM, G (2004) *The Nature of Money.* Cambridge: Polity.

KAWACHI, I and KENNEDY, BP (1997) 'Health and Social Cohesion: why care about income inequality?' *British Medical Journal* 314: 1037–40.

—— (eds) (2002) *The Health of Nations. Why Inequality is Harmful to Your Health.* New York: The New Press.

KLINENBERG, E (2002) *Heat Wave. A Social Autopsy of Disaster in Chicago.* Chicago and London: University of Chicago Press.

KNIGHT, J (2001)' Social Norms and the Rule of Law: Fostering Trust in a Socially Diverse Society', in KS COOK (ed), *Trust in Society*. New York: Russell Sage Foundation, 354–73.

LEMERT, EM (1967) *Human Deviance, Social Problems and Social Control.* Englewood Cliffs, NJ: Prentice Hall.

LIN, N (2001) *Social Capital. A Theory of Social Structure and Action.* Cambridge: Cambridge University Press.

LUKES, S (1991) 'The Rationality of Norms' *Archives Européennes de Sociologie* 32: 142–9.

MANN, M (1987) 'Ruling Class Strategies and Citizenship' *Sociology* 21(3): 339–54.

MARINETTO, M (2003) 'Who Wants to be an Active Citizen? The politics and practice of community involvement' *Sociology* 37(1): 103–20.

MARSHALL, TH (1950) *Citizenship and Social Class and Other Essays.* Cambridge: Cambridge University Press.

MATZA, D (1969) *Becoming Deviant.* Englewood Cliffs, NJ: Prentice Hall.

MEACHAM, S (1977) *A Life Apart. The English Working Class 1890–1914.* London: Thames and Hudson.

PARSONS, T (1951) *The Social System.* London: Routledge and Kegan Paul.

PUTNAM, RD (1993) *Making Democracy Work. Civic Traditions in Modern Italy.* Princeton, NJ: Princeton University Press.

—— (2000) *Bowling Alone. The Collapse and Revival of American Community.* New York: Simon & Schuster.

RIETSCHLIN, J (1998) 'Voluntary Association Membership and Psychological Distress *Journal of Health and Social Behavior* 39: 348–55.

SANDVOSS, C (2003) *A Game of Two Halves. Football, Television and Globalization.* London and New York: Routledge.

SCHUDSON, M (2003) *The Sociology of News.* New York: WW Norton.

SCIULLI, D (1992) *Theory of Societal Constitutionalism. Foundations of a non-Marxist critical theory.* Cambridge: Cambridge University Press.

SENNETT, R. (1998) *The Corrosion of Character. The Personal Consequences of Work in the New Capitalism.* New York: WW Norton.

—— (2003) *Respect. The Formation of Character in an Age of Inequality.* London: Allen Lane.

THOITS, PA and HEWITT, LN (2001) 'Volunteer Work and Well-Being' *Journal of Health and Social Behavior* 42(2): 115–31.

TOCQUEVILLE, A de (1959) *Democracy in America.* Glasgow: Collins.

TRAUGOTT, M (1978) *Emile Durkheim on Institutional Analysis.* Chicago and London: University of Chicago Press.

TURNER, BS (2001) ' The Erosion of Citizenship' *British Journal of Sociology* 52(2): 189–209.

—— (2003) 'Social Capital, Inequality and Health: the Durkheimian Revival' *Social Theory & Health* 1(1): 4–20.

—— (2004) *The New Medical Sociology.* New York: WW Norton.

WEBER, M (1978) *Economy and Society. An Outline of Interpretive Sociology.* Berkeley: University of California Press.

WILKINS, LT (1964) *Social Deviance. Social Policy, Action and Research.* London: Tavistock.

WILKINSON, RG (1996) *Unhealthy Societies. The Afflictions of Inequality.* London: Routledge.

WILSON, WJ (1987) *The Truly Disadvantaged*. Chicago: University of Chicago Press.

YOUNG, J (1999) *The Exclusive Society. Social Exclusion, Crime and Difference in Late Modernity.* London: Sage.

10

Incivilities, Offence, and Social Order in Residential Communities

ANTHONY BOTTOMS

IN THE TITLE of this chapter, I have deliberately adopted the term *incivilities*, rather than the more normal British usage of 'anti-social behaviour', to emphasise that incivilities can sometimes consist simply of behaviour that lacks civility and consideration for others. So defined, incivilities are, obviously, not necessarily grounds for any kind of formal legal intervention. However, I also take the view that incivilities can, on occasion, become genuinely *offensive* to reasonable people, in ways that may also constitute a *wrong* against them, as members of a residential community; on this basis, as von Hirsch and Simester argue in chapter four of this volume, some incivilities can legitimately qualify for inclusion in the criminal law, in accordance with the 'offence principle'. But, even where the use of the criminal law for certain 'offensive incivilities' is indeed morally justifiable, it does not necessarily follow that it is wise, in policy terms, to rely primarily on the criminal law as an instrument of social control. This is because, as will become clear, incivilities are very closely connected to the issue of *social order in public places*, and social order is not necessarily best tackled by exclusively legal means.

The structure of this chapter is as follows. After an introductory discussion based on a recent political tract, I consider various aspects of the empirical evidence relating to incivilities (or 'anti-social behaviour') in England and Wales. These data provide clear evidence that some residents—especially in the poorest communities—find incivilities both emotionally distressing and threatening to their sense of neighbourhood safety. The next section of the chapter therefore focuses upon explanation—why are incivilities seen as distressing and threatening, and why do they appear to be disproportionately concentrated in the poorest areas?

As a bridge from these explanatory questions into issues of policy, I then discuss three theoretical formulations that have become central to this field, and the empirical evidence that supports or fails to support them: these are the 'broken windows' hypothesis, the 'collective efficacy' hypothesis and the 'signal crimes perspective'. The chapter then concludes by considering what lessons for policy arise from the discussion.

Throughout, the focus of the chapter is limited to *residential communities*, in order to make the task more manageable. Some similar issues, of course, arise in non-residential areas such as city centres, but there are substantial differences of context which make it inappropriate to attempt to discuss both residential and non-residential areas within the scope of a single chapter.

I. INTRODUCTORY DISCUSSION: 'NEIGHBOURS FROM HELL'

I begin with a discussion of Frank Field's (2003) short book, *Neighbours from Hell*. Field is a respected but somewhat unorthodox (some would say maverick) Labour Member of Parliament, on the right of his party. Traditionally a specialist in welfare policy, from the mid-1990s he also became increasingly identified with the political campaign against anti-social behaviour.

In *Neighbours from Hell*, Field describes an incident that was pivotal in focussing his interest on anti-social behaviour as a political issue. A group of pensioners in their 70s came to his constituency 'surgery' in Birkenhead (2003: 10–11):

> Nothing had prepared me for the description of what they were enduring and the hell that had engulfed them. Young lads who ran across their bungalow roofs, peed through their letterboxes, jumped out of the shadows as they returned home at night, and, when they were watching television, tried to break their sitting room windows. . . . Their faces bore witness to this tragedy. They had expected to live out their time in peace and dignity. . . . They had worked hard all their lives, always adding more to society then they ever took from it. They had behaved respectfully to their elders. They reasonably expected to be similarly treated. . . . Most of their eyes were red from being robbed of the certainty of sleep.

As we shall see later, this is by no means an atypical story for our times. Field's book is an attempt to address policy issues arising from such behaviour, including some improbable-sounding proposals such as appointing the police as 'substitute or surrogate parents' in those families where 'parents . . . cannot or will not control their children' (Field, 2003: 84, 88). Despite its eccentricities, however, the book contains several very shrewd observations which, I believe, can help us with an analysis of the relevant issues. I shall select for attention here four such observations.

First, there is the question of definition. Field begins by asserting the importance of three 'social virtues' in community life: they are politeness, considerateness, and thoughtfulness, each of which contributes to 'a sense of common or shared decency in a society' (2003: 31)—or, we might alternatively say, to mutual 'civility'. He then makes the following very interesting claim:

> Anti-social behaviour [is] due to the collapse in the standards of personal behaviour which award due respect for another human being. Practically all criminal and many civil misdeeds, of course, share this characteristic . . . such actions should be countered by the existing law. In contrast, *the distinguishing mark of anti-social behaviour is that each single instance does not by itself warrant a counter legal challenge. It is in its regularity that anti-social behaviour wields its destructive force.* (Field, 2003: 44–5 emphasis added; see also 76–7.)

As Field is well aware (2003: 76), this is a narrower conception of anti-social behaviour than is often used in discussions of this problem. He claims that it is not very helpful to bracket the problem with 'general law and disorder issues', because this can deflect attention from the specific matters in hand. This is, in my view, an insightful comment upon which we can usefully build.

In chapter five of his book, Field considers some potential objections to his proposals. One of these objections is that taking action against anti-social behaviour could be said to be 'invading the private domain'. Field (2003: 55) is robust in his response:

> Everyone has a right to hold whatever views they wish. We enter a different realm, however, when these private views are expressed in public. . . . The guardians of our public space have a responsibility to consider the impact on the public peace of making private views public. . . . [Additionally], once those values determining conduct are operating in the public domain, they cease to be a private concern only, and become the stuff of politics.

While this argument could perhaps have been stated more clearly, Field is here articulating some important points. Freedom of expression remains paramount. 'Public space', however, is a communal arena where all citizens can reasonably expect to be treated with respect, provided they are using the space peaceably. When, in public space, certain uncivil values are expressed in *behaviour* (what Field calls 'values determining conduct'), then potentially the State has a right to intervene for the public good. As we shall see later, use of public space is in fact a crucial element within the incivilities debate—although not always recognised as such—and Field does us all a service by emphasising the important distinction between private freedom of expression, and conduct in public.[1]

---

[1] Field does not, however, clearly address the question of freedom of speech in public places. A correct approach would seem to be to regard this freedom as a basic right, but subject to curtailment under certain circumstances such as the expression of overt insults: see ch 4 by von Hirsch and Simester.

Field reports that another objection sometimes made against his agenda on anti-social behaviour is that 'it constitutes a new form of poor-baiting, explaining away deep-seated societal problems by blaming the poor'. To this objection, Field (2003: 63) makes a simple response:

> Politicians in touch with their constituents know that it is from working class and poorer people themselves that the most forceful pleas come for controlling the behaviour of that as yet small minority who make their neighbours' lives such a misery. . . . National surveys . . . show that the poorer an area is, the worse is the anti-social behaviour.

This demographic imbalance in the incidence of incivilities is of great importance. In the next section, I will review national data supporting Field's statement; later, we will have to consider the explanation of the imbalance.

A further and final point that I want to highlight from Frank Field's book is his criticism of the Government's overall policy strategy. Here, Field (2003: 46) usefully links the Government's anti-social behaviour agenda to its poverty/welfare agenda:

> [The Administration's concern] is to mobilise public support for an expanding array of sanctions against the perpetrators of disorder. Since 1997 the government has initiated an impressive number of counter-poverty measures. . . . The Prime Minister and his allies believe that individuals should maximise these new opportunities presented to them. More importantly, should these individuals decide not to, and behave instead in an unacceptable manner in public, the government's anti-poverty strategy secures for the Administration a moral authority to crack down on such disorder.

This kind of 'carrot and stick' philosophy is of course (although Field does not make this point) traditionally associated with rational choice theory. Field agrees that it will work with some individuals, but he is sceptical of its likely overall success. For him, 'anti-social behaviour [is] . . . caused by much more fundamental changes in society' than are addressed in the Government's approach to policy. Thus, although Field shares the Prime Minister's commitment to tackling anti-social behaviour, the two men are divided in their basic understanding of the problem.

Summing up, therefore, we can note that Frank Field has drawn attention to:

- Definitional issues concerning the term 'anti-social behaviour', which for him should focus especially upon *repetitiveness*, because it is repetitiveness that gives this kind of uncivil behaviour its 'destructive force' within local communities;
- A distinction between private freedom of expression, and the need for acceptable conduct in public places;
- A strong demographic imbalance in the incidence of incivilities, with the poorest areas suffering most;

- The fact that, in his view, the incivilities problem is caused by 'fundamental changes in society' and, unless we understand this, any policy response will be—and the Labour Government's is—inadequate.

In my judgement, this is an important set of observations. As the argument develops, it will be crucial to hold on to these insights, and to build them into our understanding and policy proposals.

II. EMPIRICAL EVIDENCE I: THE BRITISH CRIME SURVEY

I turn now to consider various aspects of empirical evidence relevant to the question of 'incivilities' or 'antisocial behaviour' in England and Wales. I begin with evidence from a large and nationally representative survey— namely, the data from the 'new module' that was added to the British Crime Survey (BCS) in 2003/4 in order to gain a more comprehensive national picture of incivilities (see Wood, 2004a or, for a shorter version, Wood, 2004b).[2]

Table 1 shows the proportion of BCS respondents who rated various specified incivilities as a 'very big problem' or a 'fairly big problem' in their local area. Unfortunately, the item at the head of the list ('speeding traffic') is ambiguous, because it does not distinguish between ordinary road users breaking the speed limit in the area, and the rather different problem of local youths attempting to use the local streets as a kind of racetrack (on which see further below). Other items listed in the table are perhaps more familiar—they include inconsiderate parking, rubbish/litter, vandalism/graffiti, teenagers hanging around, open drug use or drug dealing in the area, public drunkenness, and so on. When further asked to nominate the 'biggest problem' in their area, BCS respondents chose two items in particular, namely 'speeding traffic' (19 per cent of respondents) and, perhaps more surprisingly, 'teenagers hanging around' (17 per cent) (Wood, 2004a: 12 and Table 3.4).

There was, however, a considerable degree of variation in such responses by type of residential area. For example, using the ACORN geodemographic tool,[3] the percentage of residents perceiving 'high anti-social behaviour' in

---

[2] The BCS is an annual survey of approximately 40,000 intended respondents aged 16 or over, living in private households in England and Wales. Following appropriate weighting, the survey provides a representative sample of individuals and households in England and Wales. In 2003–2004, a new set of questions about anti-social behaviour was added to the BCS; these questions 'aimed to explore what people based their perceptions of the problem on, the nature of experiences that informed perceptions, and the impacts for individuals and communities' (Wood 2004a: 6). The response rate for the main BCS sample in 2003–2004 was 74%.

[3] ACORN (A Classification of Residential Neighbourhoods) is a tool developed by CACI Ltd, using information from the 2001 National Census, and other data sources. It combines information on households, individuals and geographical location to classify local areas by socioeconomic characteristics. In all, 56 types of area are identified, but these are also aggregated into 17 meso-level groups, and 5 broad categories. The 5 broad categories are shown in

Table 1   British Crime Survey 2003-2004: Proportion of Respondents Identifying 'Very Big' or 'Fairly Big' Problems in their Local Area in Relation to Sixteen Kinds of Behaviour

	% perceiving 'very big' problem	% perceiving 'fairly big' problem	% perceiving 'very big' or 'fairly big' problem
Speeding traffic	12	31	43
Cars parked inconveniently or illegally	9	22	31
Rubbish or litter	9	20	29
Fireworks (excluding organised displays)	10	19	29
Vandalism and graffiti	8	20	28
Teenagers hanging around	9	19	28
Drug use or dealing	9	16	25
Uncontrolled dogs/dog mess	6	18	24
People being drunk or rowdy	5	14	19
Abandoned cars	4	11	15
People being insulted, pestered or intimidated	2	9	11
Noisy neighbours	3	6	9
Racial attacks	2	5	7
Disputes between neighbours	2	4	6
People with airguns	1	3	4
People sleeping rough	1	2	3

Source: Wood (2004a: 11)

affluent suburbs ('wealthy achievers' areas) was very much smaller than in the most economically deprived (or 'hard-pressed') areas; and there was also a large area difference in the number of different types of anti-social behaviour perceived as a 'very big problem' (see Table 2, columns 1 and 2). Here, then, are the beginnings of confirmation of Field's point about the skew in the incidence of incivilities, and their particularly high concentration in the poorest communities.

Another example of variation by area type relates to respondents' nomination of the 'biggest problem' in their area. For respondents in affluent areas, 'speeding traffic' was most frequently selected (29% chose it as the biggest problem, the next being 'teenagers hanging around' at 12%); but in economically deprived areas, this order was reversed, 22% selecting 'teenagers hanging around' and 11% 'speeding traffic'. In view of the prominence of 'teenagers hanging around' as a particular perceived problem in the

Table 2. The category of greatest interest for the purposes of this chapter is that described as 'hard-pressed areas'; this contains 4 of the 17 meso-level groups, namely 'low income families', 'residents in council estates', 'people living in high rise' and 'inner city estates'.

Table 2   British Crime Survey 2003-2004: Variations in Perceptions of Anti-social Behaviour by ACORN Area Type

ACORN area type[†]	% of respondents perceiving 'high ASB'[*]	% of respondents perceiving 3 or more types of ASB as a 'very big problem' locally[††]	% of respondents in each area type perceiving 'young people hanging around' as a very big or fairly big problem
Wealthy achievers	5	5	16
Urban prosperity	20	13	25
Comfortably off	12	9	25
Moderate means	22	17	35
Hard-pressed	31	23	41

Source: Wood (2004a: Tables A4.5, A4.2 and A8.5)

[†] For an explanation of the ACORN classification, see note 3 in the text.

[*] 'High perceived ASB' is a composite measure developed by the Home Office and comprising seven 'strands' of behaviour that were found, in statistical tests, to behave in a sufficiently similar way between respondents for a valid and reliable single measure to be produced. The seven 'strands' included in the measure are: young people hanging around; drug use or dealing; rubbish and litter; vandalism and graffiti; drunk or rowdy behaviour; abandoned cars; and noisy neighbours.

[††] This measure refers to respondents nominating three of the sixteen types of anti-social behaviour listed in Table 1.

most hard-pressed areas (see further, Table 2 col 3), it seems worth taking a closer look at the detailed BCS evidence on this particular topic. That is particularly the case since this topic raises delicate questions about appropriate policy responses, given that teenagers obviously also have rights, and there is of course no necessary incivility involved in simply 'hanging around'.

Why then, in more detail, did respondents in the BCS regard 'young people hanging around' as a problem in local areas? Those who so selected it offered ten main reasons: the youths were 'loud, noisy or rowdy' (48%), used bad language (48%), were 'just a general nuisance' (43%), were drinking (31%), blocking the pavement (29%), causing litter (eg spitting gum on the street) (24%), being abusive or insulting to passers-by (17%), blocking the entrance to shops (16%), were 'generally intimidating or threatening' (11%), or were 'fighting with each other' (9%). Clearly, some of these categories are likely to be more directly offensive to other citizens than are others (eg being 'abusive or insulting' rather than 'just a general nuisance'). As

Table 3 British Crime Survey 2003-2004: Detailed Evidence About 'Young People Hanging Around' as a Perceived Problem in Residential Areas (%)

(a)	*Location* (ten most common locations listed by those who had experience of 'young people hanging around')*	
	In/around local shops	62
	In my street	44
	In other streets/street corners in area	49
	In parks/open spaces	37
	At bus stops	22
	In shopping centres/precincts	21
	In alleyways	18
	Near/outside pubs, clubs, nightclubs	18
	Near/outside schools	11
	Garage areas/stairwells/communal areas	10
(b)	*No. of people in most recent incident*	
	Two-three	5
	Four-five	26
	Six-nine	44
	Ten or more	25
		100
(c)	*Frequency* of respondents' personal experience of 'young people hanging around' in local area in last 12 months (among those who perceived this as a very big or fairly big problem).	
	No personal experience	6
	'A few times'	7
	Around once a month	6
	Around once a week	27
	More or less every day	41
	'All the time'	13
		100
(d)	*Respondents' perception of events* (among those who had experience of 'young people hanging around')	

(d) (i) Percentage of 'young people hanging around' perceived as being 'deliberately anti-social' = 64%

(ii) Percentage of respondents considering that, in the most recent incident, young people's behaviour was directed personally at respondent (includes swearing, abuse, assault, intimidation and threats) = 10%

(e)	*Timing* (listed by those who had experience of 'young people hanging around')*	
	Mornings	2
	Afternoons	16
	Evenings (6pm-11pm)	82
	Night (after 11pm)	20
	'All the time'	12

(*continued*)

Table 3 (*continued*)

(f)	Age: % of respondents in various age-groups perceiving 'young people hanging around' as a very big or fairly big problem	
	16-24	33
	25-44	30
	45-64	26
	65-74	22
	75+	14

* In these questions, multiple responses were allowed, so the totals exceed 100%.
Source: Data derived from Wood 2004(a):
  (a) from Table A 6.5
  (b) from Table A 7.1
  (c) from Table A 6.4
  (d) from Tables A 6.2 and A 6.3
  (e) from Table A 6.6
  (f) from Table A 8.6

Wood (2004a: 25) correctly comments, however, in the perceptions of survey respondents who rated 'young people hanging around' as a problem, it would seem that 'underlying all of the specific incidents . . . is the [more general] idea of the misuse of public space'. This public space dimension of the issue is further brought out when one considers respondents' description of locations where the problem of 'youths hanging about' was said to occur: the list of locations represents very much the kind of place that we may all need to pass through on an everyday basis in carrying out our routine activities (see Table 3(a)). When one adds to that the number of young people involved in the incidents, and discovers that, in nearly 70% of incidents described as problematic, six or more young people were said to be involved, one begins to see why 'young people hanging around' can be perceived as a difficulty (Table 3(b)). That point is reinforced when the relatively high frequency of this kind of occurrence is noted (Table 3(c)), especially since further data shows that this 'frequency count' is higher in economically deprived than in more affluent areas. Moreover, in two-thirds of cases complained of by respondents, the young people in question were seen by respondents as having been 'deliberately anti-social', although not usually in a manner directly threatening the respondent (Table 3(d)). None of this means, of course, that there is necessarily a case for the *criminalisation* of the behaviour described as 'young people hanging around'; but one can begin to appreciate the problematic character of some aspects of this behaviour, in the eyes of other residents.[4]

---

[4] There are, however, a number of methodological problems about the validity of survey-based data on 'anti-social behaviour', given that the data are based on the perceptions of respondents, reporting retrospectively on what they have experienced. I return briefly to some of these issues at the end of the next section.

What about the impact of incivilities on those who experience them? The BCS has some interesting data on this question, summarised (in relation to 'teenagers hanging around') in *Table 4*. The main emotional responses were annoyance, anger and frustration (Table 4(a)); it might not be unreasonable to characterise at least much of this as *resentment* at the behaviour of the young people in question, and as we shall see later such a description leads us into some interesting theoretical territory. Respondents' views about the impact of 'young people hanging around' on their quality of life varied substantially, from slight to high (Table 4(b)), as one might expect given the varied nature of the behaviour described; as before, however, the stated impact was greater in the most deprived areas. It is worth noting that a substantial minority (22%) rated the impact as 'high', and some had also made or considered specific behavioural adjustments to their daily lives because of the perceived problems (Table 4(c)); for these respondents, this was not a trivial issue.

One might suppose, from the above description, that what is at stake in all this is primarily an age conflict between the young and the not-so-young.

Table 4 British Crime Survey 2003-2004: Stated Responses to and Impact of 'Young People Hanging Around' as a Perceived Problem, Among Respondents Experiencing this Problem (%)

(a)	Emotional response (top four categories)*	
	Annoyance	54
	Anger	26
	Frustration	23
	Worry	22
(b)	Stated impact on quality of life	
	Low	38
	Medium	41
	High	22
		100
(c)	Behavioural changes made (Top four categories)*	
	No behavioural changes	47
	Avoid certain places in the area	18
	Avoid going out after dark	18
	Avoid going out on my own	12
	Thought about moving away	11

* Multiple response allowed, so percentages can exceed 100%.
Source: Data derived from Wood (2004a):
    (a) from Table A 8.2
    (b) from Table A 8.3
    (c) from Table A 8.4

While there is some more general evidence of such a divide in 'hard-pressed' areas,[5] on this particular issue that is not the case: slightly more respondents in the *younger* age-groups perceived 'young people hanging around' as a problem than did their elders (Table 3(e)). The main reason for this is, almost certainly, a question of timing: the evenings were overwhelmingly the time when this kind of behaviour was seen as problematic (Table 3(d)), and, as is well known, older people are less likely than the young to use public space in the evenings.

The BCS data have, therefore, given strong support to three of Frank Field's key points, as highlighted in the previous section; namely, the demographic imbalance of 'antisocial behaviour' as a problem, with a focus on the poorest areas; the centrality of the question of public space, and its contested use; and the importance of the frequency, or repetition, of incivilities, especially in the more afflicted areas (Table 3(c)). The data have also supported the substantial emotional impact of incivilities on a minority of respondents, and the deep resentment that can be felt.

III. EMPIRICAL EVIDENCE II: A LOCAL SURVEY

Inevitably, the evidence provided by large-scale national surveys, although extremely valuable, is broad-brush in character. It is useful to supplement it with some more local and more qualitative data, here taken from one housing estate in Sheffield.

As part of a small research study on crime, disorder and civil renewal in four housing areas, a survey was conducted in 'Gardenia', an ethnically predominantly white housing estate with high social deprivation, a high proportion of social housing, and a high crime rate,[6] which has for years been known locally as a 'problem estate' (for its history, see Bottoms, Mawby and Xanthos, 1989). The survey response rate in this particular area was 52 per cent. Here, I shall provide more detail on incivilities in Gardenia

---

[5] See for example the following comment by Wacquant (1993: 376), based on research in deprived French *banlieue* (suburban areas): 'If there is a dominant antagonism which runs through the Red Belt *cité* and stamps the collective consciousness of its inhabitants, it is not, contrary to widespread media representations, one that opposes immigrants (especially 'Arabs') and autochthonous French families but the cleavage dividing youth (*les jeunes*), native and foreign lumped together, from all other social categories. Youths are widely singled out by older residents as the chief source of vandalism, delinquency and insecurity, and they are publicly held up as responsible for the worsening condition and reputation of the degraded *banlieue*.' See also Charlesworth (2000).

[6] Gardenia was originally entirely a council estate, but changes in housing legislation meant that by 2001 its housing tenure distribution was approximately 60% social housing (council or housing association), 35% owner-occupied (under the 'right-to-buy' legislation), and the remainder privately rented. The area's police-recorded crime rate per 1000 population in 2003-4 was 270 (Bottoms and Wilson, 2006: Table 1); the corresponding rate in that year for the whole of England and Wales (including, as the Gardenia figure does not, the many crimes in non-residential areas) was 113.

Table 5   Ratings of Six Perceived Incivilities as 'a Very Big Problem' or 'Quite a Big Problem' in a 'Hard-pressed' Sheffield Housing Estate, 2005

	Very big problem	Quite big problem	Total	% of all respondents (N = 70)	Equivalent national data for 'hard-pressed' ACORN areas, 2003-2004 (%)*
'Cars being revved or driven at high speeds around the streets'	38	13	51	72.9	47
'People dumping rubbish or dropping litter'	21	14	35	50.0	41
'Drug users and drugs dealers'	17	17	34	48.6	41
'Rowdy young people hanging around'	22	10	32	45.7	41
'People damaging private and public property'	14	15	29	41.4	41
'Noisy or problem neighbours' OR 'Problem families'	10	18	28	40.0	N/A

* Source of national data (BCS): Wood 2004a, Table A 4.1. The categories were defined in the BCS in slightly different words, as follows: (i) 'Speeding traffic'; (ii) 'Rubbish or litter'; (iii) 'People using or dealing drugs'; (iv) 'Teenagers hanging around'; (v) 'Vandalism or graffiti'.

than we were able to include in the main publication on this piece of research (see Bottoms and Wilson, 2006).

One of the questions in the survey asked respondents to consider 'a list of things that are sometimes problems in neighbourhoods'. For each item on the list, respondents were then asked to indicate whether this was 'a very big problem', 'quite a big problem', 'not much of a problem' or 'not a problem at all' in their neighbourhood in the last three months. Table 5 shows six of the key items on the list, each comprising a well-known form of 'incivility', and indicates how frequently they were each assessed as 'a very big problem' or 'quite a big problem' by respondents in Gardenia. Table 6 then looks at the same data in another way, indicating how many of the 70 respondents[7] considered that all six of the listed items were a 'very big' or 'quite big' problem, how many thought five items came into these categories, and so on.

[7] There were, in all, 72 respondents to this survey in Gardenia, but 2 of them chose not to reply to this particular set of questions.

The first point to note in Table 5 is that at least 40 per cent of respondents considered *each* of the six listed problems to be, at minimum, 'quite a big problem'. this constitutes, obviously, a high degree of dissatisfaction with aspects of social life in the area. For five of the listed problems, it is possible to derive comparable data from the 2003/4 British Crime Survey (Wood, 2004a: Table A4.1) for 'hard-pressed areas' nationally; as can be seen from the two final columns of Table 5, the responses in Gardenia (which is undoubtedly a 'hard pressed' area in ACORN terms) were similar to, or in some cases rather worse than, such areas nationally. However, consistently with earlier research evidence (see especially Taylor, 2001), there was marked variation among individuals in the total number of 'big problems' that they perceived in Gardenia (Table 6). More detailed analysis showed that this variation had two sources, both of which have also been reported in previous studies—namely, (i) there was significant geographical variation by street, with respondents in some streets reporting many more problems than others, and (ii) even within the same street, different respondents sometimes had very different perceptions of the level of problems—different people see things differently.

Looking in more detail at the results in Table 5, we can also note that in Gardenia 'cars being revved or driven at high speed' seemed to be a particular issue, rated by nearly three quarters of respondents as either a very big or quite big problem. The other five listed problems all had a total of between 40 and 50 per cent of respondents rating them as seriously problematic. Besides car revving, two other matters were rated as a 'very big problem' by at least 30 per cent of respondents—they were 'rowdy young people hanging around' and 'people dumping rubbish/litter'.

To give a more qualitative characterisation of area problems as seen by respondents in Gardenia, some extracts from comments made to the

Table 6   Number of Perceived Incivilities Rated by Each Respondent as 'a Very Big Problem' or 'Quite a Big Problem' in a 'Hard-pressed' Sheffield Housing Estate, 2005

No. of perceived incivilities	No. of respondents	Percentage	Reverse cumulative percentage
0	10	14.2	100.0
1	6	8.6	85.8
2	16	22.8	77.2
3	8	11.4	54.3
4	12	17.1	42.9
5	9	12.8	25.7
6	9	12.8	12.8

research team[8] about some of the listed problems are considered below. For convenience, this will be done using as headings the six incivilities listed in Table 5, considered in the order given in the table, which is also a descending order of total 'problem ratings' (see the fourth column of the table).

1. Cars Revved/Driven at High Speed

The consensus among respondents seemed to be that this behaviour occurred 'in particular late at night', and that the driving was 'noisy and fast'. One respondent, for example, commented that there were 'noisy joyriders, youths on motorbikes and in cars flying up and down our cul-de-sac'. Another had 'contacted the council about cars being driven at high speeds around the streets, but they didn't do anything'.

Because of various problems on Gardenia, the local authority had—as in a number of such areas—appointed 'community wardens' to help keep order. One respondent told us, however, that the wardens were of little help on the 'noisy cars' issue, because 'the joyriders start at about 8 or 9 at night when the wardens finish'.

One respondent linked this issue to a more serious problem—firesetting. She suggested that 'kids dropping [stolen] cars off and firing them' used to happen 'about once a day'; now 'it still happens but not as often'.

The very widespread perception of 'car revving' as the main incivilities issue in Gardenia (see Table 5) is interesting, and differentiates this estate from most 'hard-pressed areas' nationally, where according to BCS evidence 'teenagers hanging around' outstripped 'speeding cars' as the main perceived problem (see earlier discussion). It is not hard to see why the issue was a high-profile one; if cars and motorbikes are 'flying up and down our cul-de-sac' at some speed, this not only significantly disrupts the peaceful enjoyment of public space, but the noise penetrates into the private space of people's dwellings. Hence, not surprisingly, this issue generated a good deal of emotion among respondents.

2. Dumping Rubbish or Litter

Although this item featured strongly in the numerical total of problems (Table 5), it attracted relatively few specific comments, and certainly less emotion, than some of the other incivilities in the list. People did, however, fairly frequently comment about white goods such as fridges being dumped—particularly in the local park, but sometimes also in the street.

---

[8] Such comments were made either during the research interview (interviewers were encouraged to record qualitative comments in addition to 'tick-box' replies) or, in some cases, in written responses when questionnaires were left with the respondent for self-completion.

Many of the comments were quite general, such as 'there's more litter in the streets', but some were more specific, for example complaining about 'kids chucking rubbish [from the back road] over our back gate', and a commercial organisation dumping hazardous waste: 'old batteries, spent motor oil and general scrap and waste'.

3. Drug Use/Drugs Dealing

Drug use was identified as an area problem by some respondents; their comments tended to focus either on the environmental residue ('there's a lot of needles in the road'), or the sense of discomfort created by the presence of an obviously nonconformist group ('drug users use the back of the derelict shop—though you can't say owt [anything], or you'd get a brick through your window').

Those who complained about this issue tended—as in the example above—also to complain about the drug trade being allowed to flourish. So, one respondent commented on the regular presence of drug dealers 'on the path to the XYZ estate'; he said he'd called the police, and flagged down police cars in the area, to draw attention to this, but nothing had happened. Another respondent, however, while agreeing that drug dealers did indeed frequent the area, and being very hostile to them, said they weren't really a *problem* if you weren't involved in the drugs trade, because generally speaking they ignored people unconnected with drugs.

4. Young People Hanging Around

This problem was reported rather variously in different parts of the estate. Some saw it as intermittent ('some nights there are up to twenty youths in the alley at the back—you just leave it, they might not come back for two weeks'), but others saw it as much more persistent. One of the latter commented:

> Youths hang about on the grass by my neighbour's house on the access path for the garages and allotments. . . . I don't do anything because I think the kids would cause bigger problems if I did. Some of them enjoy causing problems, so the best thing is not to react.

A frequent comment was to the effect that 'kids are getting worse—defiant 10–15 year olds', 'kids have no respect,' or, as a third respondent put it, 'they all have an attitude problem'. Three particular locations mentioned where young people congregated were alleyways (see examples above); the local shop ('there's intimidating gangs around the shop', one respondent said); and the local park, which was said by one respondent to be 'a no-go area at night because of gangs of teenagers'. Some commented on the drinking of alcohol by these groups, but this was not noted as especially problematic by most.

There was a good deal of emotion associated with many of these comments, and sometimes a sense of despair not dissimilar to that noted by Frank Field about the constituents who came to his surgery (§I above). Not everyone, however, was despairing; one respondent, while decrying the 'rowdy young people' who congregated at the end of the street, said that she would 'speak to them politely and they usually respond'.

5. Damage to Property

Police statistics for Gardenia showed that the area had a high rate of reported vandalism to homes, and this was supported by the qualitative comments. One respondent said: 'about two weeks ago my windows were egged [had eggs thrown at them]—everyone gets that round here'; and, as we have seen, the threat of having one's house windows broken was sometimes mentioned as a reason not to try to complain about a particular problem.

Public facilities in the area were also vandalised. As well as fairly frequent comments about damage to bus shelters and similar amenities, one respondent said that there had been vandalism to both the local school and the doctors' surgery, and it was well known in the area that the police had withdrawn from the bungalow which they had used as a substation, because of persistent vandalism. All this is congruent with Innes's (2004: 349) observation, in a different study, that the destruction of public amenities was an 'important recurrent theme' in his interviews; in his view, the visibility of such damage was important in suggesting to respondents an 'increased threat in public space'.[9]

Car ownership levels on the estate were not high, but those who had cars were clearly at risk of vandalism, and one respondent reported leaving his car with a relative because 'she has better security'. An act of car vandalism resulted in one of the most striking pieces of qualitative evidence that we collected: one respondent said he had witnessed his neighbour's car being damaged, and had called the police. According to this respondent, the police officer's response was not encouraging:

> from experience . . . if you proceed you're likely to face reprisal attacks. You have to think of your family. You're likely to have your windows put through, and put your family at risk. If we get them and they turn out to be under age they'll just get cautioned and let off.

---

[9] It seems possible—although as far as I am aware there is no evidence on this point—that it is not simply visibility that is at issue in such comments. Everyone knows that the relevant facilities are intended to be public and communal in character; perhaps the deliberate destruction of such facilities is seen as a symbolic attack on the community at large.

It is worth pausing a moment to reflect on the potential impact of this statement on local people. Assuming that the respondent's story is accurate, here was a representative of the official State law enforcement agency recommending withdrawal of a crime complaint, because of potential consequences to the respondent which the police might not be able to prevent. Such advice would clearly not generate confidence among the residents of Gardenia.

6. Noisy Neighbours/Problem Families

Most respondents did not report problems with their immediate neighbours, though a few did. More common were comments about 'problem families' who have 'made the area worse'. One respondent said that there were 'about three problem families, there are gang fights, and a couple of lads carry guns'. While this comment might be overstated, a respected local activist did concur with the view that 'a small number of families are responsible for a lot of the trouble'—a view more generally put forward by Frank Field (2003), who uses the term 'dysfunctional families' for such households. Sometimes, such families had been evicted from social housing elsewhere in Sheffield. Commenting on this, one respondent asked: 'Why can some people cause multiple problems and still get rehoused?'—thus, of course, raising classic questions in social welfare policy about the competing demands of need and desert.

7. Cumulative Effects and Individual Differences

It is hoped that this section of the chapter has given at least some flavour of what it is like to live on a 'hard-pressed' estate with a high reported incidence of incivilities or 'anti-social behaviour'. In concluding the section, however, two additional points must be made.

First, although in the preceding discussion I have dealt with each problem separately, respondents on the ground, of course, often experience them cumulatively. That point is well illustrated in *Table 6*, which shows that over half of respondents in Gardenia rated *three or more* of the six incivilities as 'a very big' or 'quite a big' problem; and a quarter of respondents rated five or more of the incivilities in this way. It is possible, of course, that they are exaggerating—but we need to recognise, with Frank Field (see above), that with this kind of behaviour cumulation and persistence are often a significant part of the perceived difficulty. A cumulation of different kinds of problem, or a persistence of problems despite bringing the matter to the attention of relevant authorities (see several qualitative comments above) has its own effect on residents in emotional terms, and in terms of the perceived quality of day-to-day life. As Innes (2004: 346) well puts it, cumulative exposure to a succession of perceived small problems can readily be interpreted as a big problem.

Having said that, however, it is appropriate to return to a point made earlier, namely that there were some significant differences between respondents, not only in different parts of the area (suggesting that some streets were more problematic than others) but also in the same street (suggesting that different people see things differently). This is a useful reminder of the limitations of survey data. Although the general patterns of data presented in this and the previous section seem very likely to represent an underlying reality (and certainly, our additional although limited ethnographic work in Gardenia suggested that was so), we must in the end always remember that they are perceptual data. As such, they have their own importance (residents' overall perceptions of an area can be crucial in certain respects, for example in decisions to move or stay), but they are not necessarily accurate statements of what is happening on the streets. An interesting example of this point occurred in some earlier Sheffield research (Bottoms and Wilson, 2004) in relation to another area close to Gardenia. Persistent reports were received of young people misbehaving in a certain place, but observation at that place at key times (eg Friday evenings) suggested very little action. What seemed to have happened was that there had been some past events in that place, which had been interpreted by residents as a continuing threat, but this was not matched by the current reality. It is a point that takes us seamlessly into our final source of empirical evidence about incivilities in contemporary Britain.

IV. EMPIRICAL EVIDENCE III: 'SIGNAL CRIMES' THEORISATION AND EVIDENCE

In an important paper, Martin Innes and Nigel Fielding (2002) introduced the concepts of 'signal crimes' and 'signal disorders'. These researchers, both from the University of Surrey, had been having discussions with their local chief constable, who had pointed out that police forces throughout Britain seemed to be struggling with a new problem. Overall recorded crime rates, and BCS victimisation data, suggested that most crime had been falling since the mid-1990s, but public anxiety about crime remained high, with for example most people believing that crime rates continued to increase. Why was this happening, and what should the police response be?

A key conceptual move made by the researchers in response to this puzzle was to argue that, as Innes (2004: 336) later put it, the criminological literature lacked 'a coherent explanation of the public understanding of crime and disorder, and how such understandings are imbricated in the wider symbolic construction of social space'. To fill this gap, *'the central* proposition . . . is that some crime and disorder incidents matter more than others to people in terms of shaping their risk perceptions' (Innes 2004: 336, emphasis added). Thus, for example, several spouse murders in a medium-sized town in a year would be unusual, but would not necessarily create widespread fear, or a sense of threat, to the community at large, because they would be seen as 'private matters'. By contrast, the abduction and murder of a local schoolgirl on her way to school would almost certainly generate much more fear, and a sense of threat, in the area, because of the signal it would transmit about potential risks in the community. In the light of this signal, ordinary people might freshly consider as 'risky' certain places, people or situations that they could encounter in their everyday lives; hence signals are 'social semiotic processes by which different crimes and disorders might have a disproportionate effect' in terms of fear and perceived threat (Innes and Fielding, 2002: Abstract).

These core ideas were subsequently developed by Martin Innes in his work for the National Reassurance Policing Programme (NRPP). Three formal definitions were formulated:

(i) A *signal crime* is a criminal incident that acts as a warning signal to people about the presence of risk.

(ii) A *signal disorder* is a form of disorderly conduct that indicates to people the presence of risk. Signal disorders are either 'physical', involving degradation to the environment; or 'social', involving behaviour.

(iii) A *control signal* is an act of social control that communicates an attempt to regulate disorderly and deviant behaviour. Control signals can be positive or negative.

This set of concepts was then used in a major operational way in the NRPP. As part of that programme, Innes and colleagues (2004) at Surrey University conducted detailed qualitative interviews in 16 areas across England, asking representative respondents in each area what they would identify as the key *potential threats to neighbourhood safety* in their area. Some early results from six areas are shown in *Figure 1*.[10] For each area (here designated 'A' to 'F'), respondents' perceived threats to neighbourhood safety are listed in descending order of importance; thus, for example, in Area F 'drugs' were perceived as the principal threat to neighbourhood safety, followed by 'youths hanging around' and 'public drinking'.

Three points are especially striking about the information in this figure. First, there is some significant variation by area in the details of the responses. Secondly, however, there are some common themes that clearly emerge as the first three perceived 'signals' of lack of neighbourhood safety

---

[10] Later results are similar, and are discussed in Innes *et al* (2004). *Figure 1* previously appeared in Bottoms and Wilson (2004: 387), and is published with the kind permission of Martin Innes.

Crime or Disorder 'Signal'*	Areas					
	A	**B**	**C**	**D**	**E**	**F**
1	Drugs	Youths hanging around	Youths hanging around	Youths hanging around	Youths hanging around	Drugs
2	Youths hanging around	Litter	Graffiti, litter and public urination	Vandalism and Damage	Drugs	Youths hanging around
3	Assault	Damage	Damage	Public violence and drinking	Damage and graffiti	Public drinking
4	Burglary	Public drinking	Public violence and mugging	Racing vehicles and skateboarding	Abandoned / racing vehicles	Anti-social neighbours
5	Mugging	Public violence and speeding	Drugs	Murder	Burglary	Damage
6	Public drinking	Verbal abuse	Burglary		Verbal abuse	Gangs

*   Crime or disorder signals are listed in descending order of perceived importance in each area.

Source: University of Surrey

Figure 1 *National Reassurance Policing Programme: Top 'Signals' Across Trial Areas.*

in the six areas: they are 'youths hanging around', drugs, litter/graffiti, damage and public drinking. Thirdly, it is extremely interesting that burglary does not appear in the 'top three' in any of the six areas, and only features at all in three areas.

What explains the second and third points above? The answer, of course, seems to lie in the fact that the most commonly-identified 'top signals' are all *disorderly events occurring in public space*. Thus, perhaps, they send a powerful signal to residents (in a way that residential burglaries do not) that 'my area is out of control'. As one respondent put it to Innes (2004: 348):

> Yes, it is daft, it is almost daft, but graffiti is the thing that sort of bothers me more, because it is in my face every day. I mean obviously rape and murder are more horrendous crimes, but it is graffiti that I see.

In sum, then, the Surrey research adds to our previous empirical data about incivilities in England and Wales in two ways. The first is by emphasising how different crimes and disorders can send very different 'signals' to the general population as regards threats to perceived neighbourhood safety. Secondly, the data show that even quite minor incivilities can, on occasion and especially if persistent ('in my face every day'), be perceived as major threats to local safety.

V. EXPLAINING REACTIONS TO NEIGHBOURHOOD INCIVILITIES

We have seen that, according to British Crime Survey evidence, over half of those who experience 'young people hanging around' as a problem in their neighbourhood are 'annoyed' by this kind of behaviour, a quarter are 'angry', and a fifth are 'worried' (Table 4). We have further noted that, in Martin Innes's research, neighbourhood incivilities (including, as a prominent feature, 'young people hanging around') are considered to be some of the biggest threats to neighbourhood safety—often more so than burglary. All this is so despite the fact that, according to the BCS, only about ten per cent of incidents of this kind involve behaviour directed personally at the respondent, such as swearing, abuse, and threats (Table 3(d)).

Data of this kind set us, as social scientists, an important explanatory task: *why* does behaviour such as 'youths hanging around' evoke these kinds of reactions?

Let me begin my answer to this question in an unusual way. Professor Norman Barry of the University of Buckingham, in an unpublished presentation to the Speaker's Commission on Citizenship, once sought to explain the liberal conception of society by likening it to what happens in a hotel. As subsequently reported by Raymond Plant (2001: 7), Barry developed the point in the following manner:

> In an hotel people come together under a set of rules which govern their interactions during their stay. The rules are meant to facilitate their private ends whatever they may be. Individuals are anonymous. If they wish to enter into group activities this is a matter of choice. The hotel does not itself, as a condition of being there, offer a sense of common purpose or common identity. The guests at the hotel have no positive duties to one another unless they choose to assume such obligations. The hotel is focussed on anonymity, privacy, contract and rules, not on a common purpose or a common notion of human fulfilment.

It is an elegant simile, but in fact it is unsustainable; and there are two related weaknesses. First, the simile forgets that in living this anonymous life in the hotel, with each guest pursuing his or her private ends, the guests are in fact occupants of a defined space, which they must share peaceably if they are to pursue their private ends in an undisturbed manner. Whilst a large proportion of that space (ie, the guestrooms) is, according to the rules of the hotel, private, the remainder of the space (the corridors, lifts, stairways, entrance lobby, restaurants, etc) is, for those who are living and working in the hotel, *public space*. And pursuing one's private goals in this environment will become significantly more difficult and unpleasant if, for example, every time one tries to use the lift there is a pool of urine in it, left by the last user; or if every time one walks down the corridor to one's room, other guests are there shouting personal abuse. Hence, secondly, Barry's reported summary of the hotel simile is seriously deficient in assuming that, in a hotel, 'the guests . . . have no positive duties to one another unless they choose to assume such obligations'. Clearly, they do have positive obligations to one another, that is to say, given the existence of shared space, they must respect others' rights to use that public space in at least a minimally acceptable physical condition, and without experiencing social harassment. In other words, each guest has a positive obligation to other guests to avoid *physical incivilities that constitute a wrong to other guests* (such as urinating in the lift) and *social incivilities that constitute a wrong to other guests* (such as organising posses of 'insulters' to shout at other guests in the corridors).

At a deeper level, the failure of the hotel analogy demonstrates a very important point, long understood by anthropologists—namely, that human beings are social creatures. Humans require a relatively lengthy nurturing period, which requires familial or quasi-familial structures; hence, humans live in groups. Given that human beings are also able to use language, and to act as agents, this in turn means that there have to be rules in those groups, to regulate collective and co-operative activities—hence, unsurprisingly, rules are an invariable characteristic of human groups (Fortes 1983). Even the hotel analogy recognises, in its first sentence, that there have to be rules in the hotel to 'govern [people's] interactions during their stay'; what it fails to recognise is that those rules will, inevitably, impose on the guests some 'positive duties to one another'.

In fact, however, the continual reproduction and maintenance of social order requires something more subtle than simply the existence of rules and positive duties. Innes (2004: 341) usefully reminds us of this, drawing on Goffman's work. Goffman (1972: 241) had argued that, if a given person is seen by others to be acting improperly (by the standards of that society) then, *even if there is no threat to others from this action*, nevertheless the perceived impropriety:

> may function as an alarming sign. Thus, the minor civilities of everyday life can function as an early warning system; conventional courtesies are seen as mere convention, but non-performance can cause alarm.

Innes (2004: 341) suggests that, using Goffman as a guide, we can begin to 'identify why it is that social and physical disorder should feature so strongly in people's articulations of their fear of crime and their sense of being 'at risk'. The key point, in his view, is that such disorders 'may signal to users of a location either an absent, weakened, or fragile local social order'. Although Innes does not much emphasise the point, it can be argued, following this line of thought, that the concept of *local social order* lies at the heart of a true understanding of the significance of incivilities.

Let us pursue these insights further by moving into the realm of emotions, not least since there is clear empirical evidence that emotions feature strongly in reactions to disorder. In an important text, Jack Barbalet (1998: 3) sets out to demonstrate 'the centrality of emotion to the non-deviant structures of social interaction' in everyday life. In one of his chapters (chapter 6), he tackles the question of 'human or basic rights', and argues that 'basic rights . . . require basic needs'; that is, the sense of *inviolability* which is rightly attached to the category of 'basic rights' can itself only be grounded in basic human needs. There is a tendency to think of such basic human needs as physical and individualistic, but a central part of Barbalet's argument is to insist—congruently with what has been argued above—that basic needs in human beings include 'the need for society, the need for collective and co-operative activity' (1998: 141). Given Barbalet's interest in emotions, particularly emotions as linked to 'non-deviant structures of social interaction', he then argues—crucially for the purposes of the present chapter— that '*violations of the conditions of social being generate emotional patterns which direct the action of the injured actor to restore their social standing*' (1998: 148, emphasis added). In other words, we can expect the hotel guest who routinely encounters pools of urine in the lift, and insults in the corridors, to feel certain emotions, because these physical and social conditions violate reasonable expectations of collective and cooperative activity in the mini-world of the hotel.

According to Barbalet, two emotions in particular are typically implicated when 'violations of the conditions of social being' occur. One is *resentment*, which Barbalet defines as 'the emotional apprehension of advantage gained [by others] at the expense of what is desirable or acceptable from the perspective of established rights' (1998: 137). The other emotion is *vengefulness*, which is 'an emotion of power relations'; it is 'both an appeal against an abrogation of rights and an assertion of an actor's rights both to their accepted position *and to punish those who would dispossess them of their rightful place*' (1998: 136, emphasis added). In other words, according to Barbalet (1998: 148), resentment is above all a *normative* emotion, an emotion rooted in the view that others have behaved in a way that is normatively unacceptable, and have thus violated the acceptable conditions of social living; whereas vengefulness, while sharing some features with resentment, is essentially a power-based emotion, bent upon reasserting the actor's own standing, and imposing sanctions on the person who has usurped it.

Let us for the moment leave aside vengefulness (though I shall return to it in the conclusion), and focus simply on resentment. As previously indicated, it is not difficult to believe that the reported emotional reactions to disorder of British Crime Survey respondents (annoyance, anger, worry) contain a strong element of resentment, based on their view that the peaceable and proper use of public space has been unjustifiably usurped. But, if Barbalet is right and resentment is above all an emotion based on the perception of a normative imbalance, then such perceptions must be objectively weighed in normative terms. It is clearly insufficient, in normative terms, to argue that if people feel resentment then their view of the situation must be correct— after all, the 'young people hanging around' the area also have equal rights to the peaceful use of public space. In such situations, we would therefore seem to need some kind of neutral moral adjudication, recognising the rights of all parties, and only taking action in respect of alleged wrongdoers when they really have violated the basic conditions for peaceful collective and cooperative activity in the area. It is submitted that, in this kind of context, a useful practical guide can be found in Frank Field's notion of *persistence*: 'each single instance does not by itself warrant a counter legal challenge . . . it is in its regularity that anti-social behaviour wields its destructive force' (see also the discussion of 'cumulation' in § III). To be specific, a single instance of young people deliberately blocking a shop doorway to prevent an older person entering is unpleasant, but is not itself serious enough to jus- tify invoking legal processes. If, however, the same thing happens day after day, then the older person's right to the peaceable use of public space is, in effect, being challenged; she will rightly feel resentment, and it is reasonable to consider action to alleviate the situation (*cf* von Hirsch and Simester's analysis in chapter 4 of this volume, § II.1).

I have argued, then, that the explanation of the strong reactions to neigh- bourhood incivilities lies first, in recognising the central importance of the peaceable use of public space to everyday life (a recognition that is striking- ly absent in the 'hotel analogy'); secondly, in understanding that human beings are social creatures, with basic *social needs* (for cooperative activity and a predictable social order) as well as physical needs; and thirdly, in understanding that breaches of social needs generate above all the emotion of resentment, which has an inescapably normative dimension. Along the way, two of Frank Field's basic messages—on the importance of public space, and the destructive capacity of repetition in breaches of basic co-operative social relations—have been strongly endorsed.

We are left, however, with another of Frank Field's observations, which is supported in British Crime Survey data; namely, that it is the economically most deprived areas that suffer most from 'anti-social behaviour'. How is this social imbalance to be explained? To tackle this topic fully would require a chapter in itself, but one or two points can be made here. A use- ful starting-point can be found in the following extract from an interview with a man in his late thirties, living in Rotherham, South Yorkshire in the 1990s (Charlesworth, 2000: 49):

> I mean 'alfe the [young 'uns] an't [aren't] workin' ah [are] thi? Eh? That is their
> . . . that's their lifestyle—gu'in' aht drinkin', actin' twat [daft], tekkin' a few
> drugs, chilled aht [out], innit? I mean, 'alfe'r these young 'uns don't giy [give] a
> fuck abaht 'owt [anything]. Even the'r selns [themselves].

Simon Charlesworth (2000: 50), himself born and brought up in Rotherham, comments usefully on this extract.[11] Something significant, he suggests, has changed over time in the 'dispositions and relation to self', as between the man making these comments (who left school to work in the coalmines, at a time when they were still a thriving industry) and the young people he is discussing. Causal factors in this change are the collapse of heavy industry and the catastrophic effect of this on employment prospects in the area, coupled with the more general development of a consumerist society. As Charlesworth comments (*ibid*):

> What this man sees as 'chilled out' is a relation to self less embedded in the strictures of respect for others, it is a relation to self that is based upon a public display of the body adorned with the commodified signs of fashion and sexuality. And what this man sees as their not caring is the atomization involved in their primary relation to self and others.

To elaborate this argument, in economically 'hard-pressed' areas we now see two social processes acting simultaneously. The first is that there has been a significant decline in employment prospects by comparison with the pre-1980 context, not only with the collapse of heavy industry, but also with technological advances stripping away, in particular, many previously-available unskilled jobs, especially for men. For these and other reasons, in places like Rotherham trade unions are now much less important as social institutions than they were thirty years ago; and the rather fixed gender roles of working class areas in an earlier era have been thrown into flux as more women become primary breadwinners.[12] Coupled with other changes which have affected these areas like all others—such as the relative decline of the extended family, and changes in perceptions of marriage—all this has produced working class districts that have less solidarity and more diversity than used to be the case, even in areas (like Gardenia) which have remained overwhelmingly 'White British' in ethnic composition. It is at this point that we also need to recall Jack Knight's (2000) argument—discussed by Bryan Turner in chapter 9 of this volume—that, as Turner summarises it, 'social diversity undermines community, and the erosion of common values and shared sentiments undermines trust' (see p 227 above). All this helps to produce the 'atomization' and the apparent attitude of 'not caring' to which Charlesworth refers.

The second social process relevant to the present discussion is that all of the above has occurred within a wider societal context where economic

---

[11] Charlesworth explicitly recognises that the quoted comments contain exaggeration.

[12] David Byrne (1999: 124) importantly notes that the earlier 'politics' of solidarity in working-class *residential* areas (as opposed to the industrial sphere) was to 'a considerable extent . . . carried out by women', but he does not follow through this insight by examining the role of women in post-industrial working class areas.

growth has continued,[13] consumerist messages are everywhere, and people—especially the young—are encouraged by advertisements and significant sections of the mass media to define themselves in relation to the consumption of designer goods, and hedonistic display (Charlesworth's 'commodified signs of fashion and sexuality'). In this context, one of the central insights of Bryan Turner's chapter—that offensive behaviour is typically *non-instrumental behaviour*, 'undertaken to cause symbolic affront'—is of immense significance. We lack detailed empirical evidence here, but it is not hard to see how the temptation to cause 'symbolic affront' might be particularly great in conditions of stark economic inequality, atomisation and social alienation where, nevertheless, the mass media continually transmit messages of desirable consumption and hedonism.

This chapter has so far included descriptive sections (seeking to set out clearly what is known about neighbourhood incivilities as perceived by local residents), and an explanatory section (seeking to explain some of the data patterns shown in the descriptive sections). It is now time to begin to turn towards policy, which I shall do by first examining three theoretical formulations relevant to incivilities, each of which has both an explanatory dimension and some policy implications. These formulations are the 'broken windows' thesis, the 'collective efficacy' hypothesis, and the 'signal crimes' perspective.

VI. THREE THEORETICAL FORMULATIONS

Martin Innes (2004: 335) has commented that 'with the benefit of hindsight, the almost iconic status that the "broken windows" thesis has acquired in political and media discourses on the criminal justice system appears remarkable'. So what exactly is this thesis?

As Ralph Taylor (2001: ch 3) has documented, there are in fact a number of variants of the thesis (or of other theses of a very similar kind). Of these, the most famous is to be found in an article by James Q Wilson and George Kelling (1982), summarised diagrammatically by Taylor in a figure reproduced here as *Figure 2*. In essence, Wilson and Kelling's thesis can be summarised as postulating 'a basic causal sequence of community decline whereby untreated disorder in an area generates fear of crime among the populace', which eventually (see *Figure 2* for the intermediate steps) 'leads to more serious crimes being committed in the area concerned' (Innes 2004: 335).[14]

As Ralph Taylor (2001: 123) has rather icily pointed out, it is unfortunate that Wilson and Kelling 'failed to explain' that 'prior crime levels

---

[13] See National Statistics (2005: ch 5). As a consequence, the real income differential between rich and poor households has widened since 1971 (*ibid*: 72-3).

[14] For an update of the original Wilson-Kelling thesis, see Kelling and Coles (1996).

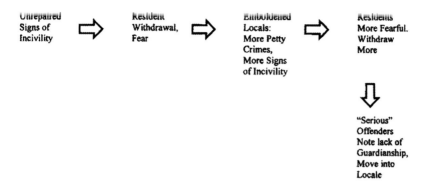

Source: Taylor, 2001: 98

Figure 2 *Wilson and Kelling's Incivilities Thesis.*

might contribute to unrepaired signs of incivility in the first place'. That point is, however, central to the critique of the broken windows thesis published by Sampson and Raudenbush (1999; see also Sampson and Raudenbush, 2001, for a non-technical summary). As part of the major Project on Human Development in Chicago Neighborhoods (PHDCN), these researchers collected systematic video and observer evidence of physical and social disorder in every street in 196 Chicago census tracts, and then sought to relate these data to other data for the same areas.[15] Of particular interest to Sampson and Raudenbush was the concept of 'collective efficacy', derived from their own earlier research (eg Sampson, Raudenbush and Earls, 1997). We can reasonably speak, they argue, of an individual having or failing to have 'efficacy' (that is, being able to achieve what he or she wants to achieve); in the same way, it is suggested, we can speak of differential 'collective efficacy' between areas, on the assumption that (among other things) all communities share the goal of wanting a safe neighbourhood. On these assumptions, the people in some areas will be better than the people in other areas at doing the things (such as intervening to prevent escalations of fights) that will help to achieve the shared goal of a safe neighbourhood. Sampson and Raudenbush then set out to test empirically the comparative strengths of the 'broken windows' approach as against their own alternative hypothesis, which mixes 'collective efficacy' with urban structural characteristics (such as 'concentrated disadvantage').

[15] Not surprisingly, this single-occasion 'systematic social observation' (SSO) approach yielded better data about physical than social incivilities (Sampson and Raudenbush, 1999: 617–9). Interestingly, however, very similar results in relation to other variables were found for both physical and social incivilities, leading the researchers to combine the 2 measures in later multivariate analyses.

To create this test, they obviously needed to operationalise the rather broad and general concept of 'collective efficacy'. They did this (see Sampson and Raudenbush (1999: 612-3, 620) by defining 'collective efficacy' as comprising two linked elements: first, the willingness of local residents (as judged by survey responses) to intervene for the common good in defined situations (such as children spray-painting graffiti on a building); and secondly, the existence or otherwise of 'conditions of cohesion and mutual trust among neighbors' (since 'one is unlikely to take action in a neighborhood context where the rules are unclear and people mistrust each other'). Thus, their concept of collective efficacy incorporates both a static 'relations of trust' dimension and a more action-oriented 'willingness to intervene' dimension.

The test of 'broken windows' versus 'collective efficacy' that Sampson and Raudenbush set up was described by them as follows (1999: 614):

> The 'broken windows' literature sees disorder as a fundamental cause of crime ...; if true, the hypothesized association of [urban] structural characteristics and collective efficacy with crime and violence ought to be largely mediated by social disorder. The alternative hypothesis we offer is that disorder is a manifestation of crime-relevant mechanisms and that collective efficacy should reduce disorder *and* violence by disempowering the forces that produce both. Our theory also suggests that structural constraints such as resource disadvantage account for both crime and disorder simultaneously. We thus test whether neighborhood disorder is an essential link in the ecological pathway that leads to predatory crime, or rather a spuriously related construct rooted in structural constraints and collective social processes. (Emphasis in original)

In the event, with the possible exception of subsequent robberies, the rigorously-analysed data favoured Sampson and Raudenbush's hypothesis over Wilson and Kelling's. However, in their conclusions the authors emphasised that although their results 'contradict the strong version of the broken windows thesis', they do not 'imply the theoretical irrelevance of disorder' (1999: 637). To elaborate this point, the authors remind us that, in their view, 'physical and social disorder comprise highly visible cues to which neighborhood observers respond'; hence, disorder might indeed 'turn out to be important for understanding migration patterns, investment by business and overall neighborhood viability', in which case it could 'indirectly have an effect on crime' (*ibid*). Although Sampson and Raudenbush do not directly make the point, the implication of this comment is that disorder needs to be studied not—as in Wilson and Kelling's formulation—largely in isolation from wider urban processes (see *Figure 2*, where the wider social context of areas is strikingly absent), but rather with a deep understanding of them.

Sampson and Raudenbush's (1999) data was largely, though not wholly, cross-sectional,[16] complicating the task of drawing inferences about causal

---

[16] They had access to police-recorded crime data for the Chicago neighbourhoods for 1 prior year (1993). The systematic social observation was conducted in 1995.

order. A more explicitly longitudinal research report on the broken windows thesis was published two years later by Ralph Taylor (2001), based on research in Baltimore—using data for 66 areas of the city in 1981, and in 30 of the same areas in 1994.

In one sense, Taylor's research results could be said to be more positive than Sampson and Raudenbush's for what Taylor calls the 'longitudinal incivilities thesis'. He did find partial support for the thesis: 'incivilities do affect some later changes in crime rates, in neighborhood fabric and in reactions to crime' (2001: 231). But there were two crucial qualifications to be made. First, 'the pattern of results has not proved robust across indicators or outcomes'. For example, 'in the chapter examining crime and structural impacts, for no single outcome was a significant impact of incivilities observed that persisted across different indicators for incivilities', and indeed these different indicators did not correlate closely with one another, which 'leaves open important questions about the validity of a broad construct of disorder' (*ibid*). Secondly, the inconsistency of the longitudinal results for incivilities contrasts with 'other, more consistent' findings in the analysis, in particular the strength of initial economic status and initial racial composition of the area in predicting later outcomes. Taylor concludes that there are 'far-reaching impacts of relative neighborhood standing' which we cannot afford to ignore in urban analysis.

Taylor's more general conclusion, arising from these results, is forcefully made (2000: 20). Theorising on incivilities, he argues,

> needs to reconnect more firmly with works in the areas of urban sociology, urban political economy, collective community crime prevention and organizational participation. Changes in neighborhood fabric, neighborhood crime rates and residents' safety concerns are each tangled topics with a range of causes. To gain a clearer picture of these processes, it is necessary to break away from [incivilities] per se, and broaden the lines of inquiry.

This conclusion is, of course, highly congruent with the implications of the results obtained by Sampson and Raudenbush.

There is no doubt that the strong version of the 'broken windows' thesis has been severely damaged by the rigorous empirical analyses of Sampson and Raudenbush and Taylor. However, neither of these alternative analyses rejects the potential significance of disorders in affecting some social outcomes, such as residents' confidence in the neighbourhood, or moving decisions. That is an important conclusion because, as Innes (2004: 340) has reminded us, criminal justice agencies such as the police have traditionally tended to dismiss disorders as 'comparatively trivial' (by comparison with 'real crimes' such as burglary). The 'broken windows' thesis was faulty in claiming almost inevitable escalatory crime outcomes from the existence of disorder; but at least it can be said to have engaged 'with the problem of why, when asked about their experiences and anxieties concerning crime, members of the public consistently attach considerable significance to . . . physical and social disorder' (Innes 2004: 340). It would seem, therefore, that we need better theoretical guidance for policy than 'broken windows' has offered us, but without reverting to a trivialisation of disorders in policy terms.

The 'collective efficacy' approach is clearly empirically stronger than the 'broken windows' thesis, but it would appear to need some development before it could directly provide such guidance. As indicated above, Sampson and Raudenbush's (1999: 614) 'alternative hypothesis' is that 'disorder is a manifestation of crime-relevant mechanisms and that collective efficacy should reduce disorder *and* violence by disempowering the forces that produce both'. While apparently correct in explanatory terms (at least on Sampson and Raudenbush's data),[17] this does not fully address the importance of disorder in everyday experiential terms, as expressed by the respondent in Martin Innes's research (above) who said that by comparison with more serious crimes, 'graffiti is the thing that sort of bothers me more, because it is in my face every day'. Moreover, in Sampson and Raudenbush's explanatory model, collective efficacy is coupled with deep-seated urban structural variables such as 'concentrated disadvantage'; so the authors' recommended policy approach of 'disempowering the forces that produce both [disorder and violence]' (above) may appear somewhat Utopian. Looked at from the perspective of the residents of Gardenia, for example, a policy prescription of 'improve collective efficacy and reduce concentrated disadvantage', while certainly relevant to the situation in Gardenia, has its limitations as a guide to action. Many residents would indeed like to improve collective efficacy, but they consider that this is unlikely to happen when the price of intervention may well be a brick through one's window (earlier as we saw); while the 'reduction of concentrated disadvantage' seems to be a very distant prospect.

So, can a third theoretical perspective, the 'signal crimes' approach, be of assistance in this context? It will be recalled from our earlier discussion that 'signals' are defined by signal crimes theorists as 'social semiotic processes by which different crimes and disorders might have a disproportionate effect' in terms of fear and perceived threat (Innes and Fielding, 2002: Abstract). Elaborating this definition more formally, Innes (2004: 342) has argued that 'all signals can be said to be composed of three components: an expression; a content; and an effect'. The 'expression' is the description of some incident or set of events (for example, 'a mugging in the town centre'); the connotative 'content' is the meaning given to that event/ those events (for example, the mugging registers as a significant event for a particular

---

[17] Other studies (eg Taub *et al* 1984, to be discussed below) suggest that in some areas high crime rates can coexist with low disorder and positive public assessments of safety; thus, the conjunction of crime and disorder found in Sampson and Raudenbush's analysis may well not be universal.

respondent, and is perceived as a risk to the safety of the respondent's teenage children if they go to the town centre); and the 'effect' is the consequential change in behaviour or attitudes (for example, the children are not allowed to go to the town centre unaccompanied). True 'signals', with these three components, are thus said by Innes to be differentiated from 'mere noise', that is, 'the plethora of incidents and occurrences that, in contrast to signal crimes and disorders, assume no real significance to people in the routines of daily life, and consequently are not consciously attended to' (Innes 2004: 342).

From our earlier discussion, it will be recalled that Innes has developed a trinity of key concepts—signal crimes, signal disorders and control signals. So far, I have not discussed 'control signals', but it is now time to take a closer look at this concept, defined by Innes as 'an act of social control that communicates an attempt to regulate disorderly and deviant behaviour'; it is further noted that 'control signals can be positive or negative'. In the qualitative data on Gardenia, we encountered a number of residents' comments that could certainly be interpreted as negative control signals, for example:

- A respondent complained about the regular presence of drug dealers 'on the path to the XYZ estate'; he had several times drawn the police's attention to this, but according to him 'nothing had happened'.
- The most complained-of disorder on the estate, 'car revving and high-speed driving' was said to occur late at night, after the local authority community wardens went off duty.
- A police officer was said to have recommended withdrawal of a crime complaint in the complainant's own interests, because the police would not be able to protect the complainant against retaliatory action from community members.

In each of these instances, the apparent *ineffectiveness* of local control agencies was powerfully communicated to residents, leading to the *effect* (in Innes's terminology) of disheartenment and withdrawal. As a converse of this, it would seem that, in principle at least, if social control agencies are able to convey a message of effectiveness, this should persuade ordinary residents that social order in the area is being seriously attended to by the relevant authorities, and this may, in turn, encourage residents to intervene more readily in problematic or escalating situations. Restating the preceding sentence more technically, it would seem that *positive control signals* should encourage, as an *effect*, residents' willingness to engage in *the interventions that are a key element in collective efficacy*. If this proposition is correct, then the 'control signals' approach should be able to help to provide some of the more short-term policy options that appear to be largely missing in Sampson and Randenbush's account (see above).

But 'control signals', on this view, would not be simply what the police do. Twenty years ago, Richard Taub and his colleagues (1984) produced evidence that two Chicago neighbourhoods (Lincoln Park and Hyde Park/ Kenwood) had high crime rates, but also (i) positive 'satisfaction with safety' scores in residents' surveys, and (ii) rapidly appreciating residential property values. Clearly, these results are unexpected: one would normally expect high crime rates to coincide with depressed property values and low feelings of safety. In both neighbourhoods, however, the authors reported that 'there [were] highly visible signs of extra community resources being used to deal with the crime problem' (p 172), and to generate confidence in the area. By no means all of this activity was initiated by the police; for example in Hyde Park/ Kenwood, those managing the regeneration (including the University of Chicago, which is located in the area) themselves invested heavily in the urban infrastructure, and also helped to obtain substantial Federal urban renewal funds for the neighbourhood; additionally, they directly addressed residents' 'safety in public space' issues by introducing a private security force, 24-hour 'safety buses', and emergency telephones on street corners. It is not hard to see how all this could send a strongly positive 'control signal' to residents; the message would be 'powerful people in this neighbourhood are taking seriously the need to halt the decline of the urban infrastructure, and the need to make the area feel safe to residents'.[18]

Is there any evidence that such an approach actually works, empirically speaking? The best evidence is very recent, and comes from the Home Office's evaluation of the National Reassurance Policing Programme (Tuffin *et al*, 2006)—to which, it will be recalled, Martin Innes's own research has been closely linked. The NRPP was conducted in 16 sites, using Innes's conceptualisation to guide police managers in consulting the public about 'threats to safety' (of the kind shown in Figure 1); in response to such perceived threats, police managers then developed appropriate action strategies. For six of the sites, Home Office researchers were able to identify viable control areas, and then to measure before-after changes in the experimental sites, by comparison with their designated control site.[19] For 10 crime and disorder outcome indicators, *Table 7* shows (in summary

---

[18] On the other hand, intended 'control signals' which appear to be potentially effective can be neutralised by other nearby developments, if care is not taken to consider social developments in the area as a whole. For a dramatic example of this, see the experience on a Hull housing estate, as described by Foster and Hope (1993: ch 6); promising environmental design modifications in one part of the estate were counteracted by an allocation policy for social housing that unintentionally allocated apartments in a high-rise block to young unemployed tenants, with destablising results (including incivilities) for the estate as a whole. This example also emphasises the importance, for many deprived British neighbourhoods, of the policies for social housing adopted by the relevant local authority and by locally-active housing associations.

[19] The Home Office research cannot, strictly speaking, be described as a formal evaluation of the 'control signals' approach, because Innes's theoretical work was still being fine-tuned when the Home Office evaluation began (Tuffin *et al*, 2006: 20). In a broader sense, however, the evaluation is, without doubt, closely connected with the 'control signals' approach, because that approach strongly underpinned, from the outset, the practical programmes put in place in the 16 sites of the NRPP.

Table 7 National Reassurance Policing Programme Evaluation: Summary of Results for Crime and Anti-social Behaviour*

	All sites combined	Fails-worth	Ingol	New Parks and Falconwood	East Wickham	Ash Wharf	Burgh-field
Crime Reduction							
Self-reported victimisation	✓	-	-	-	-	-	✓
Perception of crime rate	✓	-	✓	-	✓	-	✓
Anti-social behaviour reduction							
Teenagers hanging around	✓	-	✓	-	✓	-	-
Rubbish or litter	-	-	✓	-	-	-	-
Vandalism to bus shelters/phone boxes	✓	-	-	-	-	-	✓
Vandalism to other types of property	✓	-	✓	-	-	-	-
Graffiti on public buildings	✓	-	-	-	-	-	✓
People being attacked/ harassed because of their skin colour/ethnic origin or religion	-	-	-	-	✓	-	-
People using or dealing drugs	-	-	✓	-	-	-	-
People being drunk or rowdy	✓	-	✓	✓	-	-	-

* Ticks show a statistically significant improvement in the area(s) in question, by comparison with its/their control area(s), over a 12 month period from the start of the NRPP.
Source: Tuffin *et al*, 2006: 40

form) the one-year experimental vs control area results for each of the six sites separately, and for all of them taken together. There are two key features in the results: first, the majority of the outcome indicators (seven out of 10) show positive results when the data for all sites is combined; and secondly, there are clearly some differences in results between different sites, with two experimental sites (Ingol and Burghfield) seeming to perform particularly well. Further analysis of the results by the evaluators suggested that, in general, these positive results could be reasonably attributed to the activities of NRPP, and not to some alternative cause. Moreover, analysis of the nature of the on-site activity in the individual sites suggested that the quality of such activity was consistent with the outcomes achieved or not achieved locally; for example, 'sites that showed a significant positive change in public perceptions of juvenile nuisance . . . were the same sites that targeted problem-solving activity which was well informed by detailed analysis of the problem and where partners and the community were involved' (Tuffin *et al*, 2006: 91). In other words, the indications are, from this research study, that success in reducing incivilities can be achieved, and that success seems to derive from really listening to what residents have to say, carefully analysing the problem, and then devising targeted (and not just vague or 'off-the-shelf') solutions to these identified problems—especially where such solutions have been designed to involve the indigenous community and relevant partner agencies, as well as the police.

These are, clearly, encouraging results, auguring well for the 'signal crimes' perspective, although the caution of social scientific rigour requires one to add that further replication is needed before one treats the conclusions as definitive. Perhaps of particular interest is the possibility, raised in the preceding discussion, that the development of effective 'control signals' could help to release better neighbourhood 'collective efficacy' in a given area, thus in effect constructively combining two of the theoretical perspectives discussed in this section. To explore this possibility more fully, I will end this section with a final example which, while not in itself conclusive, is suggestive and thought-provoking.

Earlier in this chapter, I discussed residents' experiences of incivilities in a Sheffield housing estate (Gardenia). Another neighbourhood studied in the same research project was Innercity, which as its (fictitious) name implies is close to the city centre, with many of the familiar features of an inner city area, such as a multicultural population, a high crime rate and a thriving drugs trade.

A few years ago, a qualitative study by a Home Office researcher (Graham, 2000) found that Innercity residents felt very fearful and intimidated, particularly by open and visible drug use and drug markets in the streets of the area, but also by other incivilities such as litter. Innercity then received (in 2001) a large central government area regeneration grant which led to a number of improvements such as building projects; improved street lighting;

clearing up litter and fly tipping; the creation of a dedicated community policing unit; the introduction of community wardens and an anti-social behaviour team; and some installation of CCTV. Soon afterwards, there were also some city- and county-wide police operations against drugs and street crime that prominently involved Innercity; in particular, in 2003 there was an initiative aimed at key parts of the South Yorkshire drug market, resulting in a number of arrests of alleged drug dealers in the neighbourhood. In the wake of all this activity, one of the most striking results of our recent research (Bottoms and Wilson, 2006) was a marked perception of general neighbourhood improvement among residents in Innercity. It seems reasonable to interpret much of this story within the framework of Innes's 'control signals' theory—the urban regeneration activities, plus the tighter enforcement of the drugs laws, have given residents in Innercity confidence that the authorities, collectively, care about the area; and the authorities, in turn, seem to have successfully communicated a signal that they are attempting to deal with the area's problems firmly but also sympathetically.

Moreover—and this seems to be a point of some general importance—it would appear that the residents' ability to organise and develop informal social control was inhibited when there were insufficient 'control signals' from the authorities; conversely, when some significant action by the authorities was perceived, that appeared to generate a growing confidence in the area, and with confidence came an increased willingness to participate in community activities and problem-solving (see Bottoms and Wilson, 2006: Tables 8 and 11). The authorities' 'control signals', however, were not arbitrary, but were to a significant extent based on listening to the residents' concerns about a range of issues in the area; by contrast, previously the authorities were widely perceived as being unwilling to listen (Graham, 2000). Thus, the Innercity case study (see, more fully, Bottoms and Wilson, 2006) seems to provide a promising example for those interested in neighbourhood improvement, including the reduction of gross incivilities in the form of very intimidating open drug markets.

VII. PRINCIPLES FOR POLICY

In conclusion, I want to suggest five broad principles for policy in relation to incivilities. For the most part, in developing these principles I do not discuss the details of recent governmental policy on 'antisocial behaviour' in England and Wales (on which see, for example, Burney, 2005). Rather, the policy principles I suggest are deliberately general in character, although with firm roots in the research and theorisation considered earlier. General policy principles of this kind can, in my view, provide a valuable framework of guidance for those charged with developing and implementing detailed policies at national or local levels.

The first principle derives from the fact that incivilities are deeply rooted in local social order, and that social order is of central importance for human flourishing (Wrong, 1994); hence, policies for dealing with incivilities in residential areas *should always be constructed within a broader understanding of local social order*. This principle has both a negative and a positive connotation. Negatively, it means that any policy for local social order which ignores or trivialises incivilities (on the grounds, for example, that scarce public resources should be devoted to 'real crimes', rather than to minor disorders) will fail to engage with the significant concerns of residents, for whom incivilities are often more 'real' on a day-to-day basis than are officially-perceived 'real crimes'. Positively, it means that when constructing policies to address incivilities in local areas, the whole local social context should be addressed, and incivilities should not be isolated from that context (as they have been, for example, in many versions of the 'broken windows' thesis). It is certainly true, as British Crime Survey evidence reminds us, that many 'incivilities' issues are, in broad terms, perceived similarly in many different areas. But there is also significant research evidence that, in any given local area, the problem of 'youths hanging around', for example, has some very specific features which will usually require an understanding of the local history and social context of that particular area (Girling *et al*, 2000; Innes *et al*, 2004). This is why Ralph Taylor (2000) insisted that the study of incivilities—and the development of policies in respect of them—needs to reconnect criminology with topics such as urban sociology and housing markets (see also note 18 above).

Pushed to a deeper level, however, this first principle obliges us at least to touch on the some deep questions about the ultimate basis of social order (on which see for example Wrong, 1994; Elster, 1989). One possible view—although, as the texts cited nicely demonstrate, ultimately an inadequate one—is that social order is at the end of the day simply a product of the rational choices of individuals. This is an important topic in policy terms because, as Frank Field (2003: 46) has shown, there is a significant underpinning of rational choice theory in the Labour Government's current policies for anti-social behaviour (see the discussion in § I). As we have seen, Field argued that this policy approach is faulty, because anti-social behaviour is 'caused by much more fundamental changes in society' than the government's analysis allows for. In the light of the discussion in this chapter, there is little doubt that Field's conclusion here is correct, though my analysis of the 'fundamental changes in society' underpinning disorder differs in important respects from Field's.

A final implication of this first policy principle is that policy-makers need to understand the differing incentive structures of individual and collective local action in relation to local social order. This point was incisively demonstrated by Taub *et al* (1984) twenty years ago, with the following logic. Suppose that a given area seems to be declining—its local industrial base has collapsed, house prices are falling, crime and disorder are increasing. From an individual rational choice perspective, the optimum choice for a homeowner in this situation is to sell his or her property and leave the area as soon as possible. However, from a collective point of view, each person who takes such a decision actually accelerates the possibility of area decline, and potentially contributes to a 'domino effect'. An alternative possibility is, therefore, to engage in collective action to prevent such 'tipping'; this might involve, for example, trying to lever in outside resources to the area to promote regeneration; engaging in action designed to improve residents' neighbourhood safety, and so on—indeed, to engage in exactly the kind of activities that were developed by the University of Chicago and others in Hyde Park/ Kenwood, and later by Sheffield City Council and others in Innercity (see previous section). To attempt to deal with local disorder in this collective way is very much in the spirit of the first policy principle, that is, to develop policy within a broad framework of neighbourhood social order.

The second policy principle is: *enforcement alone is not necessarily the optimum way of dealing with the problem of incivilities in a given residential area.*

In differing contexts, there are many examples of the application of this policy principle. Every parent, for example, knows that when faced with bored and rebellious youngsters on a particular day, continually upbraiding them, sending them to their room as a punishment, and so forth, might well be less effective in improving their behaviour than taking them on an outing which will engage their interest. At the other end of the social control spectrum, there is evidence in the research literature on prisons that, while some prisoners are indeed more likely than others to be violent, the more violence-prone prisoners nevertheless often behave differently in different kinds of prison regime, and a change of environmental context (rather than an escalating cycle of punishments) can often be beneficial (Bottoms, 1999). Similarly, in the field of incivilities, strong enforcement on its own is not necessarily the most appropriate response. In Innercity, for example (see above), there was energetic enforcement against the drugs market, but this took place alongside the authorities' listening to residents, and several regeneration initiatives; it was the whole package, and not simply the enforcement, that apparently enabled the area to regain confidence. Or again—and in scientific terms more rigorously—in the NRPP the successful reduction in incivilities (see Table 7) took place with a primary emphasis on consultation and listening, and only a secondary emphasis on enforcement. Indeed, at a conceptual level this second policy principle can be regarded as closely linked to the first principle; for if we take seriously the fact that incivilities must above all be understood within a broader framework of social order, it is natural to look for non-legal as well as legal solutions to the problems of disorder.

The third policy principle takes us back to the previous discussion of 'control signals' and 'collective efficacy'. Collective efficacy (as defined by Sampson and Raudenbush) contains a vital element of *effective (social control) interventions by community members*, or what we might describe as 'horizontal intervention'. Control signals, as defined by Martin Innes, can also sometimes be transmitted by community members, but more usually it is necessary, in the contemporary context, for there also to be some control signals that constitute *effective intervention from a body or agency from outside the immediate locality* (or what we might call 'vertical intervention', coming in from outside). The research evidence on this issue remains provisional, but it seems to suggest that *policies to reduce incivilities are probably most effective when they contain elements of both 'horizontal' and 'vertical' interventions*. I shall not here elaborate this point further, in view of the full discussion in the previous section.[20]

The fourth principle takes us back to Jack Barbalet's important distinction between the emotions of *resentment* and *vengefulness*. It will be recalled that, according to Barbalet, these emotions differ because resentment is chiefly an expression of normative judgements, while vengefulness is predominantly power-based. Of course, Barbalet is discussing social relations in general, not the enforcement of community standards of conduct; but a similar 'normative vs. power-based' distinction can also be developed in relation to enforcement, with the lynch mob as the polar example of the exercise of power against an alleged offender, without normative legitimacy.

There are both normative and practical reasons for being opposed to policies that incorporate vengefulness, or that respond to vengefulness among community members. The normative reason is that vengefulness is straightforwardly a power-based emotion, without any necessary element of normative justification; it can therefore lead to normatively unjustifiable acts such as, for example, gross bullying or the total social exclusion of the alleged perpetrator. The practical reason, which supports but is secondary to the normative reason, is that one who is the object of a retaliatory act arising from vengefulness is likely to feel that he/she has been dealt with unjustly, and consequently to respond with defiance rather than compliance (see eg Tyler, 2003; Sherman, 1993). Accordingly, the fourth policy principle is that *policymakers should respond to normatively justifiable resentments among community members with regard to incivilities, but they should not respond to calls for action founded on vengefulness (in Barbalet's sense), nor should their own actions be based on any kind of vengefulness or apparent vengefulness.*

---

[20] I have deliberately formulated this principle in a general way (ie referring to 'horizontal' and 'vertical' interventions rather than collective efficacy and control signals). This is because later research might well suggest some modifications to the specifics of the 'control signals' and 'collective efficacy' theorisation, but the importance of combining the (more general) 'horizontal' and 'vertical' dimensions of intervention is a principle that seems likely to endure.

This fourth principle has some relevance to the topic of anti-social behaviour orders (ASBOs). As previously noted, it is not my intention to discuss ASBOs in any detail; but one point seems worth making. It has been saddening to note, at times in the ASBO saga, an apparent governmental preoccupation with how many ASBOs have been sought by different local authorities, and with what the national total has been. Such a preoccupation is perhaps the result simply of a misplaced focus on managerially-constructed numerical targets. But it can certainly send the wrong message to the public—namely, the message that the government is concerned above all with how many people are being restrained by ASBOs, and not so much with whether anti-social behaviour is actually diminishing as a result of undramatic social action all round the country. In other words, the government has at times seemed in danger of sending a power-based message of *vengefulness* against the perpetrators of anti-social behaviour ('nothing less than an ASBO will do'), rather than the much more normatively defensible message that persistent anti-social behaviour is indeed distressing and a wrong against ordinary members of communities, but that there are a variety of ways of tackling it, of which the ASBO is only one, and not necessarily the most effective.[21]

The fifth and final principle concerns the role of direct law enforcement against incivilities. From the outset of my argument, I have assumed that *wrongful offence* (as defined in the introduction) legitimately qualifies some incivilities for inclusion in the list of acts that are properly criminalised; and the empirical evidence considered in the first half of the chapter amply substantiates the view that many incivilities do cause 'wrongful offence'. However, the second policy principle, discussed above, adopts the view that enforcement alone is not necessarily the optimum way of dealing with incivilities. Is it possible to be more precise, and to specify more closely the circumstances in which direct legal enforcement against 'wrongful offence incivilities' are appropriate?

This question can usefully be considered by reference to the situation in Gardenia. Some of what was happening in that area was straightforwardly criminal, on anyone's definition, because it caused direct harm—this included criminal damage to both communal facilities (such as bus shelters and the local school), and to private houses (bricks through the window to discourage co-operation with the police). Detection for such actions is of course difficult, but where a perpetrator can be identified, prosecution creates no difficulties of principle—indeed, not to prosecute could be seen as counterproductive, as sending a 'negative control signal'. Much more difficult are acts (such as 'youths hanging around' and 'car revving') which cause 'wrongful offence' rather than harm. Here, in my view, it is appropriate to invoke Field's sound

[21] There is no rigorous research evidence on the comparative success of the ASBO and alternative measures in dealing with anti-social behaviour. As previously noted, however, and as Table 7 shows, incivilities can be successfully reduced by methods other than ASBOs.

principle of persistence: 'the distinguishing mark of anti-social behaviour is that each single instance does not by itself warrant a counter legal challenge. It is in its regularity that anti-social behaviour wields its destructive force' (Field, 2003: 44–5).

So, 'wrongful offence incivilities' justify direct legal enforcement where they are committed persistently. Even such cases, however, might well be solvable by measures other than direct law enforcement (see the second policy principle, above), so it is a matter of judgement in individual cases whether it is best to proceed by way of direct law enforcement or alternative measures. Such judgement should always be exercised bearing in mind the first four policy principles.

In short, therefore, the fifth policy principle is that *direct law enforcement against incivilities is unproblematic where harm is caused; but as regards 'wrongful offence incivilities', direct law enforcement is justified only where the wrongful offence is persistent, and decisions to proceed should always be taken bearing in mind the first four policy principles.*

So, to summarise, the five main policy principles that I would propose are:

- Policies for dealing with incivilities in residential areas should always be constructed within a broader understanding of local social order;
- Enforcement alone is not necessarily the optimum way of dealing with the problem of incivilities in a given residential area;
- Policies to reduce incivilities are probably most effective when they contain elements of both 'horizontal' and 'vertical' interventions; and
- Policymakers should respond positively to normatively justifiable resentments among community members with regard to incivilities, but they should not respond to calls for action founded on vengefulness (in Barbalet's sense), and they should avoid giving the impression that their own actions are power-based rather than normatively justifiable.
- Direct law enforcement against incivilities causing harm is unproblematic; but action against 'wrongful offence incivilities' is justified only where the wrongful offence is persistent. All enforcement decisions should be taken bearing in mind the first four policy principles.

At several points in this chapter, I have referred to recent empirical research by Andrew Wilson and myself in high-crime, high-deprivation areas of Sheffield. That research was funded under the Home Office's civil renewal programme, and is being published in a volume on civil renewal (see Bottoms and Wilson, 2006). Our conclusions—hinted at a few times in this essay— were that civil renewal and neighbourhood safety can only be delivered on a partnership basis, as between central government, local agencies such as the police and local government, and ordinary citizens. That conclusion is hardly original, and it would, in theory, be almost universally subscribed to. In practice, the number of people who genuinely subscribe to such a view is significantly smaller than the number of people who pay lip-service to it; and the

National Reassurance Policing Programme bears testimony to the fact that genuinely attempting partnership work, including a partnership with local residents, is extremely demanding. I would argue that, if such partnerships are to be truly meaningful and sustainable, they need to be based on some solid moral and social principles to which all parties can subscribe. It has been an important part of the task of this chapter to work towards such principles.[22]

REFERENCES

BARBALET, JM (1998) *Emotion, Social Theory, and Social Structure: A Macrosociological Approach.* Cambridge: Cambridge University Press.

BOTTOMS, AE (1999) 'Interpersonal Violence and Social Order in Prisons', in M TONRY and J PETERSILIA (eds), *Prisons.* Chicago: University of Chicago Press.

BOTTOMS, AE, MAWBY, RI and XANTHOS, P (1989) 'A Tale of Two Estates', in D DOWNES (ed), *Crime and the City* (London: Macmillan).

BOTTOMS, AE and WILSON, A (2004) 'Attitudes to Punishment in Two High-Crime Communities', in AE Bottoms, S Rex and G Robinson (eds), *Alternatives to Prison: Options for an Insecure Society.* Cullompton, Devon: Willan.

—— (2006) 'Civil Renewal, Control Signals and Neighbourhood Safety', in T BRANNAN, P JOHN and G STOKER (eds), *Re-energising Citizenship: Strategies for Civil Renewal.* Basingstoke: Palgrave Macmillan.

BURNEY, E (2005) *Making People Behave: Anti-social Behaviour, Politics and Policy.* Cullompton, Devon: Willan.

BYRNE, D (1999) *Social Exclusion.* Buckingham: Open University Press.

CHARLESWORTH, SJ (2000) *A Phenomenology of Working Class Experience.* Cambridge: Cambridge University Press.

ELSTER, J (1989) *The Cement of Society: A Study of Social Order.* Cambridge: Cambridge University Press.

FIELD, F (2003) *Neighbours from Hell: The Politics of Behaviour.* London: Politico's.

FORTES, M (1983) *Rules and the Emergence of Society.* Royal Anthropological Institute of Great Britain and Ireland, Occasional Paper No 39. London: Royal Anthropological Institute.

FOSTER, J and HOPE, T (1993) *Housing, Community and Crime: The Impact of the Priority Estates Project.* Home Office Research Study No. 131. London: HMSO.

GIRLING, E, LOADER, I and SPARKS, R (2000) *Crime and Social Change in Middle England: Questions of Order in an English Town.* London: Routledge.

GOFFMAN, E (1972) *Relations in Public: Microstudies of the Public Order.* New York: Harper Colophon.

GRAHAM, J (2000) *Drug Markets and Neighbourhood Regeneration* (Unpublished report available from the Centre for Analysis of Social Exclusion, London School of Economics and Political Science).

INNES, M (2004) 'Signal Crimes and Signal Disorders: Notes on Deviance as Communicative Action' *British Journal of Sociology* 55: 335.

---

[22] I am very grateful to Andrew von Hirsch for his constructively critical comments on an earlier draft of this chapter.

INNES, M and FIELDING, N (2002) 'From Community to Communicative Policing: "Signal Crimes" and the Problem of Public Reassurance' *Sociological Research Online* 7(2) [http://www.socresonline.org.uk/7/2/innes.html].

INNES, M, HAYDEN, S, LOWE, T, MACKENZIE, H, ROBERTS, C and TWYMAN, L (2004) *Signal Crimes and Reassurance Policing*. Guildford: University of Surrey.

KELLING, G and COLES, CM (1996) *Fixing Broken Windows*. New York: Free Press.

KNIGHT, J (2001) 'Social Norms and the Rule of Law: Fostering Trust in a Socially Diverse Society', in KS COOK (ed), *Trust in Society*. New York: Russell Sage Foundation.

NATIONAL STATISTICS (2005) *Social Trends No 35*. Basingstoke: Palgrave Macmillan.

PLANT, R (2001) *Politics, Theology and History*. Cambridge: Cambridge University Press.

SAMPSON, RJ and RAUDENBUSH, SW (1999) 'Systematic Social Observation of Public Spaces: A New Look at Disorder and Crime' *American Journal of Sociology* 105: 603.

SAMPSON, RJ, and RAUDENBUSH, SW (2001) *Disorder in Urban Neighborhoods: Does it Lead to Crime?* Washington, DC: National Institute of Justice.

SAMPSON, RJ RAUDENBUSH, SW and EARLS, FJ (1997) 'Neighborhoods and Violent Crime: A Multilevel Study of Collective Efficacy' *Science* 277: 918.

SHERMAN, LW (1993) 'Defiance, Deterrence, Irrelevance: A Theory of the Criminal Sanction' *Journal of Research in Crime and Delinquency* 30: 445.

TAUB, RP, TAYLOR, DG and DUNHAM, JD (1984) *Paths of Neighborhood Change: Race and Crime in Urban America*. Chicago: University of Chicago Press.

TAYLOR, RB (2001) *Breaking Away from Broken Windows*. New York: Westview Press.

TUFFIN, R, MORRIS, J and POOLE, A (2006) *An Evaluation of the Impact of the National Reassurance Policing Programme*. Home Office Research Study No 296. London: Home Office.

TYLER, TR (2003) 'Procedural Justice, Legitimacy and the Effective Rule of Law', in M TONRY (ed) *Crime and Justice: A Review of Research*, Vol 30. Chicago: University of Chicago Press.

WACQUANT, L (1993) 'Urban Outcasts: Stigma and Division in the Black American Ghetto and the French Urban Periphery' *International Journal of Urban and Regional Research* 17: 366.

WILSON, JQ and KELLING, GL (1982) 'The Police and Neighborhood Safety: Broken Windows' *Atlantic Monthly* 249(3):29.

WOOD, M (2004a) *Perceptions and Experience of Antisocial Behaviour: Findings from the 2003/2004 British Crime Survey*. Home Office Online Report 49/04. London: Home Office.

—— (2004b) *Perceptions and Experiences of Antisocial Behaviour*. Home Office Research Findings 252. London: Home Office.

WRONG, DH (1994) *The Problem of Order: What Unites and Divides Society*. New York: Free Press.

Index

abatement notices, 83, 203
abusive behaviour, 27, 29, 209
  see also racist abuse
acceptable behaviour contracts, 79,
  85–7, 206
ACORN, 243–4, 245
Adler, MD, 95
administrative regulations, 73–5
Alldridge, P, 8
Amelung, Knut, 121n11
ancillary civil prohibitions, 189–90, 192
anomie, 220, 231
anti-molestation orders, 189
anti-social behaviour
  see also offensiveness
  ASBOs *see* anti-social behaviour
    orders
  cumulative effect, 176, 184–5, 241,
    242, 255–6, 262, 278
  current public policy
    critique, 2, 190–2, 213–17
    discourse, 1–2, 27, 29
    discretionary powers of officials,
      215
    human rights, 2, 44–5, 215–16
    legislative activism, 27, 29
    poverty agenda, 242
    unpopular groups targeted, 215,
      216
    use of civil remedies, 214, 215
    vicarious punishment, 215
  definitions, 27–8, 28, 205, 214, 264
  demographic imbalance, 242, 249,
    262–3
  empirical evidence, 243–59

British Crime Survey, 243–9, 251,
  256, 259, 261–2, 274
  Innercity, 272–3, 275
  Sheffield survey, 249–56, 268, 269,
    275, 277, 278–9
  signal crimes theory, 240, 256–9
  enforcement role, 277–8
English legal history
  1986 to 1997, 199–204
  New Labour, 204–17
  previous centuries, 196–9
explaining neighbourhood reactions,
  259–64
extent, 28–9
impact, 248–9
v incivilities, 239
and local social order, 260, 274–5
and mental health, 213, 214
nature and extent, 29–34
non-enforcement solutions, 275
v offensiveness, 2, 27–8
perceptions, 256, 274
policy principles, 273–9
and poverty, 242, 262–3
resentment v vengefulness, 261–2,
  276–7
residential communities *see* neighbourhoods
and social changes, 242, 243, 274
theories, 264–73
  broken windows, 36–7, 117–18,
    127, 240, 264–8
  collective efficacy, 240, 265–8, 276
  rational choice theory, 242, 274
  signal crimes, 268–73

vicarious punishment, 215
Anti-Social Behaviour Act 2003:
  beggars, 210–11
  critique, 2, 190–2, 213–17
  environmental powers, 211
  generally, 208–12
  and human rights, 2, 44–5, 215–16
  parents, 210
  and social housing, 44–5, 209–10
  White Paper, 27–8, 35, 37, 38,
    208–9, 210–11, 216
anti-social behaviour orders
  see also two-step prohibition orders
  Anti-Social Behaviour Act 2003,
    208–12
  attempted suicide, 185n29, 191
  autistic children, 191
  breaches, 45
    burden of proof, 207
    imprisonment, 81, 188
    men rea, 187
    rates, 206
  burden of proof, 80, 207
  civil or criminal penalties, 47, 177–8,
    207
  conduct criteria, 184, 186, 191
  court jurisdiction, 207–8
  and criminology, 29
  discretion of officials, 192, 208, 215
  duration, 191, 206
  English trend, 115, 174
  extension of legislation, 207–13
  guidance, 206
  human rights, 2, 44–5, 215–16
  introduction, 205
  local authority powers, 208
  objections, 2, 45–9, 80–2, 190–2,
    213–17
  prohibited conduct, 45, 80–1, 191,
    206–7, 230–1
  proportionality, 81
  prostitution, 191
  public policy, 277
  response to offensiveness, 79–82, 91
  spitting prohibitions, 196
  statistics, 205
  targets, 33, 95, 182, 191, 206, 209
  two-step procedure, 104, 174

wrongdoing, 185n29
Anti-Social Behaviour Unit, 27, 216
apartheid, 16, 227
Aristotle, 168, 170
Armitage, R, 2
ASBOs *see* anti-social behaviour orders
Ashworth, Andrew, 2, 8, 14, 41, 42,
    44, 45, 47, 80, 174, 178n11
Askonas, P, 227
assault, 200, 231
associations:
  proscription, 12–13
  voluntary associations, 222, 223,
    224–5, 229
Auld, LJ, 41, 46
avoidability, 127–8

Baltimore, 267
Barbalet, Jack, 261–2, 276
Barry, Norman, 259, 260
battered women, 40–1
battery, 15
Baumeister, Andrea, 77n49
bawdy behaviour, 197
BBC, 32, 40
Beauchamp, G, 106
Becker, HS, 39, 219
begging, 29, 37, 38, 129, 198, 209,
    210–11
Benhabib, S, 230
Bennett, Chris, 77n49
bereavement, 224
Berkman, SL, 224
Bhatti, Gurprit Kaur, 32
Bills of Attainder, 181
Blackburn, Simon, 159
Blair, Tony, 36, 38
Bland, N, 33
blasphemy, 29, 77n51, 146
Blunkett, David, 34–5, 36, 216, 234
Boer War, 228
Bottoms, Anthony, 249, 250, 256, 273,
    275, 278–9
Bourdieu, Pierre, 222, 225, 232
Bowling, B, 36
Box, S, 36
Braithwaite, J, 156
Brandt, R, 100

Brants, C, 14
breach of the peace, 196–7
Brighton, 232
British Crime Survey, 32–3, 234, 243–9, 251, 256, 259, 261–2, 274
broken windows, 36–7, 117–18, 127, 240, 264–8
Brown, AP, 45
Brown, G, 224
Brown, KM, 230
Budd, T, 32
Bullock, K, 206
Burney, Elizabeth, 95, 201, 203, 206, 273
Burroughs, William, 42
Bye-laws, 199, 211–12

Campbell, D, 43
Campbell, S, 33, 201
Cannadine, David, 232
causation:
　Anglo-American jurisprudence, 7–8
　causes of crime, 34–40
CCTV, 121n12
Charlesworth, Simon, 262–4
Chicago, 30, 265, 270, 275
children, ASBO targets, 206
　see also teenagers
China, spitting, 195
Chirot, D, 227
choice theory, 242, 274
citizenship:
　civic participation, 222–3, 228–9
　modern working class, 231–2
　social citizenship, 228–9
civil remedies
　see also two-step prohibition orders
　burden of proof, 175
　control of criminal behaviour by, 214
　v criminal prosecution, 71–3, 175–7
　responses to offensiveness, 70–3
　seriousness threshold, 71
　torts, 198
Coburn, D, 226
Cohen, S, 232
Coleman, James, 222, 225
collective efficacy theory, 240, 265–8, 276

Colquhoun, A, 16
communication, offensiveness, 20–1, 127
community service, adequacy, 95
conscription, 230
conspiracy to defraud, 176
consumer society, 233, 264
contagion, 107
contract, acceptable behaviour contracts, 79, 85–7, 206
control signals, 257, 269–70, 272, 273, 276
Cook, D, 36
criminal law:
　Anglo-American jurisprudence, 7–8
　v civil remedies, 71–3, 175–7
　crime and offensiveness, 13–20
　equality principle, 181
　and European Convention on Human Rights, 41
　extent of criminalisation, 47–8
　fair trial, 46–7, 174, 179
　fair warning principle, 41, 174, 186–7
　generality principle, 41, 173, 181–2
　and human rights, 41, 234
　limits, 7, 173–4
　mens rea, 7, 42, 174, 187
　moral voice, 173
　over-inclusiveness, 11–13, 155–6
　penal minimalism, 14–15, 22
　private prosecutions, 71n36
　proportionality principle, 174, 178, 187–9
　public wrongs, 76
　representative authority, 173, 179–81
　restricting principles, 173–4
　safeguards, 173–4, 178–81
　symbolic legislation, 43–4
criminalisation of offensiveness:
　breach of the peace, 196–7
　debate framework, 164–71
　diversity of grounds, 124
　English legal history
　　1986 to 1997, 199–204
　　Anti-Social Behaviour Act 2003, 208–12
　　current public policy, 213–17

New Labour, 204–17
previous centuries, 196–9
public order regulation, 199–202
sexual nuisance, 212–13
German penal theory, 133–7, 146
harm principle, 15, 24, 25, 42, 57,
  58, 116–17, 124, 129, 164–71
immediacy requirement, 128–30
inconsiderate behaviour, 119–24,
  125, 126, 129
  v violation of others' rights,
    137–47
interdisciplinary perspective, 4–5
last resort, 75–9, 92–3, 110–11, 157
legislative over-reach, 11–13, 155–6
mediating principles, 124–30, 137–8,
  144, 154–5
offensiveness leading to eventual
  harm, 117–18
ready avoidability principle, 127–8
restrictions, 124–30, 137–8, 144,
  154–5
rights-centred theory, 137–47
separate Offence Principle, 7, 23–5,
  57, 58, 65, 96, 116, 118–19, 124,
  127, 129, 134
social side-effects, 126–7
and social tolerance, 125–7, 143–4
two-step procedure *see* two-step prohibition orders
wrongdoing, 58, 119–24, 149–52,
  155–7
criminology:
  causes of crime, 34–40
  criminal anthropology, 34
  feminist criminology, 36
  interdisciplinary approach, 5–7
  Marxist criminology, 36
  nature and extent of offensiveness,
    29–34, 92
  and offensiveness, 25–40
  and sociology, 274
cultural pluralism, 105–6, 163
curfew, 45, 191

Dalton, H, 137
D'Arms, J, 101
De Grazia, E, 42

de minimis offensiveness,
  14–15, 165
Deans, J, 32
deviance, 30
Devlin, P, 95, 100
Dias, M, 109
diminished responsibility, 191
Diouf, El Hadji, 196
disgust:
  basic emotion, 105
  basis for criminalisation, 110–11
  conflation problem, 101–2, 163
  contagion, 107
  cultural factors, 105–6, 163
  disgust mechanisms, 97, 103–11
  disgust realism, 97–100, 103, 105,
    107, 110, 157–64
  and egalitarianism, 109
  empirical findings, 94, 104–5,
    105–10
  expressive theory of punishment, 95
  homosexuality, 95, 152–3
  ideal observer ethics, 100, 102
  legal philosophy, 91–111
  legal remedies, 93–4, 95, 110–11,
    157
  metaphysics, 96–103, 157–64
  minority behaviour, 109–10
  reasonableness, 100, 151–7
  and sexuality, 162
  smells, 106, 123, 150
  social referencing, 106, 123
  socio-economic factors, 108–9
  subjectivism, 98–9, 153–8
disqualifications, 189–90
divorce, 224, 230
Dodd, V, 32
Dohrenwend, BS & BP, 224
domestic violence, 40–1
Douglas, J, 220
Downes, D, 30
Doyle, Arthur Conan, 37n40
drugs:
  and ASBOs, 206
  British Crime Survey, 243, 244
  Innercity, 272, 275
  neighbourhood threat, 257
  NRPP, 271

police powers, 209
post-communist Europe, 233
public policy, 36
recreational drugs, 10–11
Sheffield survey, 250, 253
South Yorkshire, 273
stereotypes, 213
drunk driving, 184
drunkenness, 27, 149, 197, 209, 233, 243
ducking stools, 197
Due, P, 224
Duff, Anthony, 9n10, 21, 76, 122, 123, 152, 154, 164, 167, 206
dumping, 28, 209, 211, 250, 251, 252–3
Durkheim, Émile, 219–20, 221, 222, 223–4, 226, 231, 232
Dworkin, Ronald, 25
dysfunctional families, 255

e-mails, abusive e-mails, 29
Earls, FJ, 265
Ellickson, RC, 184
Elster, J, 274
employment changes, 229–30, 263
environmental protection, 203–4, 211
equality principle, criminal law, 181
ethnography, 30
European Convention on Human Rights
  see also specific rights and freedoms
  criminal offences, 41
  and definition of harassment, 42
  and two-step prohibitions, 177
evidence:
  injunctions, 82
  two-step prohibitions, 80, 175–6, 183, 188, 207
exhibitionism, 110, 115, 116, 122, 141, 150, 213
extortion, 10

fair trial:
  ECHR jurisprudence, 46–7
  principle of criminal law, 174
  two-step prohibition orders, 45, 179
Fallon, RH, 186–7

Feinberg, Joel, 7–9, 14–15, 23, 57–8, 77n30, 94–5, 99n22, 104, 116, 118–19, 124–7, 133–4, 136–8, 143, 146, 154–5, 164, 167, 168
Felson, M, 36
feminism, criminology, 36
feral children, 106, 163
Field, Frank, 240–3, 244, 254, 255, 262, 274, 277–8
Fielding, Nigel, 256–7, 268
fines, adequacy, 95
fingerprinting, beggars, 38
Fionda, J, 46
Fitzgerald, PJ, 213
fixed penalty notices, 44
fly-tipping, 211
football:
  clubs, 233
  hooligans, 80
  players, 195–6
Fordism, 229
Fortes, M, 260
Foster, J, 270n18
France, 115, 220, 249n5
fraud, conspiracy to defraud, 176
freedom of expression, 25, 241, 242
freedom of religion, 25
Fuller, Lon, 228

Gardner, J, 7, 21, 80
Garland, D, 34, 36
Gelsthorpe, L, 36
gender discrimination, 15–16, 23, 36
Germany:
  collective interests, 134–5, 136
  diversionary mechanisms, 46
  Holocaust denial, 136–7
  Rechtsgut, 134, 136, 146
  penal theory, 133–7
  public nudity, 128
  public peace, 135, 137
  public trust, 135–6
  social harm, 134–5
Ginsberg, Allen, 42
Girling, E, 274
Goffman, E, 260
Gough, Stephen, 59

graffiti, 209, 211, 231, 243, 258, 266, 271
Graham, J, 272–3
gypsies, 201

Haidt, J, 106, 109
Hampton, J, 21
harassment:
    ASBOs, 27, 209
    burden of proof, 175
    definition, 42, 176
    English legislative history, 42, 201
    neighbourhoods, 204
    racial harassment, 200
    stalking, 201
    tenants, 83–4
Hardin, R, 227
Haringey, 206–7
harm:
    concept, 9–10, 116–17, 137
    criminalisation debate, 164–71
    Germany, 134–5
    harm and the Offence Principle, 15, 24, 25, 42, 57, 58, 116–19, 124, 129
    inchoate offences, 184
    likelihood of harm, 184
    offensiveness as harmful conduct, 116–17
    offensiveness leading to eventual harm, 117–18
    psychological harm, 116, 117, 166
    and resources, 116–17, 139–41
Harris, T, 224
Hart, HLA, 8, 151
Hawe, P, 225
Hayek, Friedrich von, 186
Hayward, KJ, 39
health:
    and crime, 223–6
    and social capital, 222–3
    and stress, 224
hearsay evidence, 176
hedges, 72–3, 79
Hegel, Georg, 9n10, 189
Hewitt, LN, 224
HIV/AIDS, 233
Hoggart, Richard, 231

Holocaust denial, 14, 24, 136–7, 164
homophobia, 16, 61–2, 95, 152–3
Honoré, T, 8
hooligans, 232
Hooper, J, 44
Hope, T, 270n18
Hörnle, Tatjana, 46
Housing Act 1996, 202–3, 204
housing benefit, 45
Howard, Michael, 234
Hudson, B, 36
Hull, 270n18
human rights
    see also specific rights and freedoms
    and ASBOs, 2, 44–5, 215–16
    and criminal law, 41, 234
    effect of 1998 Act, 46–7
Hume, David, 98, 158, 159
humour, 97–8
Humphreys, L, 30
Hunt, A, 22
Husak, Douglas, 8, 123, 157–63

Illouz, E, 233
immediacy of offence, 128–30
immorality, 65n19
incitement to religious hatred, 77n51
incivilities *see* anti-social behaviour
income inequality, 225–6
inconsiderate behaviour:
    v violation of others' rights, 137–47
    wrongdoing, 119–24, 125, 126, 129
infanticide, 105
Ingham, Geoffrey, 235
injunctions:
    anti-social behaviour injunctions, 209
    burden of proof, 82
    harassment, 83–4
    landlords, 83–4, 202–3
    response to offence, 70, 82–5
    sanctions, 84–5
    targeted behaviour, 82–3
Innercity, 272–3, 275
Innes, Martin, 254, 256, 256–9, 260, 264, 267, 268–70, 273, 274, 276
insults, 61–2, 65–6, 77–8, 110, 120–1, 125–6, 135

see also racist abuse
intention:
  and anti-social behaviour orders, 80
  criminal law, 7, 42, 174, 187
  offensiveness, 20–2, 61–2
  and two-step prohibition orders, 187
interdisciplianry approaches, 3–7,
  49–50
internment, 13
intimidation, 175, 209, 219
Iraq, 25

Jacobson, D, 101
Jamieson, R, 36
Janner, Lord, 31
Jerry Springer - The Opera, 32
jokes, 97–8
Jones, B, 206
Jupp, V, 39
jurisprudence:
  Anglo-American preoccupations, 7–8
  interdisciplinary approach, 5–7
  and offensiveness, 40–9

Kadish, Sanford, 43
Kahan, Dan, 95, 110
Kane, SC, 39
Kant, Immanuel, 159
Kawachi, I, 224, 225
Kearns, P, 42
Kelling, George, 36, 264–6
Kelly, L, 36
Kennedy, BP, 224, 225
Kenny, S, 230
kerb-crawlers, 212
Kerouac, Jack, 42
Keynesianism, 228
King, RD, 39
Klinenberg, E, 220
Knapp, C, 108
Knight, Jack, 226–8, 231–2, 263
Koller, S, 109
Kolnai, Aurel, 161–2
Ku Klux Klan, 24

labelling theory, 39, 232
Labour Party, 27, 30, 38, 204–17,
  229–30, 234

Lacey, N, 2, 8, 212
laddism, 231, 233
language mechanisms, 108
Lawrence, DH, 42
Leeds, 231
Lemert, Edwin, 234
Lenckner, T, 135
liberty:
  and criminal law, 14
  presumption in favour of, 92
lifestyles, 125, 128, 143–4, 146, 201
Lin, N, 222, 224
litter, 28, 32, 209, 211, 243, 250, 251,
  252–3, 271
Loader, I, 214
local authorities:
  abatement notices, 83, 203
  ASBO powers, 208
  new control powers, 211–12
  noise control, 203–4
  remedial notices, 73
Lombroso, Cesare, 34
Lukes, Stephen, 227

McCawley, CR, 106
MacCrimmon, M, 35
MacDonald, S, 47
McDowell, J, 160–1
McGaffey, R, 42
Mackie, JD, 159
MacMillan, N, 26
magic, laws of sympathetic magic,
  106–7
Maguire, M, 29
Major, John, 38
Malone, A, 16
Malson, Lucien, 106
Manchester, 205, 206
Mandela, Nelson, 12
Mann, M, 228
Marinetto, M, 230
Marshall, Sandra, 76, 122, 123, 152,
  154, 164, 167, 206
Marshall, TH, 228–30
Marx, Karl, 221
Matthews, R, 36
Matza, D, 39, 234
Mawby, RI, 249

Meacham, S, 231
media, 28, 31–2, 33, 232
mediation, 68–9, 76, 86, 87, 216
mens rea see intention
mental health:
  and anti-social behaviour, 213, 214
  diminished responsibility, 191
  and social capital, 224
methodology, interdisciplinary
  approach, 3–7, 49–50
Michael, George, 43
Mill, John Stuart, 8, 168–70
Miller, Henry, 42
Miller, William, 95, 109
minorities:
  and disgust mechanisms, 109–10
  NRPP, 271
  religious groups, 200–1
Moore, GE, 101, 160
moral panics, 201, 204, 232
morbidity, and social capital, 220, 225
Morris, A, 36
Morrison, W, 34, 39
Morse, SJ, 37
multidisciplinary approaches, 3–7,
  49–50
murder, wrongfulness, 158–9
Murphy, JG, 21
Muslims, 200–1

Nagel, Thomas, 122, 151
Narayan, U, 134
National Health Service, 228
National Reassurance Policing
  Programme, 257, 270–2, 275, 279
naturism, 59
Nazis, 12, 31
necessity, and offensiveness, 62–4
negotiation, response to offence, 68–70
Neighbourhood Noise Watch, 204
neighbourhoods:
  ACORN, 243–4, 245
  decline process, 274–5
  drugs, 257
  effects on crime, 223
  explaining reactions to incivilities,
   259–64
  hedges, 72–3, 79

Housing Act 1996, 202–3
negotiation, 69
neighbour harassment, 201
neighbours from hell, 15, 204, 240–3
New Labour regulation, 204–13
noise, 27, 29, 203–4, 209, 244, 250,
  255
signal crimes theory, 256–9
social virtues, 240–1
underprivileged, 235, 242, 251,
  262–3
working class past, 231
Nelken, D, 37, 39
Nemeroff, C, 109
neo-liberal economics, 225–6
Netherlands, 46
Neuberger, J, 92
Neumann, U, 134
new age travellers, 201
Newburn, T, 37
Nicholas, S, 32
noise:
  abatement notices, 83
  neighbours, 27, 29, 203–4, 209, 244,
   250, 255
  Noise Act 1996, 204
  offensiveness, 59
  regulation, 78, 203–4
  response to, 86
  wrongdoing, 119–20, 122, 123, 150
norm-governed offences, 60–1, 152–7,
  167
North, N, 43
nuisance:
  abatement notices, 83
  chronic street nuisances, 184
  nuisance calls, 29
  public nuisance, 84
  sensory affronts, 124
  statutory nuisance, 83
Nussbaum, Martha, 110–11

obscenity, 42, 95
obstruction, 29, 198
offensiveness
  see also anti-social behaviour
  v anti-social behaviour, 2, 27–8
  communication, 20–2, 127

criminalisation *see* criminalisation of
  offensiveness
criminology issues, 25–40
definition, 94, 96, 219
disgust *see* disgust
diversity of grounds, 124
emergence of issue, 1–2, 5, 115–16
German approach, 133–7
harm and Offence Principle, 24, 25,
  42, 58, 116–19, 124, 129
intention, 20–2, 61–2
interdisciplinary approach, 3–7,
  49–50
jurisprudence issues, 40–9
leading to eventual harm, 117–18
mediated v immediate offence,
  59–61, 122–3, 152
Mill on, 168–70
nature and extent, 29–34, 92
necessity, 62–4
norm-governed offences, 60–1,
  152–7, 167
objective v subjective offence, 98–9,
  153–8
Offence Principle, 7, 23–5, 57, 58,
  65, 96, 116, 118–19, 124, 127,
  129, 134
philosophical issues, 7–25, 96–103,
  157–64
and pluralism, 125, 128, 163, 166
previous accounts, 116–19
primitive offensiveness, 151–2, 153,
  157
profound offence, 126
ready avoidability principle, 127–8
reasonableness, 62–4, 100, 151–7
responses *see* responses to offensiveness
structures, 58–64
terminology, 232
theory and practice, 3
and trust, 230–4
wrongfulness and Offence Principle,
  58, 119–24, 277–8
Oz trial, 42

Padfield, Nicola, 2, 45
Papageorgiou, K, 137

parenting orders, 210
Parsons, Talcott, 226
Pearson, G, 33
penal minimalism, 14–15, 22
Pettit, P, 156
Phillips, C, 36
philosophy:
  disgust, 91–111
  interdisciplinary approach, 5–7,
    49–50
  metaphysics of disgust, 96–103,
    157–64
  Offence Principle, 23–5
  and offensiveness, 7–25
  offensiveness and crime, 8–20
  offensiveness and intention, 20–2
plagiarism, 74
Plant, Raymond, 259
pluralism, 125, 128, 163, 166
pornography, 29, 95, 127–8, 212
positivism, 12, 39
Posner, RA, 110
poverty, and anti-social behaviour, 242,
  262–3
pre-emptive public behaviour, 121–2,
  124
primitive offensiveness, 151–2, 153,
  157
profanity, 29, 197
professional malpractice, 189–90
property damage, 209, 231, 232, 250,
  254–5, 277
proportionality:
  and criminal law, 174
  responses to offensiveness, 87
  two-step prohibition orders, 81, 178,
    187–9
prostitution, 35–6, 191, 212, 233
psychiatric injuries, 65n20
psychological harm, 116, 117, 166
public health, 198
public nuisance, 84, 198, 211
public opinion, 32–3
public order regulation, 1986 to 1997,
  199–202
public spaces:
  destruction, 254
  freedom of expression, 241, 242

indecency, 152, 154, 155
interference with autonomy in, 121
nudity, 29, 59, 64, 105, 115, 128, 169, 213
and offensive wrongdoing, 151
pre-emptive behaviour, 121–2, 124
private and public behaviour, 241
prohibiting teenagers from, 129–30
proper use debate, 143–4
sexual acts, 115, 150, 153, 164, 165, 169
signal crimes, 258
social order in, 239
two-step prohibition orders, 182–4
universal access, 130
public toilets, 43
Puritans, 197
Putnam, Robert, 109, 222–3, 225, 226, 227

quality of life crimes, 91, 115

racism:
abuse *see* racist abuse
British Crime Survey, 244
English regulation, 199–200
and liberal democracies, 18
racially aggravated misconduct, 200
US legislation, 44
wrongfulness, 15–16
racist abuse:
basis of criminalisation, 126, 165
Germany, 135
in racist societies, 156
intended offensiveness, 61–2
primitive offensiveness, 153
Offence Principle, 23
public consciousness, 29
wrongfulness, 149–50, 152
Raudenbush, SW, 265–8, 269
ravers, 201
Raz, Joseph, 14, 15, 41, 166, 180, 187
Read, T, 33
reasonableness:
and offensiveness, 62–4, 100, 151–7
remedial notices, 73
recognisances, 197
Regan, L, 36

religion:
freedom of religion, 25
incitement to religious hatred, 77n51
minority groups, 200–1
remedial notices, 73
remedies *see* civil remedies; criminalisation of offensiveness; responses to offensiveness
representative authority, 173, 179–81
resentment, 120, 261–2, 276–7
residential communities *see* neighbourhoods
resources, and harm principle, 116–17, 139–41
responses to offensiveness:
acceptable behaviour contracts, 79, 85–7, 206
administrative regulations, 73–4
severity of Anglo-American responses, 91
anti-social behaviour orders, 79–82, 91
avoidance, 127–8
civil law remedies, 70–3
criminalisation *see* criminalisation of offensiveness
English legal history
1986 to 1997, 199–204
current public policy, 213–17
environmental protection, 203–4
Housing Act 1996, 202–3
New Labour, 204–13
previous centuries, 196–9
public order regulation, 199–202
generally, 64–79
hybrid responses, 79–87, 199
informal social control, 156, 195
injunctions, 70, 82–5
negotiation, 68–70
progress, 93
proportionality, 87
rules and regulations, 195
spitting, 195–6
strategies, 93–4, 157
toleration, 66–8, 125–7
restorative justice, 68
Rietschlin, J, 224
road traffic offences, 184

Roberto, Paul, 11–12, 14, 26, 37, 41,
46, 133, 150, 164, 165, 174
Roberts, RC, 109
Rock, P, 30
Rooney, Wayne, 196
Rorty, Richard, 159
Rotherham, 262–3
rough sleeping, 32, 244
Roxin, C, 135
Rozin, Paul, 106, 109
rubbish *see* litter
Rudolphi, H-J, 135
Ruggiero, V, 36
rule of law:
  fair warning principle, 186–7
  representative authority, 180
  requirements, 41
  and social capital, 228
Russia, 233

Sampson, RJ, 265–8, 269
Sanders, A, 26
Sandvoss, C, 233
Schauer, F, 11, 187
Schmidt, H, 106
Schonsheck, J, 76
Schudson, M, 235
Schwartz, Louis, 116
Sciulli, D, 228
Scotland, 46
self-defence, 9–10, 28
Sennett, R, 230
sensory affronts, 122–4
September 11 attacks, 200–1
sexual autonomy, 140–1
sexual nuisance:
  bawdy behaviour, 197
  and disgust, 162
  English regulation, 212–13
  sexual acts in public, 115, 150, 153,
    164, 165, 169
sexual orientation, 16, 61–2, 95, 152–3
Sharpe, K, 30
Shaw, CR, 30
Sheffield survey, 249–56, 268, 269,
  275, 277, 278–9
Shell, A, 225
Sherman, LW, 276

Sherrod, A, 109
Shoemaker, DW, 100
shopping malls, 80
Shute, S, 7, 21
signal crimes theory, 240, 256–9,
  268–73
signal disorders, 256–9, 269
Sikhs, 32, 201
Simester, Andrew, 7, 8, 17n23, 23, 24,
  42, 58, 76, 104, 110, 120, 125, 134,
  136–47, 154, 164, 166, 174, 176,
  239, 262
Sims, L, 32
Singapore, 128–9
slander, 197
smells, 106, 123, 150
Smith, ATH, 201
Smith, Roger, 2
social capital:
  civic participation and health, 222–3
  decline, 235
  health and crime, 223–6
  meaning, 222, 223
  theory, 219–35
  and trust, 221, 223, 226–30
  trust and offensive behaviour, 230–4
social changes, 242, 243, 274
social citizenship, 228–9
social constructionism, 232
social housing:
  Anti-Social Behaviour Act 2003,
    44–5, 209–10
  discretionary powers of officials, 215
  Housing Act 1996, 202–3, 204
  and New Labour, 204
  vicarious punishment, 215
Social Landlords Crime and Nuisance
  Group, 214
social referencing, 106, 123
Societies for the Reformation of
  Manners, 197
sociology:
  and criminology, 274
  definition, 220
  explanation of behaviour, 219–22
  functional theory, 226
sodomy, 95
South Africa, 16, 227

Sparks, R, 37
speeding, 184, 243, 244, 250, 251, 252, 269
spitting, 195–6, 206, 207
squatters, 201
stalking, 201
Stewart, A, 227
Straw, Jack, 216
stress, 224
Stuntz, William, 92–3
subjectivism, 98–9, 153–8
substance abuse *see* drugs
suicide, 10, 185n29, 191, 220, 224, 233
Sullivan, GR, 8, 42, 174, 176
Sumner, C, 30
sumptuary laws, 22
Swart, B, 14
swastikas, 31
symbolic legislation, 43–4
Syme, SL, 224

targeted groups:
   ASBOs, 33, 95, 182, 191, 206, 209
   dangerous classes, 198
   public order legislation, 201
   strangers, 197
   unpopular groups, 215, 216
   vagrants, 198
taste, 21–2, 59–60, 63
Taub, Richard, 269–70, 274–5
Taylor, I, 36, 39
Taylor, Ralph, 251, 264–5, 267, 274
teenagers:
   British Crime Survey, 243, 244, 245–7
   and local features, 274
   non-enforcement solutions, 275
   NRPP, 271
   prohibiting from public spaces, 129–30
   public perceptions, 32–3, 257, 259
   Sheffield survey, 250, 253–4, 277
temperance societies, 222
tenants
   see also social housing
   Housing Act 1996, 202–3
   injunctions by landlords, 83–4, 209

terrorist associations, 12–13
Thatcher, Margaret, 38, 202, 229
Thoits, PA, 224
Thorpe, K, 32, 33
Tocqueville, Alexis de, 222, 229
toleration:
   response to offensiveness, 66–8
   social tolerance, 125–7, 143–4
torts, 198
trade unions, 263
Traugott, M, 232
tree-preservation orders, 189, 190
trespass, 201, 231
trust:
   decline, 235, 263
   institutions, 221, 223
   and offensiveness, 230–4
   and social capital, 222, 223, 226–30
   and social inequality, 225
Tuffin, R, 270–2
Turner, Bryan, 220, 222, 230, 263, 264
Twining, William, 29
two-step prohibition orders:
   advantages, 175–7
   ancillary civil prohibitions, 189–90, 192
   applicants, 180
   burden of proof, 175–6, 183, 188
   by-passing constraints, 178–89
   civil and criminal character, 177–8
   course of conduct, 176–7, 184–5
   criminalisation technique, 178, 182–5
   English ASBO legislation, critique, 104, 174, 190–2, 215
   fair trial, 179
   and fair warning principle, 186–7
   flexibility, 177
   functions, 178
   and generality principle, 181–2
   generally, 173–93
   misuse potential, 178–89
   pre-emptive regulation, 129–30, 182–3
   proportionality, 178, 187–9
   representative authority, 179–81
   structure, 174–5
   targeted groups, 33, 95, 182, 191, 206, 209

trend, 115, 174
Tyler, TR, 276

United States:
  1st Amendment principle, 25
  Baltimore, 267
  Bills of Attainder, prohibition, 181
  Chicago, 30, 265, 270, 275
  citizenship, 229
  criminal law teaching, 8
  disgust, 95
  morbidity rates, 220
  obscenity trials, 42
  quality of life offences, 91
  race discrimination, 44
  responses to offensiveness, 91
  social capital, 222, 223, 225

vagrants, 198
vandalism, 28, 29, 32, 209, 219, 231, 243, 244, 254, 271
vengefulness, 261, 276
vicarious punishment, 215
vigilantism, 76, 216
Vold, GB, 34
voluntary associations, 222, 223, 224–5, 229
Von Hirsch, Andrew, 12, 17n23, 23, 24, 36, 48, 58, 76, 80, 104, 110, 116, 120, 125, 134, 136–47, 154, 164, 166, 174, 182, 190, 239, 262

Wacquant, L, 249n5
Waldron, Jeremy, 159, 168–9
Walker, A, 32
Wallace, R, 43
Wardhaugh, J, 30
Wasik, M, 190
Wayne, M, 109
Webber, J, 39, 227
Weber, Max, 221
welfare state, 228, 229, 230
Wells, Celia, 8, 201–2, 212
White, M, 44
White, WF, 30
Wiggins, David, 158, 160–1

Williams, Bernard, 159, 165, 169
Williams, Chester, 16n21
Williams, G, 7
Williams Report, 165, 169
Wilson, Andrew, 250, 256, 273, 278–9
Wilson, James Q, 36, 264–6
Wilson, William Julius, 223
Wincup, E, 39
Winlow, S, 30
witch-hunting, 197
women:
  disgust, 108
  and domestic violence, 40–1
  single women, 213
  witches, 197
Wood, M, 32, 33, 243, 247, 250, 251
Wrong, DH, 274
wrongs:
  and criminal law, 10–11
  exhibitionism, 122
  harmless behaviour, 164–71
  insults, 120–1
  interference with autonomy in public places, 121
  limit of criminal law, 173–4
  murder, 158–9
  nature of wrongdoing, 150–2
  noise, 119–20, 122, 123, 150
  offensiveness as wrongdoing, 119–24, 149–52, 155–7, 277–8
  pre-emptive public behaviour, 121–2, 124, 182–5
  sensory affronts, 122–4
  two-step prohibition orders, 185
WTO, 25

Xanthos, P, 249
xenophobic abuse, 61–2

Yorkshire, 273
Young, J, 36, 39, 232
Young, R, 26

Zedner, L, 26
zoning, 24, 211
Zuckerman, A, 11–12, 46, 174